THE LAST DEBATE

AMERICAN GOVERNMENT
IS
OBSOLETE

by William H. Lohneiss

For information concerning permission to copy selected portions of the book, write to: Permissions, Lohneiss Book Co. 2510-G Las Posas Rd. #238, Camarillo, CA 93010

Library of Congress Cataloging-in-Publication Data – in progress.
     Lohneiss, William H. *The Last Debate* – subtitled *American Government is Obsolete*
          Data to include: bibliographical references and index, government foundation, American Government, Constitution One & Two, individual sovereignty, equality, unalienable rights, title.

ISBN 0-9772009-0-6   Hardcover
ISBN 0-9772009-1-4   Paperback

Cover design by C.L.Martinez & Graphics by Kirk Fornatero

Manufactured by Delta Printing Solutions, Valencia, CA

Lohneiss Book Co. 2510-G Las Posas Rd. #238, Camarillo, CA 93010
www.lohneissbooks.com

Dedicated to my Grandchildren,

Their parents,

&

Their Aunt Ellen.

To Lori, Mark, Matt, Ian, Kyle, Elaine & Caitlin,

and with humble concern, to

everyone who has ever been a grandchild

William Harold Lohneiss

ACKNOWLEDGEMENTS

From my earliest years, I knew America was special, something to cherish.
That truth was a gift from my father, appreciated now more than ever.
And how can I repay for the value of my Mother's view of right and wrong?
This book, perhaps?

Mankind builds on the past to improve how we might govern ourselves.
Given the almost universally violent stages of government's history,
I acknowledge my debt,
our debt, to a few great men of the past.
Being far ahead of their tumultuous times, they were unable
to convince others of the wisdom of their thoughts.
But we can still learn from them today. My debt to them?
The ideals they held, the most sensible foundation for that illusive,
truly worthy government.
Perhaps we are ready to act on their long, dormant counsel.
The goal? To advance our national order, thanks greatly to them and
the authors noted throughout this book who first documented
the ongoing perfidy of American Government.

Taylor Fletcher and Albert Copeland have been welcome, essential sounding boards
for ideas; clear thinkers who helped maintain some balance
among so many alternatives.
Many a pleasant mile was spent on the trails wrestling not with critters, but with the
follies of government and the other realities of living that confound us.
My debt to such men extends also to the young people who brighten my life.
Lori, Ann, Will, Carol, Ellen have helped to keep my own perspective
meaningfully broad.

I consider myself fortunate to have been led, one might say cajoled, through a
sometimes disheartening, but always constructive edit process
to transform my written hopes from research material into this message
intended for all Americans.
With Dr. J. Michael Bennett's patient guidance, I hope I've succeeded.
The fault is surely mine if I have not.

Lastly, it's a very humbling experience to be whipped by the vagaries
of modern word processing software. Without Shirley Fisher's expertise,
guiding me through the illogical pathways of that automated world, I might still be
wondering why the words suddenly disappear.

TABLE OF CONTENTS

ix

FOREWORD

Everything comes with a price. Usually it's dollars and cents. In the case of the government, and the things we depend on government to supply, the price we pay is in dollars in ever-increasing amounts, and in something ever so much more precious, our rights and freedoms as "Sovereign Individuals."

Because we must, citizens depend on government to deal with issues we can't possibly handle. We must, by virtue of our position, trust that anyone motivated to public service will do so with reasonable honesty and dedication. These would-be officials had made the choice to take on all those nasty problems being generated in a hostile and complex world. We applaud them; we reward them well; we depend on them. Americans have trusted officials to do these things while keeping our best interests firmly in mind as their primary guide in making tough decisions. We expect these things without having the American treasure chest drained of our money or our liberties.

The government has done none of the things we have a right to expect of it. Whether federal or local, government has failed utterly to meet its obligations, or to uphold the trust Americans have extended to it. When viewed objectively, what government has done instead is to devote its efforts to extend its powers, grow to gigantic size and control obscene amounts of money, all by relentlessly assaulting individual liberty. For our part, we citizens have unwittingly contributed to the piecemeal dismemberment of America's great gift to civilization. We have done this with our money, our rights forfeited without contest and, sadly but most assuredly, by our collective inaction in the face of bad leadership and unconscionable decisions.

Our trust has been callously abused, and our treasure shamelessly squandered. By far the worst of it, however, are government's failures to promote or even preserve the very elements of American living that once made our country unique, namely our historic advancement of individual sovereignty and its attendant rights and responsibilities as citizens.

This book is a modern tragedy, not in the style of "Hamlet" or "Gone With The Wind," but far worse, because of the concentrated but sad truth it discloses. We must shamefully admit that most of the facts of America's condition have been known for a long time, known but scattered, and therefore not acted upon. The facts presented here come from the work of many dedicated, very concerned people.

1

If there is a contribution to be ascribed to this book, it may be viewed in two parts. The first is that it shows just how bad things are by compiling enough specific federal and local government misdeeds, failures and serious errors to support the nagging unease so many of us have concerning government. That recitation rests uneasily somewhere between tragedy and horror.

The second possible contribution of this book lies in the fervent belief that there is still time to counter recent history. I believe there is a solid course of action still open to us to reverse our slide toward chaos and instead advance American self-government. This part includes specific suggestions on how to begin that daunting task, taking full advantage of American good will and collective expertise. We should have within us the ability to advance from where we are today, an untenable and ominous condition, to one rededicated to our magnificent founding principles.

As distasteful as it may be, we must steel ourselves to what the facts of government actions have been telling us for so long. With characteristic optimism, however, we have reason to hope that it is not too late to do something constructive for our country, ourselves and those who come after us.

It is now ours for the doing.

CHAPTER 1
Claims & Intentions

My claim is that American government is obsolete, and to fix it requires drafting a new constitution. Government has become an organization that chooses to further its own aims rather than fulfill its obligations as caretaker of America's founding principles. The basis for this claim is evident in almost all of the activities government has taken under its aegis, and the almost universally poor performance in them all. As a direct consequence, this obsolescence is steadily leading America to ruin instead of improving national living. We have deluded ourselves into thinking that our impending demise, is far enough away in time that it can still be ignored as it has been. As forcefully as possible, I hope to show why the problem is much more urgent, why the claim of obsolescence is justified and more importantly, to show that there is a *peaceful* way out of the present morass.

The first three chapters describe the book's orientation by stating the claims against government, giving a preview of government failures that will be examined in more detail, and then in Chapter 3, philosophizing about what government's purpose should really be. I consider this latter discussion to be very important, because almost all of us have been conditioned to think that government, as it is, is the way it is somehow meant to be. It isn't, and we ought to allow o urselves to think differently about the whole institution of government.

The remainder of the book takes on the major issues. What, specifically supports the claim of obsolescence? That is covered in Part I. Then, in Part II, how can government really be fixed peacefully?

Throughout Part I, wherever appropriate, conclusions are given that relate to each government failure chosen to support the book's claims. Compare your own thoughts on the matter by testing these conclusions for logic and reason as you see it. In the spirit that motivates this book, a debate among reasonable, but dissatisfied, people can follow, a give and take I think of as "The Last debate" for a very good reason. Either we get it right this time, or we allow government to continue on its present path, which will surely lead to chaos.

Government operations have evolved from tumultuous eighteenth and nineteenth century beginnings, full of expediency, compromise and, I believe, mostly good intentions. Since the end of Hitler's war, however, government's staying power was a surety. Then with devastating effects, the collective belief of government leaders changed, along with their perception of duty, from being caretaker of our liberties to caretaker of our person. Mostly we are dealing here with important facts surrounding government actions that have followed from these new, contorted beliefs. The facts tell of misdeeds, failings, errors and even crimes by government. The issues, facts and conclusions outlined here are certainly not all that any fair indictment might include. They do, however, present a potent, and fair-minded view of the sorry extent of our plight in America chargeable directly to government at all levels of authority.

The second part of the book shows how to divert our present path toward what may well be disaster, onto a path with a reasonable chance to advance peacefully toward improved self-government. That's where debate is so essential, since no one person can know what truly is best for the people of America. Part II, indeed the entire book, is intended to be the beginning of such a debate, and includes an example of what that government might be like. The view presented here is of government that is much closer to America's needs. It is one that utilizes American founding principles directly in a new structure, and not just in the rhetoric surrounding it.

The momentum of early American, non-intrusive government has played out. We've arrived at today thinking that the lessons we learned early on from parents and grandparents still apply. They do not. The residuals, the remnants of American liberty still open to us, however, do allow us to live lives pretty much as we please. We eat and drink what we want, go anywhere, live anywhere, and moan and groan without interference about things that aren't right. Also, contrary to my thesis, we still see some examples of things being done right, giving the illusion of suitable government stewardship. If we choose to see some 'things' as still being well-tended, that's all the proof many of us need to remain sanguine about modern American government. Even for those of us who are less sure, the problems seen ahead will very likely be someone else's concern, since our own time will have passed. But what of our children? Or our grandchildren? What of them?

CHAPTER 2
Changes, Warnings & Indictments

Even though out personal lives may not have changed much over the past decade, for example, there have nevertheless already been disturbing, elemental changes in American life since the 1950s. In my view, we have been silent witnesses to unacceptable, fundamental changes in American life due directly to government acts. Examples of severe deterioration are legion. Included are such serious impositions on Americans as regimentation via government regulations, confiscation of nearly fifty percent of income, debasement of money and the consequent loss of great portions of accumulated family wealth via gross inflationary policies, the cumulative loss of individual rights, and perhaps worst of all, the disruption of virtually every home as both parents have been forced to work for wages to remain solvent. A huge chunk of the once-unique American foundation is gone, and so far, not a thing has been accomplished to slow its erosion, let alone rebuild it. Government policies have forced these major unsettling changes on Americans, and the changes are exacting great, unwarranted penalties from all of us.

None of these debilitating changes happened in a vacuum. There have been numerous warnings throughout the entire period, issued and ignored. A number of perceptive Americans, and many worthy organizations have issued alerts after careful research into government actions. Dr Milton Friedman, Attorney Clint Bolick, and research centers such as The CATO Institute and The Hoover Institution have all issued such warnings of improper government deeds. The extremely disquieting revelations from researchers James T. Bennett and Thomas J. DiLorenzo of the CATO Institute are certainly among the most potent of those ignored warnings.

Milt Friedman, (with his 'Free to Choose,' and 'Money Mischief' warnings) as long ago as thirty years, warned of dangers to come as a result of government fiscal foolishness and the ever-increasing use of destructive and counterproductive regulations. The man was absolutely right, and not a single thing has happened to change either the actions of government or the continuing consequences.

Clint Bolick has written well-documented warnings of heavy-handed and often dictatorial actions of government at the state and local levels. Bolick, an attorney with The Institute For Justice, has battled and won many legal skirmishes with local government involving the deliberate misuse of power directed specifically against individuals. Unfortunately, the means to overturn the use of such power are all after-the-fact. What is so depressing is that for every success such inspiring men have had in the courts, there are hundreds of similar instances where government persists — with impunity — in exactly the same misuse of power. And every State is different. In other words, winning court battles satisfies the aggrieved individual, but does nothing to change government's illegal methods used against citizens in general. Bolick's most recent warning has come in his new book, "Leviathan," subtitled, "The Growth Of Local Government and the Erosion of Liberty." The Hoover Institution, a research center concerned with government policy, published the book in 2004.

Among the most thorough and rigorous of warnings are those from The CATO Institute, a top organization among government watchers. In a recent report to the 105th Congress, [we're now on the 109th] were over 350 specific actions government could take within 57 functional categories, to undo some of its failures of the past. None of the suggestions have been heeded, government leaders preferring instead the benefits derived for themselves via use of their on-going methods of using power. The Bennett / DiLorenzo work, also published by CATO, was titled "Destroying Democracy," and subtitled, "How Government Funds Partisan Politics." Underneath this now-overturned rock is exposed the firmly ensconced, very clever, but illegal government practice of extending money gifts – to themselves.

Other attempts from within government have been made to warn us and to change government via its own procedures from within its present structure. Secretary Jack Kemp and Congressman William Dannemeyer, for example, regularly issued reports in their attempts to improve decisions and to keep people informed of things that weren't right. Perversely, Congress routinely negated any critically needed legislation actually enacted. This was the case when Congress was badgered by a few stalwarts into passing the Gramm, Rudman, Hollings act to limit government spending responsibly.

The net effect of all such notes of caution has been exactly zero. No substantive change has ever come when government itself was being asked to make the changes. Such actions, proper as they may be, are something leaders have shown they will not do while power rests solidly within their grasp. The fault doesn't rest with those who warn us, however. Instead, from what has been documented, on-lookers like us have been unable to integrate the myriad warnings into a coherent picture of American governance. The true scale of malfeasance, relative to the tasks asked of government, has been very hard to decipher. The appropriate steps to effect change in government operations, therefore, have remained unclear, since neither a well-formulated plan nor the means for making changes have yet been shown.

The Last Debate is meant to begin filling that void by finally offering a plan that can lead to the changes in government that Americans must accomplish.

This approach departs markedly from the usual entreaty to government to become responsible and fix itself. Change must be something quite different. What is suggested here may possibly be the only realistic approach we have to salvage America's future. Obviously, the admonition is addressed to all Americans, rather than to government.

To fix government, Americans must draft a completely new Constitution.

Constitution Two, in effect, would become a new contract between all American citizens and any person who seeks to help in the proper administration of the nation in all its complexity. The suggested change in approach to governance is very basic. It is also very necessary so that control can finally be established over those who would govern. Such control has completely vanished in America, elections, and our present constitution notwithstanding.

The goal of any effort to create Constitution Two is to find an acceptable governmental structure that can carry out only those functions which can not be done by other means. Functions and powers entrusted to government must be well defined and limited to appropriate levels. While maintaining the viability of the nation as a whole, the exercise of those powers must primarily be for the benefit of all American citizens, rather than their government.

From Kudos to Indictments

The chapters of Part I show what government has been doing wrong for a long time. In most cases there are often many government officials who know their acts are improper, but are powerless to prevent them. Their frustrations have caused many to leave public service entirely. The scary part of this whole sad narrative is that most of the examples included in this book are many years old. When one sums up all these nefarious actions, the result shows that our country is in very deep trouble. That means you and I are in deep trouble.

There are a few positives, however, so a look at what's right is appropriate before becoming immersed in what's wrong. Obviously, American government, the first real attempt at self-government, is not a complete 100% failure. There are some very important aspects of our life in the United States that are still a resounding success. All we need do to see the value of the remnants still open to us is to compare what Americans have with the sad lot of so many others around the globe. Some of this good fortune is even attributable to government. Some of it is not, being much more the result of hard work, inventiveness, and the exercise of liberties still open to us. However, to be fair, I must give due credit, and government has contributed.

No foreign power has invaded our country, terrorists notwithstanding. There is still a great deal of orderliness to living for most citizens. We have exercised the orderly transfer of political and military power at each change of federal government administrations. Our economy is stable, within limits (although that stability is in great peril). We have a military resource of the first magnitude that is soundly based on a philosophy of service and restraint, and which is clearly the most moral in the whole history of mankind. We have a body of criminal law of great value, with a balance between concern for the individual and for society as a whole. We have a homeland that is still a treasure among nations, although it now faces attacks of increasing severity. Our transportation and utility resources still serve us well and are generally well-cared-for. These are some of the major assets of great value to all of us. They are part of our inheritance from generations past, and it should be one of our goals to preserve them and pass them on in even better condition.

Every other important element of living impacted by government, however, is either in a figurative shambles or in various stages of deterioration. Without a serious, concerted effort on our part to reverse this degradation, what we will bequeath to coming generations will be chaos instead of order.

Many of government's uncontested actions include elements that are specifically, and often by intent, contrary to our present constitution. Every one of them can, and should be, cleared of constitutional questions via a reworked American constitution.

Before tackling the depressing details, a short preview of some major government failures will help to orient our thinking. Spotlighted are a mere dozen issues of the many that might have been used as proper material for review.

- Preserving Wealth   Refer to Chapter 4
One duty of government is to enact policies intended to preserve the assets of each individual. A fundamental change in the philosophy of governing, however, has been the undoing of this basic responsibility. What is the change? It is the belief that giving public money for any cause acceptable to officials is within government's power and prerogatives. That single, great error of government has had such far-reaching consequences that every American now pays continually for this government folly both in lost rights and in money. The gargantuan act of government giveaways was never authorized by the people or the constitution.

• Individual & National Security   Refer to Chapter 5

Measuring external threats to the nation is a job only government can do. It is also a task that relies heavily on experience and wisdom, commodities lacking after WW I, but much more evident following WW II. The Vietnam tragedy, and government's practice of supplying arms worldwide, is strong evidence, however, that out government's education in international affairs is very much a work-in-progress. Our method of preparing and choosing leaders is, therefore, surely open to serious question.

Internally, government's record is far worse, as the crimes committed at Ruby Ridge, Waco, Kent State and elsewhere clearly show. As sad and disgusting as those crimes were, they are dwarfed by another of government's crimes against Americans. The overriding crime of creating blameless criminals by dictate, must be among its most heinous actions. Two such acts warrant special note: drug users labeled as criminals, and some (but not all) connected with prostitution also treated as criminals. Such unconscionable and unnecessary use of dictatorial power has completely removed a person's unalienable right to choice and individual security.

• National Goals   Refer to Chapter 6

The process in use in the United States to define a national goal leaves the American people completely out of the decision loop. Nevertheless, everyone is expected to pay his 'fair share," even if his part of current national obligations is already beyond his means. Any national goal, as with our needs to assure national security, should be acceptable to virtually every citizen, since everyone becomes obligated to pay for the expenses of the project. This misuse of public funds for 'goals" defined solely by government, has added greatly and unnecessarily to our debt, and to the potential for national insolvency.

• Taxation   Refer to Chapter 7

The power now extended to government to levy taxes is effectively without limit. Use of this power has steadily escalated almost to 50% of all income for rank-and-file Americans. This is a level far exceeding that under British rule, which was a major factor in declaring American independence. Even more disheartening, once leaders became dependent on taxation to solve their money problems, they ceased to exercise leadership toward better fiscal management of the country. One of the unenlightened consequences of the entire process has actually been to degrade productivity nationwide.

• Welfare   Refer to Chapter 8

Government welfare programs in the United States are nothing but a sham and a fraud. Government's own studies s how that fewer people live in poverty when government handouts are reduced, and the reverse is true when the dole to recipients is increased. The reason these welfare programs exist is not to help people out of poverty, but to allow government to grow in size, and to control greater amounts of money. The terrible, long-standing result of this fraudulent practice has been to turn people into dependents of government instead of assisting them to assume responsibility for themselves.

- Economic Adventurism   Refer to Chapter 9

It is government's job to strive for financial stability for both the nation and each citizen. The long-standing economic foolishness practiced by government is clear proof that real stability has never been a guiding principle for money management. Instead, unacceptable adventurous forays into economics are standard practice. Adopting, and then abandoning the gold standard, profligate spending of borrowed money, chronic negative balance-of-trade practices and thefts from everyone's accumulated wealth via intentional inflationary policies all attest to such adventurous practices.

- Regulations   Refer to Chapter 10

Government's relentless drive to control money and expand in size has created a serious management problem for itself. Government's solution to this problem is to issue untold numbers of *regulations* for virtually every business and personal activity. In so doing, individuals and businesses alike have been inundated with mostly nonsense "laws," which increase intrusions and inefficiencies in every facet of life. Furthermore, most of these unilateral "devices" are arbitrary, unnecessary and often contradictory, but government is relieved of the tedium of control.

Government's overall method of operation is to maximize taxes and borrowed money, create programs to expand the amount of money that must be controlled, expand constantly the agencies of both local and federal government, and manage America via regulations. This state of affairs is the new American version of self-government. It bears no resemblance to our beginnings of two centuries ago, or to any proper method of governing supposedly self-reliant, free people.

- Special Interests   Refer to Chapter 11

This story of government perfidy bears special notice from every thinking person. We have been lied to, stolen from and robbed of our right to have a say in national affairs. This hijacking, this crime by government, is the reductio ad absurdum extension of that long-ago decision to give public money away. Today's extreme version of gift-giving has government giving away hundreds of billions of dollars to special interest groups of all descriptions, some of which then make very large campaign donations to both political parties to re-elect the givers — of our money. We are unwittingly subsidizing causes we may even abhor.

- Social Security   Refer to Chapter 12

Since its inception, social security has been a seriously flawed and fraudulent program, sold to Americans as an insured retirement plan. It is instead, the world's largest Ponzi scam. Money is collected from those in the work force who still pay social security taxes. The money paid to retired workers comes directly from these taxes, and not from a trust fund built from their own previous contributions. To make the scam complete, government confiscates any surplus money from social security taxes for the year and counts it as income to the treasury, rather than as another obligation, which is what it actually is. By ignoring this piece of the national debt, and similarly ignoring its future obligation to today's workers, government adds yet another lie when it issues reports on the national debt, since it omits its huge social security obligation.

* Public Education   Refer to Chapter 13

Government does not have the task, the authority or the wisdom to mandate universal education, nor can it show a mandate from the people to subsidize education. Neither can government claim that public education, to some level, is a proper national goal since it does not have virtually unanimous consent from the people. Education, like choices of one's occupation, home location, or the consumption of alcohol, is a matter of personal choice, which carries with it attendant obligations, and nothing more. Not only is education strictly a matter of individual choice, but also there is no logic that justifies the confiscation of one person's income to pay for another person's education.

* Local Government's Part in America's Decline   Refer to Chapter 14

The number of thefts, unjust actions, loss of rights and other crimes against individuals by local government can not be measured because there have been so many such crimes. Consider some of the more disturbing ones. There are the dictatorial acts of confiscation via Eminent Domain. There are unending assaults on first amendment rights. Excessive controls are leveled at businesses and against a person's right to work. Loss of specific individual rights is all-too-often upheld in local courts when they conflict with government plans. There is incessant local creation of bad laws aimed at small groups and specific individuals, laws faviorable to monied special interests. There is also rampant misuse of the ultimate in tyranny, namely government dictates via majority rule. Majority rule in America has come to mean one more than half of *any sized group* government agencies wish to assemble in deciding an issue, any issue.

Special condemnation is also due of local government agencies whose continuing practice of inequality is one of America's greatest shames.

* The Preservation of Unalienable Rights   Refer to Chapter 15

The net effect of all those actions taken by government, that should never have occurred, has been to gut our once-overflowing storehouse of rights to its present, greatly depleted level. Were we to grade local and federal government performance fairly, as we would students, the grade would be a resounding F for failure. Assign a plus or a minus for rights preserved or depleted. This results in a rough numerical value of government performance regarding rights and sovereignty of individuals.

11

This was done for a useful list of 24 self-evident **rights** Americans should be able to exercise. Quantitatively, all the claims of government misdeeds boil down to the following:

19 rights have lost ground, giving an overall grade of a mere 10 %, a failing grade by a wide margin;

1 right has been enhanced of the 24, (an advance for barely 5% of our rights entrusted to the government);

1 is neutral, meaning no loss or gain in that right. and for the rest I see no change.

This grade, of course, doesn't tell us anything about the degree of loss, merely that there is degradation. Privately, I have carried the arithmetic one more step, by assigning a subjective value of loss compared to the initial 100 percent we began with. Thus, beginning with 100 points for each of the 24 key rights in this exercise, (2400 points total) this subjective score of our precious rights now totals a piddling 1440 points. This leaves a bit less than 60 % remaining. Compared to the individual rights Americans had at the founding, that estimate, preliminary or not, is shocking. We should all be horrified if this estimate is borne out by further study. The loss of rights is enough to rattle anyone. What follows in this book will add substance to the reality of our loss. Even if the estimate were off by half, it would still be reason enough to act with dispatch to fix government.

After reviewing what follows, each reader may arrive at a personal summation. To me it tells of a tragedy for all Americans; one that is getting worse every year.

* * *

Clearly, evidence to support each of the claims made here is needed. Part I of The Last Debate provides the details of these disturbing and often alarming stories.

CHAPTER 3
What Government Should & Should Not Do

Everyone is vulnerable in varying degrees to the willful greed of others, and that exposure is motivation enough to look for ways to improve security, usually by joining with others. Safeguarding individuals takes many forms because enemies come in every guise and every warped philosophy imaginable. Whether the takers are foreign tyrants, religious zealots, warlords, over-ambitious politicians, petty crooks, murderers, rapists, do-gooders, fraudulent business men or just opportunists who subvert the law for personal gain, individuals need help to combat them. The plain fact is that the need is far beyond anyone's naked ability to provide for their own protection.

The world hasn't advanced to the point where force has been replaced by wisdom and maturity. That fact makes government still the only practical means to achieve security for a nation and its people. The same reasoning shows the need for force, via local elements of government, for internal security. Government's one sure use, therefore, is to combat aggressive actions with the authority and force resources supplied by those who want protection. But, and this is a critical but, in spite of the breadth of functions managed by all governments to date, there is no compelling argument that allows the use of government power to be extended to all other matters of living within a nation. The way to think about the dos and don'ts of government, and what it should and shouldn't do, is to start with a clean slate. This means not simply accepting the usual solution of history because it is so badly skewed toward the exercise of power for all matters involved in running a country.

Two useful ways of thinking about government's role in life come to mind. The first is to understand what the best mechanism should be for empowering an ideal government. The second is to think of government as a means for handling those problems that only respond to force. We may not like that we are still dependent on force to live, but being realists in today's world can lead to no other conclusion.

Consider the first perspective regarding government. The foundation for any government is the set of ideals it rests upon. From those ideals, all its major decisions are derived. History's lesson shows that the use of force has always been the foundation for governments until the Americans came along. Until then, power was universally applied first against those at home to show who is in control, and next, against anyone weak enough to be conquered. Such a foundation has been and still is devoid of all merit, because it does not recognize the sovereignty of people, nor their inherent rights. Logic is completely missing when that foundation is force, elevated to the chosen ideal for government forming.

Individuals bound to such a government have no sovereignty or rights. Nevertheless, only people can run government. The contradiction is evident. The controllers, those having decision-rights, must be special because no one else has any rights. But the thing that makes them special is the force they control, and nothing else. This is classic circular reasoning, and that can be the foundation for nothing worth while. Decisions from a government so formed, are based on how, when and where to apply power, because that's what it does. This may be starting to have a familiar ring to it for late twentieth, early twenty first century Americans.

We have to look elsewhere to know what the right foundation is when forming a government. Fortunately, it's close by, hovering just over our clean slate. Each person, considered separately, has zero power over any other person. Nor does anyone else have decision-making power over the first person. That takes force out of consideration entirely, because even if all citizens contribute their rightful power over others, it still adds up to zero. All anyone can really contribute toward a just government is that portion of their rights and fortune they are willing to yield in return for their safety and other services they deem essential. Further, there is no implication that they must make similar sacrifices for any other actions by a government.

All we have to recognize and agree upon, therefore, is that each person arrives on earth with the same sovereignty as every other person, nothing less and nothing more, and with rights equal to those of anyone else. Government based on these ideals, therefore, has the primary duty of preserving that equality while providing its shield of security at all required levels. The foundation for a truly just government, therefore, must center around such ideals.

The combined sovereignty of a large group of people willing to forego a portion of their inherent rights, sovereignty and treasure to create a fitting foundation for government can do exactly that. When that happens, the basis for an ideal government is at hand. Decisions to be made by a government based on the combined sovereignty of all its member citizens begins any debate for actions with the well-being of those citizens foremost in mind. While no government has ever been formed with such an ideal as its foundation, the early Americans did make a stab at it. Their efforts, even though they fell short of the mark, did give their descendants, you and me, all the guidance we really need to know about what a just government should be. And equally as important, by our observations of U. S. government history, the work of the founders has also shown what government should not be.

14

What A Just Government Should Be And Do

We can now state the ideals upon which government's foundation can rest solidly, and from which jointly held decisions can emanate.

Suitable government is one which rests upon only two things: the collected sovereignty and rights of all those who join together for mutual benefit, and their agreement to bind themselves together as a people under a national constitution.

The characteristics and breadth-of-power of such a government are relatively easy to jot down. The following list covers most of the essentials, but there are other salient factors that will come to mind. What this list amounts to is the target we're aiming for as we begin planning for a better way to govern ourselves. For the moment, the following comments can be made about government based on such high ideals.

- It is a government that is minimum in size, in power and in resources expended
- It creates no arbitrary rules or laws
- It is a government whose authority, functions and power are derived by agreement from virtually all the people, in accordance with a constitution drafted by those people
- Legislation is never enacted until there is proof of constitutionality
- The preservation of equality, individual sovereignty and unalienable rights of all people are placed ahead of any other goal;
- Government is charged with the responsibility to promote the stability of those elements of a society that people depend upon in normal living
    Preserve equality of opportunity in all matters
    Foster a stable social order
    Foster a stable economic order
- It is a government that adheres to the rules by which it agreed to operate, meaning its contract with the people
- Government is structured to incorporate the founding ideals directly in its makeup
- Via constitutional means, government can deal with crimes of officials to protect against unlawful acts from within government.

What Government Should Not Be Or Do

Having set the founding ideals for building an improved government, there are many actions it will not be allowed to take.

Government does not:

- Make personal decisions for citizens
- Issue licenses for normal living activities
- Become the caretaker of individuals
- Make unconstitutional law
- Confiscate an individual's property, rights, sovereignty or labor
- Confiscate almost 50 % of a worker's income
- Give away money or other national assets
- Delegate authority to another agency to meet its own responsibilities
- Create a new kind of tyranny through the control of money, or by regulating the working and living activities of individuals
- Make itself the prime beneficiary when carrying out national goals
- Murder its citizens
- Flirt with bankruptcy in its drive to control money and business transactions
- Turn the nation into the world's greatest debtor
- Compete with or subsidize any commercial enterprise
- Seek to control any industry
- Draw up the rules (the contract) by which it will operate
- Attempt to enact now those rules for which future generations should have the responsibility
- Change the purpose of government from preserving liberty, tranquility and the benefits of liberty into one of single-minded expansion of government size and sphere of influence.

Take very special notice of this sad fact. American government today is practicing every single one of these nefarious "don'ts".

And, a final extremely important fact to bear in mind, government is not a mere collection of fifty states, each claiming sovereignty and having some common goals. Neither nations nor states can justify any claim of sovereignty beyond what its citizens bestow on it, since that is a quality human beings alone can possess. A nation, therefore, is a collection of sovereign individuals with a universal need for security, and an abiding desire to live as a unified, equal and free people.

16

PART I
Government's Failures, Mistakes, Lies, Frauds & Crimes

This part of the book spotlights some, but certainly not all, of the critical failures of American government. If there were a tribunal for true justice, where the indictments that follow might be judged, the proper outcome would be to suspend the entire organization, top to bottom, and replace it with an advanced model of self government.

17

CHAPTER 4
Squandering A People's Wealth

There's really no good place to start to tell the story of American government. It's a story of failures, excesses, fraud and crimes, and because it could begin by poking into almost any activity undertaken by either Federal or local governments, we know immediately that the problem is very serious.

I'll begin, therefore, with what I consider to be the worst of the worst, government give-aways of money extracted, by force, as taxes.

Very early in its tenure, the fledgling American government debated the merits of donating money to a small group of people who had lost their homes and possessions in a fire. The natural sympathy of officials quickly moved them to pass legislation in favor of the unfortunate families, even though they had no authority to do so.

The mistake made by those officials, while quite understandable, was to confuse their compassion as good citizens wanting to help, with their duties and responsibilities as public servants. That one act could eventually lead to America's demise. Once the precedent had been set, and since there was no provision for forcing a stop to gift giving, the practice simply grew over time to the monster action it has reached today.

Being the clever and resourceful people they are, moreover, politicians have since found ways to apply gift giving so that they too benefit greatly in the process. Once again we have to become a bit more clever ourselves to cut through the political screens to understand just what has taken place since that first innocuous, but foreboding gift of long ago.

Today, Members of both political parties maneuver ever-larger amounts of money to special interest organizations. Many of them disguise their real purposes by every imaginable ruse, as something of value to various segments of Americans. Mostly they have no value at all. Their innocuous charters and statements of purpose, however, do meet government's criteria for receiving "grants." Whatever else they do with the money, large donations are made to both major political parties, the DNC and the RNC, thus helping to finance re-election campaigns. The loop is closed, as these political action groups carry out one of their main purposes, which is to support the growth of government.

The thefts, fraud, subterfuge and dishonorable acts committed in perpetuating this practice are a national disgrace. It has, by long practice, now become sacrosanct, doing great financial harm to all taxpayers, and with the potential for even greater harm to the nation.

Let me emphasize that it has become a two-party crime, since both act in unison to follow this one overriding plan to control money. The American two-party system, always marginal at best, has effectively become a one-party conglomerate, following a single, unacceptable, philosophy for control of the nation.

One might logically wonder, taking together all government spending, giving and squandering, what such actions have done to the national debt.

Ask government what the amount of America's debt is to the world and ourselves, and they will look you straight in the eye and lie to you. They've been doing it for so long now they have almost convinced themselves they are being honest. In 1992 they admitted to a national debt of about 4.2 trillion dollars. Remember this means that beyond spending every dollar of each year's take from taxes, nominally another trillion 1992 dollars, government, over the years has borrowed enough to add up to the $4.2 trillion they admit to.

What they won't tell you is the size of commitments made requiring future spending that are also part of America's real obligations. They purposely leave out huge debt items, including 'retirement' fund money for social security, railroad and military beneficiaries, and the ever-growing basket of 'off-budget' expenditures.

To my knowledge, no one outside of government knows precisely how much money has been borrowed to enable government to fund their burgeoning spending programs. There are, however, independent organizations and investigators who try diligently to look beyond the government lies to warn of America's real financial condition.

One such independent estimate for the gross (in every sense) 1995 national debt was given in a study by James Dale Davidson, Editor of the 'Strategic Investing Newsletter." The values and breakdown of the main items of the debt were given as follows:

Publicly Held Debt	$3.4 Trillion
Federal Trust Fund	$1.2 T

both debts acknowledged by the government

19

Social Security Obligation	$7.2 T
Medicare A & B Commitment	$5.6 T

these last two ignored by government, but still real.

TOTAL DEBT $17.4 TRILLION

It may be that we will never know the true picture until historians fifty years hence dig through the rubble. A real concern we should have is how big that pile of debris will be. That subset of men and women of Washington, DC, the spenders, the Right Honorable Legislators, the thieves, the liars within government have no scruples or concern for the country or its citizens. They have only contempt for us and an overriding self-interest that is leading the nation to ruin. The only unknowns are *when* chaos will begin and *what* the details of that chaotic upheaval will be like.

There are only three possible outcomes of the mismanagement and excesses of government's fiscal stewardship. Either there is full (or negotiated), planned payback of all debts over some time period, OR there is financial bankruptcy of America accompanied by chaos of infinite possibilities, OR there is violence beyond anything seen in America, as the tens of millions who have been deceived for so long finally react in a furious rage. None of the possibilities except the first can offer any hope for reasonable people, and the longer we delay the healing process, the worse will be the pain.

A fourth alternative, continuation ad infinitum, with a painless resolution by some as yet unknown process is nothing but an illusion.

Dwell for just a moment on what the consequences would be throughout the entire world, if the USA refused to honor its staggering debt. Ours is a debt owed, not just to Americans, but also to any person or nation seduced into financing it. The repercussions would be enormous. No facet of our global, tenuous civilization would be untouched.

In spite of such a specter, Congress – today – is willing to risk the unthinkable as it blithely continues to salt every spending bill with 'pork" in the billions of dollars. They have no idea where the limit of stability lies, but they are so imbued by the magnificence of their spending rituals, that they have become completely oblivious to the utter catastrophe that threatens us all, themselves included.

How & Why Has This Come About ?
Think a bit about how this financial house of cards came to be. To fund America's spendthrift programs, devised for political reasons, all congress needed was to find sources of money, preferably in large amounts, and agree to make regular interest payments. Governments around the world, investment institutions

20

and family trusts with very large fortunes need a safe haven for the money they manage. Such moneyed sources are, therefore, very pleased to have a place they believe is secure to park huge blocks of money, to stay ahead of inflation and also have spendable income. Their money is, therefore, working for them, and the demands on their time to manage large sums are minimal. It's a very neat arrangement for all.

All this globally interconnected financial structure needs to allow it to continue is the buyer's confidence that his principle can be retrieved whenever it's needed, either directly from the U. S. government, or indirectly by security resale on the global market. Confidence has been there, and the money structure has expanded with every increase in borrowed money. Therefore, for a very long time, government has had the ability to "create" operating capital merely be selling newly printed securities, which are nothing but bits of paper, and promising to make interest payments and to return the purchase price later. As long as there are buyers, the game can continue, with money being "rolled over" quarter after quarter, as the global money supply is regularly tapped. That's the plan, and that's government's expectation, to allow their foolishness to go on indefinitely.

If there are any among us on-lookers who expect the government's plan for controlling America's money to succeed indefinitely, they will very likely feel some distress due to recent news from the global financial market. A recent auction of U.S. government securities experienced its first ever indication that all the securities offered might not be scooped up by Japanese, German, Saudi Arabians and other buyers as in the past. No reasons were cited, but thinking that confidence in America's financial condition may be easing, seems like a reasonable assumption. This, too, might be seen as another warning.

This latter action by the international community, does hint at a measure of stability globally. In the judgment of lenders, if any one nation extends itself beyond some limit, these nations can protect themselves by simply refusing to buy more securities. That would certainly help our creditors, but it definitely would not solve our problem in America. Government's uncontrollable itch to spend would remain, and they would be forced to find another way to conjure up more money and go on as before. That prospect brings some very ugly thoughts to mind.

Among the group of fewer than 600 lawmakers, there are more than enough bitten by the power bug to continue leading us to future ruin. In their diligent pursuit of malfeasance, they think nothing of lying, misleading us and clouding truth to perpetuate their version of the end-justifies-the-means philosophy.

The next story of a recent warning bears special mention,

21

This warning of government-led disaster came from Harry E. Figgie, Jr. in his 1992 book *Bankruptcy 1995,* about the coming collapse of America, and how to stop it. The title may have encouraged the Pollyannas among us to take heart in ignoring such warnings, but nothing has happened since 1992 to negate his warning of impending collapse. Figgie's warning was this.

'In 1995, during the term of the president we elect now, our United States, *for all practical purposes*, will have spent itself into bankruptcy."

It behooves government and the sanguine among us to quibble about 1995 or the specific character of national bankruptcy, but the financial condition of the United States has deteriorated so badly, and our profligate ways have continued so unabated, that there can be no optimism about the impending future. The juggernaut we're riding is so huge, representing the biggest single chunk of economic activity in the entire world, that its sheer momentum will force it along. Any guesstimate of time remaining is not nearly as important as the calamity which seems to be its ultimate resting place. Whether that end looks like bankruptcy, economic ruin of a form never seen before, hyperinflation to the ultimate loss of all accumulated wealth or even bloody civil anarchy, there can be no cause for satisfaction among political leaders who chose to ignore Figgie, Peter Grace, Milt Friedman and others who cry out for reason.

Any temporary respite from such an end through less reckless spending is another possible scenario that will soothe some who hope things will still be all right. Unfortunately, the rules that have allowed excesses in the past will still be there and will be exploited again when it suits Congress to do so. The temptation to abuse government powers will not disappear of it's own accord, being so thoroughly ingrained as it is.

Figgie is an expert in business cost reduction, an entrepreneur and a CEO of a billion dollar company. He served as cochairman with J. Peter Grace on the Grace Commission, tasked by President Reagan to survey cost control measures for government. That commission documented, with cold factual data, 2478 cost-saving recommendations. Just one of those will tell of the sad state of government operations. Government Revenues, money from taxes and other sources, sit in non-interest bearing accounts until it is spent, and this practice causes the loss of billions of dollars annually. The business of government, the largest money enterprise in the world, obviously has no business manager, someone even the smallest enterprise knows it cannot do without.

Another example: The Rural Electrification Administration (REA) lends two billion dollars, at a loss of $350 million every year. This agency continues to operate long after the job of electrification has been completed, spending and losing money *because politicians can use it to buy personal power for themselves.*

The Grace Commission recommendations were submitted in January of 1984. At the time the report was submitted, the aggregate waste and inefficiency of government was found to be an astounding *one third of all tax dollars consumed.* The report soon found its way to a shelf, and to date no direct action has been taken to implement most of the cost-saving measures. A mere ten percent savings had been realized between 1984 and 1992 of the potential total identified.

* * *

Another Benchmark
As of the mid 1990s, the national debt acknowledged by Congress, the one carefully chronicled, was already over five trillion dollars, slightly less than the projections made by Figgie and Swanson in 1992. As we saw earlier, however, the debt admitted to is only part of the real total, so there is no cause for optimism.

This "surface" debt is equivalent to about $80,000 of liability per household, and is growing rapidly. Americans have become the largest debtor in world history, in real terms such as yearly wages. The build-in practice of making interest-only payments, while continuing to increase the debt principle through further accelerated borrowing, assures that we will *never* become debt free. Not only do we add to our own debt, mortgaging more and more of our future productive income, but also we guarantee by the interest-only foolishness to usurp the incomes of our own next generation and the next. This assumes, of course that by some magic, catastrophe is postponed beyond those later years.

That is what the national debt should mean to us as individual citizens. And just what is it we've been buying that mortgages our own future and those of our descendants? We're buying *Entitlement Programs* to pay other, less productive Americans, non-productive Americans and non-Americans, benefits to people whom government leaders think deserve to be subsidized with zero return to the taxpayer. The money paid is a pure gift made by government without our intent or consent; a direct outgrowth of that first innocuous gift made by government almost 200 years ago.

We are also buying the services of an ever-swelling bureaucracy whose task is to devise more restrictions on our freedoms, and more and more ways to extract the fruits of labor for their own use. Their generosity, with our future incomes, has also bought for members of Congress a renovated beauty shop ($375,000), an improved air conditioned interoffice subway, ($1 million), a renovated restaurant ($2 million), a quarter million dollar *study* of TV lighting for Senate meeting rooms, ever expanding support staffs which brought total Congressional operating costs to $2.8

23

billion in 1991. This was also aided in no small way by awarding themselves a huge pay increase to $133,644 per year, and a new retroactive pension plan that created 200 new millionaires among those already retired and 300 more prospective millionaires when they retire later. The price tag for this: almost one half billion dollars per year. Their attitude is clearly that money available for their discretionary use is unlimited and it will always be so.

We have also bought a trip to the moon for a dozen or so Americans, with a chance to gloat on the world's stage about what a superior people we are. We have bought a military capability we still desperately need, but then have allowed much of it to be sold to friends and **enemies** alike. Any net gain in our own security by these actions is moot at best. We bought a war in Vietnam to our everlasting shame. We have financed loans to other borrowers, financed gifts controlled by others to third world countries, and certainly not last or least, we have subsidized the re-election of ensconced politicians positioned to take full advantage of the greatest spending binge in history.

Little of this spending is at all essential. Too much of it has no substance at all. Some of it is perversely counter to our true goals as a nation and as individuals. You must judge whether we have made wise purchases in light of the horrendous costs involved. My own opinion is that the only justifiable reason for taking the huge risk of financial ruin, not only of our own generation but also of the next, is if we had been faced with an even worse catastrophe and had no alternative. Such was not even close to the actual condition that spawned our present cavalier method of operations.

The true reasons for the debacle are two. First was a monumental arrogance within the political hierarchy that viewed the United States as rich beyond measure, capable of doing anything it wanted. These leaders suffered from the same malady of earlier rulers, thinking they had the right to speak for us in using that great wealth. President Johnson's 'Great Society" is the perfect example of that underlying arrogance. Man's weaknesses and misplaced ambitions needed one other accomplice to allow things to go as they have. The Constitution was that ally.

Our constitution allows unlimited taxation, and it allows unlimited spending. It allows unlimited debt, and it provides no criteria by which the wisdom of proposed legislation can be measured. And, even though the known failings of men motivated the designers of American government's present structure in an attempt to contain man's deficiencies, it provided no *real limitations* on the accumulation and use of power. In fact, in one very critical provision, 'the power to suspend citizen rights in a national emergency," it actually provides for the use of unlimited government power.

24

The story of how bad our fiscal condition is and how it got that way is not yet complete, however, and it is important that it be understood clearly.

Every President and every Congress from Johnson on have fueled the fires of self-immolation. The previous 183 years had left us with a total debt of about $310 billion, with the preponderance of that coming in a period of about 20 years during and after WW II. At the beginning of G.W. Bush's second term (1/25/05), The published U.S. debt was about 7.627 trillion dollars, climbing at 2.12 billion dollars each DAY.

The approximate debt increases during each president's term in office are listed in the following table. All of these figures are supposed to be what government itself admits to, but other estimates often differ in the details. The admitted debt increase of $ 7.3 trillion in 41 years, however, is a very good indication of how spending has become the single most important activity of the U.S. Government. In a mere forty-one years, we have managed to multiply the national debt by 23.5 times the debt after our first 183 years of existence. Perhaps we might be allowed to ask where the evidence of fiscal responsibility is in any of this.

President [1]	Added Debt		Debt in Billions	Year
Johnson	$40	in 5 years	$ 358	1968
Nixon	$150	in 6 years	$ 492	1974
Ford	$120	in 2 years	$ 653	1976
Carter	$270	in 4 years	$ 930	1980
Reagan	$1710	in 8 years	$2602	1988
Bush (1)	$1464	in 4 years	$4064	1992
Clinton	$1742	in 8 years	$5656	2000
Bush (2)	$1971	in 4 years	$7627	2005

Bush the first, presided over our national well being by racking up a debt increase *in one year* that was greater than we accumulated in our first 183 years of existence; $400 billion versus $310 billion. Reagan's record binge of $1672 billion over an eight-year span was thoroughly eclipsed by Bush's record as of 1992 of $1.4 trillion. Granted, these are different dollars in each of the years listed, but their reduced values with time were mostly the result of government economic mistakes. We could go on, but such tidbits can be unfair and distract us from the real culprits, who have been the Congresses throughout this whole period. Some other snapshot facts are a better indicator of the sources of the problem.

---

[1] Source: Office of Management and Budget, the administration's arm charged with budgetary matters.

In 1974, the national clamor about our deteriorating economic condition was already a major concern. Government's attempts at maintaining full employment, regulating wages and prices, guaranteeing every citizen a "decent standard of living" through welfare (food stamps, housing subsidies, medical aid, education, income support for the poor and elderly and even recreational facilities) and the beginnings among the people of high expectations for material goods had all begun to create serious inflationary pressures on everyone's livelihood. Between WW II and 1974, the dollar had lost almost two thirds of the intrinsic purchasing power it had in 1945, and having to pay almost three times more for everything in just a 30-year span is noticeable to everyone.

1974

William Simon, then Treasury Secretary, pinpointed the main ingredients needed to correct the problem. First he targeted the demand among people for ever-increasing government handouts. We can take discomfiting note that today that demand has escalated far beyond the 1974 level and still people expect more. In fact, as new generations come along, the demand is even more strident. The attitude is increasingly one of being *owed* this subsidy from government just for being alive. In my view, that attitude of the rank and file is government-made, a direct product of the congressional strategy to buy votes with taxpayer money and increasingly with *borrowed* money. The vicious tail-chase instability of this debilitating policy is so obvious that it seems trite to have to point it out.

Unfortunately, it must not be obvious at all to the millions of voters being subsidized by other people who work to retain their independence from government but who are slowly, inexorably losing ground. And, in spite of its obvious nature and the clear long term debilitating effects on the entire country, it seems that our legislators can easily ignore such things when faced with the choice between buying votes through more government gifts or doing something sensible toward long term economic stability.

That fateful step taken so long ago, to extract wealth by force from income producers in order to give it to others — for "worthy causes" — *has become a way of life both for the recipient and for those who dole out the bounty as well.* Their entire political philosophy has become centered on currying favor among the voters. All government needed to do was to keep the handouts coming in infinite variety. They did, they succeeded in their careers, and their inventiveness blossomed into places even a lottery winner might envy. The giving has long since passed the time when the real need ended.

It has always been a necessary thing, and a charitable thing to help someone in serious need, but one cannot satisfy that need by fiat through policies that can only aggravate the problem. Those doing the giving, not of their own money but of other people's money, have an incentive to continue without any foreseeable limit because they benefit by being kept in power. Those receiving the help have an incentive to continue *eligibility* by maintaining their condition of need. The process is truly unstable since both groups have good reason to make it go on. Instead, true needs are most sensibly met by the innate generosity of Americans who are truly interested in helping the needy achieve or return to self-reliance.

Secretary Simon's next point regarding inflation in 1974 was the clearly excessive spending by government. Even at that time, he distinguished between the spending of money still under direct Congressional control (about 25% of the budget), and the remainder of spending obligations inherited from previous Congressional acts, which were termed uncontrollable. Actually, none of government spending is uncontrollable, since changes can always be made to commitments made in earlier years. All that is required is the political guts to do it (on second thought, perhaps that does mean it is uncontrollable). Simon's optimism that the 1974 Congress would lower spending proved to be misplaced as it continued the relentless rise in spending. By then, the government was already becoming very clever, and equally devious, in the manner in which reality might be obscured and spending continued, and of course, expanded. The need for more esoteric game-playing became acute as compounding of debt worked against them more seriously every year. Their potentially disastrous policies *had* to be made more palatable, and the con game of the century was under way.

Smoke, Mirrors and Lies

Like every other aspect of things, living or inanimate, government evolves with time. The evolutionary process in American government, however, goes beyond the usual progression in complexity. The single-minded goal of politicians to get themselves re-elected, created an undercurrent that became an all-important first criterion by which a pending decision would be measured. The question being asked, subliminally at first and then overtly, was not whether an action would promote security or freedom or individual liberty, or remove blockades in the pursuit of happiness. Instead, the question asked was whether the chance for re-election would be increased or decreased by what the person was about to do. The answer had to be *for* re-election first. If it coincided with the other legitimate goals of government that was a bonus, but if it didn't, then all that was missing was a plausible, logical argument (i.e. lie) to support the action. Thus the true sophistication of an evolving institution created to govern can be measured by the intricacies of logic resorted to in justifying things that are more self-serving than wise. The chicanery described below is not chronological, but it is an accurate portrayal of our Right Honorable Legislators.

- A *reduction* in deficit for the coming fiscal year is any change that makes the budgeted deficit smaller than some earlier estimate. Thus, while the new budget actually legislates a *greater deficit* than the previous year, the Right Honorable Legislators call it "a reduction in overspending." The *estimate* of possible future spending has thereby been elevated to the measuring stick by which Congress tallies its own performance grade. No one who looks at their lie is fooled, but they are self-satisfied since no one has any recourse or power to force them to change the lie. George Orwell's 1984 doublespeak is true and *reduction* means *increase*.

• A favorite tactic of the Right Honorable Legislators to conceal their actions is not to acknowledge some expenditure as a part of the national debt. They have created a whole class of expense items which are termed 'Off Budget." Thus, not included within a budgetary plan, they needn't accept their existence as debts. When these measures actually return income, as they have for many of the years since this tactic began, the money simply adds to their power base. The lie is meant only as a way of deceiving the public about their true excesses, because to date they have not even attempted to withhold payment on any of these obligations. The debts are real, payments are made, but they remain just another oddball action of government to the trusting voter.

Of course, the Right Honorable Legislators have passed a law, which "requires" them to keep certain — real expenses — *off the budget*. Their 'Off Budget" lies are therefore legal. As the listing of such high cost items below will show, they have succeeded by this deceitful strategy to make any Balanced Budget Amendment to the Constitution meaningless without including an ironclad understanding of what is to be balanced. One has the uneasy feeling that, given such an amendment, the first task of the Right Honorable Legislators would be to redefine things to allow a continuation of their unlimited spending policies. Any items that can be classified as an emergency expense, or are *created* outside the budget or have some source of income are *required* off-budget items.

• The Postal Service is an off-budget expense even though it costs in excess of a billion dollars a year, an expense paid by the government with real tax money!

• The Federal Deposit Insurance Corporation (FDIC) and the Resolution Trust Corporation are off-budget obligations. They are government insurance companies backed by United States Treasury money or borrowed money, depending on how you view it. The cost to United States taxpayers for the Savings and Loan bailout is already in excess of $500 billion. This money was spent because the fraud and theft within the Savings and Loan industry came under the *insurance* obligations of the United States Government. The expense is real. It adds directly to the real national debt, and no one in government has ever been held accountable.

• Another favorite tactic used by Right Honorable Legislators is to underestimate projected expenses. We can be confident that the tactic is a willful attempt to lie to taxpayers because **every single estimated budget** ever made during our sick fiscal period has been grossly low. In several cases, the actual deficit exceeded the estimated deficit by more than 100% (1990, 1982, 1981, and 1980, for example). The initial estimate for Savings and Loan insurance payouts was $50 billion. The true cost was more than ten times that amount.

We have to ask ourselves why our government is in the insurance business, or at the very least why such insurance losses don't qualify as real debt.

• The Pension Benefit Guarantee Corporation is another government insurance corporation. It guarantees, for a fee, to fulfill a company's pension obligations if the company is unable to do so. The obligation is an open ended one of the worst kind, virtually without limit. Because of the high fees (premiums) it must charge, mostly weak, risky companies seek such protection and the net risk to the national debt is staggering. Where did it say in the Constitution that I was willing to have money extracted from my income to pay for the future pensions of workers in risky, nameless companies? The pension obligations to employees belong to each company, and sound fiscal policy within the company is the proper answer, not some open ended insurance obligation of government.

• Federal Loans and Loan Guarantees make up another fiscal function of government that should never have started. Direct loans, made by such government agencies as the Small Business Administration and the Export-Import Bank put the government squarely into the banking business. Not only are they in competition with private enterprise, a Constitutional prohibition, but also the rules under which they allow themselves to operate are much more lenient than for private banks. For this they are rewarded with high-risk transactions, which default far beyond the banking industry norm. Such losses must be paid for with taxes or borrowed money.

Loan Guarantees for such things as student loans, FHA, VA, Rural Electrification (mentioned earlier), and Small Business Disaster Loans, are even worse business ventures. The failure, however, is not because of poor business acumen. Borrowers, among the most risky, collectively are beneficiaries of another government subsidy, both from the low interest rates allowed *and* the great numbers who default on their obligation to repay. In 1992, the student loan default debt by itself, a debt that must be paid by taxes from other citizens, was a resounding $13.5 billion. Government once again has acted on the false notion that it is their prerogative to take money by force from some to give it to others whom government decides need a handout. However it is disguised, a gift is a gift and the real *givers* had no say in the matter.

* * *

29

An Aside

The story of fraud, deceit, lies, conniving and general failure of governmental stewards goes on seemingly without end. Before going on with the worst of it, however, it's important to take a short de tour to recall the efforts of some other men of courage and integrity who opposed the drive toward financial ruin. The real significance of their saga was that they tried to correct the problem of gross financial mismanagement from within government itself. They tried, within the rules, procedures and powers open to them, that is, within the system of checks and balances established by Constitutional provisions, to correct a blatant corruption of the use of power by a branch of government — and they failed utterly. They failed not for want of trying or for making use of every legitimate means open to them, but because the structure and provisions of American government are fundamentally flawed. They literally could not correct the problem no matter what their efforts or desires might have been. All it took to frustrate their efforts were a relatively few other men of little character who wanted to preserve the status quo. Think then of the *impossibility* of correcting this source of government excess from outside government via the citizen vote. The notion would be laughable if it weren't so sad. We need to honor their efforts, however. To us outsiders this bit of government history represents a powerful reason for replacing present government peacefully, as soon as practicable. The story of those official's attempts to work within government practices follows.

The frustrations of watching the dangerous foolishness of the Right Honorable Legislators, finally reached one critical level in 1985. Thanks to the efforts of a group of determined congressional leaders, a bill was passed in December of that year with the potential to fix the problem outright. The bill, known as the Balanced Budget and Emergency Deficit Control Act, (sponsored by Senator Warren B. Rudman, R - **NH**, Senator Ernest F. Hollings, D - SC, and Senator W. Philip Gramm, R - TX) **required** with the force of LAW, that budget deficits *must not exceed* specified goals to limit budget deficits. Those goals were required by the new law to decrease in roughly equal increments from the actual deficit of $212 billion in 1985 to zero in 1991. Any actual deficit that exceeded the legal limits, *mandated* automatic cuts *by law*. Half the excess was to be cut from both defense and non-defense programs. The sacred cow of entitlement programs (those government subsidies granted to everyone who met certain qualifications, no matter how many people qualified) was never even included in the law. Including entitlements would have had ominous repercussions on the vote-buying legislation so carefully built up over the years, and could not be allowed by the spenders.

The very first test of this law came in 1986 when the deficit exceeded the limit by about $40 billion. Next, drastic cuts in spending for 1987 were so unpalatable to the spenders that they easily revised the young law to increase the allowed deficits by as much as $60 to $70 billion and extend the time to reach the zero deficit goal another two years. **Neither the old nor the new goals were ever met in any year,** as the deficits from 1988 on soared from $155 billion to almost $400 billion in 1992. Among the spenders, there had never been any serious intent to change their ways. They made this known by the ease with which they changed the allowable limits both in 1987 and again in 1990, at which time they didn't even bother to set new target dates. The law had become a farce, nothing more than just another annoyance to the spenders like the so-called national debt ceiling. When these limits were threatened, the solution was simply to raise them and go on spending.

What a clear illustration of the folly of majority rule! The hard-fought victory to set deficit limits at all was shunted aside by a simple majority vote of Congress, and big government returned easily, and shamelessly to the excessive spending of other people's money.

*   *   *

One of the Greatest Frauds of an Uncontrollable Government

Every two years we renew the ranks of our unscrupulous legislators, and the batch in power in the late 1980s deserves special mention. The social security tax increase of 1983 had for several years generated a surplus of tax revenues over benefits paid and had created a cash-rich, non interest bearing trust fund to help pay obligations to future retirees. The trust fund was like a hypnotizing narcotic to the spenders, who soon passed legislation allowing Congress to *count this money as income to the General Fund.* This allowed any real budget deficit to look smaller by the amount taken from the fund. The scurrilous fraud practiced on the public was a two-headed monster. They borrowed money and called it income (Fraud #1). They replaced the borrowed money with non-marketable Treasury bonds that have no collateral value whatsoever (Fraud #2). These IOUs are, like other government borrowing instruments, are backed by the 'full faith and credit of the United States of America," which is a legalistic way of saying they're backed by the taxing power of Congress. It's not much of a leap of logic to see that since Congress hasn't extracted enough taxes to meet its own budget, that borrowing more money from Social Security just means it is another debt that won't be repaid. Neither interest payments nor payback provisions are made in the statutes written in connection with the *theft* of this Social Security Trust Fund money. The theft to date is already in the *trillions* of dollars.

The Constitution has no answer for the crimes being committed by Congress. The Constitution gives Congress power to make law — without real restrictions — and it provides zero recourse when criminal acts are made 'legal." Clearly, the flaw is a glaring, noxious omission within our foundation document.

31

The thieves of Congress, having found gold in the Social Security Trust Fund and a temporary respite from the harsh glare of truth in front of the citizenry, have chosen to pinch the economic soundness out of *every other fund* under their direct control.   Pension funds for the military, post office, railroads and civil service; Medicare surplus and highways and airports trust funds have all been targets of Congressional avarice.   The as yet publicly uncounted obligations that attach to these scurrilous acts of *OUR representatives* have never even been acknowledged by them as obligations, yet the reality of it cannot be avoided indefinitely. For instance, now you know of the deeds.

A Discouraging Update

What's the score for 2004? On the dust cover of Joe Scarborough's 2004 book, 'Rome Wasn't Burnt In A Day," is his kind, national debt estimate of *Seven Trillion Dollars*. I say 'kind" because even he, a congressman throughout most of the 1990s, a very conscientious one at that, hadn't picked up on the gargantuan hidden debt items. His 7 trillion dollars is comparable to the   4.6 trillion acknowledged by government in 1995.

In nine short years, the acknowledged piece of our debt had jumped   52 %. Without adding a nickel of debt to the hidden debt items, (and how likely is that) the actual debt went from **17.4 T to 19.8 T** If that entire anchor and chain, the one shackled to our necks, has expanded by 52 %, (a more likely situation), our debt would be closer to 26.4 T.

Since we don't yet know the real size of the debt, consider that it is 25 trillion dollars. Spread over 280 million children, women and men, means that government has spent, given away, squandered, and otherwise wasted over $89,000 per person - - as of today, and climbing, none of it ever to be paid back.   Remarkable! Remember, this huge amount is over and above what government has spent using yearly tax money.

If we count only productive workers, workers such as yourself and myself, our debt is over $350,000 for each of us. That, Mister and Mrs. American worker is what you owe to Japanese, German, Saudi Arabian, and other foreign lenders who have helped us buy the stuff we hardly even know about.

Even more Remarkable isn't it?

CHAPTER 5
Individual Security –
A Fast Fading Treasure

Besides the attack on the 50th state in 1941, the last time an invading army threatened Americans, it triggered the War of 1812. Since that event, all security losses experienced by U.S. citizens have have been the direct result of premeditated American government actions. The most serious cuts by government into the fabric of personal safety have come since the end of Hitler's war, but throughout our entire history, an individual's security has never been given the same measure of importance as that of the nation as a whole.

In this chapter, we are concerned with the whole gamut of factors that give a person confidence in his safety, but the review shows a tormenting dualism in government's philosophy regarding national security as opposed to the safety of individuals.

The philosophical connection has been lost between the nation as an entity to be protected, and the nation as simply the composite of all its people, who must also be protected – individually – for the nation to survive. A nation can not be preserved unless its people are secure in every way that contributes to free living. Government has forgotten that truism over the years of our existence as a unified people, a nation by the choice of its people. This chapter shows why that conclusion is true, and why it is another of government's greatest failures.

The two aspects of government's security responsibilities are very different. Two entirely separate groups of people are involved, having two completely distinct sets of problems, approaches, and solutions. Even worse, those who devote themselves to protecting individuals at home, (internal security) have not been tasked with the responsibility to protect against attacks on personal liberty by the actions of government. No one has, except government itself. That fact leaves open the very real possibility of lost rights whenever officials debate options. It is too easy to miss the connection between almost any government action, national or local, and the potential harm to a person's right to a sec ure home and life, that must be guarded against.

Therefore, government has found easy pickings in what has been a very long campaign against Americans, while never seeming to be doing so. Consider first the national record.

Foreign Threats

Keeping out foreign invaders is a huge responsibility, one which government understands well. Since no foreign force has ever invaded America, in one sense, government has done its job of maintaining national security with some success. The degree of United States preparedness in December 1941, however, was at least a government miscalculation, and at worst a calculated error resulting from a poor understanding of the world political temper. The United States was involved in creating those post WW I world conditions that fomented hardships and hatred. Thus, preventing future conflicts had poor representation within the United States government at the time. The specifics of how we entered WW II are still under debate, in particular the tactics used by President Roosevelt. In my opinion those events of late 1941 are far less important than the poor long-term planning and strategies that combined to degrade the ability to defend ourselves. The fact of early 20th century vulnerability seems clear, and there must be a level of responsibility that was deficient but spread over several administrations following the Armistice of 1918. It may even be that that failure is partly the result of citizen disgust with war and military force. If that is more to the truth of things, then government *leadership* was even more at fault. Appraisal of an external threat is a job only government can do, and that evaluation was never worse than after WW I.

Government must be given its due following the Second World War, however. The lesson of its earlier failure had been heeded. With enlightened leadership from selfless men such as President Truman and General George C. Marshall, the aftermath in defeated European and Japanese lands was constructive and positive. Peace for the future was well represented, as were the American people. And the management of that strange détente with the Soviet Union, called the Cold War, ranks among our greatest achievements as a nation, a joint venture of all citizens that we should be proud of. All that was necessary was to remain very strong and to show by example that the fruits of an industrious nation were far more satisfying and rewarding than boorish conquest.

Vietnam - Again

It's hard to reconcile our actions as a nation after WW II with those of the same nation a mere 20 years later, when we sank back to a barbarian nature that took us into Vietnam. The answer to this conundrum seems clear, however. The difference was leadership. There is within us, within any large collection of people, both the good and the bad. With wise leadership, our course is sensible. With inadequate leadership, the path of action can readily be deflected into belligerence, and force can be wrongly applied. The need of societies for wise leadership never diminishes. There will likely be little disagreement, that followers reflect the attitudes of their leaders, including the gross misdirection of Presidents Johnson and Nixon during those sad and divisive Vietnam years. There were some who *knew* at the time that our nation was wrong in being there, but their cries went unheeded by an arrogant leadership. No one should be in doubt any longer about that terrible national error.

A people, a nation, follows chosen leaders. One should be very careful whom you choose as leaders. If ever you wonder about the thickness of our national veneer of civilization, just think of what was done – in our name – in that pitiful part of the world, southeast Asia, just a brief historical moment ago.

Our Civil War - Again

Think back a bit to an earlier time. How would you quantify the loss of security sustained by everyone as the American Civil War ripped into every man, woman and child in the country? Would you count those events as fulfilling a basic responsibility of government, or as a failure of unmatched proportions? And that unconscionable failure didn't end at Lee's surrender, as leadership allowed, even instigated, the gross injustices during the debacle of 'reconstruction." The grades we must give to government for rebuffing potential foreign invaders may be high, but when the invader is ourselves and people lose everything, the effect on *Security* is the same — a total loss to us, and miserable failure of government. We've thought about that devastating war often, and it continues to be a lesion in the body national that will not heal itself. It was a failure of government of the first magnitude, yet we still treat it as if it were an enterprise of greatness that made us a better nation. It was not, and it did not.

Arms Dealer for the World [2]

How would you grade a government which changes its assessment of potential foreign enemies in ways that interchange friend and foe? The American government has followed a strange logic, which allows them to become the arms supplier for most of the world, a vast warehouse stocked with all levels of latent death. The rationale may be (as it was with the Soviets) that what we sell is obsolete compared with our most advanced weapons, but the plain fact is that even a dumb bomb can kill. In local conflicts, the Sudan, Zaire, Bosnia, and every country of the Middle East there are great quantities of American munitions. Yes, some countries have acquired American war machines 'illegally," but just their availability has made it possible for people on both sides of a deadly argument to be killed by American bullets. And when American or UN service men and women are sandwiched between combatants, they too are killed by American firearms. The liberal sprinkling around the globe of goods from the United States has become a

---

[2] The following information was taken from several sources, including: The American Spectator, Aug. '95 article, Close-Out Sale at Commerce, by Kenneth R. Timmerman, US News & World Report, Dec. 9 '96, special report, Weapons Bazaar, by Peter Cary, with Douglas Pasternak & Penny Loeb.

national disgrace, an insidious and deadly one. The real motives, tawdry profits, balancing trade deficits, and re-election are exactly wrong. They don't represent the true wishes of the American people, and in my opinion, they show a failure of our government in its responsibility to keep us secure from foreign threats. The arms broadcast like so much seed, in places known for hate and volatility, have found their way to rogue governments, terrorists and drug lords who have learned very well how to use them to hurt us most. We have made it easy for them.

The Commerce Department, by another twist of government logic, has the task of selling US military equipment that is still usable, but is no longer to be kept in inventory. Clinton's Commerce Department operated like a mail-order seller, directed first to sell as much as possible. Any attention given to controlling secondary sales is a very small part of the operation. The result is that third-party buyers have little or no problem buying whatever is for sale, and virtually everything is for sale, from old obsolete aircraft carriers, to exotic stealth technology, to advanced technology.

The reason for such sales, and the lack of concern about buyers, is easy to understand from a government perspective. The government has a very large negative cash-flow problem, and anything they can do to make it look less like the abysmal deep, is to their *political* advantage. While the Department of Defense and the Joint Chiefs of Staff might think it unwise to sell $750 million of hi-tech goods to Iraq, (Bush administration), Congress had no qualms about approving the sale. Part of that sweet deal, special induction furnaces used to *mold bomb cores for nuclear weapons*, was blocked from shipment at the last minute when the *manufacturer* questioned the wisdom of the sale! This little adventure also highlighted another bit of stupidity in the whole government process when it was learned that Commerce often side-stepped the law by not obtaining review and approval from DOD or the JCS.

Between 1990 and 1993 Commerce did the same underhanded thing regarding sales of $ 60.2 million worth of missile technology items to China.

The same was true in 1995 for sale of the decommissioned aircraft carrier Bennington, ostensibly to India, but actually to China, this even after vigorous protest by the JCS. Sales of sensitive and advanced technology to other, normally friendly governments, (e.g. Germany and France), also can find their way to hostile governments because there can be no practical control after any initial sale. The usual ploy of buyers is to learn what end-uses of equipment are acceptable to Commerce Department reviewers, and simply use those reasons on their applications. Since virtually no follow-up checks are even attempted by Commerce, we the citizens are left with no responsible deterrent to foreign threats armed by our own machines of war.

The rationale of lowering government debt by selling war-making capability to anyone is dereliction of duty, and an irresponsibility of the worst possible kind. Enemies, and potential enemies, have learned about a great American weakness, and know very well how to exploit it. We are addicted to the dollar. From government official, to party hack, to most businessmen and unfortunately to most of the people, our objective is to maximize dollars first and other things second. Such a criterion among government officials is the complete reverse of their sworn duty as elected leaders and protectors of our heritage.

I make the assertion that the *potential* harm already arrayed against America by our past policy of supplying arms — whether indiscriminately or with discretion — that potential harm far outweighs any benefit we might think is ours from the sales receipts. As a nation, we must *accept* that any money used for the purpose of security, which includes all armaments, should be viewed as a total dollar loss to us, a loss we are willing to take in money to realize the gain in security. Such a loss is completely appropriate *because* it has bought critical security in the face of foreign threats for its time in use. It is not necessary to recover any money through the sale of any of it ever, (except in the form of scrap), because the added risk to security is too great. If we were ever to become super-sensible about war materiel, we would see to it that all of it is recycled, and none of it is sold — ever.

So to repeat, how would you grade government in its threat assessment abilities, and the policies that were followed?

There is also an extension to the story of government's failure regarding arms sales. Perhaps only future historians will learn the facts, (as we are now learning about past administrations from thousands of hours of recorded conversations), but the possibilities are most disturbing. Clinton and the Democratic National Committee spent more money than any candidate ever before to buy that president a second term. Preparations to fund that campaign began early in the first term when Clinton and others saw a clear opportunity to exploit the weaknesses inherent in the Department of Commerce mentioned earlier. Allegations have been made that several appointments and decisions by the president concerning Commerce were made with possible campaign contributions as an important motivation. It became public knowledge, and an embarrassment to the office of president as an inordinate number of fund raising breakfasts, other expensive fund raiser events and one-on-one meetings with President Clinton — for a high fee — became standard procedure in the Clinton White House. All this was done to build up the account for the second term campaign. Clinton's preoccupation with re-election went far beyond any previously known, and in my opinion seriously interfered with time available for real work. Some probably think that may not be all bad, but getting re-elected is not what the power of that office is intended for.

37

The administration's strategy seems to have been to use Commerce to gain favor among foreign buyers by making it easy for them to buy critical military items. For this they would obviously be very grateful and be moved to make substantial donations to the DNC; reward enough for the administration. Since no limit is placed on contributions to the major political parties, Clinton's re-election money problems would then be solved under his guidance. The policy at Commerce clearly became one of expediting sales and minimizing any blockades that might come because of security issues. As we have already seen, expediting sales has even extended to breaking some of the laws passed to safeguard against degrading US security.

Motivation for this abdication of duty gnaws at every fiber of our being. Further, where were the safeguards constitutional, and where were the officials of the other two 'independent" branches of government who should have put a stop to this blatant sale of American security merely to re-elect an unprincipled misfit who happened to be president?

The answer is easy. Justice, branch # 1, has no real means to stop such conniving. Also, a large segment of Congress, branch # 2, benefited right along with the president and had no incentive among the leadership to prevent it.

The shallowness of such men and women is our answer. There will always be such people. Therefore, any movement for changing government to deal with like people must devise ways to do what Constitution One did not do.

Clinton also appointed John Huang as Deputy Assistant Secretary for Economic Policy at Commerce, waiving aside the usual security check given to all personnel. Huang acted as liaison for Chinese purchases and was directly involved in transactions between China and the DNC for donations to Clinton's 1996 re-election campaign fund. By 1995, according to Commerce Secretary Ron Brown, super salesman at Commerce, and another hand-picked Clinton appointee, more than two billion dollars worth of military equipment was being funneled to China yearly, with much more to come in succeeding years. All of it, including aerospace production tooling, laminate and honeycomb technology, and missile electronic technology, was still very usable and very important for the design and development of modern military equipment. According to a GAO report on Commerce activities, the Department of Commerce approved 87 percent of all applications for items going to 'controlled countries." That record alone should convince anyone that we risk hurting ourselves more than any overt enemy has ever done. Why must we be so stupid? Or is it still just smallness of character, or perhaps just raw greed and self-advancement?

The sale of first-line military technology and equipment to foreign buyers has never been greater than in the period since 1993. It hardly seems likely that anyone would purposely sell his country's strength and technological edge merely to buy himself a second term as president, but that is one implication of these recent political actions. I am moved to speculate that the recent decisions and method of operation at the Commerce Department may have generated a great fear, among some people, for the future of America. It may be that these same people are determined to end the flood of unconscionable sales to governments which have no love for us. One approach, begun in 1995, is to abolish the Department of Commerce completely. Legislation to accomplish this has been proposed by Representative Dick Chrysler [R-Mich.]. Such a move might close off the biggest hemorrhage in our security fence, but it hardly seems enough to effect real change. My own opinion is that closing down Commerce would just move the fundamental problem elsewhere and perhaps hide it even deeper. The answer to the problem is to stop selling government to government. Government's role must only be to review proposed military sales from industry to foreign buyers. As long as we continue to think it necessary to sell any "surplus" military assets, however, the potential for subverting ourselves will not go away. There is NO NEED whatsoever to sell any military assets except to our closest allies, and any "lost" revenue is irrelevant compared to the real fiscal issues we face in the US.

The US and the UN

The United States government is a key member of the United Nations, an organization that alone can have the perspective of worldwide peace. Only a world body such as the UN has the *potential* to offer the world of nations a stability that can come from arbitration, binding arbitration and police restraint when words fail. No one country can assume the responsibility for thwarting renegade nations, not even the United States. We don't want to be the world's police force , but we should be convinced by now that such a force is needed. The world regularly spawns its Saddam Husseins, its Fidel Castros, its Maummar Gadoffis, its Adolph Hitlers, Josef Stalins and other brilliant misfits regularly. Their lust for power and their viciousness can only be countered by resolve from the worldwide community, and that requires the availability of force greater than any potential threat. The job of our government, therefore, is to work toward security for all nations as part of its responsibility for a secure America.

UN military successes have been joint endeavors, in Korea, in Kuwait, elsewhere in the Middle East and in many other less well-known arenas. Where resolve was lacking, as in Sudan, Bosnia, Syria and other troubled spots, success has not followed. The need, however, to restrain forcibly the gangsters responsible for criminal acts in such trouble spots is clearly apparent. It will remain so as long as there are ruthless, well-armed gangster nations, which understand only force.

The United States has garbled its role as an important member of the UN as a global, stabilizing police force by being diverted into endless debate about other potential functions of a world body. The UN should be concerned *with one and only one function* until all nations are convinced that that function, security, is being properly handled. When worldwide security becomes a reality, then will be the time to think of other matters, such as global law, trade, and the preservation of individual rights and sovereignty.

Internal Security

The second half of American government's security task lies within our own borders. Their job is to ensure protection and deterrence from harm by thieves and people of violence. This is a monumental responsibility because of the overwhelming number of ways that harm can be inflicted, and because the attacker or the thief *always* has the advantage. An organized police force, a code of law, prisons and a judicial system (in short, an orderly system to manage the criminals among us) are all institutions devised to improve individual security. The makeup and processes of all those elements of security are continually changing as the internal threat to people's safety changes. How successful authorities are in maintaining order and confidence among the people varies widely with location, with time and with living conditions. When the statistics of crime locally go beyond a certain threshold, a great deal of extra effort is applied to regain civil control. Many good people devote their entire lives in an attempt to hold down the level of crime, knowing a crime-free condition within a free society, or indeed anywhere, may never be achieved, humans being the creatures we are.

There is a way to measure the effectiveness of government, however. Simply count the number of us who, directly and indirectly, have become victims *because* of government actions taken either to improve internal security or to carry out any other functions. The view from such a perspective can be enlightening and, I believe, is much more revealing of our state of civilization, and of the balance so far achieved in America between safety from villainous neighbors, and overt harm from government itself.

In the United States the number of victims *intentionally* created by government should be ZERO. That is our reference, our measure of how well government is succeeding in this second of its five great duties. With this as our measure, we can say immediately that there are indeed failures that need to be recognized as such. Among the most recent, we can recall a number of examples that clearly show the state of our inheritance of personal safety here in the United States.

Ruby Ridge

On August 21 and 22, 1992, at a secluded mountain cabin in Idaho, three members of Randy Weaver's family were killed by law enforcement gunmen. They acted with the approval of government authorities to use deadly force, in spite of the fact that no crime had been committed by the victims, Weaver's wife, Vicki, 14 year old Sammy, and a 10 month old infant, or by the man himself. The government killers exceeded all sensible restraints we place on ourselves as civilized beings. The priority of government was clearly not people protection first. Instead, this wanton act of murder violated government's very reason for being. Their irrational priority, instead, was submit to government force or suffer the consequences, which can be life itself. On the second day of the siege, when the wife and infant were killed, 400 federal agents were used in the assault.[3]

Later compensation to Weaver could never change the reality of his being a victim of his own government, as were the three who were murdered. Those responsible for this savage abuse of deadly authority remain in authority to fail again. The safeguards remain riddled with flaws, and the only thing lacking to spark another such disaster is the next situation that hints at confrontation with authority. Tragically, that confrontation came soon after Ruby Ridge.

The Branch Davidians

The arrogance of those who control and wield police powers reached its most degraded state near Waco, Texas in 1993. A splinter, religious cult, called the Branch Davidians, was encircled and put under siege by military and police forces. The group was deemed a public threat because it had accumulated more weapons than the average Texan. At no time during its existence, however, had any member of the cult committed a crime. Nevertheless, when the showdown came, government forces opened fire with assault weapons, armored vehicles with rams smashed holes in the compound's wooden buildings, and the place was peppered with potent tear gas grenades having incendiary side effects. In other words, the place was purposely set afire by government forces, and those inside were effectively prevented from escaping by small arms fire from outside.

Cult member efforts to protect themselves did little to slow the government attack, and shortly after it began in earnest, the compound had burned to the ground with every member left inside burned to death.

Fire-fighting forces at the scene did nothing to quell the fire.

The event was the most disturbing of any such dereliction of duty by government ever seen in the U.S. for two potent reasons. Taken together, they undermine a whole lifetime of naive belief that American government was

---

[3] Ref. The American Spectator, Aug. '95, article, "The New J. Edgar Hoover" by James Bovard .

motivated by mankind's noblest virtues. Naiveté is hard to let go of, but eventually we learn the awful truth about government. When that truth is baseness, not virtue, then one is left somewhere between futility and hope with too few clues showing reason for optimism.

The first reason that this tragedy is so real and personal is that an entire group of foolish, misled people was slaughtered by our own government with absolutely no justification. How many little children must be deliberately murdered by their own government before we know that the rules under which we live are alien to our sovereignty as individuals? One? A dozen? More? With the *eighteen* barbecued children and babies were more than 60 of their parents, guardians and protectors, who died equally horrible deaths from deliberate government acts of violence. As with the murders committed at Ruby Ridge, none of these people had broken a single just law. No other person had ever been harmed by any member of the cult. Rather, they had the misfortune to harbor paranoid-like fear of their future safety and even fears about the authorities they saw around them.

They had the misfortune to be led badly by a charismatic individual who succeeded in transferring his own warped view of the world and of salvation to the sheep around him, and leading them to a strangeness that only *seemed* a threat to others. David Koresh, known also as Vernon Howard, was right and he was wrong, but his strangeness was more than the prosaic authorities could untangle and deal with sensibly. Those who followed him can be accused of being foolish, but if foolishness warrants death at the hands of brute authority, then there would likely be none of us left to police or to 'protect."

So, the first of my two reasons for seeing something sinister and evil with government handling of the brutalized, massacred Branch Davidians is that to those who did the killing, and to those who managed the killing, *the people victimized to the limits of life were of no importance whatsoever*. Only authority and control were to be preserved. The attitude upheld by all those people was one of contempt, determination to enforce the United States government's will with complete disregard for the rights, the sovereignty and the very lives of mere citizens. It doesn't matter one whit that some among the murderers agonized about their intentions and methods because, in the end, they closed ranks and did their 'job" in a manner completely in concert with the tactics Hitler used against his 'undesirables." We see here in our midst the willingness of authority to apply deadly force however it wishes and against anyone who dares to challenge — no matter how tiny the challenge. Government's action did not even come close to meeting their obligation to ensure security within our borders.

The second reason is even worse, because it shows *the extent of erosion to our national, moral foundation* that few would have thought possible. The very basis of our existence as a nation bears a festering wound that has not yet even been recognized, let alone treated.

More than eighty United States citizens were murdered by the combined efforts and decisions of duly appointed authorities *starting* with President Clinton and reaching downward to local, State and Federal agencies. On the way down this chain, virtually the entire hierarchy of power-holders did their part, from United States Attorney General, Janet Reno, to elements of the Army, the Federal Bureau of Investigation, Bureau of Alcohol, Tobacco and Firearms, Texas State authorities, and other elements of Federal law enforcement. The deed was not done in a vacuum, and it was not an accident. It was pre-planned, deliberate, and condoned by *everyone* in the chain of command.

If the killings were murders, then it follows that arrests, indictments, and trials are mandatory. To date, not only have none of these essentials for justice been invoked and pursued with the vigor that a just nation would demand, but the murderers have rewarded themselves with more time in office and all that goes with it. If the rationale is to be that what happened was just an unfortunate accident, then two things immediately follow: First, is that none of our leaders have accepted the responsibilities of leadership, and the 'buck" never stops at anyone's desk. And second, none of the men and women in the chain of command were competent to control the deadly forces entrusted to them and should NOT have retained command. The aftermath of the hideous massacre in Texas has not ended, and it will never end until the crime is acknowledged and the guilty have had their meeting with true justice in a court of law. It will not end until the United States reaffirms its dedication to the security of all citizens, not just those who bow to power.

The evidence for overhauling government stem to stern via a brand new constitution is beginning to build with some vigor.

Kent State

I'll just mention of this sad event. The divisiveness of our role in Vietnam showed itself with tragic results at Kent State University, a small school of higher learning in Kent, Ohio. The crime for which several students paid with their lives, once again was to demonstrate disagreement with national authorities. The actions of some students may have been stretching free speech, but was ending their lives the best answer government could find? One would not think so. Certainly, the founders who wrote our constitution would not think so.

Disagree if you must, but do it in private, seems to be government's attitude. Power had its way that day, and rather than admit an error in policy and end our adventurism, rather than admit an error in the vicious suppression of free expression, government continued to compound those errors until more than 59,000 service men and women had lost all security and their lives in Vietnam. Stupidity seems as uncontrollable as a raging flood, but shouldn't we take on the task of making our national selves better? Perhaps someone can explain how government arrogance displayed at Kent State is any different from that of the Chinese authorities at Tiananmen Square under communist authoritarian rule, for I can see *no fundamental difference.*

Any claim to the Right of free speech has now lost its force in law, since the government has set a new precedent by rescinding it at any time of its own choosing.

Creating "Criminals"

Just as government grants itself power by spending huge sums of money and creating vast bureaucracies to do the spending, government has also proven itself adept at increasing its powers of overt, direct control over people by first turning them into criminals.

Government has accomplished this easily, a matter of mere *definition.* The 'War on Drugs" may be just such a *stratagem.* But, planned or not, the effect on the security and freedoms of individuals is exactly the same. By the simplest of moves, by declaring certain substances as *illegal,* then all who dare to associate themselves in any way are criminals, by definition, and definition only. They immediately become subject to whatever repressive and punitive measures government may choose. The new 'rules" are familiar to everyone and they must be honored. Don't fret that the use of such stuff is a *personal* matter; government has decided for you that it is far too harmful for you to cope with, so they have made it illegal. Thus, you are no longer allowed to associate with it and, therefore, it can no longer hurt you. We have another government solution based on force, to solve a personal physiological problem. Such utter foolishness.

To make their decisions dominant (even in matters of personal choice), they have attached penalties and punishments that go far beyond the mere label of criminal. Transgressions here have escalated since the 'war on drugs" began in earnest, as have the uses and level of power applied against these new criminals-by-definition.

The use of raw power to force people to learn the truths about addictive stuff is about as unenlightened a method of handling the real problem as can be envisioned, yet it is the method of choice by our government. Perhaps the excuse is that we are being protected from a threat beyond the ability of individuals to counter. If so, then it is absurdly obvious that when methods of 'educating' people are as harmful to those same people as the thing they are being protected against, then the rationale of protection is completely false. It is merely an excuse to increase dominance. The exercise of force to dominate true criminals doing real criminal acts is a world apart from using such force against ordinary people doing stupid things that affect only themselves. It doesn't matter in the least that such people can harm themselves, and even kill themselves. They are not criminals to the rest of society and should not be treated as if they were. There may be many acts that are truly criminal in that eerie world surrounding addictive substances, but branding unfortunate victims as criminals is not the way to solve the real problems.

The extremes to which this government policy have already been carried, now extend to the *property* of any hapless and troubled individual caught in the narcotic embrace, and to any who are even close by who "might" be involved. One absurdity heaped atop another.

Notice particularly that the same government move which branded blameless individuals as criminals, also guaranteed huge profits to opportunistic suppliers. In one master stroke, both user and supplier for another human failing, have been goaded to extremes by government acts. Not surprisingly, government's choice is to use more and more force, more and more repressive measures, and greater piles of money to "protect" us all. Such tactics now can be applied against any one of us, at any time, if authorities see more of a threat to their own power and prerogatives than they care to accept. **When due process is denied to anyone, it is denied to everyone.** And we thought the constitution was our shield against this sort of repression.

The bitter lessons learned from our stupidity during the "war against alcohol," in Prohibition days, apply — exactly — to drugs. Government still refuses to learn those lessons of Prohibition and, staunchly declines to connect the two or to accept the fact that the two "wars" are exactly the same. Both bogus wars were and are criminal acts by government.

Once again, government is not only failing in its duty to protect and ensure our security, but it has knowingly become an aggressor against that very same security of individuals.

Confiscation- The Latest Offense to Security

When government acts to deny due process before taking the *lives* of some who dare to confront authority, as was done in the foregoing examples, there is really only one other vestige that remains of our liberty. That remnant is property. Sadly, that too, has now been lost to authoritarian rule. The first step was to legislate, guaranteeing obedience by the use of police force, the right of government to seize some part of the income from every person. Since no limit to this confiscation was ever set, or was subject to constitutional restrictions, there is in fact no limit beyond which they may not "legally" go. Within the tens of thousands of regulations in the tax code, the goal, well on the way to fulfillment, is to gain a controlling entrée into every conceivable money transaction possible. Government calls them "loopholes." Their intent is to allow none of them as a way of sidestepping taxes, and to foster the false notion that anyone using such government oversights, or non-rules, is really cheating the government. With automated databases and high-speed processing, cross-checking of information from several sources will make the closing of these contrived "loopholes" complete in the very near fu ture.

Only barter and an "underground" economy would offer any relief from such government control, an answer that is completely impractical for most working people, though it is a growing trend where possible. What that means is that *there is no answer to institutionalized, legalized and now computerized confiscation.*

With these facts-of-life a reality, an overwhelming blow has been administered to the security of our own property. Please remember that in trying to establish a better set of rules to live by, the founders of the American Republic had concerned themselves, at great length, with the preservation "of a man's property." They had desperately wanted to abolish the arbitrary seizure of property that had been practiced by all previous forms of government. Their intent was clear and correct. The structure and rules set up to ensure it, however, have since been outmaneuvered by the self-serving form into which government has evolved.

So, with regard to ownership, the present ruling body in America is indistinguishable from ANY previous government in history. We can now conclude, accurately, that no government has ever been in power for long without ultimately adopting the erroneous philosophy that it can legally operate as if it were the owner of EVERYTHING.

Let's linger briefly on that thought. Where might government be leading us, if we extend their policies of controlling the lives of individuals now in force? It seems that there has evolved within the members of government a compelling, mental philosophy of service to the nation that admits of little capacity among citizens for self-care. Extending such a view as caretaker of the "marginal masses" to its extreme, it is relatively easy for our parental, governmental protectors to see the need for ever more firm involvement in every facet of an individual's life. Money (control as much of it as possible), freedom of action (licensing, money flow), right of descent (Waco et-al), personal health and old age (the alcohol and drug wars, intrusion into HMOs and the entire health care industry), dependence on government for one's livelihood (welfare), and now the burden of ownership – are all clearly beyond the kin of ordinary men and women. They must be helped with all these trials of living, and since government alone has the wisdom and capacity to understand and cope with these ordeals, it (government) must assume control to

46

their logical limits, of all these complexities of living.   Or so the mantra of extremes of government logic-think goes.

The indicators are there for all to see. Whether we do, and whether we react with improved wisdom to make necessary, critical changes is very much in question.

The real coup de grace to our fond hope for responsibility in government, however, has come in the last two or three decades when confiscation developed into a standard government tool for control. A few examples will make the case.

- With some justification, police seizures from criminals and suspected criminals are routine. When such seizures are made in error, or against completely innocent people, restitution, unfortunately, is never automatic. Sadly, in the majority of cases, property is returned only if the victim persists, often at great cost. Eighty percent of police seizure victims are never charged with any crime. (From an independent survey by the Pittsburgh Press.)
- A 1984 law permits police to keep 80% of assets seized from anyone *suspected* of a crime. (Philadelphia)
- Money seized from innocent bystanders to a criminal arrest may never be recovered, especially if the arrest is drug related, and the Drug Enforcement Agency is involved.
- Between 1984 and 1992 more than $3 billion in property was seized as allowed by government forfeiture laws.
- In June 1971, agents of the Bureau of Alcohol, Tobacco and Firearms, wearing ski masks and no identification, raided, in error, the home of a newsman in Silver Springs, Maryland. When he tried to defend himself from this criminal-like invasion he was shot in the head and paralyzed. The ATF refused to pay damages, even though nothing illegal was found, and no law had been broken by the victim.
- In February 1982 a Senate subcommittee published a report which documented abuses by the ATF, citing numerous violations of Federal law. No remedial action was taken to force compliance.
- Agents of the ATF raided and sacked the home of John Lawmaster in Tulsa in Dec. 1991, while TV crews recorded the event. Nothing illegal was found, yet the ATF refused to pay damages. The only fortunate thing about this unconscionable raid by federal agents is that no one was killed. If there had been casualties, the incentive among authorities for restitution would have been no different.
- At the time of the Waco murders, that outmoded bureau, the ATF, was desperate to improve its public image back to one such as that enjoyed during the days of Eliot Ness. It hoped that the confrontation with the Branch Davidians would help them regain that status, and shows the extent to which

47

little men in powerful governmental positions will go to maintain power, and the ineffectiveness of ordinary means to prevent it.

There have been literally thousands of such acts of "legal" and illegal seizures by authorities in recent years, and ordinary citizens have no reason whatsoever to be sanguine about the security of their property.

Creating Even More Blameless Criminals

We might make the following two assertions about ourselves as human beings. Both are based on the most relevant facts about ourselves that exist today. We can conclude from our knowledge of human behavior, that one of our fundamental characteristics is that we are sexual beings, with a drive that is integral to our person, and inseparable from it. Religions, which have tried to deny this on intellectual or moral grounds, have learned the reality of it to their own dismay. The continual criminal revelations surrounding celibacy and the priesthood unequivocally demonstrate how behavior can be warped when this fact is denied. While changes in this characteristic take place with time, as they do with everything else around us, the descriptor of humans as sexual beings is valid throughout most of life.

The second point, which concerns our sovereignty as individuals, recognizes that there can be no differentiation among people, that sets one person above another wherever unalienable rights are at issue. This concept should be at the very root of how we view ourselves in relation to others. Any society built among us must be fashioned with that truth as its foundation. Even the belief in a *creator* cannot be the equal of this concept because there has never yet been complete *agreement* about creation, or creator or what it implies. There have only been emotional **beliefs**; and the differences among them are huge, and often irrelevant to the central issues and tenets of equality.

Taken together, these dual truths about ourselves show the utter folly of labeling sexual intercourse between adults who consent one to the other, as a criminal act of any degree. In our arrogance, we have labeled as law breakers, as criminals, those who choose to have sex with money as the medium of agreement. The whole notion that it can be outlawed on the basis of right or wrong denies our very nature. The notion that someone else, be he priest or politician, can decide what another will do with and for himself or herself, *denies the existence of equality* among humans. Such a denial leaves that line of logic without foundation and, therefore, bankrupt. Prostitution never was and never can be a crime except by dictate and definition. When government labels it as such, it creates more criminals where none exist, and makes them subject to repression and penalty where none are warranted. Where no crime is committed, there can be no criminal. If we persist in the travesty of dealing with it as a criminal act, then the victims of the crime are the

48

perpetrators of the crime, an oxymoron without peer. We have no basis on which to call prostitution a criminal act any more than our government would have the right to label the drinking of water a federal offense — unless it has a federal stamp on the container.

The right of choice is being attacked relentlessly by government and no action is being taken by anyone to undo the harm being done. Nor does today's constitution provide the means to prevent these government crimes.

For government, their actions have been a great victory, all at the expense of the rights of people that the constitution was intended to guarantee, but can not.

But surely, we can recognize the difference between the nature of criminals created by government definition and those made by their own acts of *harm against another*. And, surely by now, we have an understanding of how government has failed utterly in its duty to ensure the personal security of us all, done specifically to increase control over us all.

CHAPTER 6
Government Failures & National Goals

Ask any systems engineer how to identify national goals acceptable to Americans and the response would come easily. The process is straightforward and direct. It would yield a retinue of choices, with solid information about cost, schedule, returns (in terms of things we value), the means by which costs can be met or are out of reach, and finally a way of comparing the merits of those choices. The process is about as simple as can be, even though the work involved most likely would be extensive. Goals are suggested — from any source; information is gathered so that all the facts needed for meaningful analysis are at hand; and, finally, all the right calculations are made to learn about costs, returns, time, pitfalls, financing and the like. With such an array of material available, informed discussions and debate can then follow in order to reach some consensus among leaders and people alike.

Contrast such an orderly approach, or one akin to it, with the process used in America throughout its history as a nation. One man, one political party, or both parties create an idea, one with potential value in it and a lever to stir people's emotions, and **with no more thought than that**, it then becomes our great, passionate, driving, collective objective. An entire people either are indifferent to it, or have implicitly accepted the notion and become committed to it by default. At the time the idea came from the incubator almost nothing is known about it — except the golden carrot waiting for Americans to claim it. The price tag not only is unknown but also is hardly even mentioned. How any debt is to be met is a non-question just as the long-term consequences of spending are today. With a figurative wave of the arm, it becomes just another general obligation to be paid for with tax money, both our own and our children's.

Such was the 'national goal" of 'placing a man on the Moon and returning him safely to Earth before this decade is out." The carrot was to pump up American pride before any other nation could beat us to it. Cost was never a factor, and the fact that we as a nation were not paying for all our other purchases had no influence on embracing that premature goal. The decision was one man's alone, and the nation bought it on emotion alone.

Such was the 'national goal" of 'achieving the Great Soci ety." Again it was one man's doing and again it was done with no more thought than is given the choice of lottery numbers or tomorrow's menu.

Similar criticisms fairly apply to other crusades we've been led into, including 100% employment, attempts to abolish hunger, poverty and homelessness, provide health care for every citizen, and export American democracy by buying nations through subsidies. The same is true in our attempts to eliminate the threat of drugs by fiat.

The most damaging, and perhaps the most devious, crusade America has been shunted into is one that is probably the favorite of politicians. They sing its praises at every election and they devise a never-ending array of *spending* programs they can sell to voters to make it happen. What they *never* do is to disclose the full long-term costs, and they have never identified the crusade as something for discussion as a *potential* national goal. With politicians, the *need to redistribute wealth* is a given, and the only debate is how much money will be allocated this time and not whether the programs or their goals make sense. Actually, they almost never identify measurable goals to find out how effective the program is over time.

On those rare occasions when they do measure program effectiveness, as with welfare programs and the Head Start education program for instance, results that show how useless they are have no impact whatsoever on spending. Money continues to be funneled into their new rat-holes, because spending money is more important than any one program or its value to Americans.

A proper national goal is something that *virtually everyone* should agree upon, such as preventing an invasion, which is something that redistribution has never enjoyed. It has become merely a political device to enhance government power and has failed utterly in any constructive reallocation of money among needy people. Chapter 8 deals with the failures of welfare. Here we should simply note that for government to champion redistribution as a legitimate national goal, they *must* be able to show that there is virtually complete agreement from the public. Not only does no such agreement exist, but the *objectives* of such redistribution have never even been stated in dollars and cents, or more to the point, in terms of rehabilitating someone to return to self-reliance. Redistribution as it is, is *not* a proper national goal, and certainly not the way it is administered by government.

There is also another whole class of national goals that affect the way the United States uses its military power. As individual citizens, extolling our virtues to others and ourselves as a great military power, we believe that we have no desire whatsoever for conquest, that what we have is all we need or want. That belief sets the bounds of purpose. But we have been much less specific about how those forces may be used in pursuing our "national interests." What were and what are our national interests in Haiti? Or even in Panama today? What are they concerning the Middle East? Is it simply oil?

51

If we consider the flow of (someone else's) oil a national interest worthy of military intervention, what happens to that stance if suddenly an alternative power source were commercially viable, (breeder reactor or solar, for example)? Does that mean mid-east oil drops from our list? If so, how is viewing mid-east oil as OURS any different than coveting someone else's property — and land. If we treat such a region as if it had the Stars and Stripes waving above it, how is it different than selective conquest? Such questions are actually very easy to answer. The focus of government in representing America and Americans in achieving national goals should not be to covet someone else's oil, treating it as if it were our own, but to *lead* the nation in its efforts to become *energy independent*. Government's attention span regarding this, with its mercurial policies dependent only on the crisis of the instant, shows a *basic inability to lead the country in long range endeavors*.

Having discovered the Saudi treasure doesn't confer any special ownership on Americans. We are still obliged to buy what is for sale, and we are still vulnerable to the decisions of others for our energy needs.

On the one hand, Americans, myself included, have *assumed* that it was a task of government to define national goals and lead the effort to achieve them. On the other hand, that assumption may no longer be valid. The example of military projection coupled with energy *dependence* being such an obvious failure, it may well be that American government is **not** capable of leading us in our long term endeavors. If this is so, then we have uncovered another potent reason for minimizing government, a constitutional issue of the first magnitude. That conclusion will be inescapable from all its other failures examined in this book.

Conversely, there have been some worthy goals adopted, so the long used haphazard process has been at least partially successful. Quality of life has benefited greatly from improvements in water, power distribution, roads, bridges, and other infrastructure essentials. A great many of the advances, however, are due to the inventiveness and dynamic drive of American industry which, therefore, deserves a large share of the credit. Other national goals that have been important to us include the preservation of national treasures, resources, timber, wilderness areas and wildlife itself. Flood control projects, disaster relief measures, the sponsorship of scientific and medical research, exploration of the solar system, and the need to protect the environment are all beyond the capacity of individuals and doubtless have the support of a great many people even though very few have ever been queried about them. The worthiness of a goal, however, is far from the complete story, as we see from the debates that continue to rage around government handling of environmental protection, medical research and restrictions, and the mismanagement of pasture and timber lands

One national goal that has never gotten proper scrutiny is the practice of using public money to subsidize the thing called Art — in all its forms. This expenditure has never even been considered as being a goal to be pursued as a nation in spite of the fact that government treats it as such in its use of public money. No proposal has ever been voiced to the American public to support art as a national endeavor, yet it has become one, worthy or not. Actually, the public money squandered on this mixed basket of the atrocious and the inspiring is due more to the persistence of advocacy groups than to any thoughtful plan to foster American art. Any such attempt to bolster the American ego seems badly misplaced. Art and artists have their own internal drive for expression, and blanket use of public money cannot possibly represent a blanket endorsement of all Americans.

And, since the subject of *advocacy* has surfaced this early in our deliberations about government failures, I wish to introduce perhaps the most devious of all of our 'national goals,' albeit never heretofore identified as such. The government, unilaterally, has acted upon the belief that America, using public money, should adopt as a national goal the support of *political advocacy groups* ranging from A to U, from Art to Unions, and everything in between. For now it is enough to be aware that this is one very costly element of government's national goals agenda that has never been put up for any kind of approval from Mr. and Mrs. Citizen.

It should take much more thought when a national goal is set than having it come from the latest president. In all our history, this critically important responsibility of government has hardly been acknowledged as such, nor has any comprehensive plan ever been formulated in an attempt to prepare better for the future. At the present, we don't even have a *statement* of what our national goals are, let alone what they should be. We have, instead, a national budget, reworked each year, that sets the amount of money to be spent on each program and by each department.

There is not a hint of prioritization among the many, and every item is viewed as being equally urgent, no matter how that may affect the final tally. Part of the reason government has failed in its fiscal duty to Americans is its steadfast refusal to set priorities on spending programs that represent OPTIONAL national goals. The current practice is irresponsible, and unnecessary. The motivation of politicians, however, will continue to be to resist change because spending means power, and power assures more spending. The tail chase is self-reinforcing and completely unstable.

The net effect is another breakdown of government in one of its principal responsibilities, namely managing nation-wide programs essential to real current and future needs. Constitution One has no guidance of substance regarding national goals that extend beyond security of the country as a whole.

53

CHAPTER 7
Taxation & A Crumpled Government

Most people know their own preferences, the things that help to bring them contentment and happiness. They know some choices can be controlled, some only influenced and some well outside their control. Government has fashioned a monopoly on most of those outside factors that influence us most heavily. Ironically, together they have become *the most uncontrollable force in our lives*, leaving us with no way to sidestep or even mitigate them. Too often government actions chip away at chances we see for a better life, a happier one for our families and ourselves.

Taxes in general, the ill-advised, even criminal use of tax money in the creation of a warped welfare industry, bastardizing the dollar and flirting with national bankruptcy, and the creation of endless regulations affecting everything we do, are four of government's works that have degraded our own efforts toward a happier life.

This chapter and the following three, give enough of the stories behind each, to show how government has failed in each of these four categories, and to show how each failure diminishes the ability of Americans to pursue their own vision of happiness.

Progressive increases in taxes over the years have assaulted one of the most important factors underlying family living in its search for stability and happiness. Without economic stability, everything else takes on depressing shades of gray in a person's life. Somewhere along its evolutionary path in managing US affairs, government made the choice to search for ways to maximize that part of our gross domestic product under its control. That early decision has been our fiscal undoing, and a huge blow to a citizen's pursuit of happiness.

Controlling money has indeed been successful in building government power, and it has become its key strategy ever since. *If instead, government had chosen as the goal to help families achieve financial independence,* government's subsequent actions would have been entirely different, their legacy positive and their wisdom evident.

Money is basic to the way we live. If we controlled our own money, becoming financially independent in some reasonable period of time is a choice we could make, expecting to succeed. If we choose not to, for whatever reasons, it's our choice and we'll accept whatever later results come about. When government confiscation of income becomes excessive, which ours has, choice is gone and gaining our own goals has been dealt a serious blow. It may not be impossible, but for many workers it is, since discretionary money is virtually zero, swallowed up in taxes.

Tax progression in the United States is a horror story. In the decade of the 1950s a wage earner, in effect, worked without pay for slightly more than two months of the year. All wages for January, February and part of March were taken by the government to satisfy its money appetite. By the end of the 1970s, the threshold had advanced well into April. The increase was beginning to have serious repercussions on new families trying to make a start.

By the late 1990s the effective month had moved to late May, the time when a worker's efforts would begin to benefit the family, and not the government. The level of confiscation represented by five-twelfths[4] of a family's yearly income had become *the highest tribute exacted by any major government in recorded history*. Take special note of the fact that the "odious" taxation practices of King George III, because of which we convinced ourselves to wage a bloody revolution, exacted far less than is being confiscated by our home-grown government today. The whole notion that any sensible government needs that much of the labor of the people is impossible to justify.

Considered so far is the composite tax burden imposed by Local, State and Federal governments. They do **not** include the taxes hidden within the purchase price of items bought at retail. Not including sales tax, there is the increase in manufacturer's cost to compensate for the taxes levied by government on producers. Companies do not pay tax. Any such cost is immediately passed on to the consumers as an increase in purchase price. *Consumers are the ultimate, and the only, payers of all taxes.* Any talk by government of raising corporate taxes to ease the worker's burden is simply another lie.

All by itself, the tax *amount* is proof enough that government at all levels is at the very least an inefficient, wasteful organization that has no real control of itself, let alone control of things that truly matter to the people. At worst, it is an organization whose internal corruptions and bankrupt policies have moved it far beyond any rational limits for which government is instituted.

Why it Hurts so Much

As government gobbled more and more money to "process," people had to adjust to remain solvent. The single most important adjustment, and also the most

---

[4] Any good analysis of the current United States tax burden bears this out. One such study was done recently by the CATO Institute, and reported on briefly in their letter to subscribers.

disruptive of family life was the need for both parents to work for wages. When this is the only viable solution, the usual attention, care and love of children is severely cut, often with dire, long-lasting effects. In my opinion, this single forced change in the modus vivendi of American families, two working parents, has done more harm to our way of life than any other single factor. Neither wars, disease, social or lifestyle variants, or natural catastrophes have been as corrosive to the American foundation, the family unit.

To their everlasting shame, government has tried to impose upon us the notion that the need for women to work has somehow liberated them beyond those unfortunate mothers bound to kids and home. Such leadership would see the mundane as holy and the family as a thing to be avoided. This is the extreme to which government has tried to exploit a constitutional deficiency.

Taxes & The IRS

These destructive tax policies of government are put into effect by an equally heavy-handed agency that shouldn't go unnoticed. The militant collection arm of Congress is the Internal Revenue Service, whose rules of conduct have taken it beyond those of law that apply to everyone else, far beyond the limits of the Bill of Rights, and even out of the reach and purview of the Congress which created it. The IRS assumes guilt without proof, confiscates without proof of wrongdoing, and forces those so wronged to bear the burden of undoing IRS wrongs. Whether those crimes of IRS (and they *are* crimes) are due to their own error or to overt attack on *suspected* holdouts, their procedures are the same.[5]

An Example of IRS Heavy-handedness
For many years, a man who considered himself to be a conscientious objector to taxation had carefully held his income below the government limits set for filing a tax return. After several years he was contacted by the IRS, not because they had any proof of tax evasion, but simply because his returns had stopped. He refused to give any information, claiming his unalienable right to remain silent, a right clearly derived from the Right against self-incrimination, which by now we all know is explicitly protected by the Constitution — unless the IRS wants to know, a phantom proviso that the IRS takes for granted.

Time passed; five years later the man was served with an Administrative Summons issued by the IRS, which has absolutely no force in Law. The man

---

[5] The 1989 expose by David Burnham is an excellent source of that foul operation. The title is A Law Unto Itself; Power, Politics, and the IRS. The book is thoroughly documented, and Burnham's conclusion is that deficient Congressional Oversight is the chief culprit allowing the IRS to do what it does.

ignored it. Some time later a Federal District Judge was talked into issuing an Enforcement Order, still on the basis of no proof of wrong-doing. The man was ordered to appear before the IRS and provide them with all the information they wanted for the six-year period in question. Eventually he did meet with IRS agents, but continued to refuse to give information, as is the right of every person.

This extra legal battle of wills was then carried to a Contempt Hearing (granted by a federal judge) where the judge alone has the power in law, *but not the Constitutional power*, to find him in contempt of court, which he did — 40 days in jail. Mind you, the man was charged with no crime. No proof of wrong-doing was ever offered or found, yet he landed in jail for exercising a right that the IRS didn't like. The IRS abused its responsibilities and power delegated by Congress; the judge abused his power and NO ONE in government has the responsibility or can take the initiative to prevent or reverse these abuses against guiltless people.

The person whose one-sided battle with unlimited government power cost him years of undeserved harassment and at least 40 days in jail is the author, Carl Watner, who reported these government excesses in an article entitled, "Your Document for the Use of Silence, the Ultimate Protector of Individual Rights".

A Conclusion & Comment

The disgusting story of taxation in the United States has filled volumes.[6] My purpose here has been to give the essence of the *effects* of OUR government policies on ourselves as individuals in our pursuit of happiness, and the shoddy motives government clings to behind their acts.

John Marshall, Chief Justice of the Supreme Court under Presidents Jefferson, Madison, Monroe, John Quincy Adams, and Andrew Jackson (1801 to 1833), had this to say about taxation. "The power to tax involves the power to destroy." It does, - and the users of that power are doing exactly that.

We should ask ourselves as reasonable people, why such abuse of raw power must be condoned in an advanced society.

The answer is that Constitution One does nothing to prevent small-minded officials from practicing mayhem on those they should serve instead.

---

[6] Examples include:

      "The Rape of the Taxpayer", by Philip M. Stern; 1974; Random House, Pub.

      "The Hand in Your Pocket,' an essay by John T. Flynn.

      "How Taxes Destroy," by Frank Chodorov

      "The Tax Racket," government extortion from A to Z, by Martin Gross

CHAPTER 8
Welfare & Farm Welfare

In 1935, when the great depression "emergency" frightened government and citizen alike, FDR made a fateful decision. A government *safety net* was going to solve everyone's economic woes. Social Security, public works employment projects and deficit spending were the answer, and government seemed to be the natural body to carry out the solution. Government spending would solve everything. That octopus grew slowly at first, was then obscured by the real crisis of WW II, and didn't mushroom into the monster it has become until decades after it began.

Citizen and community altruism, the idea of lending assistance to individuals in obvious need, was gradually supplanted by an institutionalized, impersonal, government-run business of giving to anyone meeting certain social dependency norms set by bureaucrats. These norms later had the debilitating effect of perpetuating that class of people in need. The result became an action taken to an extreme, an excess that typifies any government process which is instituted without guiding limitations or without clear sensible goals.

Hindsight permits us now to see clearly that individual citizens can't sensibly hand over to government our power and prerogative to *give* our money to others, deserving or not. When that government is also irresponsible or worse, then the gifts go beyond any limits we might have *and* will be given for reasons of its own, not ours.

Think about how the government has taken over the job of community charity once handled quite well by the people most concerned. Given the choice, would you allocate 40% of your income to charity? The government has, and more, where the 'more' comes from a mortgage on your future taxes. And if you did want to give away that much of your income, would you want someone else to decide where it goes? Would you support another whole family - permanently - when the adults are able-bodied, but choose not to work? You are, by proxy, doing exactly that. Would you give 40% of your income to "artists" who express themselves in ways you personally abhor, or to politically aggressive groups whose aggression is exactly opposed to your own sense of right or wrong? You may not want to do these things, but you most certainly are, with government making your decisions for you.

The politician thinks of welfare in a totally different way. *Where* will it do the most good politically? For *whom*? And what is the *good* to be done? How can we, the governors, create a balance between subsidizing desirable activities (cultural, agricultural and resource management, for example) and the need to maintain coherence within these far-sighted programs by keeping the party in power? *The selling of such ideas* is on the basis of citizen need, but the actuality of 'need' supported can be anything. The give-away philosophy underlying government actions is a fraud, and has been for more than 50 years.

Of all the views we might examine to understand the prostituted notion of welfare in the United States, we'll limit our attention to only four parts of this mammoth give-away. Giving to families (i.e., traditional welfare), and Farm Welfare are the two covered here. Corporate Welfare and Political Welfare (meaning politicians giving to themselves) are the remaining two, which are found in Appendix E. Those examples should be enough to show how far the United States has sunk into the welfare pit created by the actions of Congress because there is no constitutional limitation to prevent it.

Welfare to Families

William E. Dannemeyer, United States Congressman, retired, regularly informed people within his district about government activities. His reports, always factual and topical, were quite often very disturbing because he recognized through close observation the beginnings of the fraudulent process that was evolving in Congress. One such report released in the fall of 1987 gave a clear answer to the question of whether welfare was merely perpetuating itself or was reducing the *causes* of poverty.

Dannemeyer's report listed the *Change in Poverty Rate* in each state over a ten-year period and listed the corresponding standard Aid to Families with Dependent Children (AFDC) welfare payment made to those in need. AFDC, where need is greatest, is the best single measure of need, but certainly not the only one. It is, however, a good measure of those struggling with poverty. Dannemeyer listed two groups of 15 states, each with their standard AFDC payment and the 10-year change in poverty rate. The 15 states with the highest dollar gifts all show an increase in poverty rate; the 15 lowest paying states showed a decrease in poverty rate! This result is exactly opposite to the story we are fed by government, which wants us to believe that their spending more money helps people more than if payments were to be reduced.

Recall that the federal government mandates basic welfare rules with some discretion allowed to each state.   (The raw data are included in Appendix E, Table 1.)

Government's answer to this unambiguous message *from their own study*, the House Select Committee on Children, was (perversely) to add even more give-away welfare programs with larger payments, 'to solve the poverty problem."

The Real Conclusions
When the give-away amount is above a certain threshold, poverty rolls actually increase, and below it, poverty decreases. The welfare give-away program is perpetrated by government because it benefits government to do so, not because it is solving a real human need.

Welfare - 1992 to 1995
In 1992, the Federal government spent $766 billion on welfare programs of all kinds (including social security), or almost 52% of total expenditures.[7] For that year, $766 billion ($766,000,000,000) was a little over 71% of all money taken in taxes, which totaled $1,075 billion.[8] The term entitlement is often used when referring to welfare gifts because there is a built-in connotation that (a) all those who receive our money via government give-away agencies deserve the gifts, and (b) government really has no control over this chunk of the budget and therefore shouldn't be faulted when they run a deficit.   Both notions are false, but the government continues to rely on the lie in order to soften criticisms of their actions.

That same year, interest on the $4+ Trillion ($4,000,000,000,000) national debt was $293 billion, or 27% of revenues. Together those two bills (total welfare and debt interest) gobbled up 98.5% of all the money squeezed out of the people, which for all practical purposes, means these two invoices alone required everything we paid in taxes that year to pay them off. It's even worse than that statistic would seem, because part of the $1,075 Billion in 'receipts" was the excess of social security taxes taken in, over money paid out, which 'excess" was quickly shifted into the general receipts file, itself a devious, fraudulent act, as was pointed out previously.

How has government reacted to lessons learned about welfare from the 60's and 70's, discussed earlier? The most authoritative current study that answers this question is another of the excellent works done by the CATO Institute of Washington, DC. The principal investigators were Michael Tanner, Stephen Moore and David Hartman and their results were published September 19, 1995 as the CATO Policy Analysis No. 240, one of a series of well-reasoned and factual reports

---

[7] "Bankruptcy 1995", by Harry E. Figgie Jr.
[8] Social Security will be discussed separately; here the focus is on all the rest of the gift programs.

on important social and governmental issues. The title of this report is 'The Work vs. Welfare Trade-off', which is "An Analysis of the Total Level of Welfare Benefits by State". It suits my purpose here because it gives all the facts we need to show the deterioration of self-sufficiency, self-reliance, and self-responsibility that once characterized the American spirit.

The claim I make is that government actions, seemingly well intentioned, are a *direct* cause of undermining our Pursuit of Happiness, which was recognized as a fundamental purpose for instituting American government. The following facts are taken from the CATO Policy Analysis No. 240, executive summary. Every statement is fully supported by facts and by the sensible methods used in doing the work.

- *The value of the full package of welfare benefits for a typical recipient in each of the 50 States and the District of Columbia exceeds the poverty level. Because welfare benefits are tax-free, their dollar value is often greater than the amount of take-home income a worker would have left after paying taxes on an equivalent pretax income.*

- *In 40 States, welfare pays more than an $8.00 an hour job. In 17 States the welfare package is more generous than a $10.00 an hour job.*

- *In Hawaii, Alaska, Massachusetts, Connecticut, the District of Columbia, New York and Rhode Island welfare pays more than a $12.00 an hour job -- or two and a half times the minimum wage.*

- *In nine States, welfare pays more than the average first-year salary for a teacher. In 29 States, it pays more than the average starting salary for a secretary. And in the six most generous States, it pays more than the entry-level salary for a computer programmer.*

- *Welfare benefits are especially generous in large cities. Welfare provides the equivalent of an hourly pretax wage of $14.75 in New York City, $12.45 in Philadelphia, $11.35 in Baltimore and $10.90 in Detroit.*

- *For the hard-core welfare recipient, the value of the full range of welfare benefits substantially exceeds the amount the recipient could earn in an entry-level job. As a result, recipients are likely to choose welfare over work, thus increasing long-term dependence.*

The implications of this unconscionable display of squandering your and my tax dollars are staggering. The shortsighted stupidity of creating such policies and perpetuating them is outrageous and totally unacceptable from people we have hired

61

to maintain a sound and sensible nation. The CATO conclusions tell us, with no hint of ambiguity, that people making rational decisions *for their own well being* have more incentive to settle for the trap of welfare than to become self-reliant.

What such a decision does to their self-esteem, and the lessons for living passed on to children, aren't as easy to see as the immedi ate money advantage by becoming welfare dependents. The deterioration from sensible and independent living is cumulative and is propagated to the next generation of young people who have no way to judge the harm being done. As parents, one of the most important bits of practical wisdom we must give to our children is the value of becoming self-reliant. That responsibility of ours is NOT something we should let government undermine by its insidious give-aways.

The *only* state that reduced AFDC benefits between 1979 and 1995 was Mississippi, and by so doing, it led all states in *reducing* its poverty rate. In the prior survey it ranked 14th among states which reduced the poverty rate. **The lesson is clear.**

All remaining 50 districts *increased* such payments. All 15 states cited by Dannemeyer for actually *lowering* the poverty rate (between 1969 and 1979) remained on the lower half of the 1995 list. States with the biggest increases in handouts were among those whose poverty rates had *increased* in the earlier period. This says that none of them, save Mississippi, were concerned with *effectiveness* of their programs, but only with doling money to "entitlement" families. The la rge increases in AFDC benefits in particular for Connecticut (+52%), New York (+48%), and California (+25%) for example, made each one a target for transient, hard-core welfare families who flocked to the payment windows causing even greater State budgetary problems there than elsewhere.

An example of this effect is shown by the data for Minnesota. This middle-of-the-welfare-road, high-paying state increased its poverty rate by over 7 % between 1969 and 1979. Nevertheless, it continued to increase the handout. Minnesota has experienced an increase in welfare recipients of over six times its 1977 level because of the shortsighted government welfare policy. While inflation effects have contributed to the increases cited, the lesson of *deterioration* of American family living due to an ill conceived and excessive welfare policy is still unchanged, and still unlearned, by government. In fact, the data show *increased* deterioration with each decade.

One other observation is worth mentioning. Since the general ranking of States (in welfare largess) has remained roughly the same throughout the last 30 years, the Federal Government's responsibility in *creating* greater poverty is shared by those states ranked #1 through about #20. Also, if we wish to be most charitable to

Congress, their culpability is somewhat mitigated since some of the other states were successful in avoiding excessive AFDC payments *in spite* of Federal mandates. What might be concluded from this alone is that most State and Local governments have been contributors to the decline of family living, and for the same political reasons as big brother in Washington D.C.

Effects of Other Welfare Handouts

The things we have concluded based on just the AFDC information, however, are only part of the story. When the effects of all the other welfare programs are added in, the excesses of government, and the huge subversion of American family values are indisputable.

To understand just how 'magnanimous' government has been with money that is not theirs to give, we must add to AFDC payments all the other benefits available to 'the standard needy family.'[9] Those other parts of welfare are: Food Stamps, Medicaid, Housing Assistance, Utilities Assistance, Supplemental Food for Women, Infants and Children, and lastly, Free Commodities, a small additional food program. Obviously not all recipients receive all those benefits, but a great many do.

The CATO report gives the monetary details for each of these parts of welfare. Each is accompanied by a **Federal mandate** to the states which, among other things, *requires* the state to cover all costs of the programs not paid by 'Federal money.' Federal payments range from 50% to 80%, depending on the state, with the average for AFDC being near 50% and for Medicaid about 57%. While the government payments and details are important, the thing of most interest is the staggering totals that have resulted from all the pieces. And *staggering* is exactly the right word to describe the effect on a nation foolish enough to mortgage its future indefinitely to fund programs that don't work, with money that does not belong to the giver.

One could easily trip over the mammoth stumbling block that is government welfare to families. The tabulated data for this travesty are given in Appendix E, Table 3, but the conclusions easily reached deserve our undivided attention here.

This simple collection of facts, mostly supplied by government's own documents, tells an amazing story. Dependency is a terrible trap. It is very disturbing! The reference year is 1995:

---

[9] By definition, the typical welfare household consists of a single mother over 21 with two children aged one and four. There is no father. The mother doesn't work and reports no outside income. No one is disabled in the household.

- The full benefits package provides an income that exceeds the poverty threshold in all 51 jurisdictions. This is not a helping hand; it's a free living.
- The effective welfare income in 20 states (plus Washington, DC) is half again greater than the poverty level in those states. Fifteen more are greater by 40% than the poverty level. Four of the top givers, Hawaii, Alaska, Connecticut, and Massachusetts, pay TWICE the local poverty level. All 51 jurisdictions exceed it by at least 10%.
- It makes good economic sense for welfare recipients to choose welfare instead of work. The built-in government incentive is exactly backwards. For the year 1995, more than 68% of recipients were not looking for work, and probably never will.
- The government-defined program destroys people's incentive to better themselves, creates permanent dependents of them, and is the largest single reason for expanding the poverty roster in the United States today.
- The government, by its poorly conceived welfare industry, has forced a major segment of the population to accept government decisions regarding family and home living which are clearly the prerogatives of individuals.
- The process by which welfare applicants seek and obtain welfare aid is degrading to their self-image and reinforces the economic jail they have been relegated to.

The overwhelming excess to which welfare programs have been carried, under the illogical government philosophy, is brought out in the CATO report by comparing the give-away benefits with median and entry-level wages of certain occupations.

- In 37 states and DC, welfare exceeds 75% of that state's median wage. Median wage, you will recall, is the wage at the middle of the working population, so that 50% of wage earners receive less than the median and 50% receive more. In 5 states, welfare "wage" is equal to or greater than the median (Hawaii, Rhode Island, Massachusetts, Alaska, and Maine).
- The median entry-level wage for teachers nationally is about $23,250. Nine states pay their welfare people more! (HA, AL, MA, CT, DC, NY, NJ, RI, CA, with VA, MD, and NH not far behind.)
- Nationally, a median level secretary, just beginning, earns $9/hour. Twenty-nine states exceed that in welfare benefits.
- For a janitor, the wage is $6.75/hour, and 47 states exceed that.
- For a computer programmer, the wage is $13/hour, and six states exceed that. (HA, AL, MA, CT, DC, & NY.)
- While the average time on welfare is two years, at any give time, 65% of welfare recipients have been on the program for eight years or more. You can easily visualize the incentives that motivate these people.

64

We should all be *shocked* by the arrogance of government enforcers who have no compunction at all to confiscate our earnings from real work, and then squander it on give-aways. Their program is clearly a disaster both to those who receive and to the nation as a whole, and yet government reaction is inexplicably to increase the excesses.[10]

Welfare should not be a modern-day Roman citizen-pacifier of a free living, but should instead be a temporary helping hand through rough times to regain self-sufficiency.

The task of choosing who should receive help and the task of dispensing charity are NOT government functions, they are ours, the private citizens of each community. For example, almost every church organization has a number of help programs that actually do help.

*   *   *

Farm Welfare, A Government Program Synonymous with Fraud

Government found an excuse following WW I to take over the US farm industry. The bogus rationale was that farm people weren't sharing in postwar benefits equally with non-farm consumers. Thus began a long string of Acts whose ultimate end has been to invade the industry, control decisions in every facet, and thereby build a governmental bureaucracy of immense proportions to justify the program and add power to both political parties and some key party members. The plan was a great success for government.

None of it was ever needed, nor did farm operators share of post-WW I benefits ever change one iota because of government take-over actions.

The story is a fascinating one of how government got its big brogans in the door and have been bilking us lowly taxpayers ever since. It takes an extra bit of fortitude, however, to slog through it. The details are included in Appendix E, and when you are feeling magnanimous, or strong and receptive to a true political horror story, its there waiting for you. For now, let me just state the disturbing conclusions concerning farm welfare, and point out the frauds perpetrated on us all by our own government.

---

[10] The welfare trap is even greater in large cities because of added tax burdens. CATO Policy Analysis No. 240 gives the depressing details.

Conclusion: And We Paid For It

Thirty-three billion, nine hundred million dollars spent in 1985, ostensibly to relieve farmer economic inequities, resulted in ZERO beneficial effects to poor farmers. *That* is the record of this government give-away program.

A final distressing comment in this whole sad affair is to note — in passing — that the record of helping farm workers [i.e. non-owners] was even worse. Any change in worker status came about solely because of farm owner decisions and not at all from government efforts, since interference with worker employment policies was not a part of any welfare program. Perhaps there is a small plus in this, since any attempts by government to effect improvements in farm worker lives would only have come at considerably more government spending and greater intrusion into the lives of people.

Don't misunderstand the flow of money here. Most went to buy and store surplus commodities, going to large farm production corporations, which *entered the business because a sizable profit was guaranteed*. None of this went to alleviate poverty - except incidentally.

Fraud is the Right Descriptor

Earlier I made the assertion that the US Farm Welfare program has been a fraud aimed against the American taxpayer since its inception.

I take an action to be fraudulent when there is intentional purpose to deceive someone in the hope (usually) that someone will part with money. And when thinking about government trickery, there is also fraud when the purpose is to induce someone to give up a legitimate right, such as the personal decision to plant a number of acres of a particular crop.

There are many aspects of this government action that qualify, but let's confine ourselves here to just three illustrations that label the whole program as fraudulent. Here are three deliberate practices that warrant that severe an indictment.

• **Fraud #1 Payments** — *Direct payments* to large and small farmers were made both for renting land to prevent growing certain crops and for buying surplus yields. The huge payments made to big growers, at times as much as a million dollars, became an embarrassment to politicians in confrontations with constituents. The problem was toned down partly by setting arbitrary limits on payments to any one farm, but big growers simply used the land to grow more and sell the surplus to government. The problem was also partly hidden when large sales of stored grains were made to Russia and other countries in need.

To make the embarrassment disappear from the minds of the taxpayers, however, the government cunningly devised the scheme of giving farmers payments in commodities instead of dollars. Farmers then took the gift (corn, wheat, sorghum etc.) and sold it on the open market for 100 percent profit. Farmers were happy and voting taxpayers were duped into thinking that foolish government spending had been eliminated or reduced to acceptable levels.

That is fraud, base, simple fraud.

• **Fraud #2 Program Costs** — Size alone of the Farm Welfare program in the US ensures that many attempts will be made to try and understand what of benefit the money is buying and what loses there are to taxpayers. One can imagine the difficulty of comparing independent assessments, but we should note the huge discrepancy between two cost estimates intended to be for the same elements and time period of the program.

The period was 1985. Costs that analysts attempted to quantify were for something called *Social Costs* of the Farm Welfare program. This included such things as land rental, some USDA employees, certain suppliers of resources to farmers, certain transfer payments and other peripheral programs. The Council of Economic Advisors, government spokesmen, estimated a cost to taxpayers of six billion dollars. The CATO study estimated that these same elements cost taxpayers more than $30.9 Billion. You will recall that the figure of $33.9 B was used earlier as the total cost for 1985.

Is this fraud? My opinion is that it is a fraud knowingly to declare estimates that are grossly below their true values because they might be *politically* damaging. I believe these bogus CEA study results were publicized specifically to deceive voters and to make direct comparisons very difficult. The practice is done with premeditation because government knows of the disgust and mistrust truer estimates would awaken among taxpayers. To me that is fraud.

• **Fraud #3 Program Purpose** — Discussion elsewhere of government inefficiency is an appropriate introduction to our third example of fraud. It is the fraud contained within an entire government policy that is "sold" to taxpayers as a means of overcoming poverty and want within the farming segment of the population, when in fact and practice, the program does nothing to change farm family conditions. Instead, the many programs put into effect, merely transfer money from each citizen's income over to farms and farm corporations in direct proportion to their farm size. The little guy gets a pittance and the big producer gets amounts into the millions of dollars.

Furthermore, officials responsible for these tax transfers really don't care whether the transfers make sense relative to any poverty issues because it is the *process* of administering those transfers that is important to them. To do it takes rules, staff and facilities, all of which add reasons for greater government size and the exercise of greater power and control over ordinary people.

THE LAST DEBATE

Government's purpose has become one of extending itself and its powers instead of serving people. The Farm Welfare ruse is a perfect example of that change-of-purpose, and I label that Fraud.

*   *   *

CHAPTER 9
Economic Adventurism & Stability

Stability is a prerequisite in life for making progress both personal and national. The value of money, safety of home and property, the lives of loved ones are all part of that essential stable platform for most people. Government is still the only feasible means available to counter the many ways stability can be undermined in today's globally interconnected civilization. The issue here, therefore, in the disturbing light of government's record elsewhere, is to examine how well government might be doing to preserve those elements of stability under its control, specifically the stability of money.

The intention, therefore, is to think about the effects of economic decisions made by government on the economic stability of families, or to be more precise, on the economic **instability** of families. Several critical decisions were made during the last century that degraded economic conditions so much that day-to-day living suffered, and planning for the future became untenable because of the rapidly changing economic environment. Reviewing some of these actions will tell a lot about how well government has met its responsibilities.

The fundamental relationship between the freedoms of an individual and the success of an economy has been well understood for centuries. An early explanation of how free enterprise works to the advantage of all when individuals are free to pursue their *own self interest* was clearly written by Adam Smith in his 1759 treatise, "The Wealth of Nations." Since that time, there have been enough examples of the chaos wrought by arrogant governments that have tried to warp this economic truism so that there should no longer be any doubt of its basic correctness. Nor should there be any excuse for ignoring the age-old wisdom that Smith explained so well, since several modern-day thinkers have reminded us about it regularly. Ludwig Von Mises, F. A. Hayak, and more recently Milton Friedman and Lester Thurow, have all done the same.

Unfortunately, there have always been enough overconfident government officials who chose to ignore economic facts-of-life. Actually, it's much more clear-cut than that. Politicians know they are not competent to make rational decisions on global economic matters. Their refuge, therefore, has been to seek out people with economic credentials who would tell them what they wanted to hear, and provide the learned rationale to make their bad decisions palatable to all the rest of us who knew even less.

A potent example of rogue economics – made in the USA – is included in Appendix E, a review of the FDR / Henry Wallace invasion of agriculture.

Reviewing a few more examples will help us understand the seriousness of government economic failures. I think of them as economic adventures, courting the unexpected rather than working to maintain stability.

Adventure #1 - Bastardizing An Economy's Foundation

The element that is most basic in matters economic is money, a medium of exchange beyond barter that people trust. For thousands of years gold served that function nicely, since it has intrinsic value and was universally accepted as a medium of exchange. Britain, in a rare and sensible contribution to civilization, was the first country to settle upon gold in 1821 as the standard reference for exchange. With that decision came advantages for Britain, which soon became apparent to other nations, and by 1870 just about all of Europe had adopted the Gold Standard. Gold certificates, paper, were readily convertible into the metal, ownership of gold was without stigma, and people in commerce had full confidence that the *value* in gold and in certificates was stable. Such stability remained a given during a period of significant economic advancement throughout Europe.

The United States, being a relative newcomer, didn't get itself organized economically until about 1900, when it too finally adopted the Gold Standard. This sensible move helped America become partner to stable international trade and to improved stability at home. Any imbalance between buying and selling was settled with gold transfers, which had direct and almost immediate effects on the economy. Lower gold stocks lowered the money supply, causing interest rates to rise. This in turn attracted outside money and reduced domestic investments, which then made home products cheaper and more competitive and tended to correct the trade imbalances. Very simple, very direct, and quite stable, just exactly what it takes for sensible living *conditions* for the people.

This neat, sensible monetary arrangement had one big disadvantage — as far as governments are concerned — and the US politicos didn't take long to realize it. Government could not print money at its whim to enhance its own power base. They were, instead, restricted to maintaining a reasonable balance between real money [gold] and the certificates issued by government for use in everyday business transactions.

On the other side of the ledger, besides ensuring a stable money system at home, the Gold Standard also created a sensible mechanism for maintaining parity in the balance of payments between two countries, since no one really wanted to see real wealth (gold) flow to foreign sellers.

From a non-government American viewpoint, this eminently sensible system of commerce lasted a pitifully short time, 1900 to 1921, when it was gutted by a fiscal meat cleaver by breaking the link between gold and the dollar currency.

They did so to make it possible for countries to devalue their own money system by resorting to the printing presses, and yet retain their gold stockpiles. The fiscal foolishness was officially "sanctioned" at the International Monetary Conference in Genoa in 1922.

The new system was given the misleading name of the Gold-Exchange Standard. In true political fashion, it was "sold" by misrepresenting the effectiveness of the true Gold Standard, the details of which I'll skip. What seems transparent to us now, in the behavior of our duly elected and appointed representatives, went on to completion anyway without meaningful opposition, because *there is no force to legislate responsible government stewardship.* This first phase of subverting our economy is a prime example of the reality of non-responsible American government in action. There were to be two more such acts.

The rules changed when the Gold-Exchange Standard was adopted. Now paper notes were backed up not only by gold (as before) but also by the paper certificates previously issued (e.g. Pound Sterling in Britain or Dollars in the US). Politicians figuratively licked their chops just thinking about the potential to inflate their way to greater money-wielding power.

One effect of the new "standard" was to permit purchases of foreign goods without reducing the real money supply at home. This had the further destabilizing effect of not changing the credit base. The new rules severed the fiscal connection between gold and credit, permitting (paper) capital to flow with no corresponding flow of gold reserves. In effect, the new Gold-Exchange Standard doubled the amount of money available and was a *major* factor in the wave of speculation, which brought the country to its economic knees beginning in 1929, aided by the ill-advised creation of the Federal Reserve System.

The terrible depression of the early and mid 1930s, and the disruptive trade wars that accompanied it, traumatized two generations of Americans, affecting their fundamental outlook on living and effecting *one of the worst blockades* to ordinary people in their pursuit of happiness *ever to occur.* Other government acts of stupidity and excess contributed to this sad period, but the point is made that the loss of sensible and stable economic conditions during this long period was due **solely** to failures of government. The effects were felt worldwide.

Adventure #2 – Protracted, Deficit Spending

The second economic adventure occurred a mere twenty-two years after the Genoa sojourn into the Gold-Exchange Standard. As WW II neared its end, international trade was in a shambles and the currencies of many nations were totally worthless. Inflation was hurting everyone, and in places, hyperinflation set trade back to the days of barter. A new monetary conference was called at Bretton Woods, New Hampshire in 1944; with the US not only, the strongest power militarily but also the dominant economic force. A vacuum needed to be filled and the US government was there to do just that. It was again time for economic adventurism, time to sweep away old concepts, and "fix" the international money system. Once again, *stability* lost the debate.

As we saw in the farm welfare discussion, those in power who had no proper background to decide such matters had the "expert" advice of people with strange and completely wrong ideas. Earlier during the agriculture debates, Roosevelt and Wallace had followed Thorstein Veblen's counsel based on the false notion that the agriculture industry did not follow the same supply-demand forces as other industries.

In 1944, in matters of international trade, with only the flames and excesses of war in his mind, Roosevelt again was called upon to lead where he was incapable of leading. Harry Dexter White was his choice as representative to the conference, clearly the most influential person there, the American spokesman. White's chief economic advisor, unfortunately, was John Maynard Keynes, long-time advocate of deficit spending that characterized government fiscal policy since the early 1930s. Of course, that part of Keynes' theory is what politicians absorbed and acted upon — to excess. The other half of the theory, namely to balance the deficits of bad years with offsetting surpluses from good years, politicians have completely ignored. We might be inclined to forgive some of Keynes' economic adventurism because of the folly of officials, were it not for the fact of his equally bad ideas concerning an international monetary system. His concept, and his counsel, was to abandon gold completely as the monetary reference and stabilizer, because government would not be able to *create* money, a function he felt belonged to government. A new compromise monetary system was created, the Gold-Dollar Standard, which recognized the strength of the dollar, and continued to pay lip service to gold as the chief stabilizing element. The system was fundamentally unsound.

What was decided at Bretton Woods was *a system of exchange that used the* **Dollar** *as the reference medium*, with the dollar still tied artificially to gold. Every

72

other currency, in effect, was allowed to be devalued [relative to gold] which merely allowed each country to inflate its own currency as it wished [through devaluation]. The US, however, being tied to gold, soon found itself *importing* the rampant inflation of other countries. The less-than-brilliant US team had committed to buying foreign currencies *at fixed rates* that no longer matched their values after devaluation.

Every person's net worth was summarily slashed, including government debt.

A quick example will show how this latest stupidity worked. By 1949, Britain had devalued the Pound Sterling from $4.86 to $2.80, yet we had committed to sell them dollars at the rate of $4.86 per Pound. Every other country which followed Britain's lead to devalue their currency got a similar windfall at the expense of devastating inflation in America. Between 1944 and 1971, the consumer price index [CPI] increased 130 percent. That means that whatever Americans had in money assets - savings, pension funds, cash – lost purchasing power from 100 % in 1944 to only 43 % in 1971. I would classify **THAT** as a major destabilizing force against American families, AND a major failure of government regarding our pursuit of happiness.

The sequel to this inflationary theft of people's net worth was even worse. The next two decades became the worst inflationary period in our history. By 1990 that 43 % residue of value in the dollar had dropped, in what must be termed a nightmare slide, by a *factor* of about 3.45.[11] What had begun in 1944 as 1.00 dollar and had been whittled down to 43 cents by 1971, has been mercilessly chopped to a pitiful 12.5 cents by 1990. Or turning it around, anything that cost one dollar in 1944 suddenly cost eight dollars in 1990. All told, that's the same as handing someone all your liquid wealth in 1944 and retrieving only one eighth of it in 1990.

While this shoddy government record is offset by higher wages [i.e. more cheap dollars] and inflated prices on hard assets such as a house, the fact is that government debts also conveniently disappear down the same inflation hole as your net worth.

Translation: it suited government perfectly to *allow* inflation because it diminished the true value of their enormous debt in exact proportion to the loss of value in the dollar, and it allowed officials more time at the spending booth, exactly what they wanted.

---

[11] CPI information is taken from government data sources.

Adventure #3 – The Wager Is Confidence

This next, and so far the last, money adventure took place in 1971, and as we saw, has accelerated the erosion of value in American money. That erosion, directly chargeable to government stupidity and guile, stripped the remaining soundness from the money system. And, in decades-long deficit spending, has dealt Americans continuous, water-torture-like blows that have greatly hindered the accumulation of real, personal wealth. Savings have been dissipated as the dollar value slides ever downward, and even the *practice* of saving has given way to consumerism in the hope of getting some return from money before its value effectively disappears. People whose net worth is below some threshold, fight this inflation scourge their whole lives, and government, by its callous disregard for basic economic facts-of-life, is the sole culprit.

In 1971, President Nixon formalized the world's first Fiat Exchange System for international trade. No longer would dollars be convertible into gold, and all currencies would henceforth float relative to each other, changing with the basic economic conditions in the US and worldwide. Other governments had accumulated so many dollars from our trade imbalances that the only pragmatic thing for them to do was to support the new "system."

The worst consequences of adopting the Fiat-Dollar Standard have yet to be felt beyond the inflation already discussed, and governments in general, and the US in particular, have bought themselves some more time to play economic "chicken." As long as there is enough confidence between trading partners that currencies are freely exchangeable at known rates, and as long as the *reference* currency, namely the American dollar, remains viable, valuable and (seemingly) stable, then international commerce can continue.

But CONFIDENCE is an illusive mental and emotional thing, not a known, quantitative datum, so who is to say when this latest act of irresponsibility will go beyond that confidence threshold? Our own spending habits, government and citizen alike, for a long time have not demonstrated a pattern which would instill confidence.

There is a real limit to the gross debt of America that foreign creditors will be willing to finance. I'm not capable of analyzing the world economy to be able to find the probable range of that debt limit, nor have I ever seen results from such a study. It may not even be a tractable problem, because it is so intimately tied to human behavior. We can be assured, however, that *there is a limit.* We can also be quite certain that when and if that limit is reached, the change from economic stability to economic chaos will be abrupt, will be worldwide, and will be devastating.

World leaders involved in economic decision making, led by our American government officials, have actively and single-mindedly been willing to risk the ultimate of instabilities (short of war) in order to allow themselves to create personal, party and government power structures never before equaled in history. The system so created is inherently only conditionally stable, dependent on confidence, and is of the type which will drive itself to a limit once the driving force becomes critical. It won't oscillate and give warnings of what might happen. It will just self-destruct, abruptly, once that all-important, but evanescent, confidence evaporates. The risk is far too great for us to consider these government economic adventures acceptable, and government should know what its failures in leadership and responsibility have done.

The facts of this discussion came from a 1984 essay by Jerome F. Smith, author, economist and investment advisor. The essay was called "The Big Lies," and the information used was from Part I of that work. The facts, part of the public record, were carefully researched by Smith and presented in a clear and understandable way. I look upon this essay as a very important contribution to our understanding of government excesses because of the effort needed to pull all the pieces of the story together. We should all understand the history of what went on regarding international monetary systems because that history is so fundamental to today's shaky economic condition. The facts are facts, which we all now know, thanks to Jerome Smith's work. The critique and conclusions of what it all means are opinions of my own, ones that you can evaluate against your own opinions and store of data.

The Other Side of the Coin

Taking the government to task for failures, idiocy and excesses is a distasteful but straightforward task because there are so many blatant examples. The conditions at the start of our nation, however, were so advanced in its scale of *freedoms-in-practice* and in its lack of intrusive regulations, that all of the adventurism since then has not succeeded in wiping away all the good. Far from it. There is some comfort in knowing that our condition as citizens under government continues to rank high *relative* to others.

Perhaps part of that may even be due to government decisions that have been correct or even wise. Perhaps it is merely because it will take more time under mediocre and unwise leadership to wreck things completely. It might be a worthwhile exercise to make such a study in detail. Obviously, the majority of elected representatives have been good, honest people and their efforts, without doubt, have made the difference in avoiding other failures that might have occurred.

75

Those battles could easily occupy political historians for a long time just trying to evaluate the ebb and flow of ideas, power alliances, and the wills of men and women who ultimately decide.

Credit, then, is due some unknown subset of our national legislators who have succeeded in preserving what still remains of that noble experiment in self-government. We have a snapshot of what that means as the result of a study undertaken by The Fraser Institute of Vancouver, Canada. Much effort was devoted to evaluate 'Economic Freedom of the World," a study which concentrated on the period from 1975 to 1995. The report was published early in 1996, and its key finding was described briefly in an article entitled 'The Law of the Land. " by Tom Bethell in the August issue of *The American Spectator.*

The Fraser Institute coordinated the efforts of forty five economists from eleven countries, including such men as Milton Friedman, Douglas North and Gary Becker. In ranking economic freedom within 103 countries, it found a *strong correlation* between economic growth and the *freedom* of individuals and businesses. The top one quarter of these countries, the USA included, with only 17 % of world population, produced 81 % of the total world output. Give credit, therefore, where credit is merited, but be aware that our economic accomplishments of today happen in spite of the blunders of that other, unwise segment of government that has chopped away at our heritage of economic freedoms. We should be very concerned, therefore, with the rate at which this degradation has been advancing, and try to estimate for ourselves when it will have gone too far, an event that I contend has already occurred.

In their updated report of 2004, The Fraser Institute has again reinforced the findings noted above. *Freedom is a necessary condition to realize economic advances.*

*　　*　　*

There have been discussions of late of the possibility of using an entirely new medium as the reference, or backing, for currencies. Energy or labor have been mentioned. The need for some stable, quantifiable reference, the role once played by gold, has not been lost on sensible people.

Central Banking And The Individual

The final folly I'll bring up concerning the economy and government adventurism, is another action that defies reason. Back in the dark ages, that enigmatic period from 1900 to WW I in 1918, huge pressures were again aimed at

Congress to establish a national banking system. Those who controlled the flow of money wanted to establish in the United States, a way of managing assets similar to the European methods pioneered by the Rothschilds long before. Those patient pressures finally succeeded in moving Congress to enact a money control system that was perfect – but only for the mega-money-movers in America with global ties. It couldn't have been better – for them – because they designed the institution, the control mechanisms and the legislative acts to make it 'legal.'

What was accomplished is summarized here, actions that seem incongruous.[12] The year was 1913.

- Ultra capitalists known as "The Money Trust" pressured government to become the American Central Banking System. (President Andy Jackson, in 1836, had squashed a similar attempt because he saw it as a threat to control government. He has since been proven 100% correct.)
- Those instigating the 20th century attempt at control first created an artificial banking crisis in 1907 to set the stage.
- By 1913, the hidden manipulations succeeded in having Congress establish the Federal Reserve System, which centered around three key provisions. *Take particular note that the name does not mean the thing so created is a federal government institution. It is, and always has been, a privately held group of banks and bankers!!*
- ITEM 1 - This group of private citizens, now known as the 'Federal Reserve," was granted control over Interest Rates, specifically the discount rate charged by the Federal Reserve (a set of 12 banks) to all other banks in their districts.
- ITEM 2 – The Federal Reserve was granted control over the national money supply by setting reserve requirements all banks must follow. The way this 'package" has ac tually worked, has allowed government to create dollars without limit, thereby becoming the key ingredient to allow our burgeoning national debt.
- ITEM 3 – The Federal Reserve, that astute group of private American bankers, was granted the right to be the exclusive lender of capital to the Federal Government.
- There was also a fourth provision without which none of this would have been agreed to by the bankers. It was the linchpin of this abrogation of responsibility. Congress must enact legislation giving the Federal Reserve exclusive control of marketing securities (to sell to you, me and foreign investors) against all money borrowed by the Federal Government.
- Government's so lution: Draft legislation, assisted by the Trust, which became the now-familiar open-ended income tax law that effectively uses the

---

[12] Appendix E has additional details and comments.

entire <u>labor wealth</u> of the nation as collateral for any amount of borrowing government might wish to do.

> • Finally, the "magnificence" of the system these ultra -money managers accomplished was truly something to behold. Any bank money lent by the cartel was immediately replaced by selling T-notes and other government securities to anyone, foreigner or citizen, willing to rely on the "full faith and credit of the United States of America."

The bankers were immune to any risk of non-payment, not only because of the government's new taxing power, but also because the bankers became mere middlemen between borrower and risk-taker, meaning you, me and all our foreign creditors.

What's so bad about all this? The potential disaster inherent in this money flow system is now becoming evident even to high-schoolers. Government can borrow any amount it wants, in effect printing money without limit, money that is not backed by anything with intrinsic value. Federal Reserve Bankers, acting as middlemen, sell paper to anyone, isolating themselves from financial risk. We, the risk-takers, have been unable to think beyond the interest government pays for its (almost) worthless paper because the process has endured for so long.

Notice what the true limiting factor is in this open-ended charade. It is the, as yet, unidentified maximum tax that citizen-sheep will pay without **meaningful** complaint.

Finally, I am confident that most readers have already become aware of a growing reticence among foreign creditors to continue financing our prodigious, and growing, national debt, and our ever-increasing balance of payments deficits. Picture in your own mind what a complete collapse might be like if confidence in the US economy were to evaporate among lenders.

When the financial backing behind a nation's money certificates is a state -of-mind, (for example a **confidence** in the full faith and credit of the USA) instead of a commodity with intrinsic value, that money ceases to be a viable medium of exchange.

That's what is at risk! It's hard to imagine a worse future, especially since it would be a global problem. It's even harder to believe that anyone, or any responsible government, would court such a risk for temporary personal gains. Whether from lack of foresight, or just arrogance, the only reasonable conclusion to be drawn is that American Government is not competent to manage American affairs, and **that** can no longer be tolerated. A new constitution may be the only reasonable means to become a truly responsible nation.

Other Misadventures

It seems as if this prying into government economic failures could go on indefinitely. If we choose to examine carefully almost anything government does, we would indeed find enough evidence of failed responsibility, especially regarding the noble, elusive goal of all of us, the Pursuit of Happiness.

The real dilemma is to find a practical balance between the histories of *specific government failures*, and the number of such disturbing stories needed to support my thesis stated at the beginning of this book. I've made the assumption that the record of American government already discussed in some detail, and those detailed histories of other failures covered later, offer enough evidence of failed stewardship. The issues reported above relating to economics, therefore, hopefully are enough to allow us to move on to the next botched responsibility of central government. Allow me simply to list some other economic misadventures that might just as easily have been thoroughly scrutinized to bolster my claims about government. My assertion is that the details behind these next items are just as damning as those presented earlier.

- **Minimum Wage** - Is a worthless political SOP to gain votes; a move which *always* reduces the number of jobs. It is an intrusion between small businessmen and entry-level workers, and is a usurpation of a basic *Right* between two people to agree — mutually — on work for a price. Government has no Right to interfere. Such an unwise regulation does nothing to promote family income and is clearly destructive of newcomers to the work force striving to work toward *their* long-term goals.
- **Rent Controls** - This is a guarantee from our benevolent government to force the rapid deterioration of rental property and, therefore, a deterioration of living conditions for those who think government is looking out for their well-being. Attempting to hold back the effects of government-instigated inflation in this one selected part of the economy is a fool's game, which can only shift unwanted effects, not correct them. And yet, government persists in its fool's errand because it *forces* more government intrusiveness and spending of tax dollars.
- **Government Mandates to Employers for Health Care** - Such mandates immediately remove health care benefits from being part of the competition among companies for attracting workers. Further, it is another intrusion into the exercise of individual rights. Government has no charter to mandate agreement provisions, since no such power was ever granted by the people. Also, as in so many other things government has done at cross-purposes with itself, it has been party to the outrageous increases in medical costs, through liability laws

79

and inflation, and then uses these very same increases to force more government regulation into everyday living. The socialization of medicine is not a sensible national goal, but government health mandates are leading directly to it.

• **Price Controls** - The following quotation is taken from a notice distributed in Nov. 1996 at the checkout counter of a major California supermarket, suitably decorated with the image of a Holstein dairy cow. 'MILK PRICES ARE HIGHER BECAUSE THE DEPARTMENT OF AGRICULTURE HAS RAISED WHOLESALE MILK PRICES 5 % DUE TO INCREASED GRAIN COSTS BROUGHT ON BY THE DROUGHT IN THE SOUTHERN PLAINS."

This is typical of the kind of absurdity that results when government acts in one small part of our complex economy. Its attempts to control dairy products (a small part of a much larger, interconnected industry) can only distort other parts of that economy. The actions of a free market, however, operate automatically (as has been demonstrated ad nauseam) and accounts for *all factors* involved, taking away the rights of no one.

• **Dependence on Foreign Oil** – The almost century-long lack of worthy leadership is best illustrated by America's enduring failure to become energy independent.

The 2004 sequel to an earlier oil scam is a good way to drive home the follies of a spendthrift government. Foreign creditors of US debt are indeed beginning to balk at refinancing that debt. They have begun using other economic levers to move Washington DC, specifically the price they are willing to accept from us for oil. In effect they are being very blunt about the 'value" of the American (unbacked) dollar. It is down, and it will continue to slide as long as government accumulates more debt.

Assuming war is avoided, economic realities will ultimately force the dollar to a much lower but perhaps acceptable level. What happens to Mr. and Ms. America is the pain of another round of damaging inflation. Government, on the other hand, loves the effect since it makes their ridiculous debt seem less monstrous in direct proportion to the lowered value of the dollar.   And the cycle continues…..

Another Conclusion

It seems axiomatic that something as basic and as all-encompassing as our Unalienable Right to the Pursuit of Happiness would be uppermost in the minds of people seeking election to public office. It might seem so, but the plain fact is that it is not. Their record allows us to infer that such a lofty criterion for public service is nearly the last thing politicians concern themselves with. Their deeds clearly don't match their words or their promises. Collectively, government has forgotten this particular reason for its existence. In its place they have adopted the mantle of caretaker because is suits *their* power goals. That's not what they were hired for, so it is not their job to take care of us.

Their real job, simply put, is to establish conditions that will allow people to take care of themselves.

A Post Mortem Worth Noting

Before leaving the subject of economic adventurism, it is worth knowing about some 1996 thoughts of some of the very people who participated in those bad economic decisions earlier in their professional lives. The lesson that has come through, reluctantly in a few instances, to these past economic advisors to presidents, is that American government is incapable of fixing economic problems. The issue is still with us, and as can be seen from the foregoing discussions is still a major part of my present-day indictment against our government. **It still refuses to accept the role of non-participation in economic matters**, because effectiveness is not their motive for intervention. Instead, the motive is purely to promote the power of government through the control of money, even tainted money.

The hangdog public confessions of some past Chief Economic Advisors [CEA] have been recorded in a new book, which documents this change of heart, by some former CEAs.[13] The book called *Hands Off: Why the Government is a Menace to Economic Health,* was written by Susan Lee who had first witnessed her own metamorphosis before giving government and citizen alike this badly-needed dose of economic reality. Lee had been thoroughly schooled as an economist in Keynesian theory at Columbia University. The extent of her own transformation has been complete, however.

Long observation and study of the results of Keynesian advice, as applied by several federal administrations, proved to Lee that Keynesian theory is wrong and its application does not work. With that clear realization, Lee's contribution to our knowledge of practical economics is to hammer that fact home to anyone willing to read the details. Consider these brief histories and grudging changes of past advisors who worked very hard with government, and helped create the disruptive economic events we have suffered through in the US.

- Walter Heller - [CEA to JFK & LBJ]
    - believed deficit spending was necessary to stimulate growth when economic output was below 100 % !! He also believed it was possible for government to 'fine tune" the economy, a bel ief that gave rise to even more experimentation.

---

[13] I was introduced to Lee's book by Stephen Chapman's review published in 'The American Spectator," Aug. '96.

- realizes now that output is *always* below 100 % and that deficit spending can not change that and should not be used. He realizes now that not only is 'fine Tuning" not possible, but that even rough contr ol risks destabilizing the economy.

• Arthur Okun - [CEA to LBJ]

- Believed that Johnson's income tax surcharge would slow the double - digit inflation of '68 -'69.

- Admitted to Lee that he was shocked when he realized taxation was not an answer to inflation. Such sobering realizations must have been devastating to other equally inflated egos. And yet there was no sobering counsel among these men to warn of the risks they so boldly took with everyone else's economic lives.

- Grudgingly came to realize that Milton Friedman's assessment of inflation as *always* being a monetary phenomenon is absolutely correct.

• Laura D'Andrea Tyson - [National Economic Advisor to Clinton]

- Even more ominous than those earlier voices is that of Tyson's, who believes that *balancing the budget* over the next seven years would **cause** a recession.

- Here is someone, a powerful advisor, who is supposed to understand the world of economics, yet is so lacking in its fundamentals that she sees perpetual deficit spending as necessary. Clinton relishes her advice and rationalizations.

Where do such unsound thoughts and logically deficient people come from? Why do their silly thoughts have such an all-pervasive and corrosive influence on everyday lives? Such people have always been with us, and they always will be. Their influence is out of all proportion to their distorted values *because politicians want it that way*. The practitioners of power politics, American style, merely sift through the rolls of economists for those who still think government can solve problems, and the fiction continues. In the case of Clinton, whose need for power was the greatest of any twentieth century president save FDR, Tyson's nonsense version of economics was exactly the thing to help him propagate the miserable government record in economic matters. Long-range effects on you, me and the next generation have no bearing on what he wanted to do, which was to clothe his political actions in sensible *sounding* rhetoric.

Once again we have found our way back from another failing of government, this time in the long-standing misdirecting of national economic matters, to the basic cause of the failing, to its source.

*The cause, of course, is that American government has **assumed** power far beyond its capabilities, beyond its charter, and beyond the needs of individual citizens.*

And worst of all, we citizens have not reacted to the intrusions of government and thus have *allowed* it by our silence. Like a juvenile, (and each new administration fits that appellation) government pushes against the limits of restraining guidelines, looking for ways to go beyond restraints and extend itself. Like any juvenile, something, someone must restrict the excesses and help it reach some kind of practical maturity.

Those of us who have put our trust in government to provide leadership and guidance for the nation, are coming to understand that it is not government which can lead us to lives of freedom and productivity, but it is the guidance of people whose philosophy is founded on equality and freedom, who must *guide government* and who must rework government *whenever it fails.*

This is a key job of American citizens – you and me.

CHAPTER 10
Regulations & Government Functions

Introduction

> *All legislative Powers herein granted shall be vested in a Congress of the United States, which shall consist of a Senate and House of Representatives.*
> The Constitution, Article I, Section 1

> *Each year Washington publishes some 70,000 pages of NEW regulations."* (**emphasis added**) *"Their burden already amounts to some $600 billion of lost output annually."*
> 1996 letter from Edward H. Crane, President, CATO Institute

Making regulations is part of a 72-year old disease that was introduced into government procedures long before that, almost as a time-delayed virus. Agencies of government created to deal with big administrative chores were quiet by today's standards until FDR took over in 1932. Since his tenure, the syndrome of creating bureaucracies has taken hold and expanded to gigantic proportions.

They solved the problem of having to deal with *details*, leaving Congress to the creative work ofdevising new ways to spend money. But to those caught up in the distortions that result, it has become a tragedy. Not only do the agencies make all the *decisions* of how money will be collected in taxes and then spent, (loans, purchases, grants and the like), but they also take care of the overwhelming administrative load of stipulating exactly what the conditions are that must be followed by anyone affected, meaning almost everyone. These conditions are really *laws* that have the full power of governmental force behind them, and the threat of fines or imprisonment if they are not followed. The Congress, in its arrogant drive to control through ever greater spending influence, is thus relieved of the details.

But there are two very important consequences of the way they do business. The first is that they have passed on their constitutional authority to make laws 'all legislative powers," to other bodies. The result is **unconstitutional**. One may quibble with that opinion by thinking that a hired person who merely carries out Congress' directions is still within the letter of the Constitution, if not the intent.

The reality of the process, however, is quite different. These agencies do not operate as employees would because of the second consequence, namely that congress has no real knowledge of the detailed legislative rules created by their

84

"employee s." They are instead, more autonomous than subject to Congressional control. In no sensible way do they act as employees. They merely swallow up the work load in any way they choose so that Congress can concentrate on the next spending crusade.

Not one single person in the House or the Senate has ever even read all the rules that have become **LAW** in their name, much less reviewed them beforehand for approval. They really are quite detached from the flood of paper issued every year; so much so <u>that they routinely excuse themselves from being subject to these laws, just in case</u>. They are not even surprised when Joe Bureaucrat at HUD writes a ream of law that directly conflicts with the Josephine Bureaucrat law issued by the EPA. Their rationale? Conflicts will happen, and the courts are there to clean up such messes.

The whole process has been allowed to grow purposely for power reasons, and has progressed to the level of stupidity, meaning a process lacking ordinary keenness of mind. Not only does it lack any underlying directivity based on wisdom, and on a purposeful attempt to preserve the goals outlined by the Founders, but it has also grown in its stupor to gigantic proportions of mediocrity, at best, and utter failure at worst.

There is also something else to understand about the process Congress has devised. Regulations, the product of thousands of bureaucrats, the inevitable follow-on of entitlements and other Acts of Congress, define a detailed set of *functions* that government has assumed for itself. As we review some of what regulations have done to Americans, therefore, think of them also as the new functions of government. Measure them against a more ideal set of functions (as for example those outlined in Chapter 3) that should be granted to those whom we entrust the power to rule.

It is not possible to allow any system to operate open loop (i.e., without controlling feedback) and expect it to remain stable. Instability in this critical part of government workings is shown by the:
1) *exponential* increase of regulatory law with each passing year
2) increasing occurrence of conflicting rules
3) increasing numbers of regulatory agencies whose jurisdictions overlap with little consistency among them

4) *exponential* increase in the number of government bureaucrats per capita (from 1 in 10,000 in the time of Lincoln to 1 in 20 today)

5) ever-increasing inefficiencies forced on business just to keep paperwork current

6) and finally by the *exponential* increase in costs to taxpayers to feed this gargantuan government rule-making machine

Exponential change by definition is instability. Laws, number of bureaucrats, and taxes, all increasing exponentially, cause a kind of "mechanical" instability, just like a machine without a throttle. Ultimate failure occurs when limits are reached; when taxes reach 100%, when every citizen becomes a bureaucrat at some agency, when the list of laws becomes so long that all productive activity must cease just to remain within the law; these are the reductio ad absurdum limits.

These resemble "mechanical" failures in the sense that cause and effect are directly connected, and thinking about our condition relative to these limit failures is not encouraging. Taxes at greater than 50%, bureaucrats that make up 4% of the total population (or 10% of adults, or 20% of the work force) and a load of laws that *reduce* productive output by $600 billion each year [as of 1996], which was nearly 20% of the GDP, are already at crisis levels. Guessing what levels we will have to hit before the whole social process fails catastrophically is what we must keep in mind as we try together to devise a better way to live.

A Conclusion to Dread

Government and society are a matched pair. The partner we find ourselves matched with today is *unstable*, or perhaps conditionally stable is a better term, with society being transformed from one of free men and women into one of bureaucrats and dependents.

Another Regulatory Failure – This One Related to Crime & Drugs

There is a second mode of failure of our governmental / societal machine, however, that I consider even more discouraging. Being less "mechanical", it is more difficult to make the logic connection between government actions and the consequences that hurt in subtle ways. The subtlety arises for, example, from the indirect effect that a new regulation on business will have on someone who merely buys a service. Increased cost is one possible effect, as is the requirement to provide personal information under many conditions, or fill out more complicated forms that create a personal life trail, not a criminal trail, but simply a private one, or any of a thousand other time-wasting impositions on personal freedom. The new rule, dreamed up to "solve" some real or imaginary problem of "fairness" or to help business, only succeeds in chipping away at the individual's freedom of action, or privacy, or wealth, until years of this abuse have *unnecessarily* decimated the shield of liberty we began with. Nothing useful is accomplished, and the change in individual freedom has all been negative. This loss is cumulative, with every bit of imposition degrading the singular foundation for society that has any validity, namely individual sovereignty.

Follow along on this general thesis of over-regulation as related to two governmental "wars," pressed forward for our benefit, the war on crime, and the war on drugs which has been discussed earlier.

Gun controls and the debate on what should be acceptable when denying a Constitutional right, have been elevated beyond all dispassionate reason. Each example of civil unrest, defiance against government abuses, each savage crime or act of pent up fury has been reason enough for some to demand that the right to own guns be revoked or restricted in ways limited only by the imagination of rule-makers. The arguments become even more harsh and emotion-driven when these acts of rebellion seem driven by terrorist anger. The fallacy in the whole unending debate and the regulations that have resulted, is that <u>no regulation or law has *ever* deterred any *criminal* act.</u>

Any terrorist, any murderer, any petty criminal, any Casper Milquetoast-turned-killer, intent on using weapons to harm others, will find a way to destroy the object of his hate regardless of what *gun regulations* do or do not allow. <u>Nothing</u> useful toward the protection of *individuals* has ever been accomplished because of gun regulations, no matter how oppressive and odious they are. What is *always* accomplished, however, is to impose delays, fees, disclosure of private information, suspicions and other effects on everyone else except the criminal. The load of regimentation and the structure to carry on the myth of benefiting the people is all added, via more taxes, to everyone else, and the supposed objective, to protect, is not even remotely successful.

I contend that the debate, and the legislative actions that result, are seriously misdirected. Instead of addressing the causes behind these acts of violence, all the passion and energy has been directed at peripherals which are mostly irrelevant. Since guns are never the *cause* of violence, their control can never prevent violence. The fact that real motivations and the preludes to destructive behavior are much more complex than simple gun control, that intractability has a great deal to do with the way politicians choose to deal with the issues. They know with great certainty that they are not competent to deal with human frustrations that can spark violence. *Nor are they honest enough to see the part of the crime problem caused by government itself*, i.e. the <u>excesses</u> that occupy us in this book.

Government economic and regulatory oppression, government abuses (Waco, Ruby Ridge, and the burning in Philadelphia, for example), confiscation without due process (a direct violation of the Constitution government is *sworn* to uphold), and taxation well beyond reasonable limits, all add in subtle or sometimes direct ways to the oppressive load on individuals. Likewise, almost no thought is given (by government) to the effects of overcrowding and welfare dependency on the stability and quality of life of individuals. Anger and hate, and their causes, are so

87

complex that it is easier to ignore them and "regulate" guns. The plan is stupidity in action and predictably worthless.

The "war on drugs" is an even mo re barefaced example of over-regulation by government. The stupidity of today's answer to the human problem of *addiction* has followed directly from the initial error in judgment of declaring a prohibition on the manufacture, sale and use of addictive substances. No one in government seemed to be capable of understanding the correlation between alcohol and any of the newer drugs. Lessons learned from the foolishness behind the 18th (16 Jan. 1919) and 21st (5 Dec. 1933) amendments to the Constitution really weren't learned at all.

Since this issue was discussed earlier, we needn't rehash it here, but it is important to see that the "war on drugs" is just another subterfuge of government to regulate, not to solve the underlying causes of the malady.

The saddest result to come from government's heavy-handed "solution" to an addiction problem is that it has summarily rescinded the right of choice. Choice no longer exists as an inherent right in the United States. Government has made it very clear that it has the dictatorial power over choice and will use it whenever it benefits government. Today it is drugs; tomorrow it will be b-l-a-n-k, yet to be revealed.

So finally, we have come to the real victims of overregulation. I believe that by far the biggest losers in all this are the two hundred and eighty million supposedly free Americans who summarily have been stripped, not only of Rights guaranteed by the Constitution, but also of Rights that are unalienable and inherent with life. **That is a major catastrophe**. It has set Americans back in time to a condition known to all our ancestors before America was founded. This is not histrionics. It is not sensationalism. It is simply fact. What else can you call the loss of Rights from these unconstitutional acts by our own government?

- seizure of goods without due process
- search of person and home without due proces
- loss of goods without compensation or due process
- presumption of guilt without proof
- denial of the right to decide for yourself
- the branding as unlawful, acts that can have no true connection with law

The Bill of Rights, the great foundation of American Government that sets us apart from all previous governments, is no longer in effect in America.

Please note that this time your government can not undo its drug war tyranny by conjuring up another 21st Amendment[14] for drugs. They have simply taken the power to themselves without preamble because the force is available to them. They have distorted the one truly worthwhile function of government, which is to ensure personal security, merely to add further power to government. They are quite willing to shunt aside any issues surrounding constitutionality until the rest of us finally realize what they have done.

Freedom comes hard. It is *never* permanent, as Jefferson, Washington and Madison have so clearly told us.

The 'benefits" government has sold to us while instigating their wars on crime and on drugs, all the while heaping a mountain of regulations on us, have netted us the opposite, not benefits, but **real** loss of Rights and freedom.

*   *   *

Regulations and Their Cost Effectiveness

Are regulations excessive? Are they doing the job intended? In short, are they giving us good return for the tax money government has extracted from us to spend on enforcement? It so happens that there are answers to these questions. They come in the form of hard, numerical results from two separate studies. Their scope was broad enough to tell us exactly what we'd like to know about the overall effects of *regulations* as a government strategy for attaining goals. My reading of these dispassionate, number-crunching analyses says that they tell us how cost effective government regulations are for the tax money being spent. Direct comparisons are possible because results are all in dollars spent by government to add one year to the life of one American.

The average 1994 cost to each household to comply with all federal regulations amounted to about $6,000. We all know that understanding what such an average value really means is not easy. We'd like to know a lot more of the details. At the very least we know that $6,000 is more money than we'd like to spend on paperwork for affirmative action, or licenses to handle used automobile oil, or all of the other nits government agencies have dreamed up. We might also believe that the $6,000 estimate is a fairly accurate one since the study was done by T. D. Hopkins of the Rochester Institute of Technology and published in the *Journal of Regulation and Social Costs.*[15] The $6,000 per household is merely a reference number to keep in mind. The real cost excesses and harshness of government

---

[14] Prohibited laws aimed at controlling intoxicating liquors.
[15] This information was given in an article by Ben Bolch and Deborah Pittman in 'Liberty" maga zine, Vol. 9, No. 3 of Jan. 1996.

regulations are yet to come. This information is also given in the Bolch-Pittman article in *Liberty*.

The real eye-opening study was done by a team of investigators affiliated with Duke, Harvard, and other staid institutions of higher learning that give us confidence in the veracity of the work. Tammy O. Tengs headed the team, and their method was to do a massive literature search to determine the *cost of regulations* and other interventions instituted by government for the stated purpose of saving lives. Government's purpose is a noble one. The method used is the enforced extraction of tax money from everyone and the spending of that money totally at the whim of regulators with 'well-meaning ideas" but with no real notion of how effective that spending would be. Their collective credo seems to have been that if even one human life is saved, cost is irrelevant.

As an aside, if Regulators really believe that aphorism, then you would expect every part of their own personal fortune, except what's needed to live themselves, would be donated to save the life of *anyone* at risk, no matter how slim the prospect of survival might be. Of course, none of them do any such thing! Their own fortune is not at issue. It is *other people's money* that they freely demand be spent to save that person at risk. And by their diligent work, THE biggest single error of government is perpetuated: the giving away of something that doesn't belong to them.

Back to the Tengs, et al study, as reported in a recent issue of <u>Risk Analysis</u>, Vol. 15, No. 3. The object of the study was to estimate the cost to save lives through government mandated, 'behavioral or technological strategies devised to reduce the probability of premature death among certain 'target' groups of people." By this approach, the study is as broad as can be imagined, and as basic as it gets.

It answers the question: How much does it cost (in 1993 dollars) to *add one year* to the life of *one person*:

That metric is common among all the results, and permits direct comparisons, not only of the cost effectiveness among government agencies, but also against our own *subjective opinions* regarding the premium to be placed on a life and the extent of heroic measures that are reasonable. Here's the list in order of increasing cost which, of course, means decreasing efficiency, in the use of tax dollars:

- The Federal Aviation Agency (FAA) is by far the most effective in its use of tax money. The target group is those who travel by air, which includes a large percentage of the population.
  Cost: $23,000 per life-year saved.

- The Consumer Product Safety Commission dictates regulations for an even greater number of Americans, but their cost effectiveness is only about one-third that of the FAA.

    Cost: $68,000 per life-year saved.
- The National Highway Traffic Safety Administration spends almost three and one-half times as much as the FAA saving motorists' lives.

    Cost: $78,000 per life-year saved.
- The Occupational Safety and Health Administration, OSHA, that ubiquitous governmental eye in the workplace that has been so much a regulatory thorn in every working person's life, is an even greater spendthrift. OSHA regulators spend almost two or three year's worth of your wages to add one year to a worker's life.

    Cost: $88,000 per life-year saved.

It gets worse! Much, worse!

- The Environmental Protection Agency (EPA) squanders our confiscated tax money at such a prodigious rate that any goal of saving lives must obviously be secondary to a much more 'important" goal of simply spending money. Their claim to the wise and efficient use of our tax money is seen as hypocritical hogwash of the first magnitude.

    Cost: $7,600,000 per life-year saved.

Think about this spending binge number for a moment. Taking just $5,000 tax dollars per family, this says that your government has deemed it worthwhile to spend the cumulative, confiscated 'take" from 1520 families in order to add one year to the life of one fellow citizen, saved (presumably) from environmental risks that are still not well understood. The lopsided wisdom inherent in this profligate spending of money better spent by the fifteen hundred families themselves, is beyond my comprehension. Clearly, saving lives has nothing to do with the reason for the existence of this Agency. Perhaps there is a better measure than dollars per life-year saved.

Shall we assume there is a deeper purpose? Is there reason to think that an even more noble purpose lies behind the EPA? Certainly there are many things people are doing to the environment that are killing IT at a great rate, but what is to say that this government agency is helping to undo those real excesses of mankind? As of today, this question has not been answered, but the likelihood of this agency being any different than any other government enterprise is about zero. That, of course, is merely my own cynical opinion. The question, however, needs serious consideration from everyone, especially from you, the reader, the victimized taxpayer.

As outrageous as the preceding item is, it is a mere tuppence compared to the following:

- A mandate banning asbestos has succeeded in costing taxpayers $1.4 **billion** dollars per life-year saved.
- A mandate to control benzene emissions in the manufacture of tires costs taxpayers $20 billion dollars per life-year saved.
- A mandate for the control of chloroform emissions (at a mere 48 wood pulp mills) costs an estimated $99 billion dollars per life-year saved. Please note in this instance that this does not mean that $99 billion has actually been spent to net us one more life-year. It means that the ridiculous mandates dreamed up by government agency minions have virtually *no incremental value* in saving lives for the outlandish bother and cost needed to implement them. In a word, the mandates are *worthless*.

Authors Bolch and Pittman give an apt comparison between the mindless scratching of government chickens in the garden looking for worms and the cost effectiveness of the medical profession for many high cost surgical procedures. The criticism by government 'heavy thinkers" of health care in the United States, and one of the principal reasons they are beginning to intrude seriously into the whole health care industry, is that the cost of adequate care is too expensive. High cost tends to restrict the treatment of lower income people, and only if government steps in to control things will such imbalances be corrected.

The criticism is a joke.

- heart transplants (for people under 55) cost about $36,000; and
- dialysis for kidney failure (for patients under 64), considered even by practitioners as expensive, cost only $42,000. Assume that only 5 years are added to the patient's life. The cost per life year added is lower than the government's best performer, the FAA .

One might conclude from just the sketchy review above that it might be acceptable to use the best government agency as a model for the others to emulate, and that if the incremental return on tax dollars spent were as good as that of the FAA, then government mandated regulations would somehow become acceptable. We mustn't lose sight, however, of the even more fundamental objection to the scourge of regulations and the bureaucracy that *spews* them forth every year. That reason, of course, as we've noted is the loss of freedom of action that comes with unnecessary regulation, which is to say virtually ALL regulation. That loss of freedom is a direct assault on those myriad things that contribute to a pursuit of happiness as varied as the people who work hard to better their own lives. But just to be clear that such objections, even against the best of regulators are reasonable objections, consider the following thoughts related to the best of government agencies, the FAA.

A Voluntary Approach Could Readily Replace the Best Performer, the FAA

I contend that government mandates regarding air travel are unnecessary, and that an afternoon's thought is all that would be needed to devise a voluntary approach to flight safety that is superior to the one now in use. The gist is to rely on the vested interests of airlines, airplane manufacturers, passengers and private pilots to have the very safest means of air travel possible. The commercial people want to make money, and their safety record correlates directly with passengers carried. Private flying knows it must share the air space or risk being the cause of accidental deaths, their own included.

All of these organizations could jointly fund efforts to improve air safety, much as individual engine makers invest to improve product reliability and economy of operation. There is no effort for the improvement of air travel that could not be part of such a voluntary alternative to mandated government regulations. Air traffic control systems, ground control systems, radars, satellite navigation equipment, basic studies for future upgrades, flight equipment, and every other aspect of aviation could come under the umbrella of such an approach. Such an Air Safety Organization, *a private organization* it should be emphasized, would operate via contracts with the best technological and academic organizations worldwide, which, in turn, would compete via their own best efforts.

Simply described, we have another free enterprise, the privatized equivalent of an inefficient and unfair government organization that can't possibly compete against men and women free to progress through incentives freely chosen.

And how would this be funded? Funding would come from the very people who have most to gain. The air passengers who want to get from Bakersfield to Santa Barbara, or Tokyo to Paris, or Ontario to Katmandu, with less chance of mishap than walking down the front steps after a snow storm. Without even having a detailed cost analysis to back me up, I can confidently make another assertion that any increase in ticket cost per mile traveled would be considerably less than the tax now being paid. And who would not get soaked for forced contributions to benefit faceless air travelers? All those hapless taxpayers who have no intention of leaving the ground.

*   *   *

Regulations & Health Care

Health care has been the subject of a great deal of public and political debate of late. In the US we were very fortunate to sidestep the recent onslaught of government regulators, led by none other than the First Lady herself, via a commission from President Clinton. That round may have gone to the people, but

93

attempts by government to extend regulatory powers did not end because of any such temporary setback. The mind of government is like an idiot-savant; it is one-dimensional, and attempts to increase government mandates and controls in such a lucrative industry will continue.

$$* \quad * \quad *$$

Some Final Examples

In reviewing the debacle of government regulations, we've chosen to dissect some of the most important and the worst cases. Perhaps those examples are enough to make my points, but I can't r esist the temptation to end the discussion with a quick look under just a few more slimy rocks covering some truly pathetic facts about our government in action. As we go along, think also about what these cases of over-regulation imply regarding the details of government functions actually being exercised versus functions that are proper in a country supposedly ruled by the people.

- Government is well on its way to requiring licenses for every function performed by individuals in their exercise of free choice. Choice, therefore, is no longer free and government is operating more and more on the assumption that IT is the source of Individual Rights.
- Minimum wage regulations are rammed down the throat of American business in spite of the sure knowledge that job opportunities diminish because of them. No worker is helped because of these regulations. Only our dependence on government watchdogs advances.
- In its zeal to combat drugs (government's excuse for expanded *surveillance* of all Americans) government has regulated that all monetary transactions greater than $10,000 be reported to government. The move is virtually worthless in tracking down drug money, but is an easy source of information that can be used against private individuals in their normal course of living and conducting business. What is magic about the $10,000 amount? Why is it not $1 million or even $1,000? The answer: It is purely for regimentation of average Americans, and subsequent expansion of government..
- The same is true concerning regulations — and punishments — aimed at preventing the movement of money assets into or out of the country. Such restrictions, supposedly to help ferret out money acquired by criminal acts, are worthless for such a purpose, but completely effective against honest people in their pursuit of happiness.

I quote from the "Welcome to the United States Custom s Declaration" form: 'I am/we are carrying currency or monetary instruments over $10,000 U.S. or foreign equivalent   [yes]   [no]." On the back of the form it tells us that "The transportation of currency or monetary instruments, regardless of amount, is **legal**; however, ... FAILURE TO FILE THE

94

REQUIRED REPORT OR FALSE STATEMENTS ON THE REPORT MAY LEAD TO SEIZURE OF THE CURRENCY OR INSTRUMENTS AND TO CIVIL PENALTIES AND/OR CRIMINAL PROSECUTION."

I am dumbfounded at the assault on my Right to property as a citizen of this 'free country." There is no condition under which I would agree to such a power being handed to government. Obviously, my agreement, or yours, is meaningless and will be as long as Constitution One is the legal reference.

• The handling of materials by businesses, large and small, has become so regulated that it is almost impossible to move, dispose of, mark or use *any item* without breaking the 'law" in some manner. The purpose, ostensibly to protect the environment, or the consumer or wildlife, more accurately is there to *tighten the restraints on choice*, extracting ever more fees in the process. Government has invented a new gateway into the wealth cache of ordinary working people in government's avaricious attempts to tax. Their disdain for people is once again borne out as if calling just another tax by a different name will go unnoticed. The invention has held our complaints at bay for quite a while, but even sheep eventually learn that the fence the mob in front has been jumping has disappeared.

• By far the worst example I've seen so far of regulatory madness was reported in *Liberty* magazine, Sept. 1995, Volume 9, Number 1, by Pierre Lemieux in his article "Auditing the Income Tax". Allow me to quote.

> *Mobil Corp's 1993 income tax return comprised nine fat volumes totaling 6,300 pages weighing 76 pounds; its preparation required 146,000 documents and cost $1 million.*

The utter foolishness of an enterprise that would require such nonproductive squandering of effort is compounded to even greater heights of stupidity as we note that corporate taxes *per se* are a complete sham. The ultimate payer of taxes *can only be* the ultimate consumer of anything. Corporate taxes are mere pass-through expenses added to consumer prices. Why does government even bother with all this idiocy? The only sensible answer comes from the advantage derived by government. It is the sheer exercise of POWER that explains such acts, which are pursued with cunning to reinforce its position of power and expanding presence.

*   *   *

A Reluctant, Inescapable & Sad Conclusion

Regulations, coming at the American people as an onslaught that won't stop, have become the nemesis of freedom, the mighty detractor that slowly empties our freedom bucket that once overflowed. Freedoms that were a natural result of finally recognizing the equality of all people have been spirited away almost as if regulations were a desiccant inexorably sucking moisture from the bucket. Without that moisture, there is little hope that the once robust plant we call *pursuit of happiness* can regain the vigor it once had. The trend is crystal clear; continued application of desiccants, of regulations, until decisions come only from government, relegates the pursuit of happiness to nothing but a grotesque remnant of what it had once been.

I read the condition as unhealthy and rapidly approaching the critical point. I point an accusing finger directly at government for its *failure* to meet its obligation to preserve our Right to pursue happiness, each in their own way. I read the direction of government as a continuation of past debilitating policies, a further unhealthy expansion of government functions, and I see virtually no hope that such a course will change by government initiative to rescue our national condition.

Government has failed in thousands of little ways that add up to a complete failure to understand the fundamental purpose of American government.

CHAPTER 11
Destroying the Republic -- Special Interests at Work

Profligate give-aways of tax money to special interest groups, the debacle of Social Security, government's attempts to control education and a whole panoply of like failures from State and Local government are four other "works" of government we need to understand. Once we see how these intrusive programs actually operate, we will then understand why indictments are necessary, and why any internal drive the average person has to build a happier life is akin to taking on the sheer face of El Capitan in Yosemite. As we go along this sorry path, however, keep reminding yourself that El Capitan has been scaled, and government, too, can be tamed by ordinary Americans using the right approach.

This chapter title is adapted from a book which is **the** defining work on this particular transgression by government. Not only is the subject a failure of government, involving the squandering of huge sums of tax money, but the entire process is a *criminal* one. And finally, if these government actions didn't happen to violate American Law, they would still deserve our vilification because what is taking place just isn't right.

This single method of exercising governmental power is enough, by itself, to justify government's removal and replacement by one which will finally honor American founding ideals.

As the facts show, however, the process used by government is in violation of the very laws passed by the Congress of the United States itself. The book I refer to is called <u>Destroying Democracy</u>, subtitled <u>How Government Funds Partisan Politics</u>. It was written by James T. Bennett and Thomas J. DiLorenzo of the CATO Institute, after extensive investigation of government money transactions for the period through about 1984. Recall that in Chapter 4, while describing THE most critical error of government, I referred to this example. It is one which shows just how *that seemingly innocuous first gift of public money has been taken to an extreme that threatens the very Republic itself.*

The subject of this part of our review of government failures is one that has implications in almost every responsibility handed to government two centuries ago. Whether it is preserving wealth, guiding efforts for national goals or preserving precious Rights, this shoddy government practice hurts them all. The choice to include it as another blow against our quest for happiness seems a natural one because of my belief that this is the most neglected of our Rights, and the most neglected of criteria within government as it takes action on almost any legislative business. Before government acts, it routinely avoids asking what the potential for harm might be, or how well the action might fulfill their prime obligations. Clearly government's actions or intentions have nothing to do with such lofty purpose.

Thinking about the ethics involved, it seems reasonable to expect public servants to conduct themselves in a way that is easily described. Create just laws, be very careful with public wealth, spending it only as you would your own money, and always remember you are a hired servant with profound responsibilities. With some such guidance in mind it should be relatively straight-forward to decide the particulars at decision times. The sad fact is that the giving of money, especially other people's money, has turned the process of governing into thievery, and a whole cache of public servants into thieves.

The extent of this theft of public money may never be known, but Bennett and DiLorenzo have uncovered so much of it that **the truth of failed stewardship is unequivocal**. Over the decades of spending ever greater bundles of money, the spenders have learned a great many ways to DIVERT social program appropriations to other efforts that support *political advocacy*. This diverted money is used directly and indirectly to assist in the re-election campaigns of office holders and to *expand* bureaucratic empires of public employees.

In other words these clever people have succeeded in devising ways to change the purpose of giving from a desire to help those in need into helping themselves retain power.

Giving by government for either purpose is wrong. The second of these two reasons, however, is worse by far. The temptation inherent in money has been beyond the ethical capacity of officials to remain pristine in their handling of it. As a group, they are probably no more larcenous than any other collection of people. They may even be a cut above the average in this respect. But with opportunities abounding, it is not surprising that these thefts have become commonplace. What is surprising is the scale that these fraudulent activities has reached. Clearly, the solution is to remove the opportunities (i.e. the power to spend) to the greatest possible extent.

Some idea of the scale of the potential for larceny can come from a few numbers. There are tens of thousands of contracts and outright grants given out each year via hundreds of government programs. A mere 1,000 of these programs distribute $190 billion in loans and guarantees, and a staggering $287 billion is parceled out in grants and direct payments, (1982 figures). Government largess is fair game for nonprofit organizations alone from almost 500 separate programs, initiated by legislative Acts voted into law by Congress. Individuals, State and

Local governments have entrees into an even greater number of appropriation bills. Take particular note of the fact that *there is no central point in government that monitors the distribution of these huge sums* or in any way reviews its own Acts and the means of implementing them to determine whether or not even their *intent* is being satisfied. The *opportunity* for fraud, favoritism and political advocacy is almost limitless. That is the extent to which this failure of government has evolved.

Agencies created to administer Congressional programs, a euphemism for giving money away, have little choice but to operate with very little Congressional supervision, especially regarding such mundane details as the merits of those organizations getting the handouts. Feedback to legislators comes round-about by whatever cursory procedure they themselves might have regarding the efficacy of a given Entitlement or Act on the social condition it was meant to solve. *The usual conclusion, reached when feedback is discouraging, is to increase the spending level*, without any attempt to assess the effectiveness of the whole process.

The overall cycle from Congress, to law, to agency, to recipient and back to Congress is a cascade of irresponsibilities since the chief *measure of effectiveness* is the amount of money 'processed" and not a quantification of real ben efits derived from the money. The ingredients and incentives for thievery of all descriptions are clearly there, **huge sums of money, little supervision and almost zero evaluation of results.**

Once they are created to handle the details of implementing programs, agencies are essentially autonomous, being answerable to no one except a Congress which merely stands on the sidelines, diverted to other, more urgent matters. Authority to suspend *unlawful* procedures exists only via more legislation, of which the final form is usually unrecognizable from the good intent to fix a problem. *Given charter and license to spend a given budget, the focus is on money spent rather than on its wise use.* Officials on the lower tiers of the bureaucratic hierarchy are active seekers of organizations that fit within the letter of their charter, and the game has been played long enough for a myriad of special interests groups to appear at the head of the line at money distribution time.

The Bennett / DiLorenzo report lists a huge number of federal grants and contracts made to advocacy groups. Hundreds of millions of dollars are given to hundreds of such groups each year. The Tax Gift Industry is so widespread, so large and so intricate in its operation, that even the great effort and investigative cost expended by the authors and the CATO Institute wasn't nearly enough to ferret out the whole story. Tracing money pathways for every program would be a task far beyond the resources available through CATO and other contributors. In my opinion, however, the fact that so much unlawful activity was actually uncovered is reason enough to damn the entire process.

Government is using tax money, confiscated by force (in excessive amounts), to pay its political costs to keep itself in power. This violates the very foundation of this country, the Constitution of the United States.

There is in the US a network of special-interest organizations comprised of thousands of interlocking as well as separate groups. They champion every cause imaginable, are largely non-violent, and are exercising the Right of free expression.

A large and powerful segment of this network, however, gets the money to fund its *political opinions* from the US Treasury, meaning that TAX money, extracted from everyone, is used to support minority ideas. The spending of **public** money to support the political ideas of advocacy groups is illegal, a concept and conclusion reinforced by Congress in specific Acts of Law. It is illegal for a very good reason. Under our Constitution people can not be forced to support political or any other causes with which they disagree. Unless such advocates can show support from 100% of the voters, to take public money is to break this just law.

Giving such money is also breaking the law. Congress knows this; advocacy groups know this; the one refuses to enforce the law; the others prostitute themselves in favor of the handouts. In fact the illogic of ideas behind many such groups has antagonized would-be voluntary supporters to such an extent that the groups would cease to operate without the illegal grants from government of money extorted from people who have chosen, for their own good reasons, NOT to support them.

There must be a reason that these criminal acts take place. Not only are they condoned, but over the last several decades they have actually been institutionalized. This is just a fancy way of saying that the criminal acts are made to look proper by having participants, both giver and receiver, follow a set of rules and regulations that would discourage the faint-of-heart.[16] Follow the winding green line, and at the end is the money window.

Actually, I believe there are two reasons this institutionalized theft is able to continue. The first is that We the People are completely powerless to end the practice. This is quite obvious when we note that the revelations of Bennett and DiLorenzo have been known since 1985, and absolutely nothing has happened since then to cause these criminal acts to cease. The sad truth is that the ONLY change since that time is that the amount stolen has increased every year. We should also pause briefly to note that the two other branches of our well-structured government,

---

[16] Fortunately Bennett and DiLorenzo were not faint-of-heart, and succeeded in following the money trail enough to show what is actually happening.

namely the Judicial and the Executive, have also done absolutely nothing to compel Congress to cease breaking the law.

We have a de-facto breakdown in one of the fundamental tenets underlying the structure and operation of American Self Government, namely the balance of powers among the three branches of government to assure compliance with the Constitution.

I realize the statement borders on the histrionic. It is *not* meant to do so, nor to *incite* anything except the attention of thinking, just people in and out of government. The answer to what must be done to correct this long-standing, government-run crime against our basic ideals is not to change the laws to allow the theft to go on until its constitutionality is tested in the courts, but to *end the practice completely*. That is the *right* thing to do., summarily END the madness.

The second reason theft continues is very simple and basic to the human animal. There is a clear advantage to government officials, our employees, those surrogate kings in the Senate, and their supporters in the House of Representatives, to allow it. Congress alone is not at fault, however. It takes acquiescence of the Executive Branch *and* the Judicial Branch. The benefits are shared by all, benefits derived directly from the expansion of government and of government power, which is about as basic as motivations can be. It is in the self-interest of conglomerate government to let it stand, and it does so in spite of many people within Congress itself who have tried to stop it.

The United States Government has pioneered a new kind of power-over-people, based on money and not incidentally, on the erosion of Rights through the illicit use of that money.

Who are the people who use public money against the majority? They are proponents of issues ranging from consumer protection, the environment, poverty and welfare, civil rights and energy, to social security, research and unionism. As diverse as they are, the major common factor that binds such people together ideologically is via the solutions proposed to fix whatever the problem at issue may be. The solution *always* includes greater involvement of government and the addition of more regulatory powers. A very few of the groups from among the thousands at work are listed next just to give the flavor of this self-serving industry.

- **IPS** - Institute for Policy Studies - preeminent think tank of the left
    - purpose: promote socialism and train advocacy groups.
- **ICCR** - Interfaith Center for Corporate Responsibility - affiliated with the National Council of Churches [NCC]

-purpose: replace the free enterprise / corporate structure with state and local government ownership. The buzz word attached to this movement is "economic democracy."

• **CED** - Campaign for Economic Democracy, a Tom Hayden invention.
- guiding belief: the free enterprise system is the source of most of the nation's problems;
-purpose: undo free enterprise and adopt socialist methods renamed Economic Democracy [to avoid the stigma attached to the term Socialism as perceived by many Americans].

• **AFL/CIO** - American Federation of Labor / Congress of Industrial Organizations
- decreasing membership has inspired unions to use political means to gain power over businesses, and replace the free enterprise system.
• **NTIC** - National Training and Information Center: a part of :
• **NPA** - National People's Action
- both conduct tax-funded programs to train activists, with major goals to have corporate managers change policies in line with activists demands, and to stage protests to force their ideas on government agencies, particularly with regard to budget cuts which they oppose.
• **PIRG** - Public Interest Research Groups; a movement attributable to Ralph Nader. Nader's umbrella organization is called "Public Citizen."
- Heavily responsible for the great expansion of regulations and government agencies in the 1960s and 1970s. Groups, whose tax-funded efforts have inundated companies in regulatory red tape, and have trained agency regulators whose goal has been to hurt big business. Have instigated regulatory policies targeting the pharmaceutical industry which delay approval of useful drugs beyond all reason, and work directly against the public interest they claim to champion, while failing to prevent unsafe products from reaching the market.
- PIRGs have instituted a phony tax on university students to pay for their advocacy efforts; phony because it is made to look like a part of student fees instead of a voluntary donation. The theft, from Minnesota, New Jersey and 28 other state PIRGs may total more than $4.8 million yearly.
- Nader's philosophical, utopian view behind all the disruptive activity is a desire to scale back living, abolishing all big businesses and creating small self-contained communities, with everything owned through cooperatives. Perhaps there is a nagging fear behind such philosophical nonsense that comes from valid concerns about world human population.

So much for identification. There are *hundreds* more such advocacy organizations. The fungus of special interests groups is as intricate, and as varied and all-pervasive as the spores that create mold, mildew and rot. The goals that partly unify these groups, besides expansion of governmental power and restriction of free enterprise, include others that directly oppose freedom, unalienable rights and individual sovereignty that America is supposed to stand for.

Cripple the American system through over-regulation; instigate national economic planning, with governmental allocation of capital and worker control of industry; install "econ omic democracy," a euphemism for socialism; replace private ownership with ownership by cooperatives; and institute redistribution of wealth by governmental means. All of these ideas, in various forms, are part of the pungent glue that holds these activists together. Obviously unanimity is not complete, but every one of these groups will readily prostitute any guiding criterion of its own to gain support from another on any given crusade. Bashing free enterprise, adding regulators, supporting big-government politicians or training more political activists will always win their joint efforts. My view of American ideals and the foundation America rests upon says clearly that these crusaders, and even the extremists who work for such organizations have the Right to embrace any ideals they want, whether seemingly sensible or total nonsense, but they can not steal one cent of tax money that I, and you, have been forced to hand over to government. Yet they do, and we sit and watch.

One easy deduction from the Bennett – DiLorenzo work is that this entire tribe of detractors would be vehemently opposed to any changes in government and the Constitution as described in this book. Changes would clearly mean loss of government hand-outs, and the need to hunt for gainful employment.

The Bennett - DiLorenzo work is a fascinating, disturbing journey through the intricate workings of the giant industry of political advocacy, of factions in the James Madison, George Washington sense. The tactics, the subterfuge, the cleverness and thoroughness of these detractors make an intriguing chapter in modern American history. Unfortunately much of it is criminal, and the focus here is on the *criminal* use of public money for political purposes. All of the factions listed earlier regularly receive tax money from every imaginable government agency and spent it to their own ends, as have all the others in the advocacy "industry."

A few examples of the projects **funded by tax money** will give an idea of how misused taxpayer trust and money have become.

• **IPS** - receives little or no government money directly, but establishes the social Foundation and policies taught in almost all political activist training centers as well as universities throughout the United States, which *are* also supported by tax money.

- **ICCR** - The Interfaith Center on Corporate Responsibility is the NY affiliate of **NCC** (National Council of Churches) and others who actively hate corporations. As reported in the CATO study, active investigations are actually funded by these groups to gather data useful against corporations. The NCC has even funded a reward of $10,000 to the radical United Church of Christ for 'evidence likely to lead to the arrest and imprisonment of the CEO of a Fortune 500 company," with another $15,000 if successful.

Between 1978 and 1980, NCC received at least $1,388,775 tax dollars from US government agencies including the Department of Labor, The Department of Energy, and the National Endowment for the Arts.

- **CED** - A $334,761 'Crime Control Project" grant from the Department of Justice to Communutas, a Tom Hayden offshoot, used to promote CED priorities, notably rent control. (CED is Hayden's Campaign for Economic Democracy; which when translated equals socialism.)
- **CED** - A $201,238 grant from VISTA (Volunteers In Service To America, a federally funded agency) to Laurel Springs Institute, a training center for CED activists.
- **AFL / CIO** - Unions have such potent political clout that they obtain each year *several hundred million tax dollars* to promote union political goals.
  - for example: in 1972, union strikers received an estimated $329 million in public welfare support excluding unemployment compensation. (Ref. a Wharton School study by Arnold Thieblot and Ronald Cowin.)
  - Example #2: A $2,762,956 grant from the Dept. of Transportation to organize transit workers into the union.
- **PIRG** - The National Consumers League reportedly received half of its 1981 - 83 operating budget of $500,000 from government grants.
  - The Consumer Federation of America (CFA) placed their executive secretary, Carol Foreman, as the Assistant Secretary of Agriculture (a USDA, 1978 study), who then granted $23,536 to CFA for a consumer impact study. This was more than twice the amount allowed by USDA guidelines.
  - Worse yet, the CFA had already published what the findings of such a study SHOULD conclude before the grant was even made.
  - CFA received a Dept. of Energy (DOE) grant of $85,000 (May 1978) so that CFA's position on decontrol of heating oil could be prepared. The criticisms about such use of funds were answered by DOE by giving CFA another $49,500 'to develop standards by which CFA and other consumer groups could receive grants in the future."

The list is virtually endless. And while the government spending binge continues there is never any serious thought given about the practice of funding *political advocacy*. There is no thought given by anyone that the spending, the granting of such money, is also adding to an indebtedness that is already staggering. No consistent monitoring is done by government of how such money is spent. Its uses for advocacy projects which directly assault the freedoms and Rights of individuals is never challenged by government, since government would, in effect, be challenging itself. There is no longer even a hint that the practice is unconstitutional, and the pangs of conscience about its being a criminal act have long since disappeared. There are so many people involved in the giving and the taking that they feed on each other's lack of ethics that make theft acceptable if it happens on a large enough scale. **The farce continues with each passing year.**

Before leaving this disgusting and disquieting subject of sanctioned government misconduct I will relate just a few more examples of the frivolous and foolish projects our tax money has been lavished upon. If the people who 'performed" the projects, or simply pocketed the money, actually believed there was value in them, then it is obvious it was not their own money they were using. It should be equally obvious that the TAXPAYERS never received the slightest bit of benefit from them, nor from most of the unconscionable expenditures by government for advocacy crusades supposedly done at our behest.

• The Women's Equity Action League received grants from the US Department of Education between 1978 and 1980 totaling more than one million dollars. The jargon used to describe and justify the gifts is very enlightening about the use of literary fog in this whole government advocacy charade. 'WEAL has a small but influential membership, dedicated to securing the legal and economic rights of women through a program of research, public education and legislative advocacy." !!!

• In 1985 the Free Trade Union Institute received $11,560,788 from the National Endowment for Democracy, 'to continue the broad range of programs for the development of the free independent trade unions that were begun with the support the institute received from NED in FY 1984." Clearly another good synergy between government and labor had been founded in 1984 and was likely to continue. [Why is government in the business of funding union development?]

• The Amalgamated Clothing & Textile Workers Union was awarded $317,316 from the National Endowment for the Humanities to conduct seminars 'to help members see themselves and their work in broader historical and cultural contexts." The ACTWU was a regular recipient of gifts from several government agencies for millions of dollars.

• Perhaps one of the strangest grants of all was one for a mere 50,000 dollars to Freedom House from the National Endowment for Democracy in 1984. Its stated purpose is, "To establish a network of democratic opinion leaders in both the developing and developed worlds in order to facilitate a free exchange of ideas, and end the isolation of democratic intellectuals and journalists."

Such a grandiose scope is ludicrous to contemplate for a mere fifty thousand dollars. One can only wonder at the real purpose behind the gift.

• Between 1977 & 1981 questionable expenditures of government grant money were made by PUSH and affiliates [People United to Save Humanity] totaling $4.9 million. The grants came from the Departments of Education, Labor, Commerce and Health & Human Services. Included among the purchases were:

- 10,000 Christmas cards with an autographed photo of Jesse Jackson.

- A $1 million contract to promote excellence and motivation among inner-city students, to buy basketball uniforms, and fund a high school tournament, band and dinner dance.

- $656,644 went for donations to a Chicago track club, and air travel associated with a Black Leadership Conference in Holly Springs, Mississippi.

- A *rare audit* by the US Department of Education's Office of Inspector General declared 'that Jackson had 'misused' more than $1.7 million in grants."

• In 1981 The League of United Latin American Citizens received $1,237,600 from the Department of Education for the purpose of searching for 'talent." In 1980 the gift was for $1,190,000 for the same stated purpose.

• From 1981 to 1982 the National Council of Senior Citizens [NCSC] received more than $58,000,000 from the Dept. of Labor. All activities of this group are political.

• NCSC also received a total of $212 million from six different government agencies between 1978 and 1982. One of these was a relatively new agency, The Administrator of Aging. The senior political action arena has evolved into a huge advocacy voice with an agenda that does not represent seniors. It is instead another powerful advocate of bigger, more intrusive government, and officials have responded with overwhelming generosity. It has almost achieved the status of wielding a club as large as unions, with a pipeline to government money that is comparable.

• The League of Women Voters received a total of $498,000 from the EPA for fourteen separate 'Education "projects between 1977 and 1982.

• The East Los Angeles Community Union received grants for $32,000,000 during the period from 1976 to1979. Part of the money was for 'a technical assistance interchange program that would assist community economic development organizations to formulate and implement ongoing technical transfers among themselves with the intent of bolstering each organization's capabilities in functional areas to allow an increased ability to conduct major development projects from start to finish."

No matter what the product of this program turned out to be, assuming there was to be an output, it would fulfill this ridiculous goal. An output of nothing at all would also satisfy it just as well.

Of the more than $32,000,000 given to TELACU, not **all** of it was misspent.

• The Institute for Social Justice received $201,558 from the National Endowment for the Humanities to create a history of social movements program.

• The National Farmers Union was given two grants from the National Endowment for the Humanities totaling $426,000 to conduct programs on rural life.

I must admit I was dumbfounded when I learned of the scale of this scurrilous process. It is so completely foreign to all we were taught as youngsters. I hope by what is presented here that I've transferred my amazement and disgust of this whole area of government operation to the reader. It seems only a small step to conclude that almost all of the money scattered around to most of these organizations was never meant to create anything useful, but rather to create, via money, *friends of big government* among people with no ethical inhibitions.

Where is the protection offered us by our constitution for such malfeasance?

Corporate Welfare and the Archer Daniels Midland Saga

The ADM story, another of the many which show government dereliction of duty towards Americans, can now be classified as MOTSOS, -- more-of-the-same-ole-stuff; a fitting place to leave the sorry realm of government that doesn't even understand how their actions are destroying our once beautiful republic. That story can be found in Appendix E.

It is now time to review the next appalling, regrettable record of government.

107

CHAPTER 12
Social Security

Once again the task is to understand the essence of this mammoth, long-standing government program without succumbing to emotionalism that can divert our thinking. Today's Social Security program at its core is really quite straightforward. It has become a program which extracts money from unwilling people (today's wage earners and pro ducers) and hands *some* of that money to retired or disabled people with the remainder being skimmed by government managers for their use in any way they see fit.

None of the money is invested in any way to service future obligations through long-term appreciation. It doesn't matter in the least that those same "managers" describe it as insurance against lost abilities from old age or poor health,[17] because it is not insurance. Nor does it mattter whether they describe it as funds held "in trust" for supporting earlier producers now in retirement, because there are no funds in trust. Nor is it a resilient system capable of solving its money problems again through change as it has in the past, because its only possible solution, as in the past, is greater taxation or reduction of payments, or both.

The process of taxing workers to pay current government bills and older, former workers is a scheme (no different than a ponzi con game) which *depends* on greater collections today — than payouts — today. To accomplish this, either Social Security taxes must increase as in the whopping 1983 increase and virtually every year from 1950 to the present, or the number of "contributor s"(workers) must increase, or both. Such a process *always* fails at some point since future obligations always grow faster than the growth of collections. In the case of the Social Security scam, the skimming of money by government simply shortens the time before payouts exceed revenues. It really doesn't matter WHEN this threshold will be breached. Only the fact that the process is inherently flawed is of significance. Without further drastic changes, the system will collapse like the house of cards it is. The senators and congressmen have finally realized what they have wrought, and will undoubtedly make changes to soften that implosion.

We can only guess what the form of those new plans will be, but one aspect will be certain. They will try very hard to disguise their past failures concerning social security. An example of that we've already seen in the agency's television documentary purporting to show the safely stored government securities being kept

---

[17] Ref.: the 'Social Security Handbook, 1993".

for future social security commitments. There is no such fund; they know it, and we know it.

One might reasonably question why I've chosen to view the Social Security issue as another assault on our pursuit of happiness. Certainly, as we will soon see, the failing hurts our accumulation and preservation of wealth (Chapter 4) and it impinges callously on our unalienable rights, especially those coupled so intimately with self determination and self reliance (Chapters 8, 10 and 15). The Social Security tale is also a sad chapter in our struggle to define national goals (Chapter 6). All of these fundamental responsibilities of government have suffered as a result of Social Security, and it is clearly a failure affecting them all. Perhaps it is best, therefore, while discussing it here as part of our lost opportunity for happiness, simply to bear in mind how broad an effect the Social Security failure has been.

We should take some care to understand just what it is government has tried to convince us they are providing for the Social Security money they confiscate, and how they were able to accomplish this. This is important because the sales pitch has since become a fraud, even the *intention* has long since become lost as desperate officials subverted their own integrity to find new sources of money for their general, improper use.

Originally the attraction for such a national, government-operated program was born of an awareness during the 1930s that, along with increased longevity came diminished capacity and a vulnerability to dependency. The thinking centered around two ideas. One was that with greater life span in the offing, some overt preparation was needed to assure subsistence during these later years when individuals might not be able to provide for themselves. The other was that, being a country with ever-growing wealth, the United States government could take upon itself the responsibility for *maintenance* of the elderly.

There was the growing belief and euphoria within the government and the population in general that a maturing government was slowly developing an ability to care for all the people throughout life. By some evolutionary process, not yet clearly seen, a solicitous, moral government would become more capable of providing the essentials throughout life than could individuals themselves. The sheer altruism and sheer scope of the concept might easily have prevented logical critique, if indeed altruism were the dominant force at work. It was to be a monumental social experiment, never before seriously proposed or attempted. Without weakening my own thesis here, I can even accept that true altruism and a desire to allow everyone to share in America's bounty allowed its beginning. Certainly many involved in its creation were so motivated (for example Dr. Robert J. Myers, one of those who helped define the program in the 1930s). Others, even today, are so inspired, and wish to perpetuate the thing in spite of its flawed

109

fundamentals and misguided premise.[18] All of these notions, however, were mere contributors in the national sales pitch to further a philosophy of one man who would take on the appearance of national savior.

Franklin Roosevelt's conviction that government was the proper vehicle to recognize and solve social problems became the driving philosophy that has guided government programs ever since. That conviction was wrong then, as it is now, but the proof of that wasn't to come until the failures of Social Security and virtually every other social experiment, were fully demonstrated as they have been over the past several decades.

The easy conclusion one can reach, therefore, is that the driving motivation for Social Security was *political*, good intentions and altruism notwithstanding. It became the first major round fired by government to make itself larger and more indispensable to Joe and Jane Citizen. Government was becoming a conscious entity in its own right, doing what any organism does, try to survive, become stronger and bigger. Historians of the 21st century may be able to record the complete tale of FDR's long-term social disruption of America, but today we are still in the midst of a monumental government failure that has yet to be resolved. The solution, of course, is obvious, as later discussions show.

Today's Social Security program can be characterized with just a few descriptors and facts. None of them are altruistic or encouraging in any sense. None of them show the program to be a sensible one.

- Today 15.3% of wages are paid in Social Security taxes, half each by worker and employer, on all income up to $80,000 (2004), for a total tax of $12,240. Three other benchmarks are:

1997	15.3 %	on $60,600	for $9,271.80 max
1987	14.3 %	on $43,800	for $6,263.40 max
1977	11.7 %	on $16,500	for $1,930.50 max.

---

[18] Conscientious people within The Seniors Coalition, for example, still see the Social Security program as one deserving of all efforts to preserve, a program needing to be "restored to an honest, pay-as-you-go system", even instead of a balanced budget amendment. Their concern is only with benefits for seniors, no matter the consequences to debt, no matter the consequences to self-reliance. The how of meting out benefits is not important to them; only distributions matter.

Note first that lower income workers have paid a greater fraction of their wages into the Social Security black hole than do those making more than the top income. Note secondly that the *increases* in tax are huge in comparison to wage and merit increases, with the result that these percentage tax increases dwarf normal pay raises.

Note finally that the latest taxable wage encompasses virtually all income of all workers save the topmost small percent of the work force.

The conclusion that Social Security administrators have succeeded in solving their cash flow problems only by raising taxes is irrefutable. In 1982 the desperation of administrators even caused them to begin for the first time to tax sick leave income, making the harsh change retroactive to the beginning of the year.[19]

- The other means to maintain solvency over the years has been to reduce benefits, including, for example:
   - eliminating benefits for orphans and children of disabled workers (1977);
   - postponing cost-of-living adjustments (5 mo. delay in 1983);
   - raising the retirement age; and
       taxing benefits as ordinary income.

   Obviously the program is not a bonified retirement program with known cost (to us) and known benefits; it is a *welfare program* without a shred of buyer control but with ever increasing cost.

- With 1995 as a sample year:
   Total money confiscated was $367 Billion
   Total benefits paid out was $351 Billion
   The total difference of $16 Billion was 'borrowed" by the treasury of the United States and counted as INCOME instead of an obligation to the Social Security 'Trust Fund." The 'Trust Fund", received the $16 Billion IOU with the expectation of a refund from the borrower, the United States Treasury.

The process is clearly a fraud against taxpayers and that fraud now *exceeds* $380 Billion[20] from all the transfers to the general treasury since 1985 when Social Security 'surpluses" first began. [21]

*   *   *

---

[19] Notice to employees from Hughes Aircraft Co., dated April-May 1982.

[20] Ref.: 'The Senior Coalition" publication for May 1996.

[21] In 1991 the ploy of embezzling Social Security money into the general fund was particularly useful to government since it clouded a $431 Billion deficit into looking like the mere $368 Billion deficit actually reported to the American people. (Ref.: A special 1992 report by J. Peter Grace and others.) For 1992 the corresponding numbers were: $52 Billion embezzled, a true deficit of $342 Billion and a reported deficit (i.e., a lie) of $290 Billion.

This particular fraud, however, is dwarfed by the true, total obligation of government to the present and future retirees based on current Social Security benefit schedules.

- The major obligations of government concerning retirement and disability programs are three:
  - Pensions for retired workers
  - Medicare A and B liabilities
  - Civil Service, Railroad and Military pensions
- Although required **BY LAW** to publish a full accounting of United States liabilities yearly, there is no publication from government which gives a grand total.
- One report, a 'Statement of Liabilities and Other Financial Commitments of the United States Government," comes closest to baring the governmental breast for all to see. The report, however, never sums up the pieces (claiming disparate actuarial bases; a transparent cop-out) and prints its data in virtually illegible form (reduced Photostats of hand-typed pages). Only the most diligent of reviews would succeed in understanding our true financial condition.[22]
- Another independent estimate has been attempted (besides the one given earlier) which tries to sum the total United States obligation. The analysis was done by Dr. Gary North, a respected independent analyst. His effort yielded an estimate of a gross United States indebtedness for 1990 of approximately 18,000,000,000,000 dollars, or eighteen thousand billion dollars, and not the 2.8 thousand billion dollars admitted to by government *in all its public statements*. This is certainly fraud. It is fraud on the most gigantic scale ever.

Take away the so-called 'public debt" of $2.8 Trillion, and the remainder, $15.2 Trillion, is the *hidden obligation* of government - meaning We the People. Since the civil service and military pension future costs amount to about $3 Trillion, the rest, $12.2 Trillion, is an honest estimate of money that must be paid to future retirees and disabled persons based on current Social Security rules.[23]

These pension obligations are real. Since there are no funds in trust growing and earning income to meet these future obligations, they become pure debt and can be satisfied **ONLY** out of tax revenues or more borrowing. Government continues its decades-long subterfuge of misrepresenting our obligations in order to be allowed to play the self-serving political power game for as long as they possibly can.

---

[22] Recall that an estimate was given for 1992 in Chapter 4 for this total, but without the military, RR and civil service pension obligations.

[23] The estimate of $12.8 Trillion for 1992, given in Chapter 4, is quite consistent with this value, and implies a $600 Billion increase between 1990 and 1992, which seems likely.

• A simple calculation we can make here shows that Dr. North's analysis is well within reason. If only 50 million people retire in the coming years, and each draws benefits for only 20 years averaging $9,000 each year, then a total of $9 Trillion must be paid out. While the *present value* of that sum is considerably less than $9 Trillion, that fact only helps the debtor (the government) if there is an actual trust fund growing over the years and meeting the yearly payouts. Since no trust exists, the semantics battle between *present value* and *total obligation* is small consolation to ourselves as indebted citizens. Of course we can always renege, but such a solution is not very satisfying to anyone imbued with notions of fairness.

• Getting into the present Social Security quagmire took a long time doing. The stupidity of it all, however, was established from the very beginning when the insurers (the government) chose *not* to set up trust funds. Benefits were defined politically, not as sensible, affordable payouts that result from the money paid into the program. *Social Security was, from the very beginning, just another welfare program.* The money taken in was meant only to be enough to cover *payouts* and the cost of a new bureaucracy with no concern whatsoever for future obligations. That future has become our present, and the conceptual failure of Social Security is as obvious as any failed enterprise can possibly be.

*   *   *

Another Conclusion To Add To A Growing List

There were at least three potential elements of concern that were shunted aside in those formative years which allowed the political Social Security concept to take root. These elements had to do with (a) proper government functions, (b) the specifics of the process used and (c) human behavior . All three are still with us and together have become decisive in rendering Social Security as one of the greatest shams, frauds, thefts, or failures in United States history, depending on your point of view. Considering only these three factors will explain the reasoning behind such a conclusion.

Altruism is Not a Proper Government Function

Described earlier was a government action I labeled as THE single most critical error of government, namely the giving of public money, in charity, in an attempt to help someone (Chapter 4). Confiscating money through taxes to distribute to others is not the prerogative of government, unless *everyone* agrees to establish such sharing as a *national goal*, the equal of national security. It is NOT an empowerment from the Constitution.

113

In shouldering aside the individual to assume retirement and disability responsibilities, government is telling the people that they are no longer in charge of their own later lives and that children have no responsibilities for aging parents. That notion, that concept, is 100% wrong. The individual is solely responsible for self and through planning and sharing in earlier, productive years, can build the cushion of resources and equity among loved ones to meet those later needs. Enforcement is not the answer; equal practical opportunity is.

A True Retirement Program Would Be Completely Different

Instead of having an expensive middleman (the government) between you and your retirement money, a true pension plan would invest all allocated funds in long-term securities, preferably in dividend paying, stable corporations, businesses with a long history of safety and reasonable returns.

Human Behavior Still Presides

Perhaps the most important oversight among the early Social Security planners was that those who would administer their creation would be capable of retaining purpose and altruism equal to their own. Instead these officials would and did become easily diverted by the lure of great sums of money. It became simply another source of assets to reach *political objectives.* Their behavior would be determined by *their* human drive and not by any altruistic philosophy to sustain older people. Alf Landon understood this as early as 1936, moving him to label the program "a cruel hoax" even then. It has, indeed, been a cruel hoax.

*   *   *

Another Disturbing Conclusion

Once again government's approach to providing support for people in retirement or in disability has only succeeded in intruding further into our private lives and prevented many from remaining self-reliant in their later years. Government officials have done this to further their own political ends, and have instilled a growing anger in each succeeding class of working people whose tax burden inexorably increases, and whose confidence in their own retirement lives is drained away with each passing year.

114

CHAPTER 13
Public Education -
A Rare Success of Government or Just
Another Failure?

At this point in our review of government performance, we might be forgiven if we are already suspicious as we begin a similar, jaundiced-eye critique of public education. We might expect to find the stamp of government indelibly imprinted on the American system of education. That imprint, if it matches the other government enterprises discussed so far, would, of course, be one of bureaucracy, poor social engineering, inefficiency, high cost, rife with regulations, poorly led, and very much in a quandary about goals. One might even be more than a little concerned that an unstated goal of national, if not local, government might be aimed at *indoctrination* at the expense of education. As we look into the matter, we will learn that our suspicions in fact do have merit.

For at least the last 100 years, not one person in government has ever thought to question whether education in America should be *public*, by which I mean a government enterprise. Rather, public education is taken as a given, an established truth or foundation from which all actions must flow in dealing with perceived problems. Whatever the concerns may be with learning or with the educational system, solutions should be pursued mainly through adaptations within the public school industry, whether for learning methods, curriculum changes, student scores, differences in student performance, or any other issue. The concept of education as a public responsibility has been accepted as an axiom of American life, almost an article of faith. How it became so is itself quite revealing, and history gives us some insight to the process.

More than 350 years ago, one of the earliest trend setters occurred within the Massachusetts Colony. An ordinance was issued which required any new settlement to set up a grammar school whenever its population reached 100 families (1642). The goal was to prepare students for *university* in the sense known to England, the mother country. Nothing was dictated about attendance or funding, but a precedent was implicit that government would have a say in matters of education. The event became known in the other colonies, and by the time of the Continental Congress (1787), it was quite natural to include the *Northwest Ordinance* for the establishment of *Public* schools. Thus, what might be an obvious question today was not even a question at all during those early formative days.

As the evolutionary process continued, the notion of schools as *public* had common acceptance. By 1852, Massachusetts again led the way with the first law for compulsory school attendance. The pace of regulatory change was not breathtaking, but it was unidirectional; government is boss. By 1918 all states had enacted compulsory school attendance laws, and by that time at least one statement seems to have been elevated to that of a national goal, becoming at least the sales slogan, if not a clear foundation for directing public education. The slogan was to "ass ure universal scholarship and good citizenship."

At the very best, the connection between the two goals must be tenuous, but of course there is no compulsion for them to be complementary, merely each worthy in its own right. As *national goals,* however, the one seems to be naive in the extreme (universal scholarship), and the other seems to imply that learning makes one a good citizen.

Consider the first. Within any population of students, there will *always* be some who have neither the aptitude nor the desire for scholarship. Certainly early in the last century, being proficient at a trade was far more important to many students than scholarship per se or preparation for advanced schooling. Such things were not very important to them. Even today, there are as many (in percent of the total) who are just as convinced that scholarship is not a goal of their own, for many good or even bad reasons. It seems clear the rosy, idealistic goal of universal scholarship was misstated. What was meant, or was the only logical intent, was that the *opportunity* for scholarship be open to anyone so inclined. I contend no compelling argument can be made, either for now or in the past, to *mandate* universal scholarship. Mandate is exactly what such a national goal amounts to when it comes from government.

As for the second goal, good citizenship, we should have mixed reactions to the idea. Being or becoming a good citizen requires a great many things from individuals. The whole set of citizen responsibilities that emanate from unalienable rights are part of good citizenship, and these must be learned from caring adults. Knowledge of American history also lends its support to becoming a good citizen, but is insignificant (in my opinion) in comparison with understanding responsibilities. Learning of our unalienable rights as sovereign individuals, however, has never been stressed in public schools. Responsibilities, likewise, are mostly secondary as a result. I don't think such lack of emphasis hurt the process of building citizenship, however, since so much of what is necessary must come from the home.

The disservice of public schools in this regard is in its reluctance to show clearly the relationship between the *individual* and *government.* There was far too little emphasis on the creation of government as a means of providing individuals

116

with a secure living environment, and that government is hired by citizens. The master-worker relationship was then and is now completely garbled. Government is the worker, hired to do things to help citizens who are, collectively, the master. The reverse is not the proper arrangement. Government is **not** the master, but has acted for many decades as if it were.

The ominous thing about the 1918 slogan that helped to perpetuate public education, comes perhaps only by hindsight. Learning American history was anything but a factual process. What influence or dictates of government may have operated to cause the distortions we learned, may never be fully revealed in our search to understand the past, but there can be very little doubt that there were a great many distortions of American history FACTS. One of my strong interests through elementary and high school was history, American history in particular, and I can truthfully say that virtually all of the *interpretations* of events were distorted in ways I now consider to be too important to ignore. America and Americans were always honorable, and good, and right; not in so many words, but in effect. The outcome for America was what was right and proper. Leaders were wise far beyond the norm. Heroes were important beyond any others in history, and their exploits gave us an inheritance that outshines any other.

The truth of America's history is certainly not all bad, but it is far more painful to accept than we were taught in public schools. The American revolution turned loyalists into enemies, and victims of revolutionary murderers. Every single encounter with Indians was a humanitarian disaster. The Indians were not the bad guys. They had something European invaders wanted, so they were shoved aside, murdered, lied to and brutalized. Yes, they too were savage in response, but war has always been savage. Our ancestors, those who built a new, better nation — for some — stopped short of total annihilation, but not by much. American expansion, our 'manifest destiny", is as full of greed and mayhem as any other expansion by invaders. And our wars with Mexico and with Spain had no more attributes of benevolence or innate goodness than any other past instigators of war. Benedict Arnold was not the only bad guy from our past — and we all know it.

Our picture of ourselves is partly a government painting, and government is not interested in revealing untidy parts of our nature or our background. They are interested in seeing us become good citizens, a status that accepts, among other things, the goodness and dominance of government.

In spite of all the comments above, I don't think the negatives of government controls on education had very much negative effect on people prior to 1918. In 1900, for example,[24] only about 6% of student-aged people even completed high

---

[24] Most of the quantitative information was taken from a March 1996 Liberty magazine article by Stanley Wolf, "A Short and Absurd History of School Reform".

school, so the rigors of enforcement were few. Even costs to central government were practically nonexistent since education was mostly a local matter funded by real estate taxes. The number of students going on to college was a tiny 0.25%, with cost being a major factor in determining who was able to go. But we should take particular note of the *condition* of Americans as productive and industrious citizens and as "good" citizens throughout that long period. There was little or no correlation between the level of education of a person and good citizenship or productivity. Willingness to work, honesty, and civic-mindedness were evident in abundance even though education was not. In my opinion, those characteristics among Americans were widespread, making it all the more of a mystery as to why "good citizenship" through universal education ever became the government's slogan for advancing the cause of public education. I'll not speculate here.

The next evolutionary phase of education in America (meaning public education) was one of examining and debating about teaching methods and their effectiveness. The more that teaching professionals and school administrators evolved in the industry of education, the more ideas surfaced, and the more crusades were launched to cure problems or even to "advance."

Public education, you might say, has been the site of all manner of experiments. Many books have been written about these ideas, trials and shortcomings, yet the level of contentment among parents, educators and students as well has not been one of continuous advancement, in spite of all these well meaning efforts. Before homing in on those aspects of public education that remain as consensus failures, let's first acknowledge some of the things that seem right.

With its background as a *public* enterprise, public education has not subjected students to learning religious "truths." This less -than-obvious effect might even be credited with preventing an overemphasis of religious differences among citizens with different backgrounds, which might easily have created more factions among people. Factions have always had a way of propagating themselves among large collections of people, but public education does not seem to have been one of the contributors. Rather, the general intent of working toward uniformity in subject matter has surely helped Americans reach some level of cohesiveness within the nation.

In addition, with regard to religion, students within the public school system have not been force-fed truths that are really only the doctrines of particular subsets of people. Whatever indoctrination there has been of youngsters in such things has come only from church-run schools in response to their own founding beliefs, and in accord with the American belief in freedom of religion. *The separation of religious and secular teaching has been a monumental benefit* of the American system of education and one which we dare not let slip away. This separation has endured to our great good fortune in spite of the many attempts by zealots to cram religious agendas into the culture and curriculum of the American school system. Hardly a year of the 20th century has passed, however, that attempts have not been made, mostly by over-zealous Christian minority groups, to make such changes, and there is no obvious maturing of thought among these people to suggest that such attempts will ever cease.

Uniformity of teaching, mentioned earlier, is another plus of public education, but not without some reservations. As knowledge has advanced, so too has some of the public school subject matter. The pace of basic human knowledge has quickened every decade since the 1950s, and has reached a level of acceleration today that goes far beyond anything ever known before. The great challenge today is for educators simply to keep abreast of what is being learned so the effects of new information has a chance of being reflected in elementary and high school course material.

The burgeoning storehouse of knowledge is the single most important characteristic of knowledge today. From never before understood cosmic events, to the broad range of object types in the universe, to evolution of the universe itself, to the unfolding saga of the unknowns of life from studies of DNA, the common factor that unites all life, to the vast and growing array of exotic and useful materials, to the growing realization of the interdependence of all living things, to the implications of much of this on the health of humans, we are party to a time when our fundamental understanding of everything around us is brand spanking new.

The single most important challenge to educators, therefore, is how best to assimilate this knowledge and then to integrate it into everything they are trying to teach. There is an almost unavoidable tendency to teach at levels that are easily grasped by the average mind, but a far better goal would be to develop explanations of even the most challenging concepts in ways than can be appreciated and learned by almost everyone. While some students may not be able to follow, many others will, and any winnowing of knowledge should be the result of mental filtering of students rather than by decisions of bureaucrats — or even educators — to make learning more palatable. The preference, therefore, should be to challenge all students and help any who may need help.

Those are the two chief benefits I see for public education: a course of study that is secular, and a uniformity of learning opportunity and content across the nation. Expanding knowledge demands that content change to keep pace. The trap waiting to ensnare educators is the one that would compromise the information to make it understandable at too low an academic level.

What's Wrong About Public Education?

So much of what is learned or not learned by a student is the outcome of decidedly individual factors. They are the elements that will come into play no matter who is making decisions: government, parents, school boards, or any other authority. Such things will always be with us, and the range of behavior that can result encompasses the entire spectrum from unbounded eagerness to abject indifference. Teaching problems mirror the students and can challenge educators immensely. Such problems in education, however, are not the concerns I mean to address here. Instead, the focus is on those things about public education that are wrong *because* education at the lower grades is a PUBLIC enterprise. The list of things I see wrong (because it is government run) is much longer than the few benefits discussed earlier, and in my opinion are decisive in concluding that government's record in education is one of failure.

As a preamble to such a recitation, let's first review a bit more of the history of American education, beginning about the 1960 time frame. By that time, bureaucratic entrenchment had been solidified and what was occurring had the government stamp clearly etched upon it. Had that stamp been a positive, forward thinking one, our critique might have been mostly one of gratitude. However, the record (again) is not an inspiring one.

The concept of feedback in any system was well understood in the 1960s. Norbert Wiener, Von Neumann, Shannon, Azgapetian and others taught us that understanding (measuring) the output of any system, whether it is a simple positioning machine or a complex social system like government or education, can be made useful in optimizing that output by adjusting system parameters in proportion to the measured output. If test scores are different than some sensible goals, then changes to teaching procedures can be made until results move in some desired way. With complex systems, sensitivities of results to many active parameters (subject content at different grade levels, textbook presentation, oral and written class work, etc.) can eventually be understood, ultimately to the improvement of the teaching process and the learning results. All this has been well understood since the 1950s.

However, error recognition and measurement, optimization and self-correcting systems based on feedback have been arrogantly ignored almost completely in public education.[25] None of this obviously sensible and systematic methodology was applied, due in large part to the reluctance of the hierarchy even to acknowledge that errors existed. Instead of taking advantage of an approach that holds the promise of benefiting everyone, little men preferred to hide their misjudgments in all manner of bureaucratic smoke.

---

[25] One notable exception was the use of feedback by the Navy in self-tutoring courses, with gratifying success, [ref.: Wolf's Liberty article].

Experiments in education were devised and proposed. Those that were tried depended more on how persuasive the proposal could be made than on how effective it was shown to be. In the late 1950s there was "Mastery Learning" which claimed that every child could learn anything if enough time were devoted to the task. Later, educators were motivated by the movement to promote *self-esteem* — to the benefit of no one except the bureaucracy. Friedrich A. Hayek, whom we know from his pioneering work in economics, observed that we would benefit a great deal by offering as wide a range of educational opportunities as possible because we still knew so little about the matter. He too, was ignored because of an implicit challenge to the leadership abilities of those in charge. "Programmed Learning" was next, a creation of Harvard's B. F. Skinner , without measurable benefit.

A study of American education by a team led by James S. Coleman showed clearly that differences in school *facilities* and *resources* were not significant in their effect on student achievement, but that other factors outside the control of schools were dominant. The same report showed the ineffectiveness of the "Head Start Program," another failed experiment since differences in learning ability fade away by about the third grade.

The Coleman report continues to be ignored to this day mainly *because it does not support the false concept that greater expenditures bring better results.* Government is single minded in the matter of public education just as they have always been in other programs, *that the solution to any social problem lies in greater spending.*   Education is, in the eyes of government, a political and, therefore, an emotional matter, instead of what it actually is, a matter of science and learning.[26] In spite of a growing body of data that show little correlation between academic success and success in a person's working life,[27] bureaucratic educators continue to hold lower level academics as a great ill waiting for a proper (bureaucratic) solution.

Government influences have long advocated national standards and national testing. President Clinton had taken up the banner of public education as an important focus for his second term in office, this in spite of the preponderance of meaningful work that shows two things clearly; government experimentation is *not needed* and government spending has had no real beneficial effect!

The government Standard Operating Procedure (SOP) is the thing that must be seen as directing its experiments in public education as in all other government projects. SOP calls for identifying concerns, greatly motivated by emotion, defining

---

[26] Ref. Learning to Read, by Jeanne S. Chall of Harvard.
[27] Refs.: Studies by Paul Goodman, the Batelle Laboratories, and Christopher Jencks

programs and statutes to fix those perceived problems,[28] spending billions of dollars in accordance with those laws, establishing education task forces[29] which then lead to more legislation and a continuation of the cycle, ad infinitum, ad nausium. By the government's own evaluation, all of these programs, task forces, and expenditures must have been dismal failures because this same font of wisdom, (government), is *still* telling us that American public education has reached crisis proportions. President Clinton said as much as he began his second term.

Reciting more of the specifics of government failures in public education will just raise our level of frustration at the national condition. More of that background can certainly be learned from the references cited and from the summary by Stanley Wolf in the March 1996 edition of *Liberty* magazine. Instead of adding to that misery, however, I will simply give my list of some of the things still utterly wrong in American education after correcting a small wrong of my own. At the beginning of this discussion on public education I made the statement that for the last 100 years, no one in government has even questioned whether American education should be a public (a government) enterprise. I know of at least one voice that was raised that did question the cohesiveness, the effectiveness, and the attempts by government to legislate equality of *something* in American education. The voice was that of Daniel Patrick Moynihan (Senator, D of NY) in the early 1970s. Strictly speaking, my earlier statement still holds, but Senator Moynihan did his very best to infuse some wisdom into government operations in public education. His total lack of success led him to turn his attention to other matters of government.

What's Wrong with Public Education *Because* it is a Government Enterprise?

- What is taught is decided upon democratically, which implies a majority but which actually ends up as a very small minority, those few bureaucrats involved whose decisions are essentially dictates. Voting in different bureaucrats has almost no effect on such problems. Take particular note of something alluded to earlier. The distortions in the version of American history taught to elementary and high school students are there for good reason – government wants it that way. American government has a clear preference to present American history in flattering and heroic terms, even though the term heroism most often did not apply. I'm quite sure government would like very much to create "good Americans" w ho meet government's criteria for goodness. It all starts with education of our youngsters.

- While the amount of money spent by local school boards is a known value, the cost to taxpayers from all government expenditures is an enduring mystery.

---

[28] For example: more than 700 pieces of legislation in just 1983 to 1985 alone.
[29] For example: 275 education task forces were created by government during the mid 1980s (Ref.: Donald Orlich's book, Education Reforms, Mistakes, Misconceptions, Miscues.)

• The cost of educating your child (through high school) is not borne by you alone, but by neighbors too, whether or not they also have children. *That education is without doubt a welfare benefit.* The more children in a family, the greater the welfare benefit and the greater the distortion of who pays for those benefits.

Since no definitive case has ever been made that every citizen benefits equally from such an educational subsidy (because everyone is "educated"), there can be no compelling reason for forcing the cost of education on anyone other than the parents. We have, in fact, a welfare education system in America, and *it exists because government gets to control it.*

• Whether you accept the notion of education as a welfare enterprise, there undoubtedly have been many experiments in education with which you disagree. Being *forced* to support such abortive government programs is fundamentally wrong and is a direct attack against individual rights.

• A dictated course of study, national standards and national testing, are a direct violation of freedom of choice, in this case parental choice, which is clearly a very basic Unalienable Right. The inescapable conclusion one must concede in this matter is *that government has assumed control and dictatorial power over the educational portion of a child's life*, declaring, in effect, that the prerogatives of parents in matters of education do not exist.

Stating this in such a forceful manner is an attempt to show how easy it is to lose sight and control of the fundamentals of individual sovereignty when seemingly beneficial or even innocuous programs are instituted by government.

• The uniformity mentioned earlier as a benefit of public education also has a negative side to it. That negative comes directly from a failure to recognize that real differences do exist among students. Uniformity can only hurt those whose interests and energy can carry them well beyond any "norm." Uniformity as a minimum may be sensible, but by itself is an unenlightened goal. Due provisions must be made for the wide range of preferences among young people, something that is in conflict with uniformity, but something that is second nature to an educational system based on free enterprise and the needs and preferences of those who buy its services. Such a system is familiar to us already in our colleges and universities.

• When bureaucratic decisions are poor ones, as they most often are, it is extremely difficult to fix them because of the indirect process that voters have at their disposal. Whether voting is for local school board members or for State or National education officials, the connection between the problem and the new official is almost nonexistent, making a solution highly improbable. This same effect is, by now, quite familiar since it shows up whenever poor bureaucratic performance is uncovered, as for example it has been with welfare, Social Security and other programs.

• Neither students nor parents are well-represented in the experimentation that has taken place in American education since most of it has been motivated by politics instead of the desire for true advancement. One might contrast the seemingly endless preoccupation of public education with successive crises over the past 30 or 40 years, with the unmistakable advances elsewhere in American industry. The one is dominated by government and interventions, the other is the result of free enterprise. By now we should have become smart enough to recognize that just as the agriculture industry is no different than other industries in its response to ordinary supply/demand market forces, so too is the industry of educating our youngsters tied to the forces that motivate individuals, not political imperatives. The purposes that lie behind the decisions of government are NOT the purposes of students or their parents, and they never will be.

*   *   *

What should the education goals be that America can clasp to its bosom as worthy parts of its national foundation?

• Knowing the good of our inheritance? — yes, but also knowing of things that give us no pride.
• A goal to educate all persons? — no, but rather a goal that allows everyone so inclined to learn to the very limits of their capabilities and choices.
• A goal to dictate an educational structure that will permit us to compete in the world market? — Certainly not. We have *never* depended on rigidity in any part of our makeup to be competitive. And a twelfth grade background [if that were the key ingredient of competitiveness] couldn't possibly be enough anyway. Our industry, our inventiveness, our curiosity, our innovations and most of all our FREEDOM to do as we wanted have made the difference in advancing ourselves as individuals and as a country.
• A goal to give parents and guardians the opportunity to help their children succeed through knowledge? — Most assuredly yes.
• A goal to hand child rearing responsibilities to government? The notion is preposterous.
• A goal to assure secular, scientific, artistic, business or even religious learning opportunity — or any combination? — very definitely yes. The concept is called *Free Choice,* and it is one of our inheritances that came with life itself.

124

All of the desirable aspects of education, and all of the things about education we would like to rid ourselves of can be realized by one and the same change in organizational structure. By allowing education to become *the free market enterprise it should be*, every single problem discussed here and every other problem we have faced can be fixed.

The process to accomplish that depends simply on giving people who are *motivated to find solutions* the opportunity to do so. Education is a business, an extremely important one, but fundamentally a business, not a civil servant arm of government. Educators and educational administrators can make the difference, if given the freedom to offer curricula at all levels that match the fond hopes and needs of parents at competitive costs, costs parents can meet. We would then witness a surge in knowledge never before experienced. We would surely see an evolving success story akin to what we see economically in emerging nations around the world, and ultimately learn exactly what our own national goals are in education without waiting for government to tell us what they are. We will then know what our objectives are as parents, and as one generation passing the mantle of responsibility to the next.

At the moment it may seem that cost, especially to low income families, might be the biggest residual problem. That problem, however, is no different than the desire by business to supply TVs, dishwashers or even automobiles to every family, and all the means to get that done are also available to the industry of education. Extending credit for schooling is the same as lending money for housing. Endowments, scholarship funds and contributions are powerful levelers of family debt.

In ten years, I would say, all the problems and so-called crises we agonize about concerning public education would be nothing but bad memories, provided only that *government at all levels* STANDS ASIDE. Without government disruptions, without tax confiscations, without reckless, government-instigated 'national goals," Americans have the capacity, the brain power and, most importantly, the motivation to create a superlative educational structure — for all who want to use it.

With continued government involvement, there is no reason to expect that education in America can improve.

Conclusion – Can This Really Be???
I make the rather shameful contention that grade-school America is educationally a third-world country. All we need do to see this as our present-day condition is to compare what we have and what we do, with what might have been possible if the governmental straightjacket had been removed years ago.

CHAPTER 14
Crimes Of Government At The Local Levels

Our attention throughout most of this book has rightly been on the Federal Government because it is the dominant force in America. The problem of government, therefore, is described in terms of government at the national level, and any steps to be taken to solve that problem must be directed there first. To think of the problem with American government as being only a national one, however, would leave a huge gap in our understanding of the condition of Americans as individuals who are controlled by a complete hierarchy of governors. The Federal structure is just the top of the mountain pressing down on We the People. Below that are parallel legislative bodies two and sometimes four deep, that do most of the same things done at the national level. They consist of administrations, appointed bureaucrats, legislative bodies, support staffs, cabinet-equivalent bodies and spending agencies which create state, county and city regulations. Collectively these 'local" arms of government differ only in the scope of their jurisdictions.

Two things more make them indistinguishable from their federal mentors. They learn, right along with national governors, every bit of sophistication that's useful in wielding power and spending *other people's money*. And these local elements of government are made up of exactly the same cross-section of people, with the same bias toward exercising power. There should be no doubt whatsoever that government at the local levels is capable of the same irresponsibilities, excesses and failings as their big brother in Washington DC. They are built the same, run by people with similar philosophies, and limited by constraints similar to those we have nationally, which means no real limit at all.

There are only two differences I see of significance, besides the one of scale. Local breeds of government are forced to confine their bad decisions, injustices and failings to a much smaller part of the population, which confines these failings to fewer people. The town council that adds another penny to the sales tax can only hurt local people. Secondly, most but not all, local governments have not descended to the same depths of deficit spending as the Federal government, nor have they taken on long-term debt to the same excess. Debt is not unknown, however, as New York and other hot spots have clearly shown. The recent example of excessive debt accumulation in California at the state level, is a clear warning of the possible spread of this Fed-like syndrome elsewhere. People can see it coming. Only decisive, constructive action can end it.

126

Debt locally usually comes in the form of bonds sold to raise money for specific projects, and that debt must be repaid. At least this is a meaningful difference from the federal debt. Fraud at the local level comes from the fact that these local governments pass their pet projects with that same tiny fraction of approving voters because the *process* allows it. Huge sums of money are then under the control of local politicians based on the acceptance of mere handfuls of voters, exactly as occurs nationally. Local agencies do have an advantage over national agencies in their task to convince their neighbors of the value of some project, since a percentage of the cost of most programs comes from the federal till.

So many bad decisions and so much loss of local control is hidden behind this 'free" money that people easily lose sight of what is happening to their most fundamental rights. It happens within education, business and agriculture. Federal mandates of all descriptions, and regulations are attached to virtually everything we do. All this has been discussed somewhat in earlier chapters, but the point here is that State and City governments have effectively become mere extensions of the controlling body in Washington. Those at the local levels may take offense at such a suggestion, but their operations, goals, methods and philosophies are far too well matched to Washington to think of them as independent. Any critique of local government, however, need make no use of that fact, because their own record vis-à-vis the people is more than enough to show that local government too has done *great harm* to our precious fading Rights.

If we were to dig into the long, dark histories of every state, or every city with large populations, or indeed any small city,[30] there would be enough material to guarantee numbness to any reader. Such a comprehensive undertaking would show just how common bad practices of government are locally and how similar the injuries are to the supposed inviolable Rights of individuals. It isn't necessary, however, to be quite so thorough. A few examples will make the point that individuals aren't very important to local government, any more than they are to Federal government. What **is** important to government, once again, is the ability to control both money and people. That sad fact applies to government at all levels.

Please take particular note, the comparison that must be kept in mind when evaluating local government performance, is not how it stacks up against ancient Rome, or Medieval England, or 20th century Mexico or Peru, but how it matches the idealism that became America's foundation. How well does local government fulfill the philosophy that sparked the Declaration of Independence and the Constitution? That is, after all, why this government *of the people* was instituted.

---

[30] At the level of small and medium sized cities there are a few that have remained clear of the tyranny practiced everywhere else, but they are too rare to give us comfort.

127

The following disgusting, sad, needless, frustrating and infuriating stories will illustrate our condition as the governed in American cities. None of them is unique although each is specific. Any number of other examples could just as readily have been used instead of these cases. The story of machine politics, for example, in large cities such as Chicago, New York and Philadelphia, or even smaller suburban cities like Linden, New Jersey,[31] with their unbelievable corruption and coercion, clearly show the plight of individual liberty. Or we might examine the laying of taxes by *appointed* bureaucrats who answer to no one. Or we could give the disgusting details of the political Campaign for Economic Democracy, CED, led by "activist," now *Assemblyman*, Tom Hayden. Recall that we encountered CED in Chapter 11 which dealt with advocacy politics. This bunch took over the California cities of Davis, Santa Monica and Berkeley and proceeded to strip property owners of their rights in order to force their own warped philosophy of redistributing wealth — all as a means of gratifying their own need to exercise power regardless of the consequences to the Unalienable Rights of the rest of us.

In all of the stories of local government actions that follow in this chapter, not one of the perpetrators of these crimes has ever had to answer in court, nor have any of these people lost privileges attached to government office because of what they did to our neighbors while in office. What we live with is an entire class of crimes that is *unpunishable* in present day American society. The crimes are against individual rights, and the rules of governing in America allow them.

We would do well to multiply each of the following examples by a hundred or a thousand times, or more, to see the seriousness of our condition under local bureaucratic actions. Doing so will give some idea of how widespread the assault has been. A strong case can even be made that the abuses and loss of Rights and liberty caused by local government are far greater than those due to the Federal government. Either set is cause for alarm. Together they have created a true crisis in individual Rights.

Of course, those injured by local government are always local to the particular agency causing the abuse, and so different individuals are being attacked in each case. Thus, they are divided from the rest of us and easily conquered. Very seldom can they ever join together to combat ubiquitous government. The government prefers it that way. In fact, officials rely on it to avoid serious confrontation or challenge to *an authority that creates its power from our loss of liberty.*

---

[31] This is an example of corruption and oppression, led by Mayor John T. Gregorio, whose acts finally earned him a conviction on criminal charges and removal from office. He was inexplicably pardoned by New Jersey Governor Thomas Kean and immediately cranked up his old machine, becoming Linden's Mayor once again in 1990. He later suspended the police chief, a political adversary, on a bogus charge and then appointed himself as judge when the chief appealed the suspension. How blatant must the misuse of power be before it can be corrected? The plain fact is that the little people are virtually powerless.

The source for the examples described here is another CATO publication called *Grassroots Tyranny, The Limits of Federalism.* The 1993 work was written by Clint Bolick after an extensive 5 year research effort that typifies CATO thoroughness. Mr. Bolick is a lawyer deeply committed to the task of undoing some of government's worst offenses against us. Occasionally his efforts and those of others like him succeed via the court system. The sad part of even these successes, however, is the heavy toll paid by these ordinary, blameless people in time, heartbreak, anxiety, money and health before the mayhem ends. And offsetting such successes even more are the hundreds or thousands of NEW abuses to individual liberty that took place all around the country while ONE wrong was being made right.

The process is not self-correcting. An unending battle is being waged by government on 10,000 different fronts against 10,000 individuals who are completely isolated one from another. When there are rare, local victories, they carry over only incidentally to other embattled individuals fighting the same abuse elsewhere. The situation faced by individuals who are attacked by local governments is a potent example of one of the major flaws in the American system of justice. Americans are not connected in justice to a single code of law, but face a fragmented set of legal references that refuse to be unified. This is a huge deficiency and is a fit subject for exposition in its own right.

The interconnectedness of our chief problems is again evident as we look at these few examples of local governments' misdeeds.

Five Examples of Local Government Offenses

Example 1 - The Tyranny of Eminent Domain
In 1981 the city of Detroit had an unemployment problem (18%) and the added worry of General Motors having to close two more manufacturing plants. If 500 acres could be made available, however, General Motors would consider building a new facility and everyone would benefit, that is everyone except the property owners within the region to be grabbed by the city. The site, called Poletown, contained 3500 residents, 150 businesses, churches and a hospital, but none of that deterred the government of Detroit from forcing everyone out to satisfy a perceived need for 'the greater good'. It cost the citizens of Detroit in long-term debt, approximately $200 million to make the site available, less the mere $8 million to be paid by General Motors. No one asked the voters whether the strange transaction was something they wanted, but city officials went ahead anyway. In essence, they forced people off their property, paid far less than even the assessment values they

themselves had set, typically 50%, and disrupted several thousand people *whose Right to property turned out to be non-existent.*

Telling people that their right to property is one of the great principles upon which the nation's code of justice rests (Amendments V and XIV of the Constitution) and that this Right cannot be lost without due process and just compensation, and then disavowing any of those conditions and safeguards, is a contradiction of our whole agreement for living together for mutual benefit. It is a complete contradiction to guarantee *due_process* and *just compensation* on the one hand and then on the other hand have the taker set the compensation and establish a process that denies owner involvement concerning the purpose of confiscation. There is no logic to this warped method of governing or being governed, and even worse, there is no justice in it.

I am not talking about legalities. Governments have the *power* to make *any* act legal or illegal as suits their greed, but they cannot change the fact that justice disappears and people's Unalienable Rights are rendered meaningless by such actions. We Americans have deceived ourselves into believing that our Unalienable Rights are safeguarded in this country and have taken false pride in being *better off* than other peoples because of that. The truth is that this is a lie. The very first time that "guaranteed" property is wanted by government — for any purpose — it is no longer your property. Eminent Domain, as practiced in America, meaning in every little hamlet and every metropolis, is nothing but theft, legalized by government fiat.

The sham, the theft, is aided by the court system at every level, including the US Supreme Court. In this case the Michigan State Supreme Court ruled that the theft was legal, saying in part,

> "The power of eminent domain is to be used in this instance to accomplish the essential public purposes of alleviating unemployment and revitalizing the economic base of the community. Where there is such a public need, the abstract right (of an individual) to make use of his own property in his own way is compelled to yield to the general comfort and protection of the community."

Take particular note that this legal *rationalization* was not a unanimous one, that two justices disagreed. It gives us another excellent warning about our mania for doing things "democratically," submitting to the will of the majority. While 72% of the top legal brains in Michigan thought it was legal to steal this land, 28% did not. Majority rule can be very arbitrary and it need not be JUST to be legal.

130

My opinion that eminent domain is nothing but theft is shared by many others who have had the time to trace through the bogus logic. One such thinker is Sheldon Richman who stated it nicely in his article, "The Rape of Poletown." [32]

> 'The sacrifice of some people to 'public need' is a shameful euphemism for the subordination of the rights of these people to the power of others. The travesty here is not that GM is the beneficiary, but that land is being stolen. Eminent domain, for *ANY PURPOSE*, is contrary to the principles of a free society." (My emphasis added.)

Conclusion: Eminent Domain is Legalized Government Theft

There is another process by which government takes the *use* of land away from an owner, one step shy of stealing it, but is not obliged to pay anything to compensate the owner's loss. They do this merely by *changing the regulations affecting the use of property*. This quasi-eminent domain derivative of misused power can cause even more hardships because the just compensation concept is not even active, in spite of the harm done. Bolick's book is full of chilling examples of the misuse of power by local governments, all of it done with complete impunity by bureaucrats who are not even elected officials.

Example 2 - Even Guaranteed Freedoms are Vulnerable to Local Government Tyranny

Assaults on First Amendment Rights take many forms. Bolick offers many examples of attacks on our freedoms of speech, a few of which are mentioned here.

Such as the case of Miller versus California, which built a box around the definition of *speech* and placed obscenity and pornography under the *subjective* control of community standards, a foolishness that creates as many "standards" as there are communities.

Such as the sanctions against the freedoms of Robert George of Glendale for impersonating Santa Claus and inviting disabled and terminally ill children into his version of Santa-Land.

Such as the Supreme Court opinion that strips First Amendment protection from any speech with commercial content. As Bolick notes, the Supreme Court has rewritten that guarantee to read that 'the government shall make no law abridging the freedom of speech — except commercial speech, which government may abridge with impunity."

---

[32] This quote is given in Clint Bolick's book referred to earlier. Bolick also tells us that Sheldon Richman himself was the VICTIM of eminent domain theft later in the 1980s when Fairfax County Virginia officials stole Richman's home to make way for a highway.

Such as the unconscionable majority ruling in *Posadas* by the Supreme Court of Chief Justice Rehnquist which created a pivotal exception to First Amendment protection in *commercial speech*. The Court upheld a ban on advertising for a legal casino in Puerto Rico based on the warped ordering of the priorities of government power and citizen Rights. The key passage stated that the Puerto Rican legislature could have *prohibited* gambling altogether and that, therefore, this 'great er power to ban casino gambling completely, *necessarily* includes the lesser power to ban advertising." While the Supreme Court minority opinion disagreed vehemently on fundamentals, bureaucratic majority tyranny had won out once again. The other shaky leg this USSC ruling rests on, the supposed power of government to ban gambling, is itself wrong since it too, is a matter of choice. It is not a crime to gamble, and should not be subject to government whim.

Such as the equally warped logic that allows government control of cable TV content, but steadfastly upholds the independence of printed newspapers.

Conclusion: Our Steadily Disappearing Rights Have No Real Guardian
The examples of these assaults on our basic freedoms are virtually endless and not even the highest non-political body in the American judicial system offers any assurance that reason will sustain those freedoms. Unalienable Rights exist with life, but there is no American guardian capable of assuring us that those Rights can be *exercised*.

Example 3 - Economic Liberty is Another Casualty of Local Government Tyranny

Wrapped up in this example is one of our biggest warnings yet. It is vital that we see the real nature of our condition even while just trying to earn a living. The right to earn that living is as basic and as Unalienable as the Right to life and to liberty. We have discussed this fundamental tenet before, so by now it should be clearly ingrained in our minds that government is not the *giver* of our right to work in any endeavor of our own choice. ***Instead government was instituted to protect that Right from anyone who would threaten it***. But the *condition* of that Right in America is that it is *almost* DEAD, that it has become so as the result of *government* acts, not from vindictive, personal detractors, and that government has accomplished this feat by taking full advantage of our living as individuals. The tactic has been almost 100% successful.

That conclusion can be illustrated by some events that took place in New Jersey, but it might have been anywhere. The details are enough to make a grown man cry, or give up, but we should do neither. Such a mockary of unalienable rights should motivate us to understand the full extent of our problems in self-rule, and labor to do it right the next time.

One other conclusion is also very important. The worst blows against our Rights, by far, were the actions of the courts. It is all too obvious that *the guiding criteria being used had little to do with upholding citizen Rights* when government 'rights" are involved. Review of this case, shows how easily government has allowed itself to increase **its** own benefits at the expense of We the People. It is not at all so easy to see why or how the same destructive transition has occurred within the American Justice System. The upshot of this miserable situation is that our rights exist entirely at the whim of government.

The details of this story are given in Appendix F.

Example 4 - Warped Philosophy, Bad Law and Majority Rule, vs. Privacy and Free Choice

In introducing the pitiful condition of *privacy* and *free choice* in America, Bolick cites a number of cases in which people were made to suffer — by authorities — for actions of choice which had zero effect on anyone else. The details differ in such cases but the things that are common to them all are my concern here. I believe these elements are common in all such cases where individuals are subjected to government tyranny, not just the specific examples given by Bolick. The elements are these: a distorted philosophy, leading to bad laws, misinterpretation of (or ignoring) Constitutional Rights, majority tyranny and the effect of all these on privacy and free choice. (Some details offered by Bolick are given in Appendix F.)

Two conclusions can be made out of this string of connected government elements.

First - The **privacy** of everyone has become a non-right by the actions of government.
Second - We must stop holding ourselves hostage to the unworkable concept of rule by simple majority. That warped version of majority rule now in effect has been the cause of our loss of privacy.

Example 5 - Equality the Foundation - Inequality the Practice
The story of equality in America is really a story of *inequality*, and it started with the average citizen from the very beginning. To make it last these many years, the corrupt notion that some people don't qualify for *my equality*, we Americans

have been aided by officials at every level of government, from Federal to State to City and every offshoot spawned by them.

The story has three parts, but I won't elaborate on the part with ourselves as the culprit. The contributions of Federal and local governments will give us enough food for thought about our record. As for we the people, let's merely be reminded that the attitude of inequality or inferiority, which can lead to suspicion, fear and hate, is an attitude that is *learned*. It is an attitude that is propagated by us to our descendants and it is only ourselves who can break the unfair and unfounded cycle. Every small opportunity to speak words that imply true belief of equality, every such opportunity not taken, is just another advance for inequality. We ourselves, most assuredly, are the key to creating a society of true equals. Government has done its bit, however, to reinforce inequality, and we need to see where official actions have once again failed.

The equality of *All People* was our philosophical starting point. It was there at our beginning because a few rare men showed the way to advance at a time when guidance was so critical. Equality, something never before voiced by any government, is a simple concept, self-evident and essential for a lasting foundation. Strangely, and sadly for us, it has *never been practiced in America in all its history.*

An essay which gives the essence of Equality in America is included as Appendix F. I think the message I'd like to convey at the moment will be clear enough by simply noting a few historical milestones and some conclusions that seem accurate for today's America. The sequence goes something like this.

- The Constitution espoused EQUALITY as a founding ideal, but dealt with slavery by being totally silent about it.
- The leadership of the 1850s and 1860s failed in the worst possible way to undo the inequality of Blacks, by permitting civil chaos. Six hundred and twenty four thousand men lost their lives before the constitutional lapse was even addressed.
- From the time of 'reconstruction" to the 1950s no component of government took a single positive step to undo any of the myriad elements of inequality in vogue, save for slavery itself.
- Separate-but-equal became the false legal rationale used to perpetuate inequality.
- The national legal crutch of segregation wasn't declared illegal until 1954.
- Not until 1958 was the question of federal legal decisions over States explicitly "settled" by the United State s Supreme Court. In spite of this, however, states still consider themselves as sovereign entities.

• One of the most nefarious marks of inequality was leveled at 120,000 Americans singled out in 1941, people who were stripped of absolutely every Right – except their Right to life. The reason: their Japanese ancestry.

• Once the federal court system straightened itself out, the preponderance of "legal" actions aimed at preserving inequality was continued by city governments with the assistance of State courts.

• Cities and States which stigmatized themselves by unfairness, unconstitutional acts, meanness, and persistent stupidity during this period included such places as Yonkers, NY, Fontana, CA, Starrett City, NY, Prince Georges County, MD, the State of California and Flint MI, to name just a few of the hundreds that did likewise.

• Hundreds of lesser unjust cities hide below the national horizon, but continue to perpetuate inequality in too many hateful ways.

Fair and reasonably unbiased observers of government actions from long ago to this very day might objectively come to the following conclusions regarding Equality over America's life time.

• When the US Supreme Court itself misunderstands the [sometimes sketchy] guidance offered in the Constitution, there is nowhere to turn with any hope of righting a wrong. The need to rework Constitutional instructions to all levels of government seems obvious.

• The admonition that our Constitution is "colorblind, and neither knows nor tolerates classes among citizens," has still not filtered down to all elements of government.

• The "training," the background preparation of officials regarding the Rights of – all – citizens is clearly deficient, since so many insist on using government authority to preserve conditions of inequality.

• The power of government to suspend all Rights of individuals -- in times of emergency – is completely wrong. Worse yet, the last time this power was invoked, during the non-security depression crisis, has still not been lifted. We are all in limbo with regard to our Unalienable Rights. Washington's response continues to be silence.

• The United States lacks the necessary safeguards to undo mistakes or excessive use of authority by another branch of government.

• Discrimination and inequality battles won in State or City courts do not effect changes elsewhere, and the injustices continue essentially unchanged from a national perspective. The practice of INEQUALITY continues.

• The USSC has deferred to State authority on a great many issues of regulation and control, so much so that State powers are dominant regarding individuals. The result; any advance toward equality in one State might need to be fought 49 times over to undo the same injustice everywhere else.

- In my thoughts about government misdeeds, mistakes, miscalculations, misinterpretations, mischievous mayhem, and possible ways to govern ourselves better, it seems quite clear that an overhaul must begin with the very foundation document itself, the Constitution.
- No debate entered to create an improved self-governing society can succeed unless the sovereignty of individuals has highest priority.

What conclusions do you reach concerning Equality in America?

CHAPTER 15
Indictments Against an Obsolete Government

Ideals So Easily Lost

The founding ideal which recognizes each person's right to act in ways that are most beneficial to himself or herself, is so inspiring, that being thwarted in that pursuit deserves a great deal more attention than it normally receives. To many, it is second only to security on the list of government responsibilities. It is not, as government seems to think, the mother lode of Rights ripe for trade-offs to add yet more government power. Every government activity we've reviewed was opened for closer scrutiny because of its influence on an individual's quality of life. From those discussions, you should now be able to decide how well American government has met its responsibility concerning our pursuit of happiness. My own conclusion labels it as a huge, devastating failure.

Our agony with government actions has reached the overflow level. Almost everywhere one looks, are the unacceptable results of poor leadership, bad philosophy of service and an inexplicable failure-of-purpose to serve the nation and the people of America.

Much of the huge bounty that was once synonymous with America has been scattered with callous abandon, and continues to be squandered at an ever-increasing rate.

The security of the nation is being wagered for political dollars. Even worse has been the relentless loss of individual safety, the right to property and choice of all Americans. When government murders its fellow citizens because they dare to disagree, the result is the de-facto loss of security for every American. Government has shown itself as the sole cause for all permanent losses of safety within our borders. Those who attack from outside, are transient detractors, but government executes lasting crimes for which we have had no answer. No foreign force has done as much harm to us as our own appointed officials.

Leadership regarding goals that a nation might wish to undertake is laughable, and unstructured, and without the slightest hint of planning, has been relegated to mere political fodder for opportunistic officials. Constitution One offers no guidance.

The view of America that now readily comes to mind, is nothing we would have recognized a mere fifty years ago. The terrible, cumulative loss of supposedly self-evident rights shows they are no longer ours. Repressive taxation, subversion of the family unit, debilitating regulations, profligate spending of even our future wealth, huge criminal money grants, stigmatization and murder of blameless people, and criminal confiscation of property are some of the heinous, all-pervasive crimes of government. No longer can we invoke what once were our rights to better ourselves as we alone see fit. Our once-abundant cache of rights is gone under the heavy hand of government.

The record of federal government actions is enough to appall us by its incessant attacks on those magnificent founding ideals, and their effects on the rights we once had. We now have also sadly, and with squashed hopes, become aware that local government elements are even more at odds with duty, service and preservation of every treasure we once laid claim to, surpassing even the federal government in the scope of attacks against us.

In short, we will experience more of the crimes, miscalculations, failures, mistakes, confiscations, losses of liberty and property that government has heaped on us over the last half century.

What we will not see is true, selfless leadership, a change in money management, or self-review and meaningful change in America's direction, finally to meet the true obligations of preserving America and the ideals it was founded upon.

Government has dragged us so far along the failure path that any confidence in the future, that once characterized every American, is now greatly in question. So many of our rights have been pealed away, and so much of what remains is under government control, that we can no longer hold freedom up as our standard. As of today, the world is still unaware of the real America, as illegal immigrants continue to flood to the United States in search of succor. And without practical answers from government for real problems, the deterioration goes on.

Strangely, even the officials we've elected, and their appointees seem blithely unaware of the damage they have done to our beautiful country. They, too, should step back and take a good look at their failures. **Our resilience to organized mayhem is not infinite**. Either meaningful changes are made or we will come to know much greater future sadness. Failure of that once noble experiment in self-rule is far too likely a result for conscientious Americans to ignore any longer.

*   *   *

The essence of the task now before Americans is to extract ourselves from the rigid confines of thought inherited from history. Blindly accepting that government must rely on force for <u>all</u> its works is doomed to eventual violent failure. Instead, nurture the idea that the means of solving a problem must be tailored to the nature

138

of the problem itself. Force cannot solve the problem of addiction. It cannot compel agreement with government policies, as was attempted in Waco and Ruby Ridge. Force cannot extract enough money ever, to let government succeed in building its own power if freedom and individual rights are not preserved in the process.

What must be done can be unearthed through serious, thought-provoking debate among us all. Part II, next, is offered as a point-of-departure for this critical national debate. Our future depends on what we now do.

*   *   *

Being as objective about the performance of those we have had to trust to govern with honor, caution and wisdom, the fairest conclusion is that American government has failed in its duties, and has formed itself into an obsolete organization, top to bottom. When something so important to orderly living is obsolete, the right thing to do is replace it.

PART II
How To Fix Government

Actually, there *is* a tribunal for true justice, and it is ourselves, the citizens of America. Our just verdict would be to dissolve our obsolete government peacefully, in stages, and replace it with one subject to a new contract, **Constitution Two**.

Part II shows how this change can peacefully be accomplished for the benefit of the nation and all its citizens.

CHAPTER 16
Interpreting Government Actions

Subjecting the record of American government-in-action to close scrutiny has yielded a great deal of troubling information requiring sober, serious thought from all of us. It's as if we have just awakened from a long semi-somnambulant state to find ourselves in a strange place among strangers, who look as we do, but who speak in ways difficult to understand. The words are English, but meanings are reversed. Decrease means increase, protection can mean murder, and "for your own good." means loss of something you value.

We know we have to find a way out of this mad-hatter place we know is completely wrong, but how to do so needs quiet, and time to put things into some sense of order. We need to think, not just to react. The fond hope is that first principles can do it for us. All we have to do is find a way to apply them with minimum disruption to everyone, and I do mean everyone. There are so many Americans tied so closely to the present government network, financially and philosophically, that the way they live must change if government is reworked to benefit people in general rather than officials and hangers-on. All those thousands and thousands of people who feed directly on government-controlled tax money, the thousands who are part of the federal structure and the millions tied to state and local arms of government, people on welfare and corporations being subsidized by government, the lives of all these people will be changed. We want to stop the sources of our own pain. The trick will be to make the changes without causing more pain elsewhere. Changes that are phased into operation can minimize such disruptions. That part of any plan to change government clearly would be critical both at home and for the sake of international stability. The rest of the world needs to know that America remains strong, and is leading, once again, in direct efforts to advance itself and, indirectly, all civilization.

While millions of Americans would be directly affected, hundreds of millions would not. They would simply know that their lives have been improved in fundamental ways, and things of value that were stolen from them have been restored, their precious rights in particular.

Faced with this dilemma, what we can not allow ourselves to do now is to decry the imminent end of the world, and with hyper-emotionalism, succumb to drastic reactions that would hurt even more. Because "something must be done," to end the injustices to us all does not imply the need for haste or, worse yet the use of more force. We must instead, give serious thought to what has been learned, understand why events have occurred as they have, and why government acts as it does. From that contemplation, think constructively of what can be done to rescue the things that are most important to us all. American union, America's truly magnificent founding ideals, the still unmatched bounty of our homeland, our interesting, inventive and remarkable neighbors, and our wonderful and inspiring family members are all treasures in need of our very best efforts to preserve. To excise the unwanted and unnecessary products of an unwise, obsolete government, **without harm to anyone** is a task that can only be done through the very best that is in each of us.

History will record how well suited we were to the task.

Think About & Assimilate What We Have Learned.

The entire book can be viewed as an effort to answer the question of WHY government and the Constitution should change. What I want to do now is change perspective from the simple listing of government transgressions, as given in Part I, to a more formal discussion regarding such a far-reaching change. From all those preliminaries, we have a better understanding of the real present nature of the US government, and American society that has resulted. . That understanding is essential to the success of any attempt to improve American self-government.

From the very beginning of our existence as a nation, the compromises and the structural details of government as defined by the constitution were far enough removed from the Founders' intent, that all the ills we now experience with government were *inevitable*. The genesis of the extremes and excesses of modern government lay embedded in the **constitutional compromises** and the **structural design** of government that resulted. The weaknesses of present-day government resided, unwanted but real, in the plan that was meant to champion a new philosophy, one that finally recognized equality and self-determination as key guiding principles.

That early creation, however, *did not truly implement those ideals* which effectively became buried under weighty *political* compromises. Without those principles we did not and could not become what our ideals should have led us to become.
Equality of all turned out merely to be a slogan.

Equality was *not* a criterion used to define American government or its actions. The inequality of Black people was institutionalized by default. Women, too, were singled out by default as being unequal. The fears and greed of little men who would not yield to the truth of equality, after more than 200 years of leading the *practice* of government, have finally completed the circle, ensnaring everyone in the hypocrisy of the inequality built into that government — our government. We are

142

all beneficiaries of the lie that became such a key part of our heritage, and now we are **all** feeling the sting of that stubborn inequality.

Attempts to fix the Constitution via the 13th and 14th Amendments, failed as the following 100 years of history clearly show. Moreover, that fateful flaw has evolved into something even more widespread than discrimination against the original target segments of the population. The early, overt and intentional acts of government to perpetuate inequality for Blacks, native Americans and others, now affect *everyone*. Only the specifics of discrimination are different. Black, Red White, yellow, and every other group are all uniformly being injured through the loss of Unalienable Rights that are supposedly self-evident. When the choice is made to deny Rights to some, which is exactly what inequality does, then the only possible outcome is ultimately the denial of Rights to everyone. We live in such a condition under American government today. This effect on us all, simply stated, is that government as exercised in the United States does not function FOR the people. It functions for itself and its purposes which are not the same as the purposes of the American people in all its manifistations of skin color.

Take a moment to reflect on the gulf that separates these two sets of goals. Individuals want simply to be able to exercise, in safety, the Unalienable Rights of all people, accepting responsibility for themselves and honoring the Rights of every other person. Conversely, government' s purpose is to extend its size and power over individuals, and to take away self-responsibility from the individual, replacing it with government decision-makers.

This latter effect of the actual workings of the United States government is so all-pervasive that we can't dismiss it out of hand. By integrating the excesses and failings shown in earlier chapters into a composite, we can then deduce the *essence* of American government. The result is a government, at all levels, whose goals differ widely from those of individual Americans. Nor do they match the avowed purposes of the Founders. And finally, they indeed, do not coincide with any body empowered to govern by the transfer of the inherent power of individuals over self to a proxy, which is the only proper mechanism for government-forming. The skewing of government operations toward today' s norm has been an evolutionary result, and I argue that it was *inevitable*, given the substance of our Constitution and the characteristics of behavior that so dominate the human species.

Stripped of most of the details of government acts, the essence of American government is contained in three kinds of actions, all dealing with control of money.

- gift giving
- taxing
- expanding government size & power

143

Gift Giving

Earlier I labeled gift giving as THE biggest single error of government. Giving gifts of tax money for any purpose is beyond the scope of government, yet having tested the strategy on small, innocuous but "worthy" cases, government came to understand how their own power could be opened to unlimited possibilities. FDR was the master innovator who spent us out of a depression, created family welfare, including Social Security, and subjugated the entire agricultural industry to government control through a totally different kind of welfare. This was welfare, confined initially to agriculture, that ultimately led to the involved process of gift-giving to special interests — and incidentally back to government itself in the form of campaign support and a greatly expanded bureaucracy. Welfare, in all forms, has since mushroomed to become dominant both as a means of controlling individuals and as one of the main conduits for giving away money while exacting reciprocal benefits to government. The usurped power to *give away tax money* has been the key to perpetual power for those who crave it.

Taxing

In the United States the power to tax and the process by which taxes come about are inherently unstable. Given time and normal human behavior, taxes will increase to an extreme that will cause the machine of society to fail in some unknown but catastrophic way. It doesn' t even matter what the failure mode will be because there is no benign failure from such unstable operation. *Power to confiscate some of a person' s wealth is power to take it all.* Without governmental self control, without an unequivocal limit on the wealth that can be forcibly removed, then the effective limit can only be the total of what is there for the taking. Failure — of society and of the noble experiment — will come before that limit is reached, however. The sinister game now being played by government is very like a game of chicken between two automobiles speeding toward each other. "How much can we squeeze out of people' s wealth before the producers stop producing? How effective are all our little tricks of disguising a tax? Where is that practical limit?" These are the collective thoughts of government judging by their demeanor of the past six or seven decades. They seek a limit that *they* view as practical. One not specified by Constitution or statute, but one that maximizes the government TAKE, yet does not "break" the machine of society. The likelihood of government finding such a threshold limit and then holding their avarice in check to prevent complete failure and chaos is ZERO, because there is no mastermind of government at work here. There is only the human drive for power.

In this reckless and unreasonable drive to create greater and greater governmental power, perhaps the most reckless monetary ploy has been to spend future wealth. The ever-increasing yearly take has not satisfied the government money monster, so money yet to be earned by the next generation or the next several generations became subject to today' s government. Legalities, pseudo limits and restraints of any kind are a farce. Our debts and liabilities are far beyond any prudent level, and the shocking fact is that the spending has succeeded mostly in buying us more government and very little else. The emphasis of government, so callously misplaced for so long, is on the verge of costing 100% of gross revenues (confiscated taxes) just for interest payments on the national debt. There **will be** a fiscal reckoning somewhere ahead. Government, leaderless in the realm of prudent national conduct, however, seems inexplicably content to deny that anything is amiss or that the business of governing has set the stage for ruin. Surely there must be a spark of reason somewhere, but sadly none is evident.

Expanding Government Size and Power
The third kind of action that describes the essence of the United States government is expansion. Both the taxing and the giving are used for fulfilling the prime goal of government, namely to make itself bigger and more powerful in every conceivable way. The means to do this has evolved slowly but very effectively, achieving a momentum that today seems as unstoppable as it is potentially ruinous.

The method of choice has been to expand through creation of non-elected agencies, which are then charged with spending, giving and regulating. The controllers in this process are, in effect, answerable to no one. Once Congress has created their charter, they make rules and regulations that are *never* reviewed by Congress before being put into effect. HUD, IRS, DOT, FAA, OSHA, EPA, and all the rest operate in exactly the same way, making rules by the tens of thousands, giving money away to special interest groups and funding projects that benefit government more than the voters. The ONLY time voters can influence these standard operations is when the intrusions of these tons of regulations become so blatant and odious that Congress is forced to placate the masses. So far, however, such changes have merely rearranged the details without affecting the overall process of squandering almost uncountable amounts of present and future wealth. The Internal Revenue Service is the most conspicuous of these law-making offshoots of government, but alas just one of many like-bodies.

The Glue That Holds All This Together
Government is an organization that rightly depends on the use of force to provide security. What followed in America, however, is that the same method of control has also been applied to everything else that government decides needs to be done. Collecting money for its use is a good example. With the backing of **force**, taking money started small, then grew, and grew. In America, people have no control over that growth, and so that is what is happening; escalation of taxes toward a breaking point.

Force hovers in the background when government decides it is acceptable to make dependents of people on welfare. The same is true when government turns an entire class of people into criminals for endangering themselves with addictive chemicals.

Force is there to murder those whose complaints with government go beyond its pitiful ability to cope. It's there and it is used because that's what they know best.

Force is much less visible but still present when government decides to subsidize grotesque art, or grant huge sums of money to healthy corporations and groups that advocate government expansion while also donating money to re-electing the same officials who made the grants in the first place. Force is there when government minions create a mountain of rules and regulations for every conceivable activity. Without change, what we'll get are more and more dictates, with the specter of force more evident as time goes on.

We will be stunted in personal growth opportunities as well as in advances nationally, because government leadership will continue to be poor, and tied ever-more solidly to their archaic methods so long in use. And we will see America's treasures of wealth and liberty dissipated like so much chaff in the wind – because that's exactly what government has done so far during its tenure of mismanaging American affairs.

In short, we will experience more of the crimes, miscalculations, failures, mistakes, confiscations, losses of liberty and property that government has heaped on us over the last half century. All this to perpetuate its taxing, gift-giving and expansion ways so long in use. And **force** will remain to allow government to continue to satisfy itself.

What Does All This Imply?

The manner in which our government operates is a *direct* result of its structure, its enumerated powers and the powers it has assumed by fiat. All are, therefore, traceable to a Constitution which contained major flaws from the very beginning and which, despite improvements through amendments, still does not provide the guidance for a people to create a truly proper government let alone for a government to maintain control over itself.

Consider what has resulted from a less-than-ideal Constitution and two hundred years of government evolution into its present-day form.

The most glaring Constitutional error, of course, was its failure to install *equality* as one of its principal guidelines.

146

Government took that sad flaw and produced an untold number of bad laws legalizing inequality and affecting every facet of living. A ruinous civil war, hundreds of thousands of dead bodies and 150 years of non-leadership from this government have still not been enough to undo that deliberate, compromising fact about the Constitution. The lesson of Yonkers and the Japanese-American internment camps, for example, is that inequality is still a stubborn, built-in part of the American psyche. It was put there in people's minds *because* of Constitution One, and the Supreme Court decision of Brown II in 1954 did not expunge the lingering stigma within us.

Bad law has also resulted from all the other Constitutional inadequacies that we seem loath to look at. Like religious zealots, we have accepted and perpetuated the myth of the *perfection* of that document because it *was* such a giant step forward, and because it contains the *means* to be changed. Changes to date, however important, are mostly Band-Aid fixes. They haven't even come close to addressing the fundamentals that cry out for change. Bad law still results today at every level of government, affecting society in all its manifestations. Political advocacy (with its huge benefits to government), welfare (the bane of families and individual responsibility), social security (the backward sop for retired dignity), health care control (another something-for-nothing con-game), a coercive school system that doesn't teach, a business environment rife with handouts and arbitrary rules of the most foolish kind — and almost every other enterprise of government — have been so deficient of long-term purpose and wise leadership that one would suspect the *fundamentals* must be at fault. In fact, fundamentals ARE at fault!

Lawyers will tell you that the things government does that are outside Constitutional powers, or outside wise leadership are, practically speaking, a fait accompli and have acquired legal status through long practice. Having reached that exalted status, therefore, We the People should merely accept these extra-legal acts as legal and regard such counterfeit changes as new parts of a Constitutional package binding us all. In other words, theft and irresponsibility, practiced long enough, become non-theft and responsible stewardship! Among the most potent examples of government misdeeds to acquire "legitimacy and acceptance" by such rationalization are these:

- the giving of confiscated tax money;
- the subversion of Unalienable Rights which undermine our pursuit of happiness; and
- the confiscation of property without due process.

There are others, but I consider these three to be the most far-reaching and odious of all illegal, long-standing irresponsible actions of government. (Note that taxation has acquired legal status by other means.)

147

I reject completely the notion that longevity purifies illegal actions for two reasons. The first is that theft is wrong — no matter how long it is practiced. The second is that We The People *never* had a say in the creation of such government practices, regardless of any enfranchisement.

Checks & Balances

The bad habits of American government are now virtually hard-wired into our thinking and our expectations. We continue to create bad laws at the Federal and Local levels and never once think of testing their provisions against even the existing flawed Constitution. The US Supreme Court is, sadly, a nonentity in the overriding responsibility of government to create just and wise rules by which society can gauge its actions. Like immature school children, government pushes the making of rules to every conceivable limit, without regard to constitutionality, relenting long after the fact and only when forced to retract. I am far from being satisfied, and **we** should not be satisfied with a process of governing that allows Unalienable Rights to be denied us *first*, with review for legitimacy a mere afterthought only when great harm has already been done. The US Supreme Court is not an effective deterrent to the excesses of the legislative branch of government. It is, in practice, a mere afterthought. The Executive Branch, as well, is not only not a means of preventing legislative excesses, but is actually a partner in those excesses, the real goals of the two branches being synonymous.

Thus, the *structure of government* for checks and balances is, at best, effective only in minor instances. We must somehow summon the courage and the wisdom to re-examine every element of governing ourselves, encompassing functions, powers, safeguards and limitations, goals as a people and commitments in wealth and responsibility. We must do this while stability still holds within our society, or else lose the opportunity to advance in maturity and satisfaction.

Inequality

The terrible injustices created against whole groups of people by the Constitutional flaw of inequality were not even a concern of White government for fully the first third of our existence as a nation. Inequality remained a backwater of concern until late in the civil war tragedy, and remained so even after emancipation, through the reconstruction period, through the rest of the 19th century, and throughout the first half of the 20th century. For the inequality of our Constitutional heritage finally to be faced in a serious manner required the focusing of the collective ire of nearly the entire Black citizenry and a great many other brave people who hated our unjust way of living.

It took that flood of indignation just to begin the process of change to undo effects *created by the Constitution.*

148

Fixing the problems so created is still ongoing, but at least there is directed change for improvement in our new, forced practice of equality. The whole advance in this realm of living, please notice, has been accomplished **without the slightest hint of governmental initiative**. We can say with complete fairness that *government* has made no contribution in the changes made toward true equality. That leadership came only from the people, from those with the courage of Thurgood Marshall, Martin Luther King Jr. and others like them.

Our nakedness as a people confronting an even more pervasive inequality than our national attitude toward Blacks, therefore, is both sad and frightening. To date, the whole movement of American society and American government in our battle to create and practice equality has been directed at removing *racial* injustices. What remains, almost unnoticed, is an even more insidious inequality that pits the misapplied force of coercive government against the entire body of citizens, not just one segment. Such an all-encompassing inequality, **government versus everyone else**, not only is not recognized as the problem it is, but also suffers from a lack of leadership of the Marshall & King caliber so essential to fixing anything in America. There is no equivalent, cohesive, demand, comparable to the Civil Rights effort, to examine the remainder of government excesses and crimes for the purpose of removing all the other inequities that exist in our homeland. Describing this second distorted version of injustice at the hands of government as another form of inequality is merely my attempt to get people' s attention concerning the near universal failure of American government to carry out its real responsibilities, its *only reason for existing*. Any number of other perspectives might serve as well, but lumping together all the failures of government as contributions to inequality gives an idea of the seriousness I see in the condition of modern America. Any summation of that condition must note that Unalienable Rights and Individual Sovereignty are degraded terribly from those at the beginning days of Constitutional debates. The deterioration continues at a pace that quickens perceptibly with each decade. If we have the temerity to compare that condition with one derived from a constitution *without* the flaws that now exist, the degradation of liberty is even more shocking and disturbing.

Local Government

To avoid focusing too heavily on the Federal government' s role in all this, keep firmly in mind how state and local governments have been as derelict, perhaps even more so, as they target specific people and businesses. Local government' s drive for power is no less intense than Federal. They are, however, even more successful — for themselves — because their targets are more isolated, and opposition is always weaker than government itself. Gains against racial inequality at the local level do not match those at the Federal level. The tactic locally is to delay and divide. History shows how the syndrome of inequality persists, and I suspect it will continue as long as the battles are fragmented. Fifty-two constitutions meant to guide a single society is ludicrous in the extreme, yet is a major contributor to our failure to practice equality. Every constitution or charter penned for a segment of the population MUST be directly derived from an acceptable *national* Constitution, taking away nothing of people's Rights, and adding nothing of powers to government.

While racial inequality locally is still a disgrace, the inequality of any citizen relative to local-government is every bit as bad. As with the federally-contrived inequality of individual-to-government, the condition locally is at least as serious, that of Individual Sovereignty and Unalienable Rights being lost by individuals routinely.

The changes to government discussed in this book are indeed far-reaching. It literally implies a reexamination of every single element of self government from the Constitution, to government structure, to the process and body of law so far created. It implies that everything is subject to change for the sake of improving the lives of individuals and the national life of all people. It implies, first and foremost, a restatement of the foundation principles to be used in redefining this **second generation of American self government**. It implies that sacrosanct among these principles would be true *equality*, explicit *Unalienable Rights*, recognition of *sovereignty of the individual* and *freedom of choice* in all matters of self.

What it does not imply is revolution, which heretofore has always been the world's bloody answer to change. That kind on an answer is immature in the extreme. What we look for now is a maturing of our own behavior in attempting to reorganize society, a step that is sorely needed in America. If Americans succeed in this redefinition, we will also succeed in showing how to make the *transition* peacefully from today's model to a much improved one for tomorrow. The remaining chapters of Part II discuss specific tasks that will help us find the best present-day solutions to self-rule. These are tasks that can peacefully lead to replacing a dysfunctional government with one that works FOR those being governed.

A Final Thought Concerning Today's Government
I had no preconceived idea of the severity of our problem at the beginning of this study. Years of effort, however, have dispelled any notion that American government is sound and responsible. It is not. It is an unsound entity on an unsound path evolving from an unsound foundation, and even though I have probably only scratched the surface covering our present-day condition, it is enough to show how serious our plight actually is. Present government is the implementation of a new philosophy that does not even match our founding document, which itself is deficient in certain important ways. Government needs desperately to be changed.

150

Many may disagree with my assessment of American government' s failus and the condition of liberty and Rights in America. Initially I, too, had no idea that the record and the results would prove to be so bad. The fact that it has taken so much effort and time for me to see this world of government differently probably indicates how difficult it is to understand the realities of being governed in America. Anyone consumed with making a living and raising children simply cannot devote enough energy to the task. They, as I once did, have had to rely on their elected officials to do the right and proper thing more often than they do things poorly. I have been convinced that that is not the situation in America; it is instead **exactly** the opposite! Hopefully what has been discussed here is enough to change our collective awareness of government failings. There have been far too many to expect the future to be acceptable without *fundamental* changes.

CHAPTER 17
How to Define a New American Government

During almost all of history the concept of Unalienable Rights for individuals didn' t exist. Until our own Constitution was debated and finally written, individuals weren' t of enough consequence to affect the way the dictates of government were made and applied. The lack of rights is the perspective to hold our attention, because it alone is the key to devising criteria by which modern society can learn finally to govern itself.

James Madison was a student of history and a critic of governments at the time he helped create a new approach to sensible living, an approach that concerned itself with everyone, not just a favored few. In his view, ruling bodies of the past had little to recommend as guidelines for the future. Madison, Jefferson, and those few others knew of the sad failings of the past and were convinced that an entirely different perspective was called for in defining governmental functions, powers, and obligations. Two centuries later we find ourselves in a situation, nationally and internationally, that requires we do the same as Madison et al did in their day. This need shouldn' t be a bit surprising when we consider the extraordinary changes over the last 200 years. The concept of self-rule, as implemented in the United States, as great a step forward as it was, allowed ultimately for failure as well as for success; and failure has won out.

The potential was there for great success in achieving national greatness and individual happiness in all the diversity needed by our great mix of citizens. The potential came firstly by stating the unambiguous, positive belief, for the first time ever, that all individuals are equal, and secondly, by defining and implementing a government of the *people*, a government whose role it was to help those people achieve their individual goals. The notion that government should rightly be the servant of people was well understood by the key, forward-thinking founders, but for many others, the philosophical change was just too big a leap forward to take permanent hold. As new generations of politicians replaced the old, especially within state – commonwealth heirarchies, bit by bit the early clear view of purpose for government gave way. The ethic of service became submerged, and was finally transformed to the perverted version of the Power Republic that exists now, as accurately characterized by its actions reviewed earlier.

If, then, we need to repeat the process that took place during the late eighteenth century, and I contend strongly that we do, how might we go about it? Looking back as we can to that period in history, a fair conclusion is that the process those men went through was really quite informal, and dependent greatly on the strength of character of a few and the great good will of almost everyone else. Figuratively they had a clean slate, firm ideas on the main historical ills of government, an urgent opportunity, leaders whose opinions tracked closely on many issues of the day and a great resolve to discuss, compromise and create something of greater value. Today almost none of those conditions exist, and any cause for optimism among the citizenry is almost nonexistent. There are almost no leaders with the ability to recognize fundamental problems and then to show the way they might be overcome. There is no discernible consensus of how even to approach the task of making the next great stride in self-government. The only thoughts for improving self-government are through Band-Aid fixes that sidestep the entire problem.[33] There are even too few men of good will within the political/legislative conglomerate to work together for the benefit of the people instead of perpetuating their own power industry. And the voice of true concern for individuals, the voice that tells of the true tests for acts by government, is a whisper, ignored because it is easy to ignore.

There is, however, one condition today that parallels the past. We are now being hammered about the head and shoulders by opportunity that is so forceful and urgent, but is so distorted by the political machinations of both major parties that, as yet, opportunity languishes unrecognized. There is so much political smoke being generated by little men, and some little women, in pursuit of their own self-centered goals, that there is no national recognition of opportunity.

A few thoughts seem appropriate. Opportunity can be wrapped in many garbs not easily identified. Problems are opportunities. Critical problems mask opportunity because, being obscured by crisis, they go unrecognized. Stop-gap solutions are applied and the chance for real advance passes. Worse yet, the poorly thought-out "solutions" add to problems elsewhere. Even more noticeable, attempts by government to solve problems which are outside what I' ll call its*natural functions*, fail miserably and in unpredictable ways. So, by being optimistic about problems as opportunity, we might at least tentatively accept that our overflowing bucket of problems is a GREAT opportunity, not to try and solve through government, but to see that government has not been the answer, and further to see, therefore, that we need a new definition for government, one of greatly reduced scope. The idea of limiting government is certainly not new. We will, however, finally see how it can peacefully be accomplished.

---

[33] I can't pass by this opportunity to point out the recent pitiful attempt by government to reinvent itself. Vice President Gore and his group showed an absolute and complete misunderstanding of the real problem and made an equally inept stab at solutions. Since these men and women are very bright people, the easy conclusion is that they had no intention whatsoever to 'reinvent" anything. Their purpose was to follow the political wind-of-the-moment and wait for it to subside. The result was predictable and completely worthless.

What makes **now** different than forty or even twenty years ago? It is the cumulative effect of many things. The government as constituted, and in its application of powers usurped far beyond the levels initially envisioned, has failed often and seriously. The fiscal crisis (the national debt), the trampling of Unalienable Rights (Waco for example, or rampant confiscation by many agencies), civil unrest (riots that resemble small, bloody destructive wars), a war on their own citizens called a war on drugs, foreign adventures reminiscent of past amoral governments (Vietnam, the most horrible example), social programs that trap people in poverty and propagate over generations (called "welfare"), and a succession of dictates within education that "progress" toward inferiority; these are a few that we are all now familiar with. All are new and all are very serious. The *opportunity* that comes through this sorry recitation is that we haven' t quite reached the stage of open insurrection. In my opinion, that is opportunity enough; opportunity to advance without first having to live through the agony of savage conflagration. The urgency should be obvious.

The relative calm elsewhere (compared to 70 years ago) is a positive we should not let pass. All these factors contribute toward an opportunity to make the next meaningful movement to elevate the social structure of the human species by elevating the way we Americans maintain order in America. The downside of opportunity missed or arrogantly flaunted is an easy prediction. Every major problem that is now part of our collective lives will become exacerbated to the level critical to each and erupt in its own unique way to our sorrow and everlasting shame. Stupidity, pettiness, and inaction are always easier than any attempt at mature resolve. We' ll know soon enough what best describes ourselves.

Here Is A Way to Start Something Right

Allow me, at this point, to be much more superficial than the problem calls for. Ideas are simple things, and I really just want to convey one idea of how the problem of restructuring ourselves might be handled. To carry out such an idea may prove to be a severe test of our abilities because it will depend heavily on a resolve to reach compromise on issues of great importance.

There are two essentials for progress. **The first**, I believe, lies in the wholehearted acceptance of just those few criteria by which we can measure the value of proposals to be examined. We have discussed those criteria at length throughout this book, and they are the foundation for the exercise described in this chapter. **The second** essential is the formation of a small nucleus of men and women whose personal philosophy would allow them to meet the challenges with compassion, desire and uncommon wisdom. James Madison would be a nice start. We at least have his written counsel.

154

Who Among Us Might Contribute?

I suspect that each of us has met exemplary people over the years who live lives tuned to these few high standards. They are those who readily accept the value of another person, and show understanding and compassion for the difficulties others face. Without being crusaders, they worked hard and helped others when they could. What they never did, in deference to their own philosophy, was to think of another person as somehow being less than themselves – unless that person's actions proved that they were 'lesser."

Such people are superior in the sense that they live the highest of ideals. I have had the good fortune to know a satisfying number of such people as you yourself surely have also. The only test that need be applied to know of a person's suitability for this task is this. Would you be comfortable with that person helping to plan for change? Many politicians would not pass such a filter; however, a few would. The same is true of lawyers, or for that matter, any other group. It's the philosophy of the individual that matters as to whether a person might qualify for such an important first step. From just that one simple filter, it's easy to see why so many of today's decision -makers could not be part of this process for changing government.

Ideas for the future character of our nation can come initially from a small group of such people, and I have no doubt that finding them can be taken for granted.

If I were to form the starting nucleus, there are several people I have known personally and others indirectly who would be admirable choices. Recognizable names include Milton Friedman, one of the clearest thinkers of our era, and Bill Walsh, an innovator and logical thinker. Four other men, perhaps less well known, have the mettle, the exemplary character to fill the requirement. Rubin Boxer is an engineer, innovative mathematician and technical administrator for a post-war think tank. Albert S. Copeland is a master plumber turned physicist. Milton D. Bennett is a retired US Navy Captain with a passion for reason in government. Alan A. Allen is an internationally known expert for the control of oil spills. None of these men has any idea of my equating them to such a task, but to me they represent *templates* for people with qualities essential to the task. I' m satisfied in such choices because of a close working association with each of them over many years. What I want to emphasize here is that in spite of the very large number of people I consider as misfits, people I could never trust with something so important, I also am very sure that there are men and women of compassion, wisdom, and temperament equal to the task.

The job should not be beyond us.

The Process for Defining a New Government

Any approach to lifting ourselves from the status of servants-to-government toward the inverse, is an attempt at a solution. We would like to reassure ourselves that acceptable solutions exist, but at this point it is not a certainty. So far in man' s upbringing, no actions taken can clearly be endorsed as leading to solutions that are anywhere near optimum or permanent, particularly in the matter of self-governing. So far, solving this problem has been beyond us. The Madison approach, however, should be enough of an indication that sensible government is possible provided those involved meet the challenge with the right attitude. If we succeed here in identifying to others the need for change, something positive will have been accomplished, a first step in solving it.

The introduction given next for solving the problem of *government* should give an appreciation of the complexities involved, but that these difficulties are within our collective capabilities to handle.

The process at the highest level of generality can be represented by just ten interconnected tasks. Information and ideas flow among the tasks. As new thoughts and ideas begin to gel, and as the consequences to individuals of each idea become clearer, every task will progress through as many iterations as it takes to arrive at the best possible consensus.

Guiding Criteria

From the discussion of issues covered in this book, the criteria that should be used to guide this second attempt at government, are straightforward. They encompass those same fundamentals that sparked our nation earlier, but were never used specifically when those ideals were turned into concrete instruments for governing.

- Remember the preeminence of Individual Sovereignty, and the Unalienable Rights of each person –
- Minimize intrusion on the individual in every facet of living and governing –
- Preserve choice by making maximum use of the Referendum process –
- Aspire to be a unified people, ensure uniformity of Rights, responsibilities and laws throughout the nation –
- When confronting detractors, at any level of harm, provide for Restitution rather than mere Retribution –
- In each matter of rule-making, set its longevity, its finite active life, as part of providing for structured change, and preservation of choice -
- Finally, provide procedures for continuous, permanent evaluation of government performance relative to citizen goals, and provide for extending this present task to redefine government for as long as our Union may last.

A background task of acquiring additional members of an initial organizing group is also ongoing. This will allow a permanent, yet ever-changing cadre of the very best people the nation has to offer toward this specific effort.

Top Level Tasks to Redefine American Government

The general tasks envisioned are as follows:

- **TASK 1** - Assemble the nucleus of members who can begin the work -
- **TASK 2** - Choose other candidates and how the group may change as the need arises -
- **TASK 3** - The real work begins as functions of government are suggested, (for example National Security), and the means for implementing the functions are described. At the disposal of council members for all tasks are several independent information sources that are geared to supply as unbiased and factual reports as knowledge can provide. History, in particular, in layered detail is critical because from such reports the successes and failures of past experiments in governing can be debated –
- **TASK 3a** - Local level functions are identified in a parallel effort, and each following task has its parallel for local functions. The same criteria hold for all levels of government -
- **TASK 4** – Define explicitly how a function is to be implemented -
- **TASK 5** – Making extensive use of the record of government's past actions, Identify what the effects will be on individuals as a result of the implementation method being considered, and test these consequences against the guiding criteria -
- **TASK 6** – Modify the proposed plan for implementing the particular function and iterate -
- **TASK 7** – Modify a proposed function to overcome practical problems and iterate -
- **TASK 8** – Make changes to the composition of the study group to take advantage of needed expertise -
- **TASK 9** – Make contributions to those documents that will ultimately define the new American Government and Social Structure designed according to the guiding criteria -
- **TASK 10** – Submit progress reports, updates, preliminary findings and final documents to the people to solicit serious inputs and to test the defining documents for general acceptance.
  Among the final documents will be these four:

Declaration of Individual Sovereignty & Responsibility
Constitution Two
America's Statement of Unalienable Rights
Guiding Document on the Conduct, Qualifications & Responsibilities
  of Everyone Entrusted with Governing America & Its Citizens

Some Elaboration on the Process

Any potential function that might be ascribed to government, along with its specific implementation, has to pass successfully many tests of reason, with a few of the most important being as follows:

(a) To what degree will it intrude on the sovereignty and rights of individuals?

(b) What are the specific details of how the function(s) would be implemented; and does this implementation constitute the minimum intrusion of government? (Note that the process task number 4 is closely tied to any *definition* of government function and its acceptance or rejection.)

(c) Does the function incorporate the best use of Referendum in decision-making? It must.

(d) Can the function be provided by private industry under contract to an agency?

(e) Can implementation be uniformly accomplished all over the nation?

(f) The burden of proof for adoption of any function lies with advocates, who must show as near an absolute necessity for it as judgment can require. The base position or point of departure is that *no power to govern is required for any function*. If this single test of absolute necessity cannot be passed, to the satisfaction of **everyone** in the group, and ultimately to all citizens in a referendum, then clearly it is not a proper function.

Special Note: function equates to power, and only by minimizing function can the risk of delegating power be minimized.

(g) If a function is just, proper and essential, can it be implemented via an agency (of government) that is totally independent of any other government agency?[34]

(h) What safeguards are possible? Which can be reasonably used to monitor, prevent or correct any abuse of the powers attached to instituting the function(s)?

(i) Is effectiveness of the function and its implementation overly at risk from individuals or groups having ill-will? Are there feasible counter measures?

---

[34] Implied here is the feasibility to utilize multiple, central, national agencies, each independent, each of limited power, instead of a single monolithic government. Equal power among them is NOT a requirement.

Obviously there are other tests to challenge the worth of any idea that culminates in the handing of power to anyone or any group. The list here, hopefully, is enough to show what the approach might be to this critical part of the process. We might also remind ourselves that this manner of deciding how to conduct ourselves as a society of neighbors, i.e., how to "govern" ourselves, has never been done - ever - and, like any other manifestation of life, it too will have to be refined, to change to meet the specific conditions influencing the task and decisions coming out of it. The ultimate test, of course, would come via the *referendum* for acceptance or change, but I believe that a process such as this can lead to a major improvement in living, for individuals, which of course is the primary objective.

Built into the process is the ability to make or accommodate changes whose source can be anyone inside or outside of the group. Each iteration, (tasks 6, 7& 8) aims to improve a portion of the proposed definition of government, and can be the key ingredient to a deliberate and *perpetual* process of review and refinement, thus preserving the right of choice for future generations.

There is a device, long in use for such problem solving, that should prove useful here. Two teams are formed, a Blue team and a Gold team, one to propose and one to critique. Measures of value, called metrics, are devised appropriate to the question, allowing thorough study and evaluation. Metrics such as cost and time are typical, and I suspect many ways might be found to give quantitative weight to *individual annoyance* with any given proposal. The opportunity for innovation abounds. In later discussions, Blue and Gold might reverse sides to dig out other failings or strengths, with resulting recommendations for inclusion or exclusion along with reasons why, and all weighed against the Prime Criteria.

The overall product of such an effort, after as many iterations as it takes, can be viewed in familiar terms as a **second generation constitution**, but it is more than a listing of delegated powers and a description of the structure of agencies that must execute functions on behalf of individuals and the nation. The product is also a reaffirmation of individual sovereignty, which implies and demands a renewal of individual responsibility. It becomes, therefore, *a restructuring of society itself*, a return to an earlier time in America when people had little interaction with government except at the local level, and knew they must rely on their own efforts to progress in life.

The product is simply a proposal to all citizens of the nation, and has no force of authority until it is accepted by the overwhelming majority of people. I favor anything over 85% as a reasonable requirement for adoption of this second generation constitution. The value of any proposal needs to be evident to at least that large a majority. Even at that, I would have great concern for the 15% or less

159

who demurred. Why did they balk? Has the new proposal missed the mark in some way that's repairable?

That acceptance would never be 100% is understandable in view of the large number of people to be decoupled from power. They would be unwilling to accept their own obsolescence, and unable to see that elevating each individual by this means would also elevate those who labor against it.

We have seen how government, as presently constituted and institutionalized, is totally outmoded. It has degraded itself, at all levels, city, state, and national, to the condition of obsolescence. It must be revised - drastically - to fulfill the *heritage* of all persons, which is to be allowed to exercise the unalienable rights of sovereign individuals in pursuit of their own just goals. Anything less is tyranny through the unjust exercise of raw, arbitrary repressive power, even to its criminal use. We recognize all too well the existence of criminals among us who use weapons of all lethality to steal anything and everything as they see the opportunity. By now, perhaps, we should recognize the criminal nature of the use by government of power not specifically delegated by the overwhelming majority of citizens, and periodically reaffirmed.

Local Government

One other issue needs to be highlighted and considered here, that of government at a level below national, indicated by Task 3a. The problem here is a least as bad as our situation nationally. At present there are three and at times a fourth level of local government; State, County, City, and Local Associations. I believe the same process as described for the national level could be applied to local government, with a need every bit as urgent, if not more so. The specifics are very different and the variation of issues has to be much greater because of the huge range of cultural, geographic, ethnic, and economic factors that come into play. Criteria for acceptability should not change, however, because the only proper basis for government at any level is still sovereignty of the individual.

The erosion of rights at the local level can easily be illustrated by recalling just one example. It is the overt strategy of creating public corporations, boards, districts and other 'official" agencies to perform functions that elected officials judge to be salable as beneficial to the people, but which evolve in power far beyond any inherent power conferred upon the officials themselves. It is exactly in the same mold of federal agencies created by Congress. This perfidy easily sidesteps any restrictions of any nature that are legally in place, and that the ordinary citizen assumes is working for his or her benefit. Any safeguards supposedly in operation through court action, including state and national Supreme Courts, have been totally ineffective in halting these illegal, Rights-reducing practices. The problem is rampant nationwide.

160

Once instituted, and endowed with an almost perpetual slice of the budget or Bond proceeds, these agencies evolve in power through regulations issued that are [a] at their discretion alone, [b] uncontested and unapproved by any elected body, [c] almost always beyond Constitutional limits, [d] often fraudulent through favoritism and [e] most seriously intrusive of individual rights — which are never a concern in the internal debates of the agency leading up to their adoption. The wielders of such power, (all non-elective opportunists) include zoning board members, planning commissions, school board members, environmental protection agents, business regulation and licensing agents, special district boards (water, cable TV, transportation, etc.), building regulators and other agents of almost endless scope. All at times have been given power to tax, and in this past century have only expanded in size.

Not All Layers of Local Government are Necessary

Of the three basic levels of local government, most likely two are superfluous and all are operating far beyond the intrusive threshold. It should also be apparent that all of the governmental bodies created by local government should be stripped of power not specifically delegated by referendum, and the question of function be addressed during the process of re-defining local government.

My pick for the one that should most sensibly be redefined for our second generation government is that of the City. The other two should simply be dissolved and assisted to find meaningful employment. Any process for redefining local government would, of course, need to give this whole matter the most serious of thought. As implemented now, all levels of local government are obsolete in the extreme, if for no other reason than the existing backward status of government as master over servant individuals.

A Final Word on Process

Here's a final thought to mull over concerning this process. It should be abundantly clear to everyone by now that whatever solution is generated, whether by debate and agreement (such as described here) or by simply continuing to drift into the future, it will without doubt be acceptable only for a period of time that is finite. In our view of goals and methods today we are only better than Madison and the others *because* of their pioneering and their leadership to create a better society, which meant at that time through government. If we succeed in building an improved future — in this case through a purposeful minimization of government and an elevation of the individual — then it too will have a *finite* useful life. There

161

is no way to anticipate future conditions or future needs, and that is why the suggestion is now made to allow for almost continual review and rework of ANY solution that might result. *Power will always be a problem. Coping with it will never be easy or permanent.*

The Just and permanent foundation for all such work rests upon **Individual Sovereignty.**

CHAPTER 18
A Far Better Government, Its Functions & Structure
A Strawman Proposal

Some Basics of Government-Forming

Any group of people willing to accept the heavy responsibilities of managing a nation and all the hamlets that are part of it, will have, collectively, all the limitations, infirmities and abilities common to the human breed. Thus, any charter with government must be designed with those built-in human limitations clearly in mind. The very minimum set of jobs that can be justified through reason, should be our goal. Furthermore, no one person has the ability to manage all functions of a government, be it national or local, a truism that has been demonstrated convincingly by all the American presidents of the last century, and many of the governors and mayors across the country.

It is also urgent to find a way to separate essential functions into independent parts. That is a critical goal as we redefine the new American government. Two implications of this last thought are important to note. First be very careful in deciding the functions that must be assigned to government, and second, define a structure that will allow each to be carried out independent of the others, but under the close scrutiny of other branches of government.

Once these critical preliminaries take form, and a consensus begins to emerge among the overwhelming majority of Americans, attention can then shift to formalizing the people's decisions in a new contract. Men and women best suited to perform these critical duties will then be guided by their contract which is taken directly from America's new Constitution Two. (Constitution Two is discussed in the next chapter.)

I suggest that a nationwide debate would be an extremely useful way to reach a consensus concerning government. This book is the kick-off for such a debate, and to help it get started I've made a serious attempt to define a new American government, its functions, structure and safeguards, that does away with all of the things that are wrong with government today, keeps what is good, and takes very much into account the foibles humans still fall victim to.

163

Guidelines for Defining a New Government

As part of a Strawman Proposal, certain guidelines can be stated that follow the overriding philosophy behind this entire treatise. The intention is that these principles would be appropriate to any form of government that might result from the process described in Chapter 17 and which satisfies the needed changes. Such guidelines include the following:

- Government functions will be carried out by organizations under contract to the people, with safeguards for performance, termination etc. as standard features. These are administrative contracts with established management organizations that must meet stated requirements. While staff can have longer tenure than the duration of the contract, they too must meet specific requirements for performance and adherence to American ideals.
- Most changes of substance will be via Referendum, as defined by the Constitution;
- Referendum approval for change (again, per the Constitution) requires 80 to 90 percent of the adult population;
- Policy making, for both domestic and foreign policy, is based on the intentions that they be permanent, not subject merely to the latest cadre of government office holders.
- Organizations submitting proposals to perform one or more required functions of a particular national administration (previously thought of as a government agency) must meet specific minimum requirements of competency of personnel at every level, in education, experience and philosophy, in keeping with the intent of the Constitution. The same provisos apply to proposals pertaining to local government functions.
- There is no single focal point of government power. Each Agency, assigned a specific function is given that assignment via contract which is effectively a subcontract of the overall Constitution.
- All contracts between the people and an agency are issued for periods of time that vary from three[3] years to ten [10] years depending on the function, but **none** shall be for longer than ten.
- The national armed forces shall continue to have the same relationship to the civilian government as exists presently, and shall follow the policies of civilian government which in turn are answerable to the people.
- Access to the use of force by the various agencies will be carefully stipulated by the controlling contract for each agency.
- Legislation drafted by the various agencies of government shall be required, among other tests, to demonstrate constitutionality first before enactment can occur. Availability of funding within constitutional guidelines and limits is also required before enactment.

- The **provisions** for new legislation shall not be initiated by attorneys. Their role is to write final drafts per the provisions defined by legislators who are the product of formal humanity disciplines rather than legal disciplines.
- All laws legislated by government (at all levels) have a finite life span, which is nominally 40 to 50 years, at which time it is automatically flushed from the Code. Other laws can have lesser life spans in keeping with the intent and needs of the particular laws.
- No organization to which a functional contract is entrusted can succeed itself in performing that function in the next period. This also applies to management individuals.
- The Constitution sets limitations on spending, contract terms, and terms of office.
- Establish and maintain a national Data Bank containing information on every subject of importance to national well being. This includes the background of people and their public acts (voting etc.), agency reports, reports by independent analysts of all issues and all other material needed by an informed people to make rational decisions on questions requiring a referendum vote. Full disclosure of all actions by all agencies will be standard except for national security. National security will act under a set of guidelines also set by the Constitution which recognizes the unique nature of that function. The need for people to rely on political organizations for information shall be obviated as a result of this Data Bank.
- There shall be no Judicial appointments by government agencies. All such posts are filled via separate contract with the people, for specific terms and conditions, with specific requirements appropriate to the goal of *Justice for individuals* and the *assurance of security for society*.
- The decision to declare War is too critical to be left to hired governmental agencies. A process which places the final decision with the people is to be made part of the operations of government, as described presently.
- Legal system guidelines will be created which will minimize the growing and destructive practice of law suites. This goal will be helped greatly by a complete review and elimination of bad laws, and by instituting a thorough, tough preliminary review process before acceptance as a court case.
- As part of the **Transition Plan**, all laws presently on the books will be reviewed, for retention or cancellation, and dates set for phasing out obsolete laws. Some cancellations can be immediate, others for five years hence and so forth, until the worst of the past is eliminated. (Additional thoughts on transition will be given presently.)

Criteria for Assigning Functions To Elements of Government

Empowering government, as was done 200 years ago, was an ad-hoc mixture of **proper** and **improper** ways to do the job. The men with the enlightened ideals were acting as private citizens truly working to improve everyone's life. Others were acting as *representatives* of colonial governments which already had long histories of being in power, and were jealous of that position. The resulting Constitution and government became the compromises we know. Stated in another way, the creation of an *ideal* government can not possibly be accomplished based upon a less-than-ideal process. That simple fact is trying to tell us that **only the people themselves** can form a just government, and it can be made into whatever form suits their joint purpose. The idealists of the time clearly stated the purposes for creating a new national government, one based on the highest of ideals. Those ideal aspirations are as much in force today as they were then.

There are two essential criteria for defining a government dedicated to upholding liberty and justice for the individual. Furthermore, any substitute criteria used as the basis for government would merely allow greater opportunity for repressive and even despotic rule later. The two essential criteria are these:

(a) The foundation of such a government is sovereignty of the individual and equality among all people. *Nothing else can take precedence.*

(b) Any function entrusted to government must be by virtually unanimous consent of all those to be governed, and only those functions so authorized can be performed by government.

Stated in a slightly different way, **government** does not decide what its functions are to be, and agreement for each function must have the same support of individuals extended for the purpose of security.

Notice something very important about this simple approach to identifying proper government functions. Such a ruling body can be given any task whatsoever, provided *only* that it is honorable and virtually **everyone** agrees to the job. So far in our national existence, only a single function has had that nearly 100% consent of the people. That function is security from threats, both internal and external. While the government in Washington, DC and state and local governments have taken on just about every function of control loosely called national (or local) goals, none of them have the same unqualified support as does the basic function of security. We congratulate ourselves for our practice of majority rule. Unfortunately that simple practice has been so warped that we now meekly accept government dictates derived not from any true majority but from an ever-shrinking percentage of people, ginned up for the moment, a collection of special interests that has nothing to do with any real consensus from the population as a whole.

If you accept the premise that government functions must have nearly everyone's agreement, then at least one of two things is true. Either the US Constitution allows government to usurp functions without citizen approval, or

166

government is in violation of the Constitution in many of its present day practices. We have seen that both these causes of our problem with government are at work in the United States. If you believe that requiring agreement by nearly everyone is an impractical goal, then we need to think more seriously about the consequences of that bit of democratic philosophy.

The twin functions currently appropriate to government, namely security and cooperative goals, should be the framework within which we try to decide the details of how we shall govern ourselves. Every possible derivative concern of government should also be of concern to the governed. The debate that must take place soon should dwell heavily and carefully on deciding which functions will be within the control of government. It may well turn out that all those functions that now fit within the 'National Goals" category do not have to be functions performed by government agencies

Functions For Debate - A Strawman Set of Functions

As a point of departure, this part of the discussion offers a list of independent functions that *might* be entrusted to government. It is a purposely truncated version of what exists today and is given here partly to contrast it with the all-pervasive set being used today, and partly as an introduction of ideas that need much more thought from all Americans. The motivation is to seek a simpler structure for self-government in the belief that the composition, rules of operation, complexity and the huge size of today's government are all failures and are becoming progressively worse.

Government is intimately tied to the application of force where it is needed. Thus, each of the following Strawman Functions is potentially associated with access to force at some level. As each potential government function is deliberated, the very consideration of whether force need be a part of that function, and what force level would be needed, might very well decide the question to include the function or not.

1. *Security* (the first purpose of government) requires a *National Security Function* with a military arm whose ultimate control rests with a civilian commander-in-chief or command council. Illegal immigration, is now being recognized as a modern form of invasion needing provisions never before required for control. Illegal immigration is a part of the National Security Finction, which coordinates its activities with function numbers 2, 3 and 7.

2. *Security* requires a *Foreign Policy Function*, which is predicated on a stability of attitude and actions toward every other nation, and not subject to capricious change with changes in leadership. The Foreign Policy Function includes the functions of treaty negotiations and intelligence gathering.

Regarding illegal immigration, the Foreign Policy Function also works with foreign countries to eliminate the causes for flight to the USA.

3. *Security* requires an *Internal Security Function* nationwide and at the local level, all elements sharing a criminal database and an information distribution system designed to preclude a criminal's ability to "disappear" within the system. ISF reviews and coordinates proposed NSF actions in its duties to minimize illegal immigration. Action of NSF must meet safeguards in place for the protection of individuals.

4. *Cooperative Goals* (heretofore the second purpose of government) suggests an *Infrastructure Function* which is concerned with the long term relationships between the pursuit of happiness of individuals nationwide, and the wise use of national assets. Energy production, transport and national treasures are the chief elements to be managed in assuring people the opportunity forimproved living. .

5. *Cooperative Goals* suggests an *Environmental Function* which monitors all elements of nature essential to life, including water, soil, and air. The concern is for all life, not just human life, and the intent of this function is to balance human population and the freedom of individuals against the use and misuse of these essentials to life as is then within our technological capabilities.

6. *Security* and *Cooperative Goals* both require a *Commerce Function*. That related to security is a special section of the Justice Function concerned with business oriented criminal activity. Definition of crime within the world of commerce and the monitoring and investigation of criminal activity are the main concerns here. The Commerce Function related to cooperative goals is the balancing half of commerce which is to uphold that part of American civilization that helped to make it great, namely free enterprise, an entrepreneurial spirit, productivity and a work ethic with rewards to the individual. The purview of the Commerce Functiion is world wide.

7. *Cooperative Goals* requires an *Internal Policy Function* completely analogous to the Foreign Policy Function. Its concern is with the stability of livability within the nation, which means specifically that people can rely on an even-handed, consistent and sympathetic approach in internal government policy. Monetary stability is a major concern, and internal policy must have as one of its guiding criteria the goal to see that money decisions made by young families can be expected to endure for a lifetime. IPF, as watchdog for individual rights, works with NSF to protect against improper illegal immigration countermeasures

8.   Consideration should be given for a *Citizens Advocate Function* concerned with Cooperative Goals as well as security, with direct access for individuals or groups to government agencies via the Citizens Advocate Function. By such a function it may be feasible to shorten the inordinately long time now squandered in addressing issues of most concern to the people. Not only would the Citizens Advocate Function monitor and investigate such concerns, but it would also then have direct access to other government functions involved. It would provide the oft quoted 'redress of grievances" now guaranteed in the Bill of Rights, but which is still sadly deficient 200 years after the promise.

9.   *Security* requires a *Justice Function* which is guided first by *justice* to the individual and second, by the definition of law. Governments have defined law at their whim for millennia, much of which has little to do with justice. The guiding criteria for this Justice Function, of course, will come from the constitutional contract prepared and agreed to by the people. A major task within the Justice Function, therefore, is the review of all proposed legislation **before** it can be acted upon within the *Legislative Function*.

10.   *Both objectives* of a rational government require a *Funding Function*. Such a function can be viewed as a second **independent** filter (comparable to the constitutionality filter provided by the *Justice Function*) applied to all proposed legislation. Two criteria must be satisfied. One is that the proposed legislation show all costs over the life of the bill and the means by which costs will be met. Second is that new costs, arising from the proposal, will not cause the spending limit to be exceeded in any year. A further guide to total spending in the execution of all functions of government is that government will have spending authorization comparable to families and businesses. In particular, this allows borrowing from willing lenders, but all debts require repayment of principle and interest sufficient to retire the debt within the period negotiated. There will be no interest-only debt. The cost of principle and interest for each year is a direct part of the cost of government and must be within the authorized limit for each year. Most important is that no change to the authorized limit can take place without the consent, through referendum, of 85% of all citizens above the age of 18. It is also the **goal** of citizens that all costs of government ultimately be met via an endowment process still to be defined.

11. The final possible function of government is the *Legislative Function* and is required to accomplish both purposes of national government. The legislating function does not *originate* proposed changes to law or proposed spending programs. Instead, it provides a review and an accept/reject function and then oversees preparation of the actual proposed legislative document.

Each such document is effectively a specification of an element of law or of a program to spend from the authorized general account. This function is necessarily dependent on obtaining the services of the very best and wisest from among the entire population, with a premium being placed on their selection as a result of past exemplary service elsewhere in government.

*   *   *

This set of functions is offered as a potential starting point for debate and discussion for devising an improved structure for self government. The intent is to build upon the elements of government that have served well and discard those elements that have caused such a precipitous loss of individual freedom, individual wealth, and individual initiative so critical to promoting the true strengths of America.

Nothing in this list allows those many other functions that our present government has enacted unilaterally to our great loss. Education, health care, confiscation, over-regulation of business, granting of subsidies, donations of wealth to other countries, and sales of war machines are examples of functions that deserve no further role in American self-government.

Among these excesses of government acts, their outlandish drift to ever greater giveaways deserves special attention. In a seemingly relentless quest by government to solve with money all the world's problems and, inde ed, the problems within our own borders, there is at work the violating of a very simple truth. *No one has the unilateral right to extract wealth from sovereign individuals for the purpose of giving it to other individuals or other countries, no matter what the motivations are.*

Furthermore, before using a government solution to a perceived need, remember that there are at least two other ways to help where help is needed. These are ways far more sensible than the grossly inefficient government giveaway process. Best by far is the use of voluntary offerings from probably the most generous people ever known. The plenty Americans have reaped for themselves has been happily shared with those in need, but when that same bounty is forcibly extracted through repressive taxation, the spirit of giving is damaged immensely.

A second way to extend help comes by recognizing that opportunities for commercial profit often exist within the set of circumstances surrounding the need. Cooperative efforts among private companies, individuals, and ad hoc organizations can fill many needs, even of disparate people. Inner city redevelopment through private enterprise zones is an excellent example of solving critical needs without government involvement, and in projects we've seen, done *in spite of* government restrictions.

Take particular note of the fact that government has no function to define government functions! That job is exclusively the province of the people who are seeking help to benefit themselves by commissioning jobs beyond their own capabilities.

Trying to construct a government is exactly analogous to trying to make a reliable machine using unreliable parts (in this case, people). The design, therefore, must be made fault-tolerant, where continuous monitoring for faults takes place, where agreement among *independent* elements of government must exist before any action takes place and where failed elements can be isolated (i.e. detected) and taken out of active use. Once again, this implies access to necessary police force to counter criminal activity.

The parts of such a machine (the people) must meet a minimum set of requirements exactly as automobile parts must meet certain specifications. Those requirements must be appropriate to each function, governmental and automotive, and a simple declaration by a candidate of intent to function on behalf of the governed is but a minor one of those requirements. Surely qualifications to handle governmental functions are every bit as important as those needed to perform in other demanding and complicated business functions. Political ambitions and OJT have long been insufficient for the tasks. Designing a better government means to write an improved specification for it, detailing *requirements* that then become part of a *second generation constitution*.

Elaboration of the Strawman Government

Consider now some elaboration of the particular **STRAWMAN** government introduced here. It is offered mostly to stimulate thought, since many of the ideas regarding structure, functions and guidelines depart markedly from what we have come to regard as 'normal." I have tried to test these ideas against the set of fundamentals I believe to be necessary to elevate self-government to the next plateau of excellence. Only discussion, brainstorming and debate, backed by reliable information and analysis can determine the best direction for us to take, but here is a beginning to focus upon.

How close this particular attempt at restructuring government comes to being the hoped-for solution to our problem with today's government is certainly not known. However, I will make the rash assertion that as it stands in this very form, this new government framework is easily a quantum step above today's American government. Further, I contend the statement applies for all levels of government, local and national. Every existing government body uses the same deficient philosophy, uses unwarranted force and coercion against citizens and should no longer be tolerated. I believe, however, that the process I've outlined, or something like it, must be carried out diligently in order to assure the participation of as many people as possible. The people are an essential part of any attempt to fix government, because without them, nothing of permanent value can possibly result. Without the full involvement of the people, the most likely outcome of trying to better ourselves would be extremism and militant anarchism which is just another way of saying **chaos**.

The tentative national government will be charged initially with performing eight functions as shown in the table below. These are functions required by the people to assure itself of security, stability and a means of accomplishing worthy goals as a nation in an increasingly complex world society. Three other functions are also considered for possible later addition, provided acceptable means other than government can not be settled upon. The functions are labeled as follows:

NATIONAL FUNCTION	SYM.	LOCAL FUNCTION ALSO?
• *Citizens Advocate Function*	[CA]	YES
• *Justice Function*	[J]	YES
• *Internal Policy Function*	[IP]	YES
• *Internal Security Function*	[IS]	YES
• *Foreign Policy Function*	[FP]	-
• *National Security Function*	[NS]	-
• *Funding Function*	[F]	YES
• *Legislative Function*	[L]	YES

Functions for Possible Privatization or Later Addition to Government

• *Infrastructure Function*	[I]	Possible
• *Environmental Function*	[E]	YES
• *Commerce Function*	[C]	Possible

The preliminary monitoring and approval responsibilities of each of the Agencies are indicated in the following table

Strawman Monitoring Responsibilities of Agencies
Those Monitored by Each Agency

- Citizen Advocate :: [J], [IP], [IS], [FP], [NS], [F], & [L]
- Justice :: [CA], [IS], [FP], [NS], [F], & [L]
- Internal Policy :: [I], & [E]
- Internal Security :: [FP], & [C]
- Foreign Policy :: [NS]
- National Security :: [FP]
- Funding :: [CA], [IP], [IS], [L], [I], & [E]
- Legislative :: [IP], [IS], [E], & [C]

- Infrastructure :: has no monitoring responsibilities
- Environmental :: [I]
- Commerce :: [FP], & [I]

Strawman Monitoring Responsibilities of Agencies
Each Agency - Monitored By:

- Citizen Advocate :: [J], & [F],
- Justice :: [CA]
- Internal Policy :: [CA], [F], & [L]
- Internal Security :: [CA], [J], [F], & [L]
- Foreign Policy :: [CA], [J], [IS], [NS], & [C]
- National Security :: [CA], [J], & [FP]
- Funding :: [CA], & [J]
- Legislative :: [CA], [J] & [F]

- Infrastructure :: [IP], [F], [E], & [C]
- Environmental :: [IP], [F], & [L]
- Commerce :: [IS], & [L]

Where the three Agencies, [I], [E] and [C] are still thought of as possible government functional agencies. Means other than government may be feasible.

173

The Twelfth Element of Government Structure is the Body of Citizens itself

The people will become a permanent part of the decision-making process via referendum, with those issues to be included under such action carefully defined in the new Constitution. The government agencies as defined here are no longer allowed to operate without feedback and guidance from the people. Furthermore, a completely changed set of controls and monitoring procedures are created, along with the use of referenda, to assure that the machinery of government does not become unstable in the sense of duplicating excesses of the present or other clever inventions of selfish, little people. In this context, stability means *explicitly* that the rights and sovereignty of individuals remain as the prime criteria in the making of decisions. Each function is charged to a different agency, and agencies are independent of each other except regarding specified paths of approval for their actions. The previous table shows these dependencies. The extent of monitoring responsibilities and the level of approval control to be exercised would be set by the Constitution. An objective of these monitoring assignments is to avoid mutual control, (where each controls the other) and to share responsibilities so that collusion between agencies becomes extremely difficult if not impossible. As shown, there are three king-pin agencies which demand the very highest caliber people and planning of the utmost care. They are the *Citizens Advocate, Justice and Funding* functional agencies. Mutual control exists among these three because of the nature of their functions, but the key difference here is that none of these agencies initiates legislation. Collusion should be less of a problem, therefore. If that assumption proves to be wrong, then the ultimate monitor and controller comes into play, namely American citizens, all having direct access to the [CA] agency. As will be discussed in the section which describes STEP 3, the work of an independent *Performance Monitoring Council* monitors all government activities for the express purpose of refining government operations, and initiating changes via referendum, including possible termination of an agency contract.

A few examples will help explain how to interpret the last table. The *Funding Agency* carries out the Constitutional requirements, allowances and limitations for raising all funds to be expended by government agencies, and jointly establishes budgets for each agency except National Security. These budgets then become the target contract values used by [CA] in negotiating contracts with each agency. [F] has fiscal control over agency size via the contract size set for each, but [CA] is the most important voice in final contract decisions. In addition [F] has the responsibility of maintaining fiscal control through trade-off negotiations with all agencies to assure that expenditures for the coming period will not exceed the total revenue collected during the previous period, nominally yearly, but possibly of a different duration.

Borrowing is restricted to wartime only or such other times as approved by referendum, and is limited to borrowing from American citizens only. [F] acts as a

174

mediator between other agencies regarding transfer of funds between or among them to allow some flexibility of operation. Final approval for such swaps must come from [CA]. Otherwise funding limits are set by Constitutional contracts let by [CA]. In particular [F] has the responsibility to Review and Approve proposed legislation from three agencies, Internal Security, Internal Policy, and Legislative, and possibly three others, Environment, Commerce and Infrastructure, if privatization proves to be impractical. Funding for National Security, which is primarily military needs, is set via a completely different route, beginning with the Constitution, then via [CA], through National Policy and then to National Security.

The Funding Agency, in turn, is monitored for approval of its actions by two other agencies, namely Justice and Citizens Advocate. That agency, [CA], has two primary functions as defined by the new Constitution. The first is to oversee the preparation and execution of contracts to all agencies, assuring that constitutional requirements are met. The second function is to provide direct access of citizens to government activities as a means of addressing specific grievances that may arise. Redress can be obtained via two avenues. The first is through the Justice Agency, and is intended to cover any matter of law and justice. The second entrée is via the permanent independent *Performance Monitoring Council*, a body entirely separate from government (to be described presently) which is charged with the continual review of government performance and the **perpetual task of considering changes to government**. It is the specific vehicle established to preserve choice by citizens of government form, actions and controls. This body is funded by endowment. In the event that [CA] becomes a deliberate blockade to referendum, the Performance Monitoring Council can submit them directly to the people for resolution.

The Justice Function, [J], has a drastically changed charter from that of present government. It is no longer a passive onlooker while bad legislation continues to be passed. [J] is charged with *review — and approval — of all legislation for constitutionality*. This review follows that done by the legislators themselves for the same purpose. The goal is to create law, applicable to the *entire nation*, which never again will be judged unconstitutional later as some hapless citizen struggles to undo the damage done by government. That goal will not come easily, and I fully expect that this upgrade toward true justice in the United States will need our best efforts for a long time to come. It will not be automatic even after such changes to government and the Justice system. [J] reviews all legislative proposals, all of which come to it via the Legislative Agency, [L], and in effect has monitoring responsibility over all agencies which initiate new law. There are two such agencies nationally, namely the Foreign Policy and Internal Policy Agencies, with the possibility that three others, namely Commerce, Environment and Infrastructure may be added depending on privatization decisions. [J] is the champion of Unalienable Rights of individuals, and of Justice, rather than the mere keeper of law. Justice will also have direct access to enforcement assets to ferret out crime within government agencies.

Wars - Declared & Undeclared

The making of war is an awesome enterprise. The history of wars instigated by the US government shows that officials have not met the intentions of the people on too many occasions. This requires that the guidelines be changed. Our representatives have not served well from the very beginning from actions against the unfortunate American Indians to the hapless Vietnamese. Even our international 'police" actions have often been unnecessary as independent actions. None of consequence were such as to demand action without forewarning. The change that is needed now seems very clear. Declaring and engaging in war should be a four step process, with the final step being approval by the people. The four steps are as follows, beginning with the most important one.

- Final approval to declare **WAR** is via referendum only. In no instance may war be waged without approval of the people. The Constitution requires that such an action be approved by 90% of all adult citizens.
- Justice must approve Citizens Advocate's recommendation for a War referendum. Their chief function is to insure constitutionality of such a proposed action.
- Only the Citizens Advocate Agency can give approval to recommend that a War referendum be submitted to the people. Also [CA] may initiate a War recommendation and referendum.
- The Foreign Policy Agency can submit a recommendation to [CA] to declare War.

It is conceivable that [FP] might actually want to instigate war for selfish or illegal purposes, and succeed in withholding vital information from the people and from [CA]. Another check is, therefore, needed, and is provided by requiring that both [CA] and [J] have full access to all classified information generated and collected by the Foreign Policy and National Security agencies. No information may be withheld from that segment of these two agencies charged with oversight responsibilities for foreign affairs.

There is one other critical aspect of War that must be emphasized. An earlier discussion singled out the constitutional error regarding this, and the error must not be repeated. **Under no circumstances** is government allowed to diminish the fundamental, Constitutional, Unalienable Rights of the people by any measure whatsoever.

These preliminary responsibilities of government agencies and others are shown in the following Table.

176

Function Responsibilities of Strawman Government Agencies

Citizen Advocate	Justice
Interface directly with the people, provide entrée to government.	Review & Monitor all legislation for constitutionality
Legal representation is not required	
Prepare all Referendum submissions	Review CA contracts with all agencies
Create framework for US Foreign Policy per Constitution	To pass, a US Supreme Court decision must be unanimous
Has final decision to submit War referendum to the people	Act with Citizens Advocate on removal recommends from PMC
Create contracts for all agencies; Change per PMC requirements*	Monitor all government functions with CA
Devise requirements, tests etc. for Justice contracts per Constitution	Review any War referendum for approval or rejection
Review legislation & test whether it is for referendum, or meets national goals requirements	Monitor enforcement units of Internal Security for performance with regard to Individual Rights **
Act with Justice on removal recommendations from PMC	
Establish funding for National Security per Constitution	Is charged with minimizing law suites within the US
With Justice, Monitor recommendations from Funding Agency	Collaborate with the new Justice Agencies as needed to preserve Rights& Sovereignty affected by criminal and civil investigations
Create career profiles for all Government functions	
Create & maintain national government data base	

Internal Policy	Internal Security
Draft internal legislation, demonstrate constitutionality, & submit	Create national crime data base, track criminal cases nationwide
proposed bills to Legislation Agency	
Administer Internal Policy programs approved via referendum	Create & maintain national forensic labs & R&D
[e.g. disaster relief, medical other R&D, space programs]	Provide surveillance, data gathering & investigation
Draft proposed referendums for national goals	Provide special national response force

Foreign Policy	National Security
Draft long term policies for each nation	Maintain national armed forces, & their readiness
Provide diplomatic liaison	Administer R&D for military needs per policies of FP Agency
Draft legislation, demonstrate constitutionality & submit to Legislation Agency	Create & maintain intelligence service units

177

Foreign Policy – (Continued)

Provide civilian control of national armed forces

Gather intelligence, maintain an open and a restricted data base

Propose aid packages to CA & J for proposed referendum

Can submit recommendation for war to CA

National Security - (Continued)

Respond to overt attacks by foreign nations or forces

Funding

Review all legislation for funding availability & constitutionality

Establish budgets for all agencies

Enforce constitutional limits on funding via control of the money

Establish contract budgets for CA

Mediate budget negotiations between agencies

Collect and invest sales tax proceeds to pay for government expenses for the **next** year

Legislation

Review all legislation submittals for constitutionality

Write final form of all legislation with no add-ons

Submit legislation to Justice for final approval

Coordinate with F for funding availability

Enact legislation once all approvals are obtained

*Performance Monitoring Council [PMC] a non government body

Measure performance of all agencies against guideline goals

Collect & study all inputs for possible future changes to government

Prepare recommended changes to government for submission to CA & to J for referendum; iterate as needed

Submit recommendations to CA & J for cancellation of an agency contract, or change in personnel; or submit directly to referendum,
with high percent needed to enact the recommendation.

THE PEOPLE

Vote on all referenda submitted; high percent approval needed to enact or change anything.

Remain informed via national data base

Interact with Citizens Advocate Agency for judicial and constitutional matters

Retain **final** decision with regard to War via referendum only

Vote on CA contracts with all governmental agencies

Elections, Voting and Representation

One of the visions Madison, Jefferson and the others had was to include the common man in the decisions of government as a means of protecting him against abuses from that source. Equal Representation was the criterion they felt was essential if the people were ever to maintain control over government excesses. They were correct in their comprehension of its need. What went wrong was a combination of two things that contribute to true representation. Both of these failings have been discussed earlier, but it's fair to recall them here to understand the motivation for proposing an entirely different method to reach the same objective. As it stands now the concept of equal representation requires that each person's vote have the same weight in decision-making, and that decisions be made on the basis of a majority, for one side or another. In practice here in the US, neither element of the concept operates to enable true and equal representation. In virtually every case *majority* approval for government actions has been so warped that it is now negated completely. Diligent searching for any example showing where truly one half of the people have shown agreement *for any action* will come up empty, because there are none. Votes are segmented so thoroughly that *the outcome of every government move* is decided by a mere handful of voters or their representatives.

Becoming involved in a war in Vietnam is as bad an example of the distortion of the hope for true representation as I can recall, but it is a potent indicator of just what I mean regarding representation. In effect no individual of group had a meaningful say in this, an action that was as important as one can imagine. The manner of implementing Representation, as embodied in the present Constitution, failed utterly at the most *fundamental level* of representation, namely keeping us out of war.

The method of equal representation likewise fails in every other instance of citizen participation in deciding on actions by government. The main difference between issues such as war against Vietnam and other government acts, is that less potential trauma rides on these other decisions, but each one usually amounts to another "legal" intrusion into citizen rights. The cumulative effect of these intrusions, however, in my view, does rival in seriousness the debacle of Vietnam, it has been that bad.

Representatives can not represent anyone except themselves when a vote is taken. Constituents at home who happen to agree with a particular vote seem to have been represented, but the likelihood that such a vote has majority approval is almost always near zero. It is also a cold reality that legislators rarely even concern themselves with the majority consensus when they vote on legislation. Being representatives, they vote as they understand the issues, as they must. Whether their vote represents a majority opinion among their constituents is a non-factor to them.

For those at home who disagreed with that vote, their representation was in fact zero. Their voice had no champion, no representative, because they themselves were excluded, having no possibility of being heard directly or indirectly.

The present method of assuring citizens a voice in their own future does not work. They are not represented equally, and in effect, they are not directly *represented* at all. Today's government structure has handed the power to vote *on all issues* to a small subset of people by removing the citizen vote from all decision procedures except via referendum. That is precisely why politicians work so hard to prevent its use, because the referendum is much more effective as a means of controlling government actions. Perhaps the closest to achieving equality of vote is the use of State-wide balloting on Propositions in California and a few other States. Here, at least, the final step in the sequence to act is referred to the voters at large. All the other deficiencies remain, however.

Lest we forget, the most barefaced inequality of representation is actually an integral part of the constitutional structure of the national government and state governments as well. Two 'representatives," called Senators, assemble from each State to decide on critical national issues. Whether a State has thirty million people or one million, it has two senators. The foolishness of this arrangement is so obvious, and the inequality of representation so obtrusive, that its existence is dumfounding. Clearly, these men and women should not be speaking for their respective States, and must have a national perspective in what they do. If that is so, then why are they chosen two to a State, an artificial breakdown of the national total? Why is this huge, erroneous holdover from colonial days never discussed? Possibly the answer to that lies in tradition, which we all agree has great value. But traditions in ritual, in family, in schools and the like should not be confused with traditions in *dictates* from government which can not balance violations against the rights of sovereign individuals. The structure of government, which may have been a logical one at the end of the eighteenth century, cannot stand the test of logic today. The tradition of handing these senators the power they hold and allowing them to decide national matters, simply because that is the way things began some two hundred years ago, is poor reason to think it must continue unquestioned. Much more likely is the possibility that the structure of a Senate within government represents a now defunct sop to the supposed sovereignty states still attribute to themselves.

States have erroneously viewed themselves more as independent nations, with privileges and sovereignty befitting their exalted stations, than as part of a unified nation. National oneness has never been as strong as our regard for our own State — except during wartime — and the battle between national and local governments has been a persistent characteristic of the United States since the founding. One might argue that the two protagonists help to control each other; to which the obvious reply is, in what way? At the very least, assuming that a Senate were to remain as part of government makeup, its members must be chosen on the basis of completely different criteria, experience, philosophy and wisdom. To think otherwise is to be tricked by confusions surrounding tradition and government.

From one perspective, this can be seen as a strong indicator of why government has failed across the spectrum of agencies to carry out the prime objectives of self government.

There has never been even nominal control, by the people, of government actions in all of our history, because the means to exercise control has never existed.

Enfranchising citizens as we have (to vote on representatives only) does not do it in the least, and it should be no surprise that the very act of exercising that franchise has slowly dissipated with time. The People clearly have been perceptive enough to realize that their vote is essentially worthless as a means of controlling foolishness and excesses within the nation. And that very same condition exists within each state and each city, which are structured and guided in the same improper way. The resulting value of a citizen's vote is essentially worthless as a means of control. Power has been placed in the hands of a small number of people called representatives, but they exercise that power according to their own agenda and not as representatives of the rest of the people.

The real agenda, therefore, is essentially that of the two, indistinguishable major political parties, which in turn are controlled by a mere handful of individuals.

That power was put there by today's Constitution, and we the voters keep it in their hands whether we vote or not. One is forced to conclude that **representation** can not work, that each person must represent herself or himself. It is quite clear from government's actions over the past two hundred years that the conclusion must be correct, since the people are effectively non-participants in the business of governing themselves. As added corroboration, we know this is so, because in failing their honor-bound duty to the people, the consequences to officials have been completely nonexistent. For me to be comfortable with the concept of representation, i.e. where someone else makes MY decisions for me, I must have a great deal of confidence in that representative. I know of pitifully few in whom I have such trust. The greatest extent to which I would be willing to delegate representative tasks is to *trust certain people* to generate **options** from which I might then make my own selections. But that is the limit to which I am willing to accede to representation. The process of representation, like voting, is not a workable one, as proven by the results of its two hundred year test period.

Majority Rule

The second half of the method used to assure citizen control of government supposedly comes via the concept of **majority rule**. This issue has already been discussed at length. The summary notion is that if a true majority ever actually did decide a matter, either nationally or locally, then the wishes of the other half of the voters are disregarded completely. The 50 % dividing line between go and no-go is completely without merit. In considering why such a threshold came into use there seems to be no satisfying answer. Concern about non action may be part of it, but the consequences of doing an action when half oppose it has led to chronic *errors of commission* in the fear of a **possible** error for doing nothing. That threshold must change, and the Strawman proposal does just that. In the process it whisks away all of the ills that have become attached to representation as we know it now.

The vote that people cast for representatives is essentially worthless, and the net effect has been the mountain of bad legislation to come out of Washington DC and **every other local legislative body** in the nation. The few positives to come from them, and there are very few, can not be argued to have balanced the disasters on the negative side of the ledger.

The proposal, therefore, is to do away with elections for representatives. In its place will be an entirely different, two element process that assures that a great deal of control will reside in the hands of the people while still accomplishing what truly needs to be done.

First, all those issues defined in the Constitution that are to be settled by referendum, require citizen vote for passage. Furthermore, those issues can not be written in such a way as to create a lose- lose, or a win-win result which would subvert the intention of the Constitution. They must be written in such a way as to require approval of the **threshold majority** before action can be taken. Negative 'approval" is not allowed, and the Justice Agency will assure that this provision is met in all matters submitted to the people as a referendum. As part of this procedure, that *threshold majority* required for approval, will be in accordance with Constitutional provisions, as previously approved by the people when they adopted Constitution Two. The assumption being made here is that these levels of approval thresholds will be set very high, so that MOST people will indeed be represented upon passage of critical issues, *or it won't be passed.*

As an addition to its normal responsibilities, the Citizens Advocate Agency will carry out a thorough study of the reasoning behind those who disapproved a particular referendum. The purpose is to search for any potential fundamental problems in the governing process as evidenced by the negative vote, and thereby be prepared to recommend future changes in government toward preserving the rights of all individuals and of society as a whole.

The **second** element of the process that puts control back into the hands of citizens is assured via their part in approving the contracts to all government agencies. These too are referendum issues. Each cycle of contractual review for an agency includes voter review and approval. This would occur once the preliminary work of the Citizens Advocate and Justice agencies is complete. Since each agency contract has its own term duration, such referenda will not be a yearly event for all agencies, but will be staggered to meet Constitution requirements. The final item to mention is that each contract is partitioned into a number of viable parts which are voted upon separately. The entire contract is not a go, no-go ultimatum, and Constitutional provisions exist to handle the situation where approval is withheld by the people on all or part of the proposed provisions.

The conclusion one should come to regarding voting and representation is that the new structure and procedures discard today's useless approach and replace it with one that actually does place control of government in the hands of the people. This is not a matter of day-to-day micromanagement, but is an effective means by which citizen goals remain preeminent in government actions. Voting is used not to elect representatives, but for referendum issues only, of which there may be many. This is done instead of perpetuating the pretense that representation works and is an untouchable institution.

The vote of today has become as useless as politicians could possibly hope for, having become just another tool for political manipulation. Since we recognize this, the proposed structure transforms the vote back into a useful tool of the people instead of politicians.

Operating Procedures
Some of the thoughts related to government operation have been mentioned already. A few others will give an extended view of the interactions, safeguards, controls etc. that would apply as this new form of self government deals with the American presence in today's complex world.

To simplify the discussion, assume that the transition from old to new government is complete, and that the function set allotted to government is the minimum. Functions include only the following: Citizen Advocate, Justice, Internal Security, Internal Policy, Foreign Policy, Funding, Legislative and National Security. There are also two other very important assumptions to note. First, all the information generated by and about government is available to every adult citizen via an updated version of the Internet, with enough public access sites to accommodate anyone who doesn't have a home computer. That same system will also be the means for voting on referendum issues, with suitable coding for security and verification.

The second assumption is that the hierarchy of government, national and local, has been decided upon, and that the nation has **ONE** Constitution, not 51. This is a huge assumption. It is made here in the belief that differences in fundamental guidelines for governing can not **justly** exist between different locations within a unified nation. We are either forming a single social entity called America, or we bow to meaningless differences among us and create fifty different nations. Since there are no real differences in the Unalienable Rights and Individual Sovereignty of the people in all the fifty States, then the assumption must hold. The very act of approving the new Constitution nationwide would validate the assumption. Therefore, before leaving the subject, a few more of the operational procedures within the new government will help give a better picture of this new institution for self-governing.

- **National Security** [NS] is the civilian administration agency for all military resources, intelligence gathering resources and defense research & development assets. Justice [J] and Citizen Advocate [CA] have joint responsibility for **review and approval** of [NS] actions and information which may be outside the requirement of full disclosure to the people. [NS] has no responsibility except advisory related to declaring war.
- **Foreign Policy** [FP] is charged with maintaining stable policies with regard to every other nation in the world, taking due regard for theirs toward the US. Only [FP] can recommend that a state of war be instituted against another nation. In such recommendations, they are accepted or rejected jointly by [CA] and [J], and when accepted, the recommendation is submitted to a referendum vote of the people, who have the **final** voice in the matter.
- A progression of career advancement paths will be established through the various agencies of government which are meant to utilize to the fullest the capabilities and experience of individuals. Rigidity among such steps is not the objective, but opportunity for advancement and prerequisites for most functional assignments is, while maintaining constant vigilance against excesses within government. Entrenchment in most of these posts is to be avoided. Those entrusted with government posts have every bit as much a need for meeting requirements as do those in military service, and merely being an American citizen, or having a willingness to exercise power are not sufficient for most cases.
- All agencies are subject to formal reviews, to be devised, which are reported to the people and to the independent Performance Monitoring Council. Chairmen of review boards serve for short, specified periods.
- Expenditures are limited, absolutely, to the actual receipts collected during the previous period, nominally one year. Money collected is done so in

accordance with the Constitution, and no change of any sort is allowed without referendum approval of 90 % of the total adult population.

• No government agency is allowed to give away any asset placed in its charge, nor can any agency sell US military assets to another country. Military support of allies in perilous situations, of which many exist today, is possible in accord with constitutional provisions and limitations, **or** via Referendum.

• The Constitution establishes certain funds for specific purposes approved by the people as the means of accomplishing shared national goals. These funds build up over time in accordance with the allocations approved and, until used, are invested for gain, and may not be used for purposes other than that intended. Disaster relief is an example of such a fund. Others might include space exploration, scientific research or pure R&D for potential advancements desired and approved by the people.

Local Verses National Government

In a nutshell there should be no difference between local and national governments in their structure or manner of operation. The Constitution that controls national activities and national level contracts, is also meant to control any other government body. The only difference between local and national is their jurisdiction. Individual rights are exactly the same, the prerogatives toward goals are the same, and the responsibilities of government toward security are the same.

Compartmentalization of the territory of the United States has been by States, Counties, Cities and Villages. Size, whims, and colonial holdovers have all played a part in creating this mix. The outcome has been an unending string of worthy and interesting traditions derived from local culture and conditions, and an ungainly mess of overlapping administrative organizations that chew up tax assets with no regard whatsoever for productivity, or performance.

An important part of the national debate must center around local government. We need to extract ourselves from the morass and abuses of local government every bit as much as from the national government. Choice must be returned to people, which means that local politicians must be divested of the powers they have usurped that have chipped away at the rights which belong to individuals. Without upsetting any of the traditions gained over time of the type involving states, counties and cities, **a totally different breakdown of *administrative regions* can and should be created,** where each can support a functionally oriented government similar to the national structure described earlier. A city orientation is my own choice, where rather loose boundaries are set which can enclose every chunk of land. The rules of operation within each such region would be the same as for national government, and the cross checks, limitations and extent of delegated powers also match those set in the Constitution.

Other Questions Regarding The STRAWMAN Government

Many questions arise from the structure outlined here. The details of how all this can be made to work properly cover a great range, and all of the issues need to be considered in detail if the major goals are to be reached. Clearly the job has just begun; precisely why I believe **a national debate is necessary to arrive at a reasonable end result**. Before moving on to the matters of drafting Constitution Two, and making the transition to a much improved government, let me list a few of those questions that come to mind.

- What checks can be made to set and approve the budget for [CA] ?
- Will the administrative review function of Justice over [CA] be enough to maintain a workable control ?
- Should the Legislative agency be used to *approve* actions of any other agency ?
- Should National Security be given an approval function of another agency ?
- If Infrastructure becomes a government function, is there a review and approval task for it as well ?
- I have argued that the Federal Reserve system is unnecessary. Does this require any other functions of the Funding Agency ?
- While direct quantitative performance monitoring is clearly possible, what is the optimum way to monitor the activities of Justice ?
- etc.

What Government Does NOT Do

Almost all of the things I've found fault with regarding government have been their errors of commission. They chronically do too much, and most of what they do beyond the scope of an IDEAL government has been wrong, or fraudulent, or unconstitutional, or excessive, or criminal. Therefore, we should be very clear about what the new government *does not do*. I take the case of government being structured as described here for the Strawman proposal, having eight functional agencies. The following is a list of some of the things *government will not do* that present government has done so poorly for so long.

- Government, of its own volition, does not give away any asset acquired by any means whatsoever.
- Government does not sell military surplus or any material to offset costs of national security or any government obligation. The transfer of military assets to allied nations requires that Foreign Policy includes such recommendations, and that they in turn have been approved according to the Constitution.
- Does not tax without referendum approval; therefore, there is no IRS. Initially, funding for government is provided by receipts from a national sales

tax for example, with appropriate items exempted, and agreed upon termination.

• Government is not in the health business, insurance business or education business.

• It does not deliver mail of any kind.

• It does not support Political Action Groups, the Arts or political campaigns for any individual or group. It does not subsidize any industry, company or group of people.

• It does not regulate or license any activity involving decisions of individuals or their property, for example regarding the manner of earning a living. Government's role is limited to the prevention of harm to Americans, and maintaining order under the constitutional principles.

• etc.

The list goes on and on, with government removed from untold numbers of improper enterprises it is now engaged in.

CHAPTER 19
The Best Hope to Advance American Government - Change the Constitution

Every modern government rests upon a defining document that states the founding ideals, the goals of union based on those ideals, the composition of bodies to govern the nation, the delegation of powers, their limitations, and the essential guidance on how that government shall operate. Some nations, Ireland for example, include the code of laws that will be followed. Doing so, however, can confuse the difference between guidelines and laws. The US constitution keeps the two separate, and any new constitution should do the same.

This chapter is an exposition of thoughts meant to show why the American constitution must change if our government is ever to be diverted from its present dangerous path to one which can elevate it to a truly great institution.

The American Constitution, therefore, must be our starting point. For once we must try to view it realistically to see our way through the present dilemma with government.

There is a remarkable paragraph that appears in the section called "A Word to the Reader," in a 1992 book by William Lee Miller. The book is called "*The Business of May Next*," a reference to the monumental work of James Madison at the founding of our nation. The paragraph is remarkable because in a few succinct lines, Miller summarizes all those achievements we should remember and be eternally grateful for as our legacy from these men. These thoughts, quoted next, focus our minds on the time and on the beginnings of a brand new philosophy for building a far better society than had ever existed.

> *Among the meanings concentrated in those years and in that founder are these: that good fortune offered this nation an unusual chance at ideal nation-forming and that some honorable leaders seized that chance; that this nation was founded not only, as all nations, on the triumphs and heroes of the battlefield and the palace and the podium but also on the quiet work of thinking and reading; that this reading and thinking did not start from the ground but build upon centuries of Western history; that the version of Western history that it particularly drew upon had a shape and featured a distinctive strand, the best short name for*

which is republicanism; that the Americans did not so much
invent the received republican ideals as give them new and lasting
institutional expression; that this republican institution-making
was not the work solely of scholars in their studies but also of men
with experience in the institutions they were thinking and writing
about; that this thoughtful republican institution-making was not
the work of one man only, a single great lawgiver, but was a
collaboration; that the institutions thus designed were not
complete but contained within themselves provision for their own
continuing alteration; that the revisions made possible by these
changeable institutions included the overcoming of great evils the
founders themselves only partly — but partly — recognized; that
a primary insight underlying this collaborative thought-and-
experience-based republican institution-making was a sober
wisdom, which is not the same as cynicism or pessimism, about
the conduct of human beings in the large and across time to the
great matters of collective life.

Those were the accomplishments, and because of what was done, there was another gift as well, one of showing the way. Begin with fundamental truths, find men and women of selfless intent, learn from history and devise a structure, rules and the means to adapt to change and what can result is a true advance for people. Governments are not important. People living in harmony is. The real worth of government is measured by the successes of people in all the things that are satisfying to them in life. Stability, security, achievement, respect, love and freedom being among the most rewarding. Government is there not to bestow these things, because it cannot. It is there to see that opportunity is not stolen from individuals as they seek and work toward their own goals.

As Miller reminds us, the founders realized that an unprecedented opportunity was there for them, and they followed the course. There was a common fear of foreign adventurism, a wide-open and uncontested land, a relatively close-knit people with many common values, a governing vacuum at the national level, and a time and an expectation to build a better future where individuals were important.

Today, we have no such obvious opportunity. The fear of foreign powers is low; the land is full to overflowing with people showing a growing divergence of values and attitudes; the 1780s governmental vacuum is replaced by a stultifying, intrusive thing that threatens to engulf our lives; and our time and condition seem more of an impending disaster than an opportunity. Perhaps our opportunity is just well disguised in the dress of impending crisis, a do-something-or-else condition we had better heed. Perhaps it is just a growing fear that we will fail as all others before us have, and that failure will be of our own doing. The signs around us say we had better see opportunity here — and follow it — or the consequences might be far worse than if today' s Constitutiorhad never come into being. The distracting cacophony of vested interests must not be allowed to prevent an honest reappraisal of ourselves, our condition, and our direction as a people.

Madison and the others did the best that could be done with the conditions and attitudes of the time. What they did then was proper for their time. There were, however, clear cases of expediency and others of trial solutions that have not been nearly appropriate. Our job is to recognize them and aim for that next higher level.

One such solution is the piecemeal approach to change, which works for things that pertain to refinements, but which have no hope for success for more substantive change. The Constitution was created by consideration of the whole social-political condition of the time. Change, which possibly may end up being modest, cannot be most wisely confronted unless the whole social-political condition of today is re-examined. To be forthright about it, however, I would expect that Constitution Two has to be greatly different from Constitution One because its deficiencies are so compelling. The perspectives of the two approaches to change are entirely different, the one to Band-Aid problems, the other to find a more optimum solution to the complete problem of governing a nation.

Where the founders had the issue of slavery to deal with and failed, we have another issue that, if allowed to perpetuate, could easily defeat any effort to improve our condition. The process of taxation and confiscation *without limit*, which allows the little people of government to propagate without restraint the misuse of power, is not one that can be solved simply by setting a ceiling or two. The entire legislative process is involved, and it is faulty. Changing the process would not even suffice. The entire structure, goals, and guidelines to government are inseparable parts of the puzzle, and all must come under review.

The process of change envisioned by the founders and included in our Constitutional make-up has fallen short of being effective in part because of a very large temporal gulf in the two main effects at work. On the one hand has been the accelerating pace of social change resulting both from technology and from government experimentation. On the other hand, that pace is a rapid one only when compared with the Constitutional process to adopt change. The most recent proof of this has been the attempt to adopt an amendment to balance the Federal budget and deal with the national debt. While the present unwieldy and tortuous process has helped to prevent its passage, government innovators have honed their legislative excesses to negate the *intent* of such an amendment even if it were to pass. Any chance at improvement has been side-stepped by a sophisticated government despite the clear, united voice of voters to limit government spending in some sensible and effective way. Likewise, the slow unidirectional push from

190

restrictive laws by direct congressional legislation and indirectly by rules from an army of regulators are given no guidance whatsoever in our founding document. All of this is effectively outside any real control, either by legislators themselves or by the public.

In short, our inherited process of change to remain a great people has been effective for a few crises and completely ineffective in others that are more serious.

Those men who led the way 200 years ago could not anticipate the timing realities of change and of events. They did not anticipate the extent of a creeping corruption *nor the creeping subversion of an ideal*. Little men, and even men with good intentions, have decimated individual liberty by their actions which show more concern for their own gain than any consequence to people. Yet the consequence has been an endless series of tiny ruptures in the body of individual sovereignty and a slow metamorphosis to something now unrecognizable.

Think seriously then, about the need for change to be fundamental. Change can rightly encompass every element of government. That should be the new perspective.

Few of us have even thought about whether the Constitution needs to change, let along what such changes might actually be. How to go about suggesting what an updated Constitution might embody, therefore, is no small concern.

It's useful to think of the constitution as a *contract*, and the contract can best be created by the buyer, by the collection of buyers who want certain services and are willing to pay for them. Thus, a buyer can agree to empower a police force at the cost of some money and that part of their right to privacy, for example, that allows police to search under clear, prescribed conditions. It' s a tradeoff to be judged by each individual and reflected in the rules for search. As part of the agreed contract, security is improved and everyone benefits.

An individual cannot, however, empower a government to take money from a second person and give it to yet another person. All one can do is to give government carte blanche on the money that individual has himself or herself.

As an extreme example of what an individual cannot do; he or she cannot empower their contractor, their government, to declare war, invade and take by force anything belonging to someone else. There is no rightful claim and, therefore, the individual cannot transfer it to government. This has great implications on what a just government can conceivably perform as proper functions in the name of sovereign individuals.

Lastly, government is not qualified or appropriate to be the initiator or the preparer of the contract, Constitution Two. It represents the transfer of assets which belong to individuals in exchange for services anyone can perform, and only the individuals have a say in what they are willing to spend and what rules shall apply to those who agree to provide the services.

*   *   *

1 Summarizing Why Constitution One Must Change to Fix Government

Throughout this book dozens of Constitutional shortcomings were mentioned. All have played a part in allowing government to become a mere caricature of what was envisioned at the founding. In the discussion to follow, are summarized many of those points made earlier under seven headings that I consider to be key reasons for change. Where inadequate provisions or failings exist in our present Constitution, (Constitution One), they are noted and used to show the need for change. The urgency for change, however, is not stressed here since the entire book is really an attempt to hammer that very point home. We begin at the beginning.

Bedrock for any just government lies in the primacy, the sovereignty of the individual. In their desire to be secure and to be part of enterprises beyond their own capabilities, people join together to form institutions to reach those objectives. Americans tried to do this first over 200 years ago, forming a new kind of republic, defining and empowering an institution to guarantee self-rule. The agreement of empowerment, based on Rights relinquished by the people, became Constitution One and it is really a contract between two groups, citizens who need certain services, and anyone from among their number who is willing to accept responsibility for providing those services. **A *just* government cannot exist except by an act of creation by the people.**

The following subsections highlight important facts about Constitution One that taken together could, and did, add up to today's compelling reason to change the constitution in a fundamental way. In effect, these facts are very like the indictments made earlier against government, and are prime reasons for constitutional change.

a) The People Had No Say in Constitution One

It's immediately apparent that ConstitutionOne doesn't match the description above or the criteria for government-forming. Well represented as they were by Madison, Jay, Jefferson, Washington, and some others, individual citizens, i.e., the people, had virtually nothing to do with the process or the government so defined. It may seem unlikely that the product would have been improved with their participation, but still there is that question, and the sobering fact that government

192

itself, albeit lower level government, wrote the whole contract. The assumptions hidden in the philosophical makeup of that group must, therefore, contain a bias which grants to government certain inherent RIGHTS which it cannot have unless agreed upon by the people.

The foundation for Constitution Two, therefore, must expand beyond individual sovereignty to include the obvious truth that such a contract can *only* be created and approved by the people, all the people. It is unequivocally a non-government function to write a contract for services wanted by the people.

The cost for these services, as the people well understand, comes from the only two sources of value we own, wealth and Unalienable Rights. The contract, therefore, becomes a statement of how the desired services will be paid for, meaning specifically what money will be available, and what degree of specific individual Rights the people are willing to relinquish to make the services feasible.

The ideals and purposes for which American government was first formed were an inspired set. The same set still applies today. To form a more perfect union, establish justice, ensure domestic peace, provide security, promote the welfare[35] of all and thus achieve lasting liberty are truly enlightened goals. Part I of this book translated those goals into six critical areas of living under government and how they have been subverted by that government. Part I was devoted to showing that these ideals and purposes have not been achieved by that government so created. Particular emphasis was given to the pursuit of happiness, the forgotten Right. The specifics of government failures consistently worked directly against this Right and this goal. A very broad conclusion seems justified, therefore, that the product, Constitution One, has not met the goal of creating a *just* government in the manner envisioned. Judgment of the severity of this overall failing is a matter of individual interpretation, my own being described here.

b) Band-Aid Fixes to Constitution One Won't Do It
To meet these still worthy goals, therefore, requires a drastic departure from Constitution One because the means, the contributors, to these ideals are infused throughout such a document. Granting too much power, providing too few restraints, and allowing compromises that undermine the very foundation of the structure could and did allow failure. Thus the most effective solution is to begin again with the foundation, restate the goals and rewrite a new contract, Constitution Two.

---

[35] Where "promote the welfare" is understood to be accomplished by ensuring conditions of stability and uniform fairness that remove blockades and allow people to take charge of their own welfare; the emphasis being on promote and not on welfare.

It should be obvious to everyone that in holding up **equality** as a centerpiece for establishing the nation, that ideal was never used as one of the criteria for defining the particular structure of government. Constitution Two can leave absolutely no doubt in anyone's mind that *equality* encompasses every single person, and that there can be no differentiation whatsoever with regard to public matters.

c) Constitution One Has No Guidance Regarding Crimes by Government

Concentrating physical power in the hands of government to ensure security increases the risk of that power being used against individuals. Ruby Ridge, Waco, the "war" on drugs, and dozens of other instances in recent years have confirmed that the risk of harm *directly from government actions* has increased over the years and is essentially uncontrollable since the real culprits are the controllers. Constitution One does not provide any effective means by which the crimes of government officials from one branch can be countered and corrected by another branch. The leaders and the triggermen involved have actually rewarded themselves when, in fact, indictment and trial should have been invoked without second thought. The Attorney General and the President were directly involved in approving the actions which took place and which ultimately resulted in the murders at Waco, and Constitutional provisions have had nothing to say on the matter. **Constitution One is totally ineffective as a guide to handle crimes of government** — except the most rigid of offenses by a president. The extent of this deficiency of Constitution One is most widespread in the matter of government's wars on alcohol and on drugs. Those two wars made criminals of huge segments of the population, and unilaterally stripped everyone of their Right to decide for themselves. Constitution One allows this foolishness, and even the repeal of Prohibition (Amendment XXI) did not fix the fundamental deficiency with Constitution One OR with the problem of government intrusion into matters of individual choice.

d) Multiple Constitutions???

Amendment XXI also dramatizes an even more basic failing of Constitution One in that IT is not *the* defining constitutional document in the USA. State Constitutions are prime in unnumbered matters of law. The concept of a national Constitution not being *the reference* in all matters of Rights, laws and powers of government is untenable. Furthermore, it is unnecessary. What exists today is another divisive remnant of that first attempt to build a nation. Constitution One was the product of the several Colonies which viewed themselves as "sovereign" States, a status that did not come via agreement from the people.

We continue to hold, under the cloak of nation, a collection of more-or-less similar, sovereign states that still covet their own powers, derived not from the people but from early colonial provisions, philosophies, and points of view purposely installed without full adherence to Constitution One.

From the citizen' s point of view, our codes of law are a polyglot of parochial provisions that often contradict, and do little or nothing constructive for individuals. What they do accomplish, of course, is to preserve power in the hands of state officials and obstruct the application of US Supreme Court decisions, thereby further restricting Unalienable Rights.

Any effort to create a new national Constitution must, therefore, be a nationwide effort so that the product, Constitution Two, becomes THE Constitutional reference for the entire nation. Moreover, I have argued that the artifice of states may very well be an obsolete feature of governmental hierarchy, and that Constitution Two must encompass within its scope of governmental structure — *all levels* of government — whatever the hierarchical breakdown may end up being. As you must recognize, I am *assuming* that the people of all 50 states see more value in being part of one nation than in remaining a solitary, sovereign state. We would then all be committed to finding a way to raise our nation to the next plateau of excellence.

e) Pass Laws Without Review for Constitutionality???

There is no provision in Constitution One that requires laws created by legislators (at any level) to be Constitutional, nor that they be reviewed beforehand for that purpose. An assumption was undoubtedly made that no one would knowingly or willingly propose and pass into law any unconstitutional act. Once again, the safeguards were badly deficient since such contrary laws are routinely made and passed. The burden of proof has fallen on those most hurt by the bad law, exactly opposite to sensible, just governing. The burden of proof for the *need* of any proposed law and the *Constitutionality* of it *must* be on lawmakers themselves.

In this light we can also see that decisions by the US Supreme Court should automatically apply to every governing body from Federal to the lowest Local level. It should not be necessary to argue the merits of every variation of an issue because of variations in State Constitutions.

f) Changes to Government Must Come From The People

Constitution One, in the matter of adapting for change, had been introduced earlier. There is another aspect to change that needs comment, and that has to do with the rigidity of structure of government. Change in structure has only come about by actions of government itself, the most important being the creation by Congress of regulatory agencies. None have been instituted or achieved by the action of citizens. The effect of this inverted process for change has ensured that for more than ten generations since the founding, there has been no CHOICE open to

195

each new generation regarding the whole edifice of government. Defining and initiating a proper means of self-government is NOT a one-time process, never more to be attempted. It should be, and obviously so, that changing social conditions require review and rework of earlier decisions on roughly **a continual basis**, which may be generational at the very least. CHOICE, an inherent Right of the people, should be accommodated in Constitution Two by a defined process which makes it possible to exercise such a Right.

Briefly, this simply means that the effectiveness of government to carry out each Constitutional duty should be continuously measured by independent, non-government groups. With factual information available on every action prescribed by the contract, Constitution Two, the need for change is also continuously known. Then by providing a periodic process for contract review and change, each generation can exercise its right of choice, and the means to achieve continued improvements in self-government will exist. In other words, the process followed by the founders and the review and debate in progress today about our social-governmental condition is one that should effectively be continuous, not intermittent at 200-year intervals.

g) Abrogating The Very Foundation of Individual Rights???

The final serious indictment of Constitution One, related to its foundation, is another misdeed against our Unalienable Rights. Power was explicitly given to the Federal government to *suspend individual Rights* in a wartime emergency. This must be thrown out, if only on the basis that not one individual non-government person ever agreed to it. Such rights do not come from government and, therefore, government cannot rightfully withhold them. They can only be denied at gunpoint in an obvious criminal act against *all our Unalienable Rights*. Sadly, there is an addendum to this huge error on the part of the Founders. Government chose, without constitutional justification, to extend the power of suspension to a non-wartime problem, instigated by FDR during the 1930s Recession. We live today under a government, which has *given itself* the power to deny, at any time, any Right of individuals it so chooses. This single flaw makes the failings of Constitution One complete as the definitive guardian of individual sovereignty, since it has never provided such protection.

* * *

There are a large number of other deficiencies in Constitution One as well. I'll simply list some of them to reinforce the conclusion that constitutional change is imperative.

- Representative government as structured is not representative.
- The bicameral structure of government is part of the deficiency in representation.

196

- Recognition of the inherent personal power within an individual is virtually ignored in Constitution One, and almost completely ineffective in contests with government.
- Other than the test of amending Constitution One to include the Bill Of Rights, improvement in American government via the Constitution One change process has been mostly of the Band-Aid variety rather than in fundamentals such as the dichotomy of State – Federal authority.
- The basic structure of American government was distorted by a misunderstanding of the relative threat to harmony of foreign powers to that of built-in constitutional inequities, as exemplified by slavery and the status of females.
- Individual Sovereignty, equality, freedom of choice and other Unalienable Rights could not possible have been uppermost in the minds of those helping to form American government because of the very fact that the American Union was one of Sovereign States, and not of a unified population of sovereign individuals.
- While no power was given for gift giving, neither was there a restriction against the practice.
- The "all other powers" provision in Constitution One, was so nebulous, and so lacking in specific guidance that it accomplished almost nothing concrete to guide future decisions regarding the exercise of powers.
- Individual Sovereignty was never a true, explicit part of the foundation of American government.
-

2 Government & Excessive Powers

Fully two thirds of the faults I have found with government and Constitution One have to do with excess power, usurpation of power (usually over the Rights of individuals), and the lack of Constitutional provisions to limit that power. In my view, this shows the utter bastardization of the lofty concepts set forth when the American nation was formed. The reason that government stewardship has been so one-sided and so divested of honorable results (if not intent) can only be attributable to a defining contract that did not assure government compliance with those ideals. Constitution One, by the record of government in the United States, has clearly failed completely in the *preservation* of the rights and freedom of individuals since the stockpile of these precious assets has dwindled continuously throughout our history. The fundamentals of government formation demand a foundation that is unequivocal, empowerment that is fully defined and precisely limited, a process for redress of government errors, failings and crimes that is absolutely effective, and a process for change of contract and structure that works to stabilize misjudgments in any provision. *Constitution One has fulfilled none of these requirements.*

With regard to limiting powers, let me simply recall a few of the overwhelming number of abused powers.   Taxes are unlimited and destructive of families, spending is without limit, and both are major flaws; government has taken absolute power over Unalienable Rights; seizure of property without due process is now standard governmental procedure; projection of military power is poorly guided as is the sale of weapons; & majority rule, even with the 50% threshold, is a non-workable process in American life because of government subversion.   That extension of government power has been taken to the point where *most* laws are now enacted by individual regulatory agencies, meaning passage by a minority approaching zero percent of the population.

The next eight subsections show how the wide range of abused powers can be viewed to help search for practical means to control them.

a) Government & National Goals

Government has treated the concept of national goals as unfettered license to do any project that allows it to exercise power. From invading Vietnam to landing men on the Moon, to subsidizing pornographic "art" and advocacy groups which lobby for more government, to usurping control over the entire agricultural industry, the government has recognized no limitations whatsoever — and they are right — there are no effective Constitutional limitations. That condition must end or soon the human tendency to excess will surely complete the 200-year old slide toward ruin.

There are many more examples of abused power but the aggregate effect is merely to reinforce the inadequacy of Constitution One to provide control of government against abuse of power. In addition, the Constitution must recognize that basic differences exist for functions relating to security and to national goals, and as such, the whole process of law making might sensibly differ for the two. In particular, any debate for the purpose of establishing national goals should be much more widespread and cautious, and all other avenues outside government should first be exhausted.

b) Define Government Functions Explicitly

All of this discussion amounts to the most far reaching concern for establishing the set of *functions* that will be required of government. That is where our national debate must be centered and our greatest caution exercised. People, meaning ourselves, cannot be entrusted with power beyond our abilities to control, because those who tend toward abuse and excess would soon dominate.

A Conclusion

We must begin to understand that to provide for our own security from foreign and internal predators does NOT require that the institutions empowered to achieve that security also be given every other power to control.

198

The two functions are unrelated, and in defining government functions, clear separation of security from all other matters is absolutely essential. THE shining example of Constitutional oversight here is its failure to disallow the give-away of public money.[36]   The mere forbidding of gifts, however, needs much more Constitutional attention to force legislators to abide by the intent of restrictions against this unwanted practice.

The attention given to limiting powers of government 200 years ago has proven to be totally inadequate. In our attempts today to avoid that same error, the charter we hand to government should contain an absolute minimum number of tasks it is expected to perform.

In the United States our rules for self governing should be set based *First* on the premise that accomplishing *anything* should be via private enterprise, and only when this is not feasible, should the use of government be considered.

c) Our Guidelines to Those Who Govern
The mindset of the principal founders, I think, was that they were dealing with honorable men. I believe that they were, so it is easy to understand that directing and guiding the forthcoming actions of government need not have been exhaustive, or perhaps even adequate for the most obvious of counsel. History has proven that without specific and continuous reminders, men in government, and women as well, inexorably drift from a charted course for what are perceived to be valid reasons. The effect is exactly that of any "system" that is allowed to operate without the stabilizing effects of feedback. Drift, uncorrected, progresses toward an unstable limit, and we are well on the way to that unknown limit today.

Redefining government should be done with an entirely different and much more pragmatic mindset. Assume that inadvertent or overt skullduggery is likely at every possible opportunity and that there will always be some percentage of petty men more interested in personal gain than in honor. Such an attitude should be an overcompensation for human behavior, but there will be no loss in achieved excellence by being overcautious. Conversely, being too trusting — again — will surely ruin the eventual outcome. The intention in all this effort is to spare future generations the kind of hurt caused by the failures and excesses of our present government.

---

[36] As a cynical aside, one can readily envision congressional discussions of how such a restriction might be negated. Simply redefine money distribution so that everything becomes a needed purchase and is no longer a give-away.

d) Laws Must be Constitutional – Before Enactment

Procedures of the present government are deficient in some important ways, and perhaps the most serious is the manner in which laws are written and approved. The issue has surfaced earlier but deserves extra emphasis. The onus of assuring constitutionality of any law, Local or Federal, must rest with lawmakers. People confronted with bad law are doubly penalized, first in their confrontation with police and the judicial system, and second when it becomes necessary to force the issue to the high court, usually with several traumatic steps along the way. None of this would be necessary if the backward procedure of law making were changed. The goal SHOULD be to create law that is *never* unconstitutional.

e) USSC Staffing & Performance

Another glaring example of the lack of balance among the branches of government is the manner and the process for staffing the US Supreme Court.

The purpose of life-long tenure was to spare the court undue influence from the political arena. Yet every appointment is precisely political and the only check on a person' s fitness occurs at unstructured hearings where other politicians try to assure themselves that their own political philosophy prevails. The result, at the people level, is that we have the prospect of being controlled in important ways for decades, with relief dependent entirely on death removing any irritant. The whole process of selection and tenure is unacceptable, and especially so since the people themselves are denied any involvement whatsoever.

There is no review of court performance, and the threshold for passage of any court opinion is pegged at one more than half of the nine justices and, as mentioned before, the whole court is relegated to after-the-fact judgments on issues that consistently spawn bad law from legislatures across the entire country. The definitive review of law should take place *before* it becomes law, not after it has done its harm.

f) War, & Power to Wage It

The guidance to government by Constitution One in matters of the use of military power is essentially non-existent. Again, the assumption was made that honorable men would prevent its use for less than honorable, or offensive purposes. In the absence of directional guidance — from the people via Constitution One — the wars we have instigated have NOT all been honorable, and that situation is intolerable.

g) Define Citizen Rights & Guidelines to Government Officials More Fully

Part of the cause of significant loss of Rights is that they are not fully defined anywhere. Any occasion where infringement of Rights might occur lost out to power and regulation because no specific guidance exists. Make law first and worry

200

about unconstitutionality second — if at all — is the government approach to law making. The process has worked for government, and the glaring lack of specific guidance has done its part in undermining our Unalienable Rights in wholesale fashion, with rules that usurp the Right of CHOICE being most invasive. The "war on drugs" is a striking example of the loss of Rights by unconstitutional government actions — as was prohibition — where specific guidance was sorely lacking. Individual choice seems to be such an esoteric concept to regulators that they obviously require more specific guidance on the issues they face.

I envision a companion document to Constitution Two which would not only enumerate all Unalienable Rights to the fullest of our ability to define (with accompanying responsibilities), but also serve as a guide to governing. Such a guide would be far more explicit of our expectations of the actions of public servants and would be the basis of evaluation of their conduct in office. In effect, it would be a code of law specifically addressed to government officials at all levels, just as the legislated code of laws is addressed to all citizens. A very specific provision of such a companion code for officials is as follows. They can never excuse themselves from any law which applies to citizens-at-large.

h) Government Should Be the Last Means to Achieve National Objectives

As a final note on the lack of guidance in Constitution One, just consider how much grief we might have avoided if the founders had thought to take a stand on the *giving-away* of public money, and the *taking* of wealth. It is worth repeating: Rather than handing a task to government, all other means of accomplishing difficult objectives should be exhausted first before the function is handed to government.

3 Government Structure, at all Levels is Part of the Constitution

This discussion is concerned with all levels of government, Local and Federal, and the structure of that government. At the present time there is a huge disconnect between elements of Local government and the Constitution, supposedly of the people. The connections between them are so informal that they are subject to the vagaries of State legislatures and the good will of state officials. There is nothing automatic about the law of the land propagating from central government (the keeper of Constitutionality and the preserver of Unalienable Rights of individuals) to every scattered jurisdiction and individual in the country. Instead we have States enacting unconstitutional laws unilaterally, denying Rights of choice because of Local bias (also unconstitutional) and subversion of US Supreme Court decisions for the same petty, juvenile and hateful reasons.

As a single entity with common justice and goals, the United States **isn' t.** That disjoint, structured reality could not be more pronounced than it is and still be considered as a union of 50 states into a single nation. This huge deficiency is another remnant-legacy of the expediencies forced upon the founders. That deficiency must be addressed and resolved if the purposes for our joining together are ever to be achieved.

One goal in this new approach to government-forming is to reduce the number of governmental levels to an absolute minimum. At the present time, that minimum number should either be two or three, depending upon how controllability and order would fare under Federal and City levels only, compared to the alternative which retains the intermediate level of State. The variations in city size actually overlap state size (in population) so population is not the determining factor. While state-level militia seems sensible, the need for state as intermediary among groups of cities seems superfluous. Many issues involving groups of cities such as commerce, water, roads, power, environment, are issues that go beyond the artificial borders of states to become national and regional concerns.

Such thoughts as these are merely introduced to point out that the structure of government, considered as unified and as an ocean-to-ocean entity, need not be taken unchanged from what exists today. The hand of oppressive government is *most* heavily felt as applied by Local levels of government. Any potential for relief by minimizing the number of levels of government is change in the right direction.

The Federal government has often tried in its heavy-handed way to force compliance of rules by mandates. Such things have covered the full range of bad-to-beneficial actions that have been discussed at some length in the book. But the point of most relevance is that in many instances, such mandates have infringed on powers supposedly belonging to the States themselves, but which truly are reserved to the people.

The ambiguities, the informalities of structure and the total lack of a unifying Constitutional base which is supreme over all governmental elements accounts for the disjoint codes of laws that exist.

Ours is a society of individuals committed to the rule of just law, yet we are still unable to claim that we have it.

Functions expected of government must be defined for the complete hierarchy of government if there is to be order in the way we govern ourselves. Functions finally settled upon will have a great influence on what the optimum structure of government should be. The inescapable conclusion is that the task to be undertaken — by the people of America — is to prepare a new Constitution that encompasses allocation of functions, governmental structure, rights of individuals, accountabilities and limitations pertaining to every level of government hierarchy.

We either have a single, unified nation or we do not. If we do, then what we create to maintain order must be build upon that fact, something that Constitution One cannot claim.

The following seven subsections may help to view the subject of government structure differently than in the past. Particular elements of structure need to be understood as we try to find that illusive minimum government.

a) Separate the Functional Powers of Government

In designing governmental structure, there is nothing that requires that powers for different functions be collected within a single element of government. Separation of functional powers among independent branches may be one means of controlling the effects of governmental failures. In other words, we should not limit our thinking about structure any more than about the functions themselves. Whatever the optimum structure might be, the goal of unity of purpose will be paramount.

For debating what the functions of government are to be, the starting point should be that there is only one that *must* come under the authority of government, and that is the function of security. Police for domestic order and military strength to counter foreign threats are the only needs of the people that truly require government to carry out. No other potential function has an equal compulsion to be handled by government. The choice of placing a function of national or Local interest under government purview and control comes only if there is no better method of providing the services of that function. Whether it be infrastructure, foreign relations, commerce, environment, funding, education, grievances, or a host of other social and national issues, the opening position should be that non-government methods will suffice. Only when that *proves* impossible should the function become a government one.

Having reluctantly been passed to government, since no other practical means exists, then a similar filter regarding structure should be applied. Here the go, no-go filter settles the question of whether that function can be done by an independent branch of government or *must* be included under another branch to which other powers (functions) have been allocated. The use of multiple independent functional branches is much the preferred choice.

b) Who Is To Govern ???

In our zeal to convince the world and ourselves that we have achieved self-government we have placed no restrictions on who may apply. What we have ignored in taking that approach is that certain qualifications exist for every job, but in regards to government, are never insisted upon. Opening up the application window to public service to everyone does not mean that the job lacks requirements

203

of the applicant. Perhaps the opportunity for fraud, favoritism or manipulation is so great if certain qualifications were to be required, that insisting upon them is impractical, That, however, has never proven to be the case for any other non-government job from janitor to CEO. It seems an obvious oversight in our attempt to govern ourselves that all that' s required is intent. As we begin rightfully to demand better of our public servants, part of that demand lies in an insistence upon a level of competence and a philosophy that values truthfulness and high principle from all who would seek to govern. It seems rather obvious that salesmanship, sloganizing, histrionics and emotional appeal have had their fair turn at determining election winners. Qualifications should replace all that, and deciding what those qualities should be is an important issue that should have a direct effect on Constitution Two.

c) Human Behavior Must be Reckoned With

We are captives of our own behavior and will forever harbor within our number just enough larceny, immaturity and selfishness to impede the social progress we seek. As it happens, handing power to someone is often the surest way to bring out the worst in that person. Like Madison and the other founders before us, all we can do is use that knowledge of disruptive and destructive behavior to minimize its effect. There are some explicit ways to minimize the harm that might be done by little men and women while others work to improve society. Because I' ve tried to be brief about them shouldn' t lead anyone to think they are unimportant. I believe that doing these things can help us be successful in reaching that next plateau of effectiveness in self-government.

The criticism I have of Constitution One is simple. Besides the fact that the founders mindset assumed government was the answer, they were unable to use effectively their knowledge of human behavior in their government-forming task. All of the items I' m about to list were either not applied at all or were used only incidentally in the process. In short, the founders were *not nearly cautious enough* when they designed and created the government of the United States of America.

The lust for power is the first human behavioral failing to which we turn our attention as we try to devise sensible ways to counteract it.

To counter the lust for power, use tactics such as the following:

- Spread out the Power — If there are two governmental jobs to be done, give it to two independent contractors (i.e., parts of government). Do not concentrate power in a single entity as Constitution One does in Congress.

- Minimize Power — Minimize the powers associated with any task handed to government, because even power that seems small and well contained can be badly distorted by those who wish to do so. Exhaust all other possible means of providing a service, adding it to the government list only as a last resort.

A quick example. The United States Forest Service has dominion over national parks, including those with the last of our unspoiled forests. Since the United States Forest Service makes up the rules, they have decided it was all right to use tax money to build logging roads and to allow private lumber companies to strip-cut huge areas of forest. The damage being done is extensive, unsanctioned by the owners of those parks, namely We the People, and it is criminal. No one told these little men they didn' t have the power to sell our resources for a pittance, or to use our money to cut destructive gashes called roads. No one told them not to, so they just used the power we foolishly gave them to do something only they and the lumber lobbyists thought was okay. The level of control by Congress is essentially non-existent, with a few "hearings" and promises to take better care of the forests, enough to let their destructive use of power continue. Caring for such a treasure is obviously not a task to be handed to men with power, real or implied, to use that treasure, so the fault we must find with the present system is that the intricacies of modern society have gone far beyond our ability to cope, via Constitution One,. Explicit issues must have explicit attention, and that means explicit limitations. Constitution One provides none of that either in its defined structure of government or its guidance to officials regarding their conduct.

• Monitor the Use of Power — This is probably the most important task associated with the entrustment of power, yet it was handed to the very same people holding and using that power. It should be ludicrously obvious to anyone that the user cannot be the evaluator. This is a major fault of Constitution One, but one that is readily fixed.

• Charge Officials Directly with Responsibility — Willful actions to harm, such as denying Rights or confiscating wealth, are crimes that are committed by people. Worse yet, they are the crimes of officials cloaked under the folds of bureaucracy and left unattended. But crimes are planned by people and carried out by people. Crimes are ultimately traceable and those individuals responsible for them must be held *personally* liable for their actions. In effect, present government, Local and Federal, holds no one accountable for acts done in the name of government. The logic is exactly backwards. If government acts are done to benefit, then there will be no crime and no official will incur liability. If government acts are criminal, then people are hurt and such acts should be stopped in the most decisive way.

The analogy of legislative actions to police actions is a good one. In those (rare) instances when police have committed criminal acts, sometimes hidden behind legitimate police business, the system allows, even demands, that legal action be taken against those who violated their public trust. The few are not allowed to ruin the whole structure of law enforcement. With law makers, however, there is free reign for their actions and immunity from responsibility for any harm done. The result is a *totally different attitude among legislators* and an ineffective method of control which has caused a great deal of willful harm to people who seek only fairness.

- Reluctant Officials — I must admit that following the rule of handing power to those reluctant to use it is one that is hard to implement. There are such people, however. They are people whose interest lies in serving. Any changes we make in the process of training and selecting public servants that provide extra incentive to such people, or even just help us identify them, will be to our lasting benefit.

- The Boundaries of Power — As a final counter-measure to the human lust for power, the contract with power holders must clearly define the limits of that power along every conceivable path where it might be exercised. It is this very concern that provides us with the most telling argument for instituting an almost continuous process for changing the contract, Constitution Two. It is nearly impossible to anticipate the ingenuity of those more interested in serving themselves than in selfless service. The need to undo the corruptive use of power is axiomatic in any drive to create and maintain a just government. Thus, when the bounds of power are breached, change would again be needed.

*   *   *

d) More on Human Behavior
There are other human behavioral characteristics that continue to frustrate attempts to improve national life. Being aware of them should help in planning Constitution Two. People can become over compassionate, and if they see government as a solution to social ills, their whole approach is to perpetuate. They see the pain and suffering and cannot see the causes. Only when they see the pain subsiding will they begin to understand there are means other than government to effect improvements in American quality of life.

There are others whom we might be tempted to classify as zealots, but who may really just be sincere people who are easily misled. They take at face value those real power-hungry leaders who prey upon their faith to enlist support. Men have created a base of power for their own purposes by this very means, and as long as the words continue to sound pious, support continues. The "crime" in all this is that in projecting such biased power, the **Rights of others will be sacrificed,** all in the name of a set of beliefs that are not shared by all people. Any approach to government which seeks to fashion a set of rules-of-conduct dictated by one particular view of religious faith, MUST become an infringement on the Rights of others who believe differently.

By far the worst of human failings, however, is larceny, used here in its broadest sense. In public life, this can take on any number of shapes and degrees from favoritism to accepting kickbacks to extortion and even to the warping of legislation for dishonorable ends. All of these aberrations in behavior were with us in 1788, are with us now, and most likely always will be. The greed of little men is a fact of life. From what we have seen of the performance of government officials, the effects of such men are felt much more at the Local level than nationally, since it is so much easier to work against isolated individuals. It is done all the time. To combat it takes more than hand-wringing or hope for enlightenment. It takes overt action in the planning of how a country or a city is to be run. It takes the application of all the monitoring, the vigilance, the laying of responsibility, the punishments and the ability to change that must be part of an advancing society, as long as it contains people, which is to say, forever.

e) How We Change Must Change

The need for change is seen in the change process itself, which has already been touched upon to some extent. Constitution One makes no provision for people to exercise the Right of choice for any of the fundamentals of government. Spending levels, the basic functions expected of government and the structure of government itself are examples of things essentially outside the control of both government itself, and the people as well. Such things are not something that can be set for all time. They must be made subject to the will of society by means of a change process which fits the needs of that society. The process in use today is as non-responsive and so indirect that it is almost never invoked, having come into use only 26 times plus one more still pending. We have nurtured the notion that *change* in our instructions to officials is something to be avoided, something dangerous to national stability. Change is actually our greatest tool for salvage, and without meaningful and timely revision, the worst of government failings are simply perpetuated. Two hundred years of following the implicit logic of maintaining the status quo, should be ample proof of *its* failure. Change, well-considered and thoughtful change, should be embraced and used wisely to elevate our national lives.

Government functions in particular are the focal point of any such planning for change because both structure and spending can be derived from the list of tasks to be entrusted to government. *The change process, therefore, must rely on a continuous review and appraisal of how well government performs.* (Refer to the next section.) When you are clear about how well something performs, or more to the point, how poorly something performs, then measures to change that something to improve what it does are within your grasp.

The process to institute change at the Federal level under Constitution One relies on other, lower level *government bodies*. **Nowhere do individual citizens become involved**. We are once again back to the issue of representation as the means of following the will of those being governed. That process clearly does not work, as we have already seen from countless examples. The referendum works fine but is not used, and the people are without a real voice in the thing that should be most responsive to them. To repeat, the government is not the thing of importance here, the people, and only the people are.

Obviously there are practicalities to contend with in knowing the consensus of a large population, but the technological means exist today to implement the referendum in matters of key national and local business. Computers and appropriate reference databases can readily be applied to a decision process that truly returns the Right of choice to the people.

f) The Referendum Takes the Guesswork Out of Knowing Citizen Needs & Desires

One can envision a referendum process throughout the nation that would first be applied to the new Constitution Two. The response might be acceptance, acceptance with specific changes, or rejection of the version as proposed to the people. The process would very likely involve several iterations before approval. When a consensus is finally reached on a new national and internal contract, Constitution Two, the same procedural network can then continue its usefulness as each referendum-level issue is addressed. As an example of how such a network might be assembled, one only has to see the existing university and college structure as an almost ready-made resource of high integrity for such a purpose. Augmented by a growing computer-literate population with personal at-home computers and the extrapolation of use to national and city business is straightforward. This, coupled with a sensibly high approval threshold, then becomes the essence of true self-government, unhampered by all the shortcomings of today' s "representative" form.

Proposals for actions meant to cope with city-wide or nationwide issues could, for example, be initiated by anyone or any group. The belief that only those versed in law can write legislation is unfounded. What that approach has given us is a series of codes interpretable only by lawyers, and a built-in requirement that virtually all interactions within a society are utterly dependent on the legal community to accomplish anything, usually at exorbitant cost. The key legal issue with new legislation is its constitutionality, and presently that is never established until after the fact. To become a voting issue, any proposal, from any source, **must** be subjected to a complete battery of tests and reviews. Constitutionality, need, alternate means, cost not only in dollars but also in individual Rights, funding and the like must all converge to place the question before the voters. None of this is required now. Most such information does *not require the actions of government to* *prepare*. The opportunity for misleading voters seems ever-present, and safguards must be devised that can be done elsewhere outside of government, again taking advantage of university resources and private analysis organizations. Multiple, independent, private resources can be used to generate much of what is needed for people to create an informed opinion and vote on such key issues.

Constitution Two would include an initial listing of those public issues to be decided upon only by referendum (both city and national) and those which *initially* can be entrusted to agencies under contract in accord with Constitution Two. Both, of course, would be subject to continuous monitoring and change as need be. Choice would be firmly in the hands of the people, and the unending and often frivolous binge of legislation would cease. Constitution One accommodates none of this ability, thus preventing people from exercising choice.

At the Local level, the absence of voter choice is even worse than it is nationally. Whether from the State Legislature or City Council, ideas and decisions are made by a mere handful of individual officials who need not be responsive either to the need or choice of voters. Constitution One and the semi-independent, lower level Constitutions and Charters have no effective countermeasures to these kinds of widespread abuses.

In our deliberations for change to our present method of self-government we must recognize that a fundamental difference exists between the two incentives for forming a government, that for security and that for achieving national and local goals. Each purpose should be given *independent consideration* and debate appropriate to it and not be constrained by the assumption that all government actions can be resolved by a single process.

g) Fix Bad Law Now on the Books
Lastly, in relation to government structure, it is worth adding emphasis to the need for a much better approach to handling bad laws. The consequences resulting from laws that should never have become laws, have been devastating both to individuals and to the rights of all people. The inadequacy of Constitution One to deal with this problem and the untenable looseness of State constitutions and City charters makes of this problem one that is intimately enmeshed with our basic structure of government and the processes in use for creating law and dispensing justice. Theft of property via eminent domain, theft of property without due process, whether via IRS action or our ridiculous war on drugs, or criminalizing acts of free choice, are all potent examples of how bad lawmaking-by-fiat can become and has become in this country. Extrication is too often impossible and *always* destructive of individual Rights. A case can easily be made that the winner in these confrontations is always the government, which is not the purpose of government in the least.

A practical ability to deal effectively with abusive laws is a change that is long overdue.

4 Monitoring the Performance of Government

The United States Federal government and all elements of our existing Local governments comprise THE LARGEST business enterprise in the entire world. Unlike a business of any size, however, it operates without the faintest hint of how well it performs against any measure of effectiveness. It has no goals for the performance of any task; it has no procedures even for evaluating performance; it has no procedures for minimizing cost for a given service return or conversely maximizing its return per dollar spent; it has no feedback whatsoever on what incremental benefits result or should result for increases in spending. It has not even devised what measures of effectiveness are meaningful for most of the programs that become commitments that must then be honored by the American people. Likewise there are no means for evaluating the effectiveness of any official' s performance in the many leadership roles within government. In fact, the only requirements for leadership are those placed there by leaders themselves, which are to assure reappointment by being best at the stratagem of politics.

Reviews and evaluations are essentially non-existent, either for the product of government, which is service to the people, or for the performance of officials toward that same end. Poor performance is rewarded as handsomely as good because rewards are controlled by the performers. Informal evaluations of the miserable people-records of officials (and there have been many) are ignored and, of course, are completely ineffective for improving government operations. One of the best recent evaluations of government at the Federal level is the 1997 "CATO Handbook for Congress." The book is a compilation of sensible changes suggested to Congress, where each suggested change is clearly derived from government's poor performance for that particular function. Thus the CATO book is the step *following* evaluation, a much more subtle way of telling the government it has performed very poorly, and here are some very specific suggestions to improve that performance. It addresses 57 specific topics, and for each it lists from two to a dozen unambiguous actions that the 105th Congress *should* take to begin to make things right. Those 57 topics range from the connections between Congress, the courts, and the Constitution, to controlling the budget, to abolishing agencies, to adhering to the Constitution, to regulation, to foreign policy, and on and on into almost all the activities of government. A few of the specific suggestions for improvement will give an understanding of how thorough the *Handbook* is and, by simple deduction, how bad the performance of government has been.

- abolish the Department of Education
- abolish HUD
- enact law *only* after confirming its Constitutionality
- subject Congress to the rule of law by identifying specific Constitutional authority before any action
- abolish corporate welfare, subsidies
- privatize social security and return control of Social Security deductions to the individual
- terminate more than 100 major Federal programs and agencies (listed, total savings $168 Billion)
- privatize $100 Billion worth of Federal assets, lowering the national debt with the proceeds
- end subsidies to arms suppliers
- eliminate trade barriers used to protect special United States firms
- replace the income tax with a national sales tax and abolish the IRS
- abolish the Department of Energy and most of the programs it manages
- withdraw from culture and art activities
- eliminate the Department of the Interior, including NASA, TVA, and a host of other sub-agencies
- repeal existing, specific laws that infringe on the Rights and liberties of individuals (initial list provided)
- restore Constitutional immunity against double jeopardy
- downsize the Federal government
- etc. . . . .
- . . . . .

The CATO list is comprehensive, sensible, addresses real excesses and failings of government, and is a monument to the extent that government has strayed from its true purpose.

Government is an enterprise, a monopoly that has safely weathered all criticisms of conduct and ineffectiveness because Constitution One places no demands whatsoever on services or officials. I consider this to be a glaring deficiency of Constitution One. The result, even without assuming the worst in human behavior, could not possibly have been the coveted advance of American society. Even without intent to do so, without the means and guidance from Constitution One, what must come about did so. That result is undirected, inefficient, incompetent and costly services, where the cost in lost Rights has been even more devastating than the cost in wealth.

The Constitutional deficiency extends to the lack of guidance on the handling of national wealth, a factor of small concern at the end of the 18th century, but one which now dominates in any evaluation and indictment of government performance. It was inevitable that this Constitutional shortcoming would lead to the failings and excesses of government that have come about, because that is exactly the nature of the human animal.

The CATO handbook is interesting to me for two important reasons. In its structured way, it addresses many if not all of the faults of Federal government that have concerned me here and which are the major reason for the deterioration in American life. I take this as almost complete corroboration of the facts of government actions and perhaps an endorsement of many of the opinions I have expressed along the way.

The second thing of interest is the divergence of opinion on how to remedy a bad situation. CATO suggests explicit steps to Congress that would help greatly, showing a faith in the American system and officials. There is no thought or discussion of Constitutional change. The steps suggested are legislative, and while the aggregate effect would be a sweeping change in the way government operates, one can easily view the whole process as orderly and potentially very satisfying to everyone except those in government who would need to look for other employment. I see a great deal of merit in the CATO approach because it is a positive one, blaming no one, yet simply moving on in a much more sensible way.

The solution I have discussed in this book is much more idealistic. Return to the Foundation Principles of life, equality, Individual Sovereignty and Unalienable Rights, redefine what the tasks of government shall be and restructure completely the institution of government, national and Local. The contract with that government then becomes a new Constitution, THE reference for all levels of government for as long as it represents what the people want of government. Where CATO assumes the good will of present officials to do these sensible things, I have zero optimism that any voluntary change will occur. Just as the Grace Commission identified thousands of steps Congress *could* take to improve operations, CATO has identified hundreds of steps that are even more far-reaching and sensible. But just as Congress ignored the Grace Commission recommendations, so will they ignore the CATO ideas. I wish I were totally wrong about this, but unless Congress is FORCED to undo the excesses and failures IT has created, it will do absolutely nothing substantive. That is simply the nature of the thing created by Constitution One and the innate behavior of humans. Forcing change, however, does not even imply insurrection, for that would be the absolute worst way to achieve sensible and essential change.

Knowing the thoroughness of the CATO Institute, I am also sure they recognize that even if Congress implemented every change suggested under their 57 topics, the job of fixing American government would only be partly completed. Turning functions over from national to State governments, for example, would be no improvement at all for individuals. State meddling in education is as bad as Federal meddling. Neither level of government has any charter from the citizens to dictate matters of education. Majority tyranny is worse at the Local levels than Federally, and eminent domain is an issue that has never been resolved, one that always hurts vulnerable individuals. The injustices to individuals from State and City laws that deprive people of their Right of choice are so widespread and haphazard that we live in a land of 52 codes of law instead of one. These are potent reasons to reexamine the whole problem of self-government, and any long term view will, of course, do that.

The present Constitution, enlightened as it seemed to be 200 years ago, nevertheless contained, from the very beginning, a number of fundamental flaws that must somehow be corrected. The failings and excesses of the US government, Federal and Local, are directly traceable to the Constitution. The only way fundamentals can be honored is to begin again at the foundation and build a structure that adheres to those fundamentals.

CHAPTER 20
Transition & Other Steps to Better Government

England set an example for relatively peaceful transition of government power in the 19th century, some time after America declared its independence. Philosophically, that change was even greater than is being suggested here for America, since the country went from a Monarchy to a Republic centered on partially elected officials. Conversely, the American philosophy will presumably be the same as it has always been, equality, individual sovereignty and government of the people. Only the mechanisms for decision-making and levels of authority will change.

Actually, you and I both know now that the American underpinning has never been based on those lofty ideals. States Rights have been the real basis for law making since earliest days. Fortunately, there are many who still believe in the founding myth so that it should still be there expediting our decision to change government.

Even so, I believe that changing American government to this new model is much more comprehensive than in the case of England, and, therefore, potentially more disruptive. When England made its change only the Royal Family had to adjust to their new position as a showpiece and reminder of presumed past glory.

In America, millions of people will have to adjust. Planning for transition, therefore, will be critical, because in that planning NO ONE should be made to feel like a second-class American. Every single person is, and will remain equal and of value to the country. If it is done sensibly, every group, every person directly affected, will become a 'line item" in that plan, the objective of which is to minimize personal trauma to the greatest possible extent.

Those laboring in the agencies to be phased out can be assisted via a generous severance package. Look at it this way. Any money so spent would have continued to be paid if their agency remained in operation, and the worker would continue to do things we want to stop. With closure, the wasted money would be the same for a while because of severance, but the governmental attacks against all the rest of us will have ended.

There is another interesting line of reasoning, a similarity between the two times of government-forming that is not so obvious. Two hundred years ago, there might have been a rather simple solution to the slavery issue if someone had thought to pay slave "owners" for their "property," inste ad of waiting decades and then killing anyone who disagreed with the notion of equality. In fact that is exactly what England did when faced with the very same issue early in the 19th century. Severance is not much different, and ever so much more civilized.

Elected officials at the federal and state levels have already provided for themselves with generous "retirement" plans, and of course, they must be honored. Any attempts by present government to augment such gifts to themselves would represent a wrinkle in the transition blanket, requiring more attention.

Elected officials at the local levels are very likely to be much less of a concern, because there will still be great need to carry out duties locally, albeit with changed authority. Appointed officials, extended staffs, government appointed corporations, are other candidates for sensible severance packages. Every city will need to help in its own readjustment, and the business of transition itself can rely on those people with the right organizational skills.

Needless to say, police, fire, city maintenance, water and other utility activities will be virtually unaffected, as will many chain-of-command structures now in place.

The major elements of transition will require careful timing and sequencing so that changes can be absorbed in a seamless and almost routine manner.

More Thoughts On Transition to Sensible Government

How long might transition take? Computer processing and internet distribution of information will take much of the drudgery out of the project. A first draft of the new Constitution in two to four years seems within reason. Another two to three years of review and revision should give time enough to produce a serious and enlightened Constitution Two ready for submittal to the people, with high expectation for overwhelming approval, since so many have contributed directly to the new foundation document. Implementation is more difficult to judge, but as a first estimate, ten years may be enough time to allow people to adjust as individuals and as organizations to minimize the inevitable negative effects both financial and otherwise. National security would probably be the least affected by a changed Constitution, since the relationship between the military and our civilian government is among the few successes of government and bears little need for fundamental change. The details of making the transition, of course, are another extremely important part of the whole rework process, with the transfer of authority over military and police forces being a critical, early event.

215

I want to emphasize that *none of this activity requires the approval of present government.* That organization was empowered by the people, (at least theoretically) and it is the people alone who have the authority, **by mutual agreement,** to change the rules under which a governing body shall operate. Those rules include the transition plan to take us from today's system to a better one, and the stages of change can be clearly defined. The only means by which present government can block the changed will of the people would be through force. I believe, as an optimist, that government would not resort to such a foolhardy tactic, that instead, they too would see the wisdom of the changes wrought by the people. In all likelihood, being mostly good people, politicians would finally, although perhaps reluctantly, have embraced the new direction for government. I'm quite sure many practical ideas would come from them for this hugely complex enterprise, the United States of America. Any such ideas would have been welcomed, and weighed along with all others against the basic criteria upon which the new Constitution is drawn. That situation would give us the best of all possibilities.

Besides being critical to our survival as a cohesive and **JUST** society, there are two, added, very attractive features surrounding the creation of an enlightened government. The process needs and allows the participation of any and all citizens, giving back to them the *right of choice* so long denied. That precious right was lost so long ago that few among us have even been aware of its loss.

The second feature preserves that regained right of choice as the *new process for changing government* is made a permanent part of the Constitution. Review of government performance, and the changing needs of the citizens of the United States of America will continue to be the basis for future change. The entire procedure of review, reevaluation, revision and resubmittal via referendum will be an ongoing one, thereby removing the unworkable method now in use, yet assuring that changes cannot become frivolous. I contend that choice in the manner in which we are governed is as cherished a right as any other self-evident right, and because it has been so thoroughly denied, effectively if not intentionally, during our entire history, government excesses were as inevitable as they have proven to be. A discussion of this ongoing monitoring activity is given below in **STEP 3** of our solution to the problem of government.

Important Steps To Begin ASAP

There are four additional steps, beyond writing Constitution Two, (Chapter 19), that bear further thought as part of our preparations for fixing what needs to be fixed. Each is discussed in the remainder of this chapter. The four steps are these:

216

STEP 1 Devise a completely new process for choosing leaders.
STEP 2 Institute **Truth** into learning, especially with regard to history.
STEP 3 Monitor government performance & citizen needs to allow continuous, orderly & necessary revision of government, thereby preserving choice.
STEP 4 Implement choice via the Referendum process.

Each of these tasks would add to our ability to change government and are undertakings that can begin whenever Americans finally see their value.

[STEP 1] A New Way To Choose Leaders

This step ordinary citizens can take is to learn how to choose leaders. While this may seem to be a non-problem to some, history has shown all too clearly that it must be an extremely difficult chore because it has been botched consistently. A rough estimate of how many *satisfactory* leaders there have been from the time of the Greeks to today might generously be set at about 1%.

If we restrict our attention just to Presidents of the USA, the percentage of acceptable leaders rises a bit from that historical average, but the number of *exceptional* men who have led us is again a mere handful from among the total. Even the one leader revered most by historians and ordinary people alike failed utterly in his most fundamental of duties as he led us into a needless and horribly destructive civil war. In more recent times, the president alone can not be singled out as being wholly responsible for failures, because so many others have become part of the decision process, but their collective leadership has also failed grievously, leading the nation into disasters of a different kind from the past. Roosevelt began the forced process of creating dependents of government out of people who have the right to choose and work for themselves, and while so-doing have lost unalienable rights in great measure. Every president from L. B. Johnson on has spent us further into needless debt as his leadership continued that transition process of making responsible, self reliant people into wards of the state. Kennedy and Johnson turned us into an aggressor nation, as we ravaged Vietnam in as ruthless a manner as any killer country from history, all unsanctioned by even a scant majority of the people.

Consistently, at the polls, we have been given the choice of men with demonstrated marginal or non-existent principles, who then proceeded to translate those failings into foreign and domestic policies that continue to degrade the US stature in every decade. The once worthy principles that first bound us together as a nation, and which most individual citizens still hold as the ideals we would hope to

217

be identified by, have slowly but relentlessly eroded over the decades. We are not what we want to be, and the sole reason for that truth is because of failed leadership.

The US government's record, so painfully examined in this book, is thus due largely to two factors, bad leaders and our own failure in choosing them. We have failed to insist upon being given choices among men and women who were much more capable of leading a nation, or a city or a state. By now it must be obvious to anyone thinking about the problem, that the job of leading the most advanced nation in history is extremely demanding, calling for exceptional people. Yet the *requirements* that are placed on those who are presented to us at the polls, have virtually nothing to do with the needs of the posts established to carry out this difficult role. Hoopla, innuendo, denigrating opponents and histrionics have absolutely nothing to do with leading a nation, yet these vacuous tactics are the norm rather than the exception in our choosing of leaders. One might compare the succession process in a monarchy as more to the needs of the office, since the Queen-to-be is at least exposed to a lifetime of training for the job. Since succession-by-birthright is as foolish a process as can be imagined, where then do we rank one that is inferior to it?

The failure has been complete at *every level of choice*. It has been a failure because the process that first produces and then settles upon those choices has been completely inappropriate for the need. Two political parties offer candidates who adhere, in virtual lock-step, to a single philosophy for governing. There is no meaningful difference between the two. Both work for the continual expansion of government functions and size, differing only in the time it takes to do roughly the same, wrong thing, and both spend most of their interactive efforts with the public trying to convince us of the wisdom of new government initiatives. Supplied with such choices, voters are actually given no choice at all, and government goes along in its usual way, failing as it has done for so long. Perhaps worst of all is that the qualifications for a government post are tied foremost to having accumulated years of experience carrying out that same party philosophy at the lower levels, demonstrating to party controllers (not to the people) that they know the routine thoroughly, and endorse it completely. Entrenchment of the two parties has been so complete in the United States that every attempt to carve a niche for a third party has been foiled. It is quite unrealistic to think that the process will ever change of itself, or that choice will ever improve, of itself, for the benefit of the people. The leaders, offered to the voting public, will continue to sport the same stripes, and their collective records will still offend the olfactory glands at least as much as in the past, regardless of the good intentions of those elected. One can honestly say that most of those elected do, indeed, have every intention of doing better than the last wave of winning politicians, but in the end the results are the same, and unacceptable. The reason clearly is that the all-pervading philosophy of governing is wrong, and the direction it takes us in is the slow emaciation of a once vibrant national character. The plan being followed by the nation's political industry has evolved over a long period of time. But it's not even a real plan; it is a haphazard method of choosing our kings, big and small, our decision-makers, and is as unacceptable as most other aspects of modern American government.

I'm not being unkind or picky in the least by such a characterization of the process, as two quick comparisons will show. In jury trials, especially high-profile cases, the effort spent in choosing jurors overshadows by far that of choosing political candidates who will serve the people. That effort is spent in finding those who will best serve the party 'platform." Jurors are screened for their philosophy, experiences of like kind, biases regarding race, religion or education, and a host of other personal factors that give an indication of how they might decide the questions at issue. This screening is solely to impanel the best group that either side can have, not to be the most fair or accurate, but to give the best winning chance to each side. Many prospective jurors are offered, but many are rejected for the job as the two sides see it to be.

Perhaps the best example, however, is the contrast one sees for choosing leaders of companies, colleges, banking institutions and hospitals, i.e. most private enterprises, versus that for any government office. The difference lies in insisting that capabilities of the applicant match the needs of the position. For every such position there are specific and detailed requirements a person must meet before even being considered, and that process is extremely successful. Anyone is at liberty to try for these posts, but to do so they are well aware that their background education and experience must prepare them as thoroughly as possible. Only those fully prepared rise to such positions. Occasionally, when someone unqualified takes over it isn't long before the mismatch is evident and changes are made.

Notice two more things about this process compared to government. Each product that private enterprise offers to the public is good for them or it suffers in the market place; a choice completely under the control of the people. Marginal products, whether they be for higher education, banking services, hospital care or beer, are the measure of leadership performance, and are soon improved to customer satisfaction or it's no sale. On the other hand, government products, the result of unqualified leaders and appointees, are most often inferior, especially long term, but the feedback from the 'buyers" can never be directed at the product i tself but only indirectly at the polls. There is never a direct relationship between the two. The connection between inferior government products and official philosophical incompetence is so tenuous that corrective measures can not effectively be made. Government products continue to be poor to bad, and the process of installing poor leaders goes on as if everything offered by government were acceptable.

The second thing to note is that the effective method used throughout industry to offer acceptable products to the public, is done so without public vote of any kind regarding the choice of *leaders* responsible for producing the products. An acceptable product depends on the competence of an entire organization, which in turn depends on the competence of its leaders and staff. No organization can produce acceptable products with incompetent people or the wrong notion as to what people want, yet we continue to thrust huge responsibilities on incompetent or ill-prepared people within our governing organizations and expect their products to be what are needed. *It can't be done*, and we surely must recognize that fact after so much government failure in the things they have produced.

An analogy. Suppose people were given complete freedom to accept or reject each government dictate, whatever it may be. Those who accept would abide by it; those who reject it would be free of it, not contributing to it (through taxes) nor bound by it. It takes little imagination to visualize what the split might be among the people for and against the many laws, regulations, tax increases and other products to come out of government. Most would lie fallow on the "shelves" of the government "store," because most are inferior products, unwanted by most people (my opinion). In the analogy, voting for representatives has been replaced by a "market place" vote at the government store, and the ineffectiveness of our method of choosing leaders is sidestepped completely. Those leaders who didn't have the vision or the ability to see what was truly needed by the people would soon be out of a job, and the organization would soon learn how to prepare its leaders and staff better or they, too, would be out of business entirely.

There has been a tacit assumption, inbred among Americans, that all one must have to be an acceptable candidate for public office is American citizenship. I challenge that assumption as being a misinterpretation by the people of our freedom to govern ourselves. It is merely the start point to gain any office. Beyond that simple prerequisite are a whole set of real requirements that should be met before anyone can be considered qualified for any office, from the lowest to the most exalted.

Thus, the process of choosing government leaders is deficient on fundamental grounds, and the means to control effectiveness of the organization, through workable feedback, is non-existent. Control is also deficient concerning the capabilities of individuals, since it is almost impossible to remove inept people until their term of spreading incompetence comes to an end. This leads to the obvious conclusion that the process should change, or else mediocrity will continue, and the consequence will be more failures from government. The methodology to redefine government was discussed previously along with a Strawman organization based on that method and the underlying principles of American life. The second ingredient needed to drag us up from an unworkable governing philosophy, is to change the method used for selecting leaders at all levels of government.

Education of Leaders

The solution to this thorny issue of choosing leaders, after first recognizing it, is to initiate the same kind of preparation and filtering methods used everywhere else to select people whose abilities must match the needs of the job. It isn't enough just being a mother, or a father, to serve on a school board, or to live in a given location to serve on a city council. It isn't enough just being a lawyer who can write legalese to serve in the Congress, or just being a citizen to be president of the country. Every one of these offices, even now, should have educational requirements attached to them that fill in great holes that now exist in a person's background, yet are needed to perform competently. Formal courses in government operations are a must, courses which include analyses to compare those existing operations to other countries and to our own historical beginnings. People who aspire to lead others and to make decisions **for** others *must formally understand the true nature of the responsibilities they want to assume*. It is not enough simply to be willing or even anxious to ram you own beliefs at others, without also having a full appreciation of *their* rights that are being affected, possibly even being trampled by fiat. Perhaps the best example of what not to do is provided by President Clinton's own preparation for office. His education was complete from an academic sense, all aimed first to benefit what he believed were his own needs to assume power. While it may be an oversimplification, however, his education was completely lacking in those aspects of public life which cover responsibilities, the humanities, high moral principles and the sovereign rights of every single person he sought to lead; and that background is the product of an entire lifetime of learning, formal and informal. That biased formal background was further distorted by his experiences in Arkansas, where instead of having to exercise qualities of exceptional leadership and service, the art of power politics was all he had need of. That part of his preparation he learned with great skill as the country now surely knows from the record of his presidency.

President Clinton's mental blocks regarding service and responsibility are not an isolated case, since the rights of individuals are not understood by most officials. Sadly this is true *within all levels of government* throughout the nation. The formal training people have had in this area of study alone is almost nonexistent. Even allowing that High School curricula can satisfy the 'formal" requirement, what has been taught does not satisfy either of these first two requirements for substance. The rights of individuals, of all other people besides self, is almost never taught. Likewise, the failings of government in its creation of legislative products is never brought out by being compared in depth with the philosophy that founded the nation. Every aspect of government is glossed over or even whitewashed in an altruistic and misguided attempt to present government in the most positive light. The same has been true for most of the documentaries seen on television. The net effect is non-education concerning reality, and by default, the continued propagation of the grade school notion that we are the Earth's example of perfection in self government.

Each crop of new leaders carries this subliminal understanding with them, and the rusted chain of today's philosophy for ruling remains unbroken.

As there is in the military academies, there is an overwhelming need for formal training in leadership for public service, and that need is quite different among the several identifiable levels of responsibility. None of this vacuum is being filled today, nor has it ever been. We have become so accustomed to letting things just happen, taking what comes along, that it is little wonder American leadership is so poor. It takes a truly exceptional person to develop leadership qualities by himself or by herself. Pitifully few of our political fellows have measured up, a truth from the very beginning that is still with us today. The solution for this great deficiency is quite obvious. The need for an Academy to train Statesmen and Leaders of Society is acute. One can readily envision such a place of training akin to West Point, Annapolis, Coast Guard and Air Force Academies, devoted to a need for leadership that is our greatest. Such an Academy, with affiliations to the very best of our existing universities, would be a most sensible way to extract ourselves from the mediocrity that confounds us continually.

A New Cadre of People
Study of the humanities should also be an important part of the curriculum. While home study can easily be part of the overall effort to fill the formal education gap, examinations can not be the take-home, multiple choice pap so often seen in time-filler courses. The whole matter under discussion is an extremely serious one, and the manner in which we fill the need is likewise as serious as one can imagine.

Education is the key to improvement in choosing leaders. And the requirements should be progressively greater for posts of greater responsibilities. Testing should be extensive, as it would be in any good course of study, and the results of those exams should be public. Anyone who wants to make decisions for others, must contend with **full disclosure** of his or her regard for the rights of others, as well as having a thorough understanding of the consequences of choices made in the past by earlier political leaders. Many of the CATO publications should be on the required reading lists for such studies, as should many of the classic works of social philosophy. Finally, there should be a series of public tests, preliminary and final, for each level of government, which are completely analogous to those given for the Bar or Professional Engineers exams. The testing of individuals seeking government posts should not be limited by party membership, nor should the appearance of candidates on ballots be restricted by party membership. The monopoly exercised by the two major parties for offering candidates must be ended,

222

and the fiction of seeming to offer choice via useless primary "elections" will become clear to the public through changes of the kind described here. Being a member of either political group can not possibly be a requirement to become an effective leader or legislator, yet that is exactly the implied assumption under which our political system operates. Rather, the candidates offering themselves for elective positions should be those most qualified as evidenced by new educational requirements and background experience.

Under Constitution Two, of course, most elective positions would be replaced by negotiations between the people (via the Citizens Advocacy Agency) and organizations competing to carry out the functions of government. Leadership requirements for such organizations would remain as described, however. Moreover, those positions that are elective (via referendum, for example) would only be filled by candidates prepared as described here.

As almost an afterthought, it should be quite clear that *the practice of making political appointments* can not be reconciled with the new demand for competence among the leaders and staff doing tasks beyond the scope of individuals. Appointments for these posts has no merit whatsoever as its practice has shown. The purpose of appointments, which is to allow a "winner" the means of rewarding those who helped him win, makes losers of all the rest of us by sidestepping completely the need to satisfy requirements for critical positions. Once again, voters have no part in such appointments, and our failure to choose the right leaders continues. Staffing correctly is accomplished through sensible reviews of those meeting qualifications.

Since I am assuming government must be redefined, most of this discussion for choosing leaders has quite a different connotation than merely outlawing appointments or having the right people placed on a ballot, which presently is a disgrace.

Rather it implies the creation of a completely different, far more qualified cadre of people interested in serving the nation and its people toward a more optimum form of self government.

At the same time a satisfying career path can be carved out for such dedicated people. The power hungry will not like the idea at all, but such people are not the ones we want to satisfy. The concern we should keep clearly in mind is the truly enlightened goal of improving the life of ordinary people by respecting each and every Right due them as sovereign individuals. From a cadre of knowledgeable, dedicated and qualified people such as described here, will come the staffs and the leaders needed to carry out those functions that **must** be performed by agencies of government under contract to the people, and limited to those functions that can not be handled by individuals themselves or private, non-government organizations.

[STEP 2] Institute TRUTH Into Learning, Particularly Historical Truth

People believe what they are taught. This is axiomatic with youngsters. Since we're concerned here with improving the way we govern ourselves and the things that might be done to help achieve that, it follows that any school lesson in government should be factual. Otherwise there is no basis for evaluation or change. The understanding a young person has surrounding the way we are being governed and the specifics of government actions, is critical to their own decisions to be made later in life. Generally what is being taught now, however, is a whitewashed version of history, and too little critical analyses of the actions of men who have made our decisions in the past. We grow up with a firm belief in the innate and total virtue of the United States of America and, therefore, in most if not all of its government actions. It seems likely that if fantasy were removed form the lessons prepared for all students, the building up of a national ego might initially suffer, but the expectations of growing adults regarding government would be much more realistic and far different than at present. What I'm addressing here is but one step in overcoming our built-in gullibility by being as consistently rigorous in what we teach about history and government as can possibly be. Obviously, for many things, mankind has not learned all the truth there is to know, but the truth we have learned, especially regarding government, is impressive nevertheless. Moreover we know how to handle that issue. Teach fact as it is known, accompanied by the caveat that parts of the story, any story, can have holes and here they are.

The goal of truth and the teaching of it is an illusive one because it is so easily obscured. Anyone with an intent to confuse understanding can easily do so simply by questioning the issue and entering half-truths into a discussion. Immediately we see the importance of motive, another intangible human attribute that can easily work against us. The most deliberate examples of this kind of obfuscation are seen in the court room, especially in high-profile cases. The O.J. Simpson criminal case illustrated the malady in sharp relief. The man murdered two people; the forensic evidence was absolutely conclusive; yet the extraneous screening, half truths, volumes of tangential material and unending disruption of the flow of facts by clever, little men with dishonest motives,[37] was enough to obscure truth and frustrate justice. All the conclusions just mentioned were proven in civil court after the murderer was allowed to go free.

Truth is an extremely hard commodity to collect and pass on to the next generation, and the main reason is precisely because of people and their distorted motives. Government, likewise, is motivated to distort history, past and current.

---

[37] They will excuse their actions in this case by saying they were just trying to give the defendant the best possibly defense, all their actions being allowed by law. I contend, however, that this isn't good defense, it is willful distortion of TRUTH condoned by a flawed System of Justice.

With the passage of time, the organization called government takes on a momentum of its own, and it wants to survive both for good reasons (like stability) and bad reasons (like the drive to increase power). Staying in power is an overriding goal of government as we saw when Lincoln led us into civil war, and as we see today in its attitude toward groups of people who have a low tolerance for intrusion by government into their lives. With some insight, we also see it in just about every legislative action taken that adds power to government and diminishes sovereign rights of individuals. Government has a vested interest in presenting itself in a virtuous light, and there is little question that in their capacity as enforcer of 'public" education, they influence the text books that drill our children. Obviously five and six year olds aren't ready to debate the details of history, but there should be no surprise at how receptive they are to distortions knowingly put before them, when truth would just as easily have been received and accepted.

What is the truth of a thing? The dictionary defines truth as "actual fact, conformity with fact or reality, a verified or indisputable fact or principle." The last says it best, I believe, but it needs to be restated, with added emphasis on *indisputable*. Something is Truth if *everyone can reasonably accept it*, i.e. if no one in good conscience disputes it. Immediately we see the classic conditions for tail-chase logic. Since our conscience is tuned to the things we are taught, then, 'in good conscience,' we can hold on to things that are not true and meet the definition of truth. By learning a different truth, one based on new or better facts, then the old truth gives way, or should give way, to a new and better truth. Truth is a boot-strapped treasure of society as it slowly learns facts and unlearns old things previously thought to be facts. It is **applying** newly learned facts to revise old lessons that slowly lifts society up from superstition to reality, and is the thing that is noticeably lacking in the US education system regarding government. All of the lessons learned so painfully, some as unsettling revelations given earlier in this book, and there are many, show the opposite side of the stories being delivered in public schools now. This too is a failure of leadership.

Regarding government, in spite of our having a collection of facts now that are worthy in every respect, and that belie the unfounded lessons still being taught, there is little or no attempt to change that pattern of untruth that still distorts our direction as a society. We still throw the same unfounded stories of government virtue at the kids, and they still come away with the same distortions we ourselves had, and which many still have. The tail chase is still in frantic progress, now dominated by the newer myths of today's government. One subliminal message, or stated another way, the integrated effect of today's distortions, is the notion that government is the solver of all social problems, and dependence on government becomes a natural thing. Subtlety is indeed subtle, and that mien of government is greatly responsible for keeping us captive to the general drift toward greater dependence on government.

There is a rebuttal to my thesis concerning government that may be worth considering. William F. Buckley, the superb editor of National Review, would have us believe that "We are winning, ...our ideas are winning. Theirs are losing." He is speaking of the torrent of untruths that continue to pour from government, as I have contended. He too has focused his attention on truth — because it is so rare. The notion, however, that truth is beginning to displace the lies of government, 'to our great relief' shows far more optimism than I can conclude. Government excesses and crimes against the people are far from being limited to lies fed as truth, and passive response will not change the realities of their distorted brand of Americanism. My firm conviction is that only overt, peaceful changes, such as outlined here can effect the real changes needed in how we are governed, and formally embracing **TRUTH** is one such important change.

We continue to delude ourselves about our history; to believe that those craving power want to help us; and to believe that bad people will be punished and good people (like ourselves) will finally be rewarded — in a later life, and that trying to change things, therefore, is not all that important.

Everything that can't be **verified** is opinion. Learn to recognize TRUTH which can be unearthed from society's pile of refuse by **testing** everything against ever more and better facts, thereby swelling the ranks of those who can reasonably accept it as truth. The step we wish to take to improve the way we govern ourselves, therefore, is to wipe away the pap being taught, and instead make full use of truth known from facts . The effects of such a change will come slowly, but the long term well-being of the nation is dependent on it. It is quite all right to allow our national ego to suffer, since it is now out of synch with reality anyway. Yet prideful ego would be far more deserved if we were to begin seriously to adopt truth as part of our national makeup and behavior toward ourselves and the rest of the world.

[STEP 3] Monitor Government Performance & Citizen Needs for Continuous Updating of Government

The thing that makes us smarter today than Madison, Jefferson et al were at the end of the eighteenth century comes from our having been witnesses to the last 200 years of US history. They had triggered an entirely new experiment in social-political interaction, having been convinced that governments of old did not fulfill the real needs of the people of a country. They were completely right about that. Unfortunately what they could not know for certain was how well the newly devised government would do what they hoped it would do. We, however, have seen that in spite of being quite clear about the fundamental criteria needed as the basis of government, the use of those criteria as determinants for national actions has not been automatic at all.

That same situation holds true today. Nothing is automatic. Good intentions do not make government automatically act the way it should, nor can we today be any smarter than they were about what might happen in the next two hundred years. This leads directly to the conclusion that **change is not a one-time need,** but change for the sake of continuous improvement is essential, and may be for a long time to come. Providing for a workable means to change, therefore, is essential. Those early founders also saw such a need, and sought to satisfy that requirement by the current means of changing the Constitution. Today we're also smarter about that process through 200 years of use. It too does not work in a way that can satisfy the real needs of change. I believe that a fundamental overhaul of government is called for, yet the current method of making changes is so limited that *such basic rework is not feasible by that existing process.*

Thus, I have strongly argued that the process itself must change in order to handle the real needs of constructive change. Based on that line of reasoning, I've suggested a method that is essentially continuous in the monitoring of government actions and citizen needs, coupled with use of the referendum to decide on the change(s) themselves. This section is an elaboration of earlier discussions on monitoring government performance. It will show how a continuous review process can be organized to give the people quantitative information on how well government is doing its job as defined by a new Constitution. Instead of just sitting back for the next one hundred years and absorbing whatever government does, formal monitoring can give a running appraisal from which further sensible changes in government can be devised and presented for approval.

Monitoring, in fact, can be formalized for present government, and would be an ideal starting point for the task.

Change Must be Orderly

Changing government in an *orderly* manner is the only mature way to go about it because any other means gets people killed, as history proves. Killing is the worst possible way to try to improve living conditions; it defies all logic if not history. It does exactly the opposite of upgrading the rights of people, especially for those murdered during transition. Change, however, may not be a never-ending legacy of these proposals. With the right process for change in place, and effectively being used as the need arises, then it seems quite reasonable to expect that the *need* for change will slowly diminish. Big changes give way to lesser ones as that elusive ideal of optimum government is slowly approached over time. The whole gamut of functions for which the people must rely on government to carry out must ultimately be resolved into a final acceptable set, requiring little or no further change. The same may hold for the means of funding government expenses, and the checks and balances used within government agencies to negate human failings. Changes at that time may ultimately boil down to handling the unknowns of interacting with the other peoples of the world, which will probably always be with us.

Evaluating Government

At the moment there is no existing group which evaluates government in the manner suggested here. There are, however, many Action Groups which do a fraction of the job, each concentrating on the parts of government which seem important to them. CATO, The Hoover Institute, The Chicago School of Economics and some of the investigative journals do excellent watchdog work now, but are usually reactive rather than comprehensive. CATO is perhaps the closest example of what is needed, but it too does not follow a structured nor comprehensive regimen in their evaluations. Conversely, there are a great many respected organizations capable of such work, JPL, MIT, RPI, GRC, Cal Tech and SRI among them. Also it is quite likely that grants and endowments could provide much of the early funding, later to be augmented by document sales. Cost to taxpayers might then be nil, but the service would be indispensable. Government is supposed to do certain specific things as have been discussed, and their successes and failures while doing them are the things which must be graded. Grading, however, is far from an academic exercise, since the results will be used directly to initiate corrective measures on the part of the people through the Citizen Advocacy Agency, or its equivalent. Personnel and staff can be let go, whole contracts with functional agencies can be canceled, functions can be modified or discontinued, new functions can be contracted for, or any of the other elements of government structure can be reworked to try to improve government performance.

The era of open loop government operations should be brought to a close just as soon as possible, and diagnosing government performance, followed by corrective action, is the way to do it.

Today's government does all the hundreds of things covered earlier in the book, and my informal evaluation resulted from an analysis of its performance. I concentrated on the six major responsibilities of government and gave it a failing grade on all of them. All these duties were also deficient in a wide range of contributors to those basic six, and many were discussed at length. Still, that appraisal was certainly informal because of its limited scope, and because not all the analyses were done quantitatively. Due note is also made that the manner used to quantify loss of unalienable rights was still more subjective than it should be or can be. Formal analyses will slowly upgrade the *subjective* into *more rigorous results* as more and more agreement surfaces among people on the relative values of our Unalienable Rights.

Therefore, the proposal here in [STEP 3] is to formalize what this book attempts to do in shortened form by subjecting the whole spectrum of government actions to more rigorous, quantitative scrutiny.

Every function that government carries out, presumably for the people, can be quantified in some manner, whether in percentages, amounts spent, authorized goals accomplished, or rights subverted. Comparisons can be made at every crossroad on the true benefits to people versus their loss in freedom of action, unalienable rights, property, money, ability to make choices, and a whole host of prerogatives innate to sovereign individuals. The consequences of what government does can be directly linked to the prime purposes of government and their measure of performance taken. That is the key to knowing what must be done to keep improving the way we manage the business of governing ourselves.

The formal process for measuring the effectiveness of government will be described presently, as soon as the people half of our goal is noted. Government is created by the people to do what they want done but can't do as individuals. Remember, *The People* does not mean 51 percent of them, it means virtually all of them. Again, Security is our ideal example. Everyone wants to be safe, not just 51 % of the people, and since almost everyone can agree on this need, positive measures can be taken — by government — to work for everyone's safety. The way to assess the true needs of the bulk of the population is to ask for specifics in the form of referenda. As more such questions are asked and answered, the unknowns slowly give way to real information about the things that matter most to people.

Desires are another matter entirely. In my view desires come under the heading of potential national goals, not *imperatives*, but *options* to consider. The people, being given a choice in such things, will also soon remove the mystery by saying just how much they are willing to give of their earnings to fund these optional enterprises. Great societies, trips to the moon for a dozen travelers, journeys to Mars, high speed rail lines between New York and Chicago, and all manner of 'good and worthy goals' can be decided easily. Simply ask for subscriptions as part of the referendum. The results will come without ambiguity.

The Monitoring Process
We're back to System Engineering 101. The government is nothing but a big system, with a lot of unreliable moving parts, many of which are defective in unknowable ways. (For example, a bad philosophy in a person can hurt immensely, but knowing about it beforehand is extremely difficult.) Nevertheless, measure the output of the elements, the various subsystems and the overall system itself and you have all the information necessary to know where improvements are needed. Conceptually the process is as simple as those we've met earlier. It relies on

229

progressively upgrading a data base, both in scope and in fidelity to American life. It makes use of a set of models representing all the functions charged to government, and whose outputs are *comparative measures of government's success in preserving rights and accomplishing goals*. Proposed government actions have consequences, and an evaluation model will do two things. First it will evaluate what has been done, the consequences of a move. Second it can be used to predict the likely outcome of proposed legislative actions. At the highest level, the model can be visualized as an extensive, three dimensional matrix representing Rights, Goals and Proposed Actions, and at each matrix intersection there are influence coefficients which relate the effects of each on the other factors. These 'coefficients' are themselves the result of other lower level analyses of cause and effect, made quantitative through experience with the models, and the metrics chosen to relate actions with consequences.

A top level view of the overall process shows it as a list of interactive tasks, all continually being upgraded as events and information change. Independent teams allow for the use of competing analyses, but the objectives are the same:

- define metrics both for government performance and for citizen Rights -
- define and create models of government actions, and their effects on Rights –
- apply metrics and analyze the effects of proposed actions on both the stated goals, and on individual Rights –
- Do extensive model testing using historical data –
- then apply model and other analyses to evaluate proposed new legislation.

The expected feedback to managers would include the cost in loss of Rights to achieve a national objective. Such work has the potential to find the best course of action in terms of minimizing that loss of Rights to achieve a critical goal, and thus be more acceptable to individuals.

As before, it should be understood that each part of the process is expanded and detailed during planning to the point where analysis requirements are established for every part of the monitoring task. Most likely the first version of the analysis itself will not do all that is wanted, but as is true in all such problems, each upgrade brings the work closer and closer to what is needed. As more elements are added, the scope increases and the results are more meaningful. As firm referendum information is generated, unknowns are replaced with numbers. And as the detailed history of government acts is analyzed for the last two centuries, and particularly the past few decades, then the effects of real actions become quantified, and questions of what future acts might do become fewer.

A Guideline To Help Maintain Focus

The loss of unalienable rights and wealth already suffered because of government actions is the crux of the whole problem with present government, and the analyses, the models, and the data offered here are all tailored to add rigor to our subjective displeasure with the record.

The nature of the monitoring job allows it to be chopped into many parts, so that many different groups and organizations can participate. Several independent teams can be used for those parts where subjectivity might remain an issue, and where consensus must finally be achieved. Such teams would be formed with representatives from many disciplines including analysts, historians, managers, mathematicians, economists, military analysts, social analysts and legal and constitutional experts. One of the first chores, after creating a preliminary set of requirements for the monitoring function and the working teams to match, would be to begin generating a complete set of metrics[38] by which the elements of performance can be quantified, and the factors involved can be related functionally and quantitatively. The whole long history of US government actions can be used as fodder for these early tasks, and can be used as **test cases** for all the model elements. For such tests, the "answer" is essentially known fr om the record, and calibration of the overall model becomes more straightforward once consensus is reached on a preliminary set of values to be attached to citizen Rights.

It is extremely important to keep the objectives of this work clearly in mind. Everything comes with a price. In the past, government acts have exacted a heavy toll in citizen wealth, and an even more costly, but less obvious, squandering of Rights. The trade-off between Rights and wealth on the one hand, and the objectives of government on the other, has all been skewed heavily in favor of those interested mainly in power; the real costs all borne by the people.

That lopsided tradeoff must be replaced by one that compares Rights and Wealth with joint objectives of the people, not government. That is the question to be answered — and only by the people via referendum. *That is the measure that must be quantified* so everyone can understand exactly what they have been giving up to buy the deficient products of government. The goal, of course, is twofold; (1) prevent government from creating future defective products, and (2) know exactly what the tradeoff will be for any proposed action. *Decisions then made by the people can be made with full knowledge of the consequences to liberty and treasure.* Reminders such as this will be ever-present as the work gathers

---

[38] Such as money spent on asbestos cleanup, per life-year added (ref. Chapter 10), or the benefit to safety [or improved quality of life] per dollar spent on art endowments vs. DNA diagnostic equipment — and hundreds of other similar metrics. The MO of government in its spending practices makes it easy to create meaningful metrics for evaluating performance.

momentum, and as it progresses, citizens, once held in contempt by government, will be lifted out of the dark and made fully aware of what is being done on their behalf and done **TO** them as a consequence.

Testing Procedures to Evaluate Methods

In order for any analytical model to be acceptable, there must be confidence in its use. Rigorous testing is the way to gain that confidence. Testing makes use of a number of *benchmark events* in American history such as the Civil War period, the Spanish American war, the great depression and the New Deal, Vietnam, and funding special interests of the Bennett – DiLorenzo variety. Tests compare the results of two methods of analysis, those of the developing models and those taken from the historic analyses of these same benchmark cases. The objective is to refine the models, which use firm quantitative data, until model results yield essentially the same evaluation of performance that came from an interpretation of the historic work. While interpretation will always be a necessary part of evaluation, the specific metrics and reasoning behind conclusions will be abundantly clear. It will, therefore, be possible, and desirable, for each voter to decide what his own level of confidence is in the work, and vote each referendum question accordingly.

Extending these methods of analysis to cities, large and small, is easy to visualize.

With history as the means of testing the confidence one can place in analyses, attention can then be focused on current government activities. The new rules under which government will operate (making the necessary assumption of a new Constitution) then become the basis for the next set of tests. Such questions can be asked as the following:

- How would the new Constitution have altered government acts of the past?
- What would the loss of Rights have been limited to over a given period, and how significant might that be?
- What would the expenditures of government have been like if profligate spending had been removed as a function of government?
- How else might history have been changed for the better under the new guidelines?
- Or possibly for the worst?

Admittedly, some of the results coming from this work might be taken as requiring clairvoyance to have implemented such directives, but that would not be the purpose of the exercise. Had different rules been in effect over the last sixty or seventy years, our gains and losses would be different than they are. Some measure of what those differences might be would help greatly to gauge what might be in store for us ahead into the time when nothing can be foretold with confidence. A model with an ability to yield mature, factual results for historic events will then provide the kind of evaluation information needed by voters to decide on proposed future moves. If later those decisions prove to be deficient in unforeseen ways, then the process for change is invoked to bootstrap ourselves upward notch by notch to better self government.

Every set of results gives more complete knowledge of the analyses themselves and leads to improvements where they are needed. Repeated use and refinement of the elements raises the confidence level of the methods, the data and our interpretation of what the results are telling us. When confidence in the entire process is raised to a point where judgment dictates, then analyses can begin in earnest on current questions and decisions. At that time the microscope of factual appraisal will have replaced the subjective and often childlike emotionalism presently in use. What results ultimately from all this effort are reports which assure that the people are kept fully informed about government proposals, decisions, actions and their likely consequences. Details and summaries of every aspect of the work are there, and nothing is kept hidden. I contend that for self government finally to become a workable concept, that **the people** must be able to exercise their right to choose, to decide, and that when fully informed, their decisions will be orders of magnitude better than those of *representatives* who can not truly represent anyone but themselves.

What government is called upon to do at the request of the people is too important to rely on trust alone. While trust in leaders is still a goal to be sought, it is not something we can be complacent about because it has so often been abused.

Thorough monitoring of government, minimizing government functions and the continuous exercise of choice by the people can take us to the next goal, a higher plateau of self government which has been slowly fading from hope for so long.

[STEP 4] Referendum vs. Representation

It may seem irreverent, or foolhardy or even worse to propose that representative government be replaced by one which requires people to make their own decisions via referendum. Therefore, the issue must be given much more attention. The essence of the matter is contained within the simple question of whether the desires of the people can be determined and implemented more faithfully by having someone speak for them in formal gatherings (the Assembly, Senate, House, Town Council or other body) or by allowing them to speak for themselves in response to a referendum. The common sense answer is obvious. No one can speak better FOR someone than that person, but of course that is not the whole story.

233

People have the self-evident right to govern themselves. That tenet has been acknowledged from the beginning. The accompanying debate, however, was not about the principle, but about how to implement it in the 1790's, and still get something accomplished, especially for self defense. Europe still harbored greedy leaders who thought stealing from anyone who was vulnerable was acceptable conduct, and America was a tempting prize. Representation was the only sensible answer back then because *information* was shackled to horse or ship, and time to act was usually short. It would have been completely impractical to survey the people every time a decision was needed. For military matters, central control was required, and in truth, those sent as representatives did know what the people wanted because they had frequent personal contact with them regarding security. Representation was faithful and much more efficient than any direct citizen vote could possibly have been **at the time**.

The world has changed completely since those days. Now information — to everyone — is essentially instantaneous. The threat from beyond our borders is well known and we are well prepared. The task that remains is to stay alert, and continue to advance our ability to defend ourselves. Even the decisions required to remain prepared are not those that must be made in an instant. The press of time even for defense is no longer as it once was. The old worry, no longer spoken of today, is that the country would not be able to act in a timely manner during a crisis if it were not for the ability of representatives to make timely decisions. Even that rationale, however, can no longer be supported in today's world of instantly available information. Nor can any logical argument be made regarding decisions for everyday, non-time-critical, issues.

Representatives make all our decisions, but, in truth, there has never been a valid reason for that for any issue except time-critical questions.

While we're at it, there is also no good reason to institute the representative concept to overcome a supposed lack of education or ability among the people to understand. For domestic issues, the people, who are the nation, are quite likely *better* qualified than surrogates, who become politically motivated rather than practical about the issues that affect people directly. The **only** reason that representation is still being used to control the country and all the local fiefdoms, is because the controllers want it that way. The capability exists today to create a system of distributing information *relevant to any issue* and having the people vote directly on it in a timely manner. **Representation is clearly obsolete,** at least as far as reaching a final decision is concerned.

Proposing legislation to be voted upon, the next important part of the legislative process, however, is actually where the greatest gulf exists between the needs and

234

desires of the people and the actions of government. That is where the money is controlled. It is the step in the American governmental process where true power is exercised, and it is at this step that most of the poor decisions of the past have been made.

One can view the whole incentive to create a new governmental structure, with new Constitutional guidelines, as a way to break the political stranglehold that the present, unworkable representative government has on America's wealth.

The myriad abuses from both federal and local government bodies have reached the level where we risk national suicide if fundamental changes are not made — soon. The proposed Strawman government, therefore, includes legislative steps only for those few functions suited exclusively for government agencies, functions considerably reduced in scope from those of the present. The spending lid is set by the people at a predetermined level, based on *money that is available*, rather than as a consequence of legislative spending, which is exactly backwards, and ultimately destabilizing of American society.

Representative government, therefore, which does not actually represent the people, can be replaced with something that does work — for the people — instead of for representatives. Limited functions are defined in a new Constitution; proposed legislation is written by separate, monitored functional agencies; and voting on referenda replaces the fiction of representation via legislative bodies. In addition, drafting a referendum is not limited to legislators, nor do legislators have any approval function whatsoever for submitting such choices to the people.

Finally, it should be a *constitutional* matter as to the *level of approval* required for passage of a referendum or other legislation, depending on the type of issue to be resolved. There is no compulsion whatsoever to retain the concept of a simple majority to gain consent. That threshold is arguably the most unfair element of American government, and is one that can not logically be defended.

As to the use of votes via referendum, instead of representatives, their effectiveness can readily be seen from examples of its use. Over a decade ago, Howard Jarvis risked his own political career by opposing the entrenched party regarding taxes. As spending splurges continued in California, politicians sought to increase taxes in any way they could. Real estate had become a favorite target for repeated increases in previous sessions of the Legislature. To counter that regressive trend, Jarvis fought hard to place Proposition 13 on the ballot, a measure specifically designed to limit real estate tax increases. The vote was *overwhelmingly approved* by Californians, leaving no doubt whatsoever what the people's decision was regarding such taxation. Their representatives, however, had other desires, and

235

immediately used every possible means to overturn or negate the will of the people. Ultimately the politicians won that war, because, having failed to overturn the decision, they soon succeeded in subverting the **intent** of the vote by redefining the elements that make up the tax levy attached to real estate. They were soon back in business as usual in the matter of spending money as **they** see fit regardless of the unambiguous will of the people in the matter.

A more recent example, again from California, concerned the language of use in public schools. In some areas, the percentage of Spanish speaking students had become greater than those speaking English. Bilingual classes became commonplace, and the use of Spanish increased to the point that Spanish actually replaced the use of English in many classes even though there were still students in the class who understood only English. Evidently school authorities, in trying to accommodate those who did not speak English, forgot about those students who did. The matter had to be decided by referendum, Proposition 227. Again the people approved overwhelmingly the English-only guideline for public instruction. They had clearly made their decision. The teaching of English, as a second language, obviously continued, but the use of another language to instruct English speaking students was discontinued. And what was the reaction of our representatives? They immediately waged political war against this clear mandate through court action and every end-run tactic possible. The people's decision has held so far, but it did so *in spite of elected representatives,* not because of them.

The wisdom of this voter-approved change in public education seems to have won the day as other states with similar quandaries about language are debating the issue. Arizona, for example, is trying to end government mandated bilingual education because of the California successes. The debates triggered by this issue, however, still show much disagreement among people. Nevertheless, if we step back far enough from the details of the issue, two important lessons become crystal clear. **Firstly**. use of the Referendum in California corrected another government error of intrusion into education. **Secondly**, it was not a matter that should have been mandated in the first place. Without government involvement in what is just another matter of choice, the needs of all citizens, Spanish speaking and English speaking, would have been satisfied in the market place. Private educators can fill both needs, and that is the Just way to handle such problems. It never was a go, no-go issue. It was always an issue of choice for individuals and should be handled that way, no matter what the second language may be. Those who have emigrated to another country have always been faced with learning a new language to help themselves live. If they choose not to bother, then the consequences are just a result of their own choice, a responsibility of their own, and no one else's. Clearly government has no Just say in the matter.

236

I'll repeat an earlier statement; ***representatives are incapable of representing anyone except themselves,*** and the concept of using surrogate voices in place of those of the people themselves can not function properly where self-government is the goal. It is the concept that is at fault, not those who try to represent others. Only in the rarest of instances can such substitution effectively ensure that the will of the people is followed, and in such cases the real need for a formal vote is quite likely unnecessary.

EPILOGUE

Any machine or system that no longer does what the user wants done, is obsolete. The recitation in Part I of this book of government actions shows decisively that American government fits that description remarkably well. The proof is in its failures to manage properly what is needed, and its badly mismanaged national and local projects that shouldn't even be done. Costs to us, the trusting citizens of America, are excessive both in wealth, and in supposedly guaranteed individual, unalienable rights.

That mismanagement of American affairs has covered the gamut of transgressions from simple errors, to abject premeditated crimes against our own laws. Even more serious are the same spectrum of offenses against the citizens of our once unique country.

All attempts to date, have failed to inject control into government actions. Citizen expectations, the stewardship Americans have a right to demand of officials, local and federal, have been rebuffed summarily for far too long.

The great hope one can take from this book, however, is that returning government to its real purpose of serving Americans, and redirecting American society that takes its form and attitude from government, is for us to begin again. Take the first decisive step, peacefully, to advance American self-government. That step, which can only be taken by the people, is to draft a new Constitution, and in it, to redefine functions, including the role of citizens, and redesign government structure with guidelines and limitations to authority that are appropriate to modern America.

How to go about accomplishing these weighty changes occupies the latter half of this book, and every indication is that the task is within our collective abilities.

A FINAL ADMONITION

The correlation between a defective government, by any measure, and a system of Law that is also destitute, is clearly one hundred percent. The American system of justice is not limited to bad law, however. There are far more serious deficiencies we should no longer tolerate.

But that is another story; one that is addressed in a companion book devoted to **THE LAST DEBATE.**

APPENDICIES

APPENDIX A

The BILL OF RIGHTS[39]

The First Ten Amendments To The
Constitution
of the
United States of America

Amendment I.

Congress shall make no law respecting an establishment of religion, or prohibiting the free exercise thereof; or abridging the freedom of speech, or of the press, or the right of the people peaceably to assemble, and to petition the Government for a redress of grievances.

Amendment II.

A well regulated Militia, being necessary to the security of a free State, the right of the people to keep and bear Arms, shall not be infringed.

Amendment III.

No Soldier shall, in time of peace be quartered in any house, without the consent of the Owner, nor in time of war, but in a manner to be prescribed by law.

Amendment IV.

The right of the people to be secure in their persons, houses, papers, and effects, against unreasonable searches and seizures, shall not be violated, and no Warrants shall issue, but upon probable cause, supported by Oath or affirmation, and particularly describing the place to be searched, and the persons or things to be seized.

Amendment V.

---

[39] Ratified effective December 15, 1791.

No person shall be held to answer for a capital, or otherwise infamous crime, unless on a presentment or indictment of a Grand Jury, except in cases arising in the land or naval forces, or in the Militia, when in actual service in time of War or public danger; nor shall any person be subject for the same offense to be twice put in jeopardy of life or limb, nor shall be compelled in any criminal case to be a witness against himself, nor be deprived of life, liberty, or property, without due process of law; nor shall private property be taken for public use without just compensation.

Amendment VI.

In all criminal prosecutions, the accused shall enjoy the right to a speedy and public trial, by an impartial jury of the state and district wherein the crime shall have been committed; which district shall have been previously ascertained by law, and to be informed of the nature and cause of the accusation; to be confronted with the witnesses against him; to have compulsory process for obtaining witnesses in his favor, and to have the assistance of counsel for his defense.

Amendment VII.

In Suits at common law, where the value in controversy shall exceed twenty dollars, the right of trial by jury shall be preserved, and no fact tried by a jury shall be otherwise re-examined in any Court of the Unites States, than according to the rules of the common law.

Amendment VIII.

Excessive bail shall not be required, nor excessive fines imposed, nor cruel and unusual punishments inflicted.

Amendment IX.

The enumeration in the Constitution of certain rights shall not be construed to deny or disparage others retained by the people.

Amendment X.

The powers not delegated to the United States by the Constitution, nor prohibited by it to the States, are reserved to the States respectively, or to the people.

APPENDIX B
Unalienable Rights Generally Agreed Upon Since 1791

Unalienable Rights Generally Agreed Upon Since 1791

RIGHT NO.	STATEMENT of UNALIENABLE RIGHT	COMMENT
1	The right to retain American citizenship, despite even criminal activities, until explicitly and voluntarily renouncing it.	There are heinous crimes for which the just punishment is *death*. Such a sentence certainly strips a criminal of citizenship in a most permanent way. Short of execution, there are other crimes that show unsuitability for citizenship — because there has been a vicious demonstration of not meeting even the minimum requirements of Responsibility, the other half of Individual Sovereignty. The human predator of other humans (child molestation to the point of murder, for example) should never be allowed back among unsuspecting new potential victims. The problem of where to send these deviants probably prevents the practical use of loss of citizenship as a deterrent to crime, but the Unalienable Rights of citizenship must carry with it some minimum level of responsibility.
2	The right to receive equal protection not only from the states but also from the federal government.	This right is stated poorly. "Equal protection" is obviously ambiguous. Likewise "equal" cannot be resolved between Federal and State government responsibilities; in matters of individual security, the two levels of

Unalienable Rights Generally Agreed Upon Since 1791

RIGHT NO.	STATEMENT of UNALIENABLE RIGHT	COMMENT
		government have widely different rules. What is probably meant — and should be stated as such — is that Individual Sovereignty must be the main *criterion* that both sets of governing officials apply when forming decisions about government actions.
3	The right to vote subject only to reasonable restrictions to prevent fraud	This is a restatement of Paine' s right to equal representation, and its derived MISUSE in majority decisions, about which discussion has already been given. The Right, however, is clearly fundamental, and the badly deficient implementation so far given to it does not change its fundamental nature. Implementation, in fact, has negated this right, and those responsible for that state of affairs have carte blanche to gloat about how successful they have been in shunting it aside. As offered earlier, it is my opinion that this essential Right can never be justly claimed by individuals as operative, until questions decided by vote become effective ONLY when the decision is supported by the OVERWHELMING MAJORITY of the total voting-age population.
4	The right to a presumption of innocence and to demand proof beyond a reasonable doubt before being convicted of a crime.	It is unnerving to think that this Right was not a basic element of the Bill of Rights. It seems almost to be an afterthought, and, of course, the justice system reflects that attitude in its decisions.

Unalienable Rights Generally Agreed Upon Since 1791

RIGHT NO.	STATEMENT of UNALIENABLE RIGHT	COMMENT
5	The right to use the federal courts and other governmental institutions and to urge others to use these processes to protect their interests.	Yes, but again implementation places restrictions along the path, including cost, that make the exercise of this right overly difficult.
6	The right to associate with others.	Derived from Amendment I, freedom of assembly, but properly broadened.
7	The right to enjoy a zone of privacy.	This is an abused right suffering greater incursions with every passing year. The history of abuse against this Right led finally to its enumeration, but the inventors of abuse seem always to be ahead of laws and court restrictions aimed at ensuring the right.
8	The right to travel within the United States.	This right implies the absence of boundaries, and the commonality of laws within the entire US, conditions that do not exist.
9	The right to marry or not to marry.	One would think it is unnecessary in the exercise of choice — in personal matters — to need enumeration beyond the underlying Right of Individual Sovereignty and freedom of choice. Court action dealing with such questions must be viewed as frivolous and unnecessary, and *therefore never allowed serious legal debate*, because none should be needed. Swimming in ice water, being tattooed, divorcing, marrying or overeating are all far outside the concern of any government and hardly need enumerating. Marriage is an agreement between two people, and only those two.

Unalienable Rights Generally Agreed Upon Since 1791

RIGHT NO.	STATEMENT of UNALIENABLE RIGHT	COMMENT
10	The right to make one's own choice about having children.	Rights that need to be enumerated are those that might come under attack by government, other groups or individuals. While it may be conceivable that this matter of personal decision might come under legal attack, it is really no different than any other matter of personal choice (as noted in #9), and therefore should be summarily dismissed from legal action of any kind. It cannot be a difficult question to resolve, and two seconds ought to be enough time to waste on the attacker. The statement of right must be coupled with the number of children, however, which is not unlimited.
11	The right to educate one's children as long as one meets certain minimum standards set by the state. [See note 1]	I believe this "Right" as stated is completely wrong and violates the very foundation of Individual Sovereignty which is freedom of choice. No State, no Government can set minimum requirements in education, because no citizen or group of citizens handed that right to anyone or any body other than themselves. This mistaken philosophy and its implications need considerably more discussion.
12	The right to choose and follow a profession.	This is another in the long list of personal choice rights. I'm quite sure that it shows up here because rogue governments have subverted it shamefully. An extrapolation comes to mind. If we were planning to

Unalienable Rights Generally Agreed Upon Since 1791

RIGHT NO.	STATEMENT of UNALIENABLE RIGHT	COMMENT
		institute a rogue government, or if we recognize that our own government is drifting into practices that emulate the rogues, then a reminder that this is a Right of individuals to be protected and preserved probably is appropriate. But if we here are trying to define Unalienable Rights and have full intentions to create a means for preserving that right, then the right to be preserved is the one of Free Choice in ALL matters of self. That is where the emphasis must lie.
13	The right to attend and report on criminal trials.	The foundation right of consequence here is the right to know what government is doing in discharging their obligations to individuals. National Security seems the only acceptable reason for withholding information, but too often the reason has been merely to protect someone in government who has stepped beyond his bounds of responsibilities. Iran-Contra, Watergate, and Waco are familiar, very disquieting examples.

Notes

[1] One of the most insidious attacks on this right, allowed by the improper proviso that effectively negates the right, is the recent drive by government to remove parental prerogatives through a United Nations Convention [Treaty] on the Rights of the Child. The danger is immediate and the possible consequences far-reaching.

APPENDIX C
The Hierarchy of Unalienable Rights -
Rights That Come With Life

The table below is my own elaboration of our Unalienable Rights, listed under six categories that seem basic and helpful. The particular breakdown is of far less importance than the content, but it helps to show rights that are supportive or are derived from others. Such an agreed, expanded set of Rights should be an integral part of any new American Constitution.

A companion table also exists (but not printed here) which reminds us of the *responsibilities* that accompany the exercise of each right. *Responsibilities* are man-made adjuncts to human Rights that come with birth, and are part on an attempt to improve society. They are the balance between the rights of self and the equal rights of everyone else.

THE HIERARCHY OF UNALIENABLE RIGHTS -
Rights That Come With Life

1. LIFE   (Declaration of Independence)

1.1 Right to life, to their own person, the property of no one else.

1.2 Right to join with others for security.

    1.2.1 Right to pay for protection and Right to change agreements when cost [however measured] is too high or performance is deficient.

        1.2.1.1 Right to decide through negotiation, acceptable compensation for those hired to perform government functions.

> [In most instances, government is the term used here for the organization tasked to provide security. History, and many people today, however, have shown an erroneous bent for thinking of government as much more than a means for collective security against foreign and domestic criminals.]

    1.2.2 Right to define the organization for protection and the rules under which they will function, and therefore, to redefine them.

        1.2.2.1 Right to remove individuals from that organization or change a contract.

        1.2.2.2 Right to change the political Constitution to advance their interests and happiness.

        1.2.2.3 Right to Representation in government acts. [Equal is not the issue, because there is no sensible definition of equality. Disagreeing with a majority view is enough to assure zero representation on an issue, which is unacceptable. A major improvement in assuring some representation is to require a high percentage of agreement before acceptance. Thus minority representation is upheld by not allowing actions where a mere 1 more than 50% wants to do something.]

> An idea to consider: A striation of the population by age into several groups - each group permitted to review and decide on different kinds of issues; e.g., roads, everyone; war, 60 years and up; trade issues, 50 and up; etc. ...

1.2.2.4   Right not to be thrown into confusion, ruined or detested by government.

1.2.2.5 Right to revolt against oppressive government [Thomas Paine # 3]

1.2.3 Right not to be deprived of Rights by security organizations.

1.2.4 Right to defend life.

1.2.4.1   Right to learn (for all three basic reasons (Life/Decisions/Fruits)) means a Right to information that will help protect self.

1.2.4.2 Right to own and bear arms for self protection, protection of family and property.

1.2.5   Right to expect only truth and honesty from all government officials, whether elected, appointed or hired.   Failures serious enough warrant dismissal, and harm done as a result of dishonesty or untruth, are crimes, warranting prosecution.   Any person seeking to be part of government must understand the seriousness of the commitment to uphold this right of those being served, and to demonstrate a philosophy that supports this commitment. This is our Right to truth from all *hired* people and organizations whether government, courts, police, manufacturers, lenders, teachers, advisors (including the spiritual type) etc.

1.2.5.1 Is there an Unalienable Right to truth from every other individual? This is framed as a question because the logic that applies would seem to indicate otherwise.   I have only an opinion on the question.   Since individuals have the Right of free speech, that freedom must include the Right to speak nonsense and the freedom not to speak truth.   There is a basic contradiction between the Right of one person to receive only truth from all others and the Right of all others to freedom of speech. The only real restriction is that exercising free speech should not result in harm to others. The more basic Right, therefore, must prevail.

The assumption must be made that no one can be forced to speak only truth because that conflicts with their individual Right. The use of untrue and misleading statements is so common in human society that it is dumbfounding to see how often truth is expected of another just because the question might be an important one. The record of governments, business, salesmen, witnesses, law-enforcement officers, clergy and individuals hoping for any advantage shows where truth resides in modern society. This issue is thoroughly dissected, especially in Volume II. Clearly many of those entrusted with upholding collective security have routinely violated a basic Right of those being protected.

1.2.6 Right to have the Rights and well-being of individuals within society placed *ahead* of the personal goals and ambitions of members of government. While tests before the fact may be difficult to devise, demonstration of actual failure to abide can be just cause for dismissal. It should not be unreasonable to ask each person seeking to act as a servant of society to meet this requirement.

1.3 Right collectively not to be the object of hate by government.

1.4 Right to be secure, and Right to Privacy for their persons, homes, papers, information and possessions, including reputation.

1.4.1 Right against unreasonable searches and seizures shall not be violated and no warrants shall be issued except upon probable cause, etc.,...(Amendment IV). This right to security is specifically addressed to security **From** government excesses in the use of force and incursions. [Note: thought should be given to requiring agreement of more than one person before issuing a warrant]

1.4.2 Right to Privacy. In the litany of Rights, the wording of the Right to Privacy is among the more outdated and inadequate of them all. The concern addressed by the Fourth Amendment centered around the arrest of citizens, attempting to remove the arbitrary ways of earlier governments. It' s not at all surprising that there was no recognition and no accounting for the other major ways to invade a person' s privacyincluding the stealing of information. The advent of high speed computers and surveillance equipment have changed the whole meaning of privacy. They have added a sophistication for invading privacy so that it has become almost impossible to exercise the right successfully. Information concerning the public history of a person is outside the privacy cloak, but *any* other matter about a person, business or family comes under the right to privacy, and releasing any information pertaining to it is at that person' s sole discretion. An example of how Amendment IV might be revised is as follows:

> *The Right of individuals to be secure in their persons, homes, possessions, papers, private information and effects, whether physical or informational, against unreasonable searches, seizures, duplication or surveillance, shall not be violated. No Warrants shall be issued, except upon due cause supported by oath or affirmation, and particularly describing the place to be searched, and the persons or things to be seized. This Right is specific protection of individuals against intrusions by government which has no authority for*

such invasion of privacy granted by the people, except as allowed herein.

1.5 <u>Right to control elements of government through restraints, rules of operation and any other means to assure compliance with the contracts (Constitution) agreed to.</u> All Rights to changing government reside with the people. [The people would be well-advised to contract with the several arms of government via agreements of no longer duration than 20 years and phased so that reviews and updates occur with one or more arms every 5 years. For example, if there were four government functions, one contract might be renegotiated every five years.]

1.6 <u>Considering the present, end-of-century condition that exists between government and We the People, the Right to change might be feasible to exercise as follows</u>: In a two-stage process, the exercise of decision-making for all those functions usurped by the Federal Government but not so empowered by the present Constitution, is to revert to the people in whom these rights reside as part of their heritage. The first stage will entail the overt transfer from National Government to State Governments. The second stage will entail similarly the transfer from State Governments back to the people. Envisioned here is the rather simple act of government renouncing government actions on those elements of wielding power that have never been relinquished by the populous. {Please note that this process is a limited one, correcting only part of the misadventures of government. It should be viewed as only one element of a transition plan to change the government from its present form to one fully cognizant of the sovereignty of individuals. [This Volume I expands on the needs for government redefinition and a plan for transition to the new.] }

1.7 <u>Right to resist oppression</u> - Clearly this is a fundamental Right of all individuals. To exercise this Right, or to have it "guaranteed" by a government dedicated to negating it is a contradiction. If government is not causing oppression, no guarantee is needed and the need to exercise the Right never arises; an ideal condition of social life. If government is causing oppression, then a guarantee is worthless and the Right can only be exercised outside of government-defined laws.

Therefore, rules of conduct for government bodies must include as clear and complete a statement of limitations, which, if honored, will assure the companion Right of not having to resist oppression — because there is no oppression. The Right is fundamental, however, because the definition of 'oppression' is not static, so that people must be aware of this Right along with all the others.

1.8 <u>Right of equality of human class with all other people.</u>

1.9 <u>Right of individuals not to be dictated to in any action involving only personal matters of the individual.</u> [See also Items 3.]

1.10 <u>Right of individuals not to be dictated to through law based on religious grounds</u>. Religious superstitions and overzealousness have no place in creating laws that every person is expected to follow. The potential mischief from religious groups (prohibition again comes to mind, or the oxymoron scientific creationism) might not be great provided all such "offerings" were decided by referendum and required a huge majority (say 85% or more) for adoption. Such a means of control against ill-conceived ideas from religious communities, however, is not part of any Fundamental right. It would rightly be only a part of an improved Constitution which is yet to be recorded and adopted.

1.11 <u>Right to Citizenship</u>. In a just society citizenship can be taken as one of the most treasured of possessions. It is clearly an attribute, an Unalienable Right that comes with birth or naturalization. It is not subject to cancellation by any other individual and, therefore, by any other group of individuals, including those under Constitutional contract to society, namely government. No Just society must be forced to absorb undue abuse, however, without some means of protecting itself, short of execution of criminals or imprisonment for life. By their own choice, individuals who go beyond some threshold of behavior against other citizens effectively remove themselves as an acceptable part of society. Loss of citizenship is an answer that should be seriously considered. If a workable means of banishment can be devised, the threatened or potential loss of citizenship could prove to be a deterrent to crime, where others have failed.

1.12 <u>Right to Death</u>. The truth of this Unalienable Right seems so clearly obvious that one wonders why society has gone to such lengths to prevent responsible individuals from exercising the right as he or she sees that ultimate need. In my opinion, the misguided force of society against this right is the direct result of dogmatic religious teachings, warping and subverting the right of some who do not agree with that same superstition. No one else has the right to decide life or death for another person, or to prevent that person from exercising that Right.

1.13 <u>Right to be free of physical and mental abuse from any other person</u>.

2. BASIC FREEDOMS

2.1 Right to life and freedom from subjugation
2.2 All people are born with equal Individual Sovereignty, possessing exactly the same Unalienable Rights.
2.3 All power is originally vested in and consequently derived from the people, and government is instituted by them for their common interest, protection and security; (New York delegation on the Bill of Rights). Government's

power, therefore, can be no more than the accumulation of incremental powers received from individuals.

2.4 Freedom of Speech.

2.5 Freedom to create, print and preserve.

2.6 Freedom to assemble peacefully.

2.7 Freedom to confront and petition government for a redress of grievances.

2.8 Freedom to keep and bear arms for security and with the approval of no one else.

2.9 Freedom to make all decisions regarding use of home and property so long as the rights of others are not threatened or violated.

2.10 Freedom honestly to buy and sell.

2.11 Freedom to pursue happiness as defined by self.

2.12 Freedom to exercise each inherent Right.

3. DECISIONS FOR SELF

3.1 Liberty   (Declaration of Independence)

   3.1.1. Right to make own decisions.

   3.1.2 Right to let others decide or not.

   3.1.3 Right to defend liberty against security organizations such as government and courts.

   3.1.4 Right to meaningful choices - particularly with regard to existing conditions at time of reaching the age of responsibility.

   3.1.5 Right of following own conscience in all matters of religion and belief.

3.2 Right not to be bound by decisions of others from before own life - or not actually agreed to by self. Thomas Paine noted that no one has the power to barter away the rights of the unborn, or for that matter, those already alive [Thomas Paine #1].

3.3 Right not to accept responsibility — Knowing that the consequences can be partial or complete loss of Unalienable Rights.

3.4 Right to decline military service on decision of conscience.

4. FRUITS OF LABOR

4.1 Pursuit of Happiness   (Declaration of Independence)

   4.1.1 Right to acquire property.

   4.1.2 Right to keep possessions.

      4.1.2.1 Derived directly from the rights to acquire and keep possessions, *is the right not to be taxed*. (See also 4.1.2.2.)

         Taxation has been the means by which the costs of doing government functions have been paid for. From our very beginning the extent to which taxation is allowed, meaning the restrictions on government in its use of the power, has not been a condition set by the people. Instead government itself has set the rules, effectively usurping a basic Right of the People. Having taken the Right by force [penalties of greater payments or even jail for non payment being all the force required], government has, of course, refused to honor any *limitations* on the ensuing confiscation.

The fundamental Right in effect is the Right of individuals to join together for greater security by contracting with something called government. All the conditions of such a contract are a matter of preferences of the People, including the functions and limitations, the means of payment and the amount, and all the provisions for changing any contract agreement.

Government, in fact, in accordance with the true source of Rights, has no say whatsoever in defining any of the Constitutional Provisions.

Nevertheless, if "legal" pathways can be established by government which allows this unilateral confiscation through taxation, then the contractual relationship between the people and its servant, government [at all levels], must be corrected. The plain, self-evident fact is that the Right to establish all rules of government resides with individuals alone and not at all with the instrument, the servant of the people.

4.1.2.2   Right to be free of confiscation (land, taxes, assessments, fees) (derived from right to property and to keep property) (See also 4.1.2.1)

4.1.3 Right to defend possessions.

4.1.4 Intimately tied to the unalienable rights of acquiring, holding, using and defending property and wealth is the right of disposing of that wealth after death.   Government has *no just claim* to any of this property, and confiscation is a direct violation of an individual' s Unalienable Right to same. This right is one solemn means by which the financial strength of families can be improved from one generation to the next, gradually increasing with time the abilities of later individuals to become fully self-sufficient, and responsible, the basic foundation of individual sovereignty. Individuals must be able to exercise the Right to transfer wealth between generations, a concept that can be a long-term solution to financial security for individuals. This part of a basic Right is a vastly superior solution than the government concept of confiscation and redistribution we know as welfare. The first concept is lasting and productive; the other is debilitating and regressive.

4.2 A person' s Unalienable Right of ownership is not subordinate to any other claim. The right to ownership of property, however, is *not protected* by the present implementation of Amendment V of the Bill of Rights as understood and implemented.   It is an easy matter for government, particularly at the local level, to confiscate property, land and wealth, "for public use" and without "just compensation". [This abuse of a basic human right is discussed explicitly in Volume I.] Nor does the French Declaration of Rights give better guidance, being even more tolerant of abuses.

A suggested restatement should allow that anyone being "asked" to relinquish property for the public good (that person also being a member of the public) shall have the Right to set the value of the property satisfactory to the owner before transfer of ownership. Those who want to confiscate (steal) should not also have the power to set compensation. The present wording of Amendment V puts no restriction on what "just compensation" means, resulting in gross abuses against a person's Unalienable Right to property. (Refer to. item 4.1.2)

4.3 The right to acquire, keep, sell or use property of any kind is coupled with the right to engage in the free trade of property, within a framework established by society.

4.4 The pursuit of happiness does not only depend on acquiring property. Also part of that basic right are the following:

  4.4.1 The ability to exercise all Unalienable Rights with a minimum of intrusion.

  4.4.2 The right to choose and pursue any occupation or profession in any locale.

  4.4.3 Right to find a mate.

  4.4.4 Right to create.

  4.4.5 Right to conceive and to rear offspring. [see also 4.4.8]

  4.4.6 Right of choice of recreation and the manner in which to spend wealth.

  4.4.7 Right not to do any of these things.

  4.4.8 Right of parenthood. The most fundamental right of existence, after self preservation, is the right to conceive and rear children. As long as the basic responsibilities to offspring are provided by the parents and physical means of control are within society norms, then no other person, group, government or organization can dictate the decisions of parenthood.

This Right, freely exercised throughout history, has finally led to a growing mismatch between our numbers and the ability of the Earth and the evolutionary state of society to cope with those numbers. With each passing decade, the growth of human numbers gives us cause to question their contribution to the greater and greater suffering we see among people. Whether the trend in population might be our ultimate undoing, or is at least a problem of major concern warrants our serious attention. While the Right remains, the corresponding responsibilities of procreation change because of the total population vying for the same resources. Volume IV gives my view of the problem of population which begins by first trying to understand more clearly what the 'population problem" is.

The concern here is to try to decide what new responsibilities we have collected by the actions of our ancestors and ourselves who are seniors, hopefully then to be used in solving this dilemma.

4.5 Right not to have to compete with any monopoly created by government.

5. RIGHTS IN LAW AND JUSTICE

The condition of Law and Justice in America is such that it has become another of the four major problems we as a society face today. As such, an examination is attempted that occupies an entire book, and the discussions of Volume II give much of the background behind the abbreviated comments in this Table.

5.1 Right to fairness by the law and law enforcement. The law enforcement system must be impartial, and like government, people in the system are employees of society, empowered by the people and under contract to them. The system exists for the sole purpose of providing security for all individuals, and so the prime criterion of operation is to protect the sovereignty of individuals. That function, often a dangerous one, nevertheless must presume innocence until proven otherwise, and must be carried out amidst the confusion of a mixture of innocent bystanders, *victims* and criminals of all stripes.

5.2 Amendment IV states:

"The right of the people to be secure in their persons, houses, papers, and effects, against unreasonable searches and seizures, shall not be violated, and no Warrants shall issue, but upon probable cause, supported by Oath or affirmation, and particularly describing the place to be searched, and the persons or things to be seized."

Rights acknowledged and protected by this Amendment are the cornerstone of justice for individuals. Government attacks against these Rights, so prevalent today, show the need for change in the way they are to be protected. Refer back to item 1.4.2 of this table where the right to privacy is the issue of discussion.

5.3 Fairness under the law is expanded through the enumeration of Rights covered by Amendment V of the Bill of Rights. The practice of enforcement through the centuries, up to the Founding, was more arbitrary and violent than fair, and Amendment V identified four areas of law enforcement that had trampled most heavily on the Rights of individuals. This acknowledgment of the four Rights that follow was certainly one of the most important contributions to humankind by any set of leaders — ever. As we shall see, particularly in the discussions of Volume II, Law & Justice, society has long since passed the point where this great beginning needs to be updated to counter newer practices that continue to deny people' s Rights.

The Rights dealing with property, also emphasized in this amendment are even more fundamental, and as we saw in Items 4.2 and 4.1.4, such rights have become non-rights. They desperately need a renewed acknowledgment by expanding the definition of The Right to Property. [Refer also to Item 5.4.]

5.3.1 Right to indictment only by a Grand Jury. *["No person shall be held to answer for a capital, or otherwise infamous crime, unless on a presentment or indictment of a Grand Jury, except in cases arising in the land or naval forces, or in the Militia, when in actual service in time of War or public danger;......"]*

The Grand Jury too often has become the rubber-stamp of district attorneys. If the purview and powers of a Grand Jury are not going to match the needs of protecting the Rights of individuals, then the Grand Jury is not a protection but merely a sop. Change **must** be instituted.

The Amendment proviso of this "Right" further diminishes the true Right which holds that a person is due protection from capricious imprisonment by those in power. *All* persons are due this protection whatever their occupation, and military cases must have a method equivalent to that intended for the Grand Jury. Actually it may be that the protections afforded by the military approach to this basic Right are better than that of the Grand Jury as now implemented. At the very least two changes are needed in this statement from Amendment V; the proviso, [intended as a restriction on the Right], should be removed, and the definition and duties of a Grand Jury — or equivalent in military situations — must be explained more fully. Mere reference to a Grand Jury is far from sufficient in an attempt to define protection for people in such cases.

5.3.2 Not to endure Double jeopardy; *["....nor shall any person be subject for the same offense to be twice put in jeopardy of life or limb,...."]*

5.3.3 Not to incriminate self; *["....nor shall be compelled in any criminal case to be a witness against himself,...."]*

5.3.4 Due process to be deprived of life, liberty, property; *["....nor be deprived of life, liberty, or property, without due process of law;...."]* (Refer to comments in Item 4.2.)

5.4 Just compensation for confiscated private property. *[".... nor shall private property be taken for public use without just compensation."]* This needs to change. The right of eminent domain is only a license to steal, and has been used for exactly for that purpose. [Refer to Item 4.2.]

5.5 Amendment VI is further elaboration of the Rights of individuals under the law. Rights enumerated under Items 1., 2., 3. and 4. are all *Unalienable Rights*, while Rights pertaining to the Law are derived from them. As such they are much more subject to opinion as we shall see. With the benefit of two hundred more years of experience under the Bill of Rights, we are now in a better position to evaluate those early opinions and to offer changes.

257

5.5.1 Speedy public trial; *["In all criminal prosecutions, the accused shall enjoy the right to a speedy and public trial,...."]* Trials today are anything but speedy. They are public, perhaps too public, but far too often trials take much too long to begin, and drag on for long periods, sometimes years. The manner in which these shams are conducted, too often show that justice and truth are not the objectives of the system. All we need to do to be convinced of the unfairness of the present system is to contrast the two following methods to achieve justice. On one hand no case decided by Supreme Court action has taken more than a few days [normally hours] for presentation. Deliberation to arrive at a consensus may extend for several weeks or more, but this time is simply wait time and not trial time for the petitioner.

On the other hand, Jury trials have lasted for *years* and then resulted in a not guilty verdict. [The McMartin Preschool trial is an example.] This is hardly speedy and is certainly without fairness. Even when the opposite verdict is reached, the process is badly deficient, so much so that *Justice can not be attained*. Clearly the system used in the public case is deficient in major respects and must change.

5.5.2 Trial by jury - a must ??? *["....by an impartial jury of the state and district wherein the crime shall have been committed; which district shall have been previously ascertained by law,...."]*

One of the elements of the Justice System, and one that Madison and others singled out as essential is the derived right to a Jury trial. Clearly they sought impartiality, and back then it was reasonable to expect that jury functions could be fairly and competently accomplished by the "man in the street." That is no longer true, as too many recent examples clearly show. The net result is a major cog in the Justice machinery that no longer applies, and instead of being a Right is actually a deterrent to protecting an individual in the exercise of more fundamental Rights.

5.5.3 Informed of charges and witnesses; *[".... and to be informed of the nature and cause of the accusation; to be confronted with the witnesses against him;...."]*

Implementation of this Right is deficient, even to the point of catastrophe for some defendants.

5.5.4 Compulsory process (subpoena) for defense; *["....to have compulsory process for obtaining witnesses in his favor,...."]*

5.5.5 Counsel; *["....and to have the assistance of counsel for his defense."]*

5.6 Amendment 7: *"In Suits at common law, where the value in controversy shall exceed twenty dollars, the right of trial by jury shall be preserved, and no fact tried by a jury shall be otherwise re-examined in any Court of the Unites States, than according to the rules of the common law."*

5.6.1 Civil Suits - Trial by jury must change. Similar to earlier comments, a jury is not able to decide civil matters any better than criminal questions because of the lack of background, pertinent information and information to know who is lying and who is not.

5.6.2 Re-examination of facts. This seems to be a non-right since it allows such reexamination simply by allowing authorities to define the rules in any way they choose.

5.7 Amendment 8: "*Excessive bail shall not be required, nor excessive fines imposed, nor cruel and unusual punishments inflicted.*"

5.7.1 Right to fairness in bails that are not excessive. Another of the failings of the present Justice System is in the powers ascribed to Judges. Discretion, tenure, capriciousness of rulings, functions and consequences of arbitrary "Contempt" citations are a few of the things that need change. The Right to fairness is not upheld by the way the court is allowed to function. [See Volume II for further discussion.]

5.8 Right not to be accused, imprisoned or held under arrest except as prescribed by law. [French Declaration of Rights of Man] This is a poor statement of rights covered more adequately under Amendments IV, V, and VI [See items 5.1, 5.2, and 5.6]. The reason for listing it here is to note how poorly this "Right" is worded, in effect not showing it as a right at all, since no conditions are placed on the law that is to apply. Our own Bill of Rights suffers in similar ways, albeit in different degrees.

5.9 Right to humane treatment by police. [French Declaration of Rights] Any person accused of any crime is to be presumed innocent until proven guilty. This *extremely important Right* is nowhere stated as a condition in the people' s directions to American government.**This major oversight** is far from a mere philosophical glitch, because the presumption of innocence is often not the rule followed by law enforcement officials. It is a matter of deficient teaching of recruits that follows directly from a fundamental misunderstanding of the rights of individuals.

5.10 Right to just punishment, free of cruelty. This Right is certainly a proper one, in keeping with an attempt by society to demonstrate greater maturity than the criminals with whom it must deal. The criterion by which society deals with criminals, however, is only 50 % proper; the other 50% is totally missing. Thus we must add to the list 5.11, the *Right of Victims*.

5.11 Victims of crimes have a Right to expect from the Criminal Justice System *restitution* of losses suffered, to the fullest extent possible. Since society did not cause the harm, the burden of restitution must rest mainly on the criminal who caused the harm. The responsibility of the Criminal Justice System, therefore, lies in seeing that restitution is carried out.

6. SPECIAL RIGHTS.

6.1 <u>Habeas Corpus - The Great Writ of Liberty.</u> This is the writ which guarantees that the government cannot charge us with any crime and hold us, unless they follow the procedure of due process of law. This writ also says, in effect, that the right of due process of law cannot be suspended, and that government cannot operate an arbitrary prerogative power against us, We the People. Unfortunately, the Founders included within the Constitution itself, the very means of negating the Great Writ of Liberty. Thus this basic Right, one enumerated in the Constitution, can be lost to us. This book shows, in fact, how it has been lost.

6.2 <u>All Unalienable Rights that are accepted as self-evident by a society have another attribute</u> that, until now, has only been implied, and must now be made explicit. Failing to include it has allowed the greatest cumulative loss of freedom in the entire history of America. None of these self-evident Rights should come with the proviso that they apply only so long as there is no national emergency. If such a proviso were included in the Constitution, that alone would be an oversight in the wording that would give power-hungry men in government the excuse to allow themselves to create extraordinary powers. National Emergency, however, was considered as a special situation by the Founders, during which *Rights can be suspended*. Thus, the Constitution in fact *does* include overt and direct *means* within its articles to allow Constitutional provisions, those of Rights of citizens and limits on government, to be *summarily suspended*.

The means has been discussed thoroughly in this volume. The implementation was through the use of "War & Emergency Powers," enacted as of March 9, 1933. Those powers have allowed government (meaning themselves) to "suspend" all necessary rights of individuals during the self-declared emergency. This sad excuse for a law was warped by Franklin Roosevelt to include the financial crisis of the great depression. The "emergency" was a sham, and the fact that the "legal" condition of Emergency has *never been removed* to this day,[40] means that all Americans can "legally" only exercise those self-evident, Unalienable Rights that our benevolent government says can be exercised. The Constitution of the United States of America has been suspended since 1933. This has only one meaning: all of those self-evident Rights we think are being honored by our government are no longer in effect. Our heritage of Rights is non-existent, and the foregoing enumeration has been an exercise in political self-deception — unless we achieve a new beginning that must begin with a new Constitution.

---

[40] "War and Emergency Powers," A special report on the National Emergency in the United States of America, by Dr. Gene Schroeder et-al, 1994.

I contend further that the whole notion that the Rights of individuals must be suspended in wartime is *exactly wrong*. That is precisely the time when Rights must be cherished and held sacrosanct above all other times.

The implied Right in explicit form should be to the effect that all Rights of individuals continue in effect for all time. The only test for continuation, is lawfulness of the individual within the full set of Unalienable Rights as adopted by society.

* * *

APPENDIX D
The Genesis of Government's Gravest Error

My contention is that giving away money has been the **greatest** source of our national undoing. This story of an act by an early Congress is true. With that action, they opened the dike to the great flood that followed of your and my money and that of future generations, an act that now threatens to end the noble experiment in an unthinkable catastrophe.

Back To The Early Nineteenth Century

One day in the House of Representatives, a bill was taken up appropriating money for the benefit of a widow of a distinguished naval officer. Several beautiful speeches had been made in its support. The Speaker was just about to put the question when Representative Crockett rose:

"Mr. Speaker — I have as much respect for the memory of the deceased, and as much sympathy for the sufferings of the living, if suffering there be, as any man in this House, but we must not permit our respect for the dead or our sympathy for a part of the living to lead us into an act of injustice to the balance of the living. I will not go into an argument to prove that Congress has no power to appropriate this money as an act of charity. Every member upon this floor knows it. We have the right, as individuals, to give away as much of our own money as we please in charity; but as members of Congress we have no right so to appropriate a dollar of the public money. Some eloquent appeals have been made to us upon the ground that it is a debt due the deceased. Mr. Speaker, the deceased lived long after the close of the war; he was in office to the day of his death, and I have never heard that the government was in arrears to him.

Every man in this House knows it is not a debt. We cannot, without the grossest corruption, appropriate this money as the payment of a debt. We have not the semblance of authority to appropriate it as a charity."

Today it is a simple conceptual matter to institute a check of any proposal as to whether it would violate either the Constitution or any other existing statute. All that is required is a complete database of law and suitable query capabilities. We have in this example our first indication of the pitifully slipshod way that Congress typically conducts business. The routine involves the stipulation of spending measures set forth in hundreds of pages of legal text. The marquis provisions of a Bill, the ones from which a popularized name is derived, are the main topics of debate and reasonably well understood by the representatives. But the literally *hundreds* of add-ons not only are never read by those debating the question, but also

262

are never given the checks for legality that should be standard operating procedure for so-called lawmakers. Any proposed action that can't pass such a first test of its legitimacy must NEVER be allowed to be put to a vote concerning adoption of any provision. If a thing is contradictory to law, no vote should be possible. A go, no-go test such as this would seem elementary. We return to the Congressman From Tennessee:

"Mr. Speaker, I have said we have the right to give as much money of our own as we please. I am the poorest man on this floor. I cannot vote for this bill, but I will give one week's pay to the object, and if every member of Congress will do the same, it will amount to more than the bill asks."

He took his seat. Nobody replied. The bill was put upon its passage, and, instead of passing unanimously, as was generally supposed, and as, no doubt, it would, but for that speech, it received but few votes, and of course, was lost.

Later, when asked by a friend why he had opposed the appropriation, Crockett gave this explanation:

"Several years ago I was one evening standing on the steps of the Capitol with some other members of Congress, when our attention was attracted by a great light over in Georgetown. It was evidently a large fire. We jumped into a hack and drove over as fast as we could. In spite of all that could be done, many houses were burned and many families made houseless, and, besides, some of them had lost all but the clothes they had on. The weather was very cold, and when I saw so many women and children suffering, I felt that something ought to be done for them. The next morning a bill was introduced appropriating $20,000 for their relief. We put aside all other business and rushed it through as soon as it could be done.

Had there been no earlier precedent, the country now had its crack in the dam. Giving away what was not theirs to give only requires a reason acceptable to a very few with the power to spend.

"The next summer, when it began to be time to think about the election, I concluded I would take a scout around among the boys of my district. I had no opposition there, but, as the election was some time off, I did not know what might turn up. When riding one day in a part of my district in which I was more of a stranger than any other, I saw a man in a field plowing and coming toward the road, I gauged my gait so we should meet as he came to the fence. As he came up, I spoke to the man. He replied politely, but, as I thought, rather coldly.

'I began: 'Well, friend, I am one of those unfortunate beings called candidates, and —'

"Yes, I know you; you are Colonel Crockett . I have seen you once before, and voted for you the last time you were elected. I suppose you are out electioneering now, but you had better not waste your time or mine. I shall not vote for you again.'

'This was a sockdolager ... I begged him to tell me what was the matter.

"Well, Colonel, it is hardly worthwhile to waste time or words upon it. I do not see how it can be mended, but you gave a vote last winter which shows that <u>either you have not capacity to understand the Constitution, or that you are wanting in the honesty and firmness to be guided by it.'"</u>

The same admonition applies today to every single man and woman in both houses of Congress because every single one of them has given away charity money that was not theirs to give.

"In either case you are not the man to represent me. But I beg your pardon for expressing it in that way. I did not intend to avail myself of the privilege of the constituent to speak plainly to a candidate for the purpose of insulting or wounding you. I intend by it only to say that your understanding of the Constitution is very different from mine; and I will say to you what, but for my rudeness, I should not have said, that I believe you to be honest.... But an understanding of the Constitution different from mine I cannot overlook, because the Constitution, to be worth anything, must be held sacred, and rigidly observed in all its provisions. The man who wields power and misinterprets it is the more dangerous the more honest he is.'

'I admit the truth of all you say, but there must be some mistake about it, for I do not remember that I gave any vote last winter upon any constitutional question.

"No, Colonel, there's no mistake. Though I live here in the backwoods and seldom go from home, I take the papers from Washington and read very carefully all the proceedings of Congress. My papers say that last winter you voted for a bill to appropriate $20,000 to some sufferers by a fire in Georgetown. Is that true?'

'Well, my friend; I may as well own up. You have got me there. But certainly nobody will complain that a great and rich country like ours should give the insignificant sum of $20,000 to relieve its suffering women and

*children, particularly with a full and overflowing Treasury, and I am sure, if
you had been there, you would have done just as I did."*

The trap of logic is so beguiling that it is small wonder we, our government,
have not been able to avoid it. We, the richest country on Earth, can surely afford to
help these unfortunates.

The question is one that fits snugly under the umbrella *function* of carrying out
other national goals than that of security. If there were one hundred percent
agreement for such a giveaway, then there would be no debate. There is no such
agreement, and it is not within the powers handed to legislators to do so. The logic
of wealth, means, and need are irrelevant, and most certainly the seemingly small
amount of money at issue is *not* the issue.

*"It's not the amount, Col onel, that I complain of; it is the principle. In the
first place, the government ought to have in the Treasury no more than
enough for its legitimate purposes. But that has nothing to do with the
question. The power of collecting and disbursing money at pleasure **is the
most dangerous power that can be entrusted to man,** particularly under our
system of collecting revenue by a tariff, which reaches every man in the
country, no matter how poor he may be, and the poorer he is the more he pays
in proportion to his means. What is worse, it presses upon him without his
knowledge where the weight centers, for there is not a man in the United
States who can ever guess how much he pays to the government.'*

Does this have the ring of familiarity? [My emphasis added in the paragraph
above.]

*"So you see, that while you are contributing to relieve one, you are
drawing it from thousands who are even worse off than he. If you had the
right to give anything, the amount was simply a matter of discretion with you,
and you had as much right to give $20,000,000 as $20,000. If you have the
right to give to one, you have the right to give to all; and, as the Constitution
neither defines charity nor stipulates the amount, you are at liberty to give to
any and everything which you may believe, or profess to believe, is a charity,
and to any amount you may think proper. You will very easily perceive what a
wide door this would open for fraud and corruption and favoritism, on the one
hand, and for robbing the people on the other. No, Colonel, **Congress has no
right to give charity.** Individual members may give as much of their own
money as they please, but they have no right to touch a dollar of the public
money for that purpose. If twice as many houses had been burned in this
county as in Georgetown, neither you nor any other member of Congress
would have thought of appropriating a dollar for our relief. There are about*

*two hundred and forty members of Congress. If they had shown their sympathy for sufferers by contributing each one week's pay, it would have made over $13,000. There are plenty of wealthy men in and around Washington who could have given $20,000 without depriving themselves of even a luxury of life. The congressmen chose to keep their own money, which, if reports be true, some of them spend not very creditably; and the people of Washington, no doubt, applauded you for relieving them from the necessity of giving by giving what was not yours to give. The **people** have delegated to Congress, by the Constitution, the power to do certain things. To do these, it is authorized to collect and pay moneys, and for nothing else. **Everything beyond this is usurpation, and a violation of the Constitution.'**

"So you see, Colonel, you have violated the Constitution in what I consider a vital point. It is a precedent fraught with danger to the country, for when Congress once begins to stretch its power beyond the limits of the Constitution, there is no limit to it, and no security for the people.'"*

Can any warning be more clearly stated? With the view of another century and a half of observing the consequences of this very clear disregard of the Constitution, the fact of debts that hold our grandchildren hostage to our arrogant ways was inevitable.

"I have no doubt you acted honestly, but that does not make it any better, except as far as you are personally concerned, and you see that I cannot vote for you.'"

'I tell you I felt streaked. I saw if I should have opposition, and this man should go to talking, he would set others to talking, and in that district I was a gone fawn-skin. I could not answer him, and the fact is, I was so fully convinced that he was right, I did not want to. But I must satisfy him, and I said to him:

'Well, my friend, you hit the nail upon the head when you said I had not sense enough to understand the Constitution. I intended to be guided by it, and thought I had studied it fully. I have heard many speeches in Congress about the powers of Congress, but what you have said here at your plow has got more hard, sound sense in it than all the fine speeches I ever heard. If I had ever taken the view of it that you have, I would have put my head into the fire before I would have given that vote; and if you will forgive me and vote for me again, if I ever vote for another unconstitutional law, I wish I may be shot.'"

266

I dare say that if each member of Congress had lived up to such an apocryphal oath, over say, the last 30 years, that either not a single bill would have made it into law, OR there would be a cemetery full of Congressional Representatives, dead of gunshot wounds.

'He laughingly replied: 'Yes, Colonel, you have sworn to that once before, but I will trust you again upon one condition. You say that you are convinced that your vote was wrong. Your acknowledgment of it will do more good than beating you for it. If, as you go around the district, you will tell people about this vote, and that you are satisfied it was wrong, I will not only vote for you, but will do what I can to keep down opposition, and perhaps, I may exert some little influence in that way.'

'If I don't, said I, I wish I may be shot; and to convince you that I am in earnest in what I say I will come back this way in a week or ten days, and if you will get up a gathering of the people, I will make a speech to them. Get up a barbecue, and I will pay for it."

"No, Colonel, we are not rich people in this section, but we have plenty of provisions to contribute for a barbecue, and some to spare for those who have none. The push of crops will be over in a few days, and we can then afford a day for a barbecue. This is Thursday; I will see to getting it up on Saturday week. Come to my house on Friday, and we will go together, and I promise you a very respectable crowd to see and hear you."'

'Well, I will be here. But one thing more before I say good -bye. I must know your name. 'My name is Bunce.' Not Horatio Bunce? 'Yes.' Well, Mr. Bunce, I never saw you before, though you say you have seen me, but I know you very well. I am glad I have met you, and very proud that I may hope to have you for my friend."

'It was one of the luckiest hits of my life that I met him. He mingled but little with the public, but he was widely known for his remarkable intelligence and incorruptible integrity, and for a heart brimful and running over with kindness and benevolence, which showed themselves not only in words but in acts. He was the oracle of the whole country around him, and his fame had extended far beyond the circle of his immediate acquaintance. Though I had never met him before, I had heard much of him, and but for this meeting it is very likely I should have had opposition, and had been beaten. One thing is very certain, no man could now stand up in that district under such a vote."

Such is not the case today. It almost doesn't matter what a politician has done, how he or she has voted, or what their reverence for the Constitution might be. The success of their campaigns is more dependent on money spent, favors given and inner office deals made than adherence to loftier principles represented in the Constitution. Such traits of government, shown in the body of this book, are ample proof of the that conclusion.

'At the appointed time I was at his house, having told our conversation to every crowd I had met, and to every man I stayed all night with, and I found that it gave the people an interest and a confidence in me stronger than I had ever seen manifested before.

'Though I was considerably fatigued when I reached his house, and, under ordinary circumstances, should have gone early to bed, I kept him up until midnight, talking about the principles and affairs of government, and got more real true knowledge of them than I had got all my life before.

'I have known and seen much of him since, for I respect him — no, that is not the word — I reverence and love him more than any living man, and I go to see him two or three times every year; and I will tell you, sir, if every one who professes to be a Christian lived and acted and enjoyed it as he does, the religion of Christ would take the world by storm.

'But to return to my story. The next morning we went to the barbecue, and, to my surprise, found about a thousand men there. I met a good many whom I had not known before, and they and my friend introduced me around until I had got pretty well acquainted — at least, they all knew me. In due time notice was given that I would speak to them. They gathered up around a stand that had been erected. I opened my speech by saying:

"Fellow citizens — I present myself before you today feeling like a new man. My eyes have lately been opened to truths which ignorance or prejudice, or both, had heretofore hidden from my view. I feel that I can today offer you the ability to render you more valuable service than I have ever been able to render before. I am here today more for the purpose of acknowledging my error than to seek your votes. That I should make this acknowledgment is due to myself as well as to you. Whether you will vote for me is a matter for your consideration only.'

'I went on to tell them about the fire and my vote for the appropriation and then told them why I was satisfied it was wrong. I closed by saying: And now, fellow citizens, it remains only for me to tell you that the most of the speech you have listened to with so much interest was simply a repetition of the arguments by which your neighbor, Mr. Bunce, convinced me of my error.

'It is the best speech I ever made in my life, but he is entitled to the credit for it. And now I hope he is satisfied with his convert and that he will get up here and tell you so. He came upon the stand and said:

"Fellow citizens — It affords me great pleasure to comply with the request of Colonel Crockett. I have always considered him a thoroughly honest man, and I am satisfied that he will faithfully perform all that he has promised you today.'

'He we nt down, and there went up from that crowd such a shout for Davy Crockett as his name ever called forth before. I am not much given to tears, but I was taken with a choking then and felt some big drops rolling down my cheeks. And I tell you now that the remembrance of those few words spoken by such a man, and the honest, hearty shout they produced, is worth more to me than all the honors I have received and all the reputation I have ever made, or ever shall make, as a member of Congress.

'Now sir," concluded Crockett , 'you know why I made that speech yesterday. There is one thing now to which I will call your attention. You remember that I proposed to give a week's pay. There are in that House many very wealthy men — men who think nothing of spending a week's pay, or a dozen of them, for a dinner or a wine party when they have something to accomplish by it. Some of those same men made beautiful speeches upon the great debt of gratitude which the country owed the deceased — a debt which could not be paid by money — and the insignificance and worthlessness of money, particularly so insignificant a sum as $10,000, when weighed against the honor of the nation. Yet not one of them responded to my proposition. Money with them is nothing but trash when it is to come out of the people. But it is the one great thing for which most of them are striving, and many of them sacrifice honor, integrity, and justice to obtain it."

The essence of this story is direct, easily understandable, and fundamental. I think we can take it as an accurate description of the event that helped one man to grow. Congress, government, has no funds that are not taken from citizens as taxes. However, since government [presently] has no independent treasure of its own, and since the Constitution grants no power of charity, Congress has no power whatsoever to grant money gifts to anyone, any group, or any country.

The flawless logic behind the story and the illegality of such actions, however, didn't prevent an early Congress from stepping beyond its constitutional bounds to make that first watershed grant. Whatever the first giveaway was, I haven't learned, but it *was* made and the most devastating precedent to United States government operations came about. Once the innocent and, I'm sure, altruistic gift was made, it was as if a hairline crack had shaken into being in an earthen dam. Each new choice for giving came easier, the trickle loosed became a steady flow and then a flood as our national wealth, extracted from Mr. and Mrs. taxpayer, disappeared.

APPENDIX E
The Pursuit of Happiness, Our Forgotten Right

1 – Some Details of American Government's Fraudulent Welfare Excesses

Government's own study shows that adding more money to welfare programs increases the poverty rate and dependency, and reducing welfare money decreases poverty rate and dependency. Government's answer to the unambiguous message from their own data was to add more welfare spending.

That backward result is shown by the *government-generated* facts in Table 1. The truth of the matter is exactly opposite to the political sales pitch hawked to taxpayers, which says that government will solve our nasty problems simply by spending more money on them. The irony of this particular little story is that the information was generated by the House Select Committee on Children, Youth and Families, i.e., by Congress itself.

Table 2 shows that these same perverse actions by Congress of adding more money to welfare programs, continued on into the 1990s. Nor has anything changed since then.

Obviously the purpose for the welfare program is not to reduce poverty or assist those with temporary problems, but to increase government size and power through control of greater amounts of money. That is the reason I've labeled their actions as *fraudulent*.

Another Way to Look at Government's Welfare Excesses
Look closely at Table 3. For each jurisdiction, column 3 gives the total 1995 benefit paid to the *typical* welfare household. Column 4 shows what a wage-earner would have to be paid to equal what this welfare recipient gets without working. In more familiar terms perhaps, is the hourly wage shown in column 5.

Table 1 PERCENT CHANGE in POVERTY RATE Between 1969 & 1979

HIGHEST AFDC PAYMENTS					LOWEST AFDC PAYMENTS			
RANK	STATE	PMT $/MO	% CHANGE in POVERTY RATE		RANK	STATE	PMT $/MO	% CHANGE in POVERTY RATE
1	Vermont	524	+ 20.9		1	Texas	140	- 13.8
2	California	487	+ 19.7		2	Tennessee	148	- 16.3
3	Washington	483	+ 17.3		3	Alabama	148	- 19.5
4	New York	476	+ 49.6		4	Georgia	170	- 12.4
5	Michigan	470	+ 41.5		5	Louisiana	187	- 21.7
6	Wisconsin	458	+ 16.9		6	Arkansas	188	- 25.2
7	Minnesota	454	+ 7.3		7	North Carolina	210	26.8
8	Connecticut	446	+ 46.2		8	South Carolina	229	- 26.8
9	Iowa	419	+ 13.9		9	Florida	230	- 3.6
10	New Hampshire	392	+ 19.0		10	Kentucky	235	- 13.3
11	North Dakota	389	- 10.1		11	Arizona	239	- 7.8
12	Utah	389	+ .9		12	New Mexico	242	- 17.2
13	Rhode Island	389	+ 16.2		13	West Virginia	249	- 23.9
14	New Jersey	386	+ 53.2		14	Mississippi	252	- 26.4
15	Massachusetts	379	+ 48.9		15	Missouri	270	- 2.0

Payment Standard is for a 4 - Person Family

Table 2 COMPARISON of AFDC BENEFITS Between 1979 & 1995

HIGH RANK '95	'79	STATE	1995 PMT $/MO	1979 PMT $/MO	LOW RANK '95	'79	STATE	1995 PMT $/MO	1979 PMT $/MO
1		Alaska	923		25		Nebraska	364	
2		Hawaii	712		24		Wyoming	360	
3	4	New York	703	476	23	12	New Mexico	357	242
4	8	Connecticut	680	446	22		Colorado	356	
5	1	Vermont	638	524	21		Virginia	354	
6	2	California	607	487	20		Nevada	348	
7	15	Massachusetts	579	379	19	11	Arizona	347	239
8	13	Rhode Island	554	389	18		Ohio	341	
9	10	New Hampshire	550	392	17		Delaware	338	
10	3	Washington	546	483	16		Oklahoma	324	
11	7	Minnesota	532	454	15		Idaho	317	
12	6	Wisconsin	517	458	14	9	Florida	303	230
13	5	Michigan	489	470	13	15	Missouri	292	270
14		Oregon	460		12		Indiana	288	
15		Kansas	429		11	4	Georgia	280	170
16	9	Iowa	426	419	10	7	North Carolina	272	210
17	14	New Jersey	424	386	9	13	West Virginia	249	249
18		Pennsylvania	421		8	10	Kentucky	228	235
19		Dist. of Columbia	420		7	6	Arkansas	204	188
20		Maine	418		6	8	South Carolina	200	229
21		South Dakota	417		5	5	Louisiana	190	187
22	12	Utah	414	389	4	2	Tennessee	185	148
23	11	North Dakota	409	389	3	1	Texas	184	140
24		Montana	401		2	3	Alabama	164	148
25		Illinois	367		1	14	Mississippi	120	252
26		Maryland	366						

Payment Standard is for a 4 - Person Family

TABLE 3 Excess In Anything - Even Altruism - Is Always Destructive

1	2	3	4	5	6
col. 4 Rank [a]	Jurisdiction	Total Yearly Welfare Benefit (Tax Free)	Pretax Yearly Wage Equivalent (non welfare)	Equivalent Hourly Wage	Benefit as % of Poverty Level
1	Hawaii	27,736	36,400	17.50	234.7
2	Alaska	26,849	32,200	15.48	227.2
3	Massachusetts	24,474	30,500	14.66	204.6
4	Connecticut	24,176	29,600	14.23	207.1
5	Dist. of Columbia	22,745	29,100	13.99	192.5
6	New York	22,124	27,300	13.13	187.2
7	New Jersey	21,968	26,500	12.74	185.9
8	Rhode Island	21,541	26,100	12.55	182.3
9	California	20,687	24,100	11.59	175.1
10	Virginia	19,386	23,100	11.11	164.0
11	Maryland	19,489	22,800	10.96	164.9
12	New Hampshire	19,964	22,800	10.96	168.9
13	Maine	19,018	21,600	10.38	160.9
14	Delaware	18,486	21,500	10.34	156,4
15	Colorado	18,457	20,900	10.05	156.2
16	Vermont	18,754	20,900	10.05	158.7
17	Minnesota	18,441	20,800	10.00	156.1
18	Washington	18,730	20,700	9.55	158.5
19	Nevada	18,456	20,200	9.71	156.2
20	Utah	17,838	19,900	9.57	151.0
21	Michigan	17,560	19,700	9.47	148.6
22	Pennsylvania	17,574	19,700	9.47	148.7
23	Illinois	17,492	19,400	9.33	248.0
24	Wisconsin	17,389	19,400	9.33	147.2
25	Oregon	16,959	19,200	9.23	143.5
26	Wyoming	17,780	19,100	9.18	150.5
27	Indiana	17,192	19,000	9.13	145.5
28	Iowa	17,335	19,000	9.13	146.7
29	New Mexico	17,368	18,600	8.94	147.0
30	Florida	17,268	18,200	8.75	146.1
31	Idaho	17,028	18,000	8.65	144.1
32	Oklahoma	16,642	17,700	8.51	140.8
33	Kansas	16,687	17,600	8.46	141.2
34	North Dakota	16,812	17,600	8.46	142.3
35	Georgia	16,405	17,400	8.37	138.8
36	Ohio	16,551	17,400	8.37	140.1
37	South Dakota	16,688	17,300	8.32	141.2
38	Louisiana	16,290	17,000	8.17	137.9

1	2	3	4	5	6
col. 4 Rank [a]	Jurisdiction	Total Yearly Welfare Benefit (Tax Free)	Pretax Yearly Wage Equivalent (non welfare)	Equivalent Hourly Wage	Benefit as % of Poverty Level
39	Kentucky	15,807	16,800	8.08	133.8
40	North Carolina	16,007	16,800	8,08	135.5
41	Montana	15,814	16,300	7.84	133.8
42	South Carolina	15,953	16,200	7.79	135.0
43	Nebraska	15,725	15,900	7.64	133.1
44	Texas	15,470	15,200	7.31	103.9
45	West Virginia	15,202	15,200	7.31	128.6
46	Missouri	15,102	14,900	7.16	127.8
47	Arizona	14,802	14,100	6.78	125.3
48	Tennessee	14,582	13,700	6.59	123.4
49	Arkansas	14,088	13,200	6.35	119.2
50	Alabama	13,817	13,000	5.25	116.9
51	Mississippi	13,033	11,500	5.53	110.3

[a] rank changes somewhat for the various columns   Payment Standard is for a 4 - person family

2 - Central Banking And The Individual

There is a story of government misadventure and the creation of the central banking system of the United States, called the Federal Reserve, which is part of a much more comprehensive tale. I discuss here just enough of the Federal Reserve background to show how the government has failed in yet another of its endeavors that greatly affect everyday living. The repercussions of this poorly handled responsibility may even be the most serious of all its doings. Certainly it is as catastrophic as those government misadventures that have forced both mother and father to become wage earners, in an effort to meet the tax burden and to make a better future for their family.

See also chapter 9 for more on the Federal Reserve. The potential for degrading individual freedom and individual sovereignty is as ominous as I can imagine, but for now it is only a *possibility*, not yet a fait accompli. In contrast, the failure of government in its handling of a central banking system *is a reality* and we need to be fully aware of it. The year 1913 was a critical turning point in American monetary and economic history for two very important reasons, creation of the Federal Reserve System, and passage of the Sixteenth Amendment and the income tax.

The Federal Reserve System

In 1913 the federal government finally buckled under to the relentless pressure of the most powerful political action committee ever, namely that of the ultra capitalists known at the time as "The Money Trust." For decades, those top-of-the-heap Americans who had amassed great wealth from steel, timber, oil, railroading, coal and other basic enterprises, and their select banking industry thirsted for positive means of preserving those fortunes as well as to make them grow. As they grew in sophistication, they adopted the same strategic approach which had been pioneered and perfected by the Rothschilds and others in Europe during the nineteenth century. The solution [for The Money Trust] was to become established, via legislation, as *the* central banking system within the United States.

As early as the 1830s Andy Jackson had to dismantle the forerunner of today's Fed, namely the Bank of the United States, which operated between 1816 and 1836. He did so because he saw its actions as a naked attempt to *control the government,* and as a *chief cause of economic distress* to the American people. Moneyed people and institutions do not just go away, however. They merely withdraw, accumulate more wealth and return at more favorable times [for them] to try again for control. There is never any need to hurry or to panic in trying to achieve their goals, as we will clearly see later in the book.

Success had to wait until after the beginning of the 20th century. In the meantime, every crisis was used as an excuse to extol the virtues, and the need, for a *central* banking system, to smooth out such crises. Perseverance finally paid off when the banking PAC was able to engineer yet another economic crisis in 1907 that completed public indoctrination to accept that banking concept. J.P. Morgan, through rumor, spread the lie of insolvency against the Trust Company of America and triggered bank runs that escalated to crisis proportions. While not all historians agree about the cause of the 1907 bank crisis, few can question the fact that the Morgan-led group became pre-eminent in the US banking industry following 1907. In the background, besides Morgan were such stalwarts of the banking industry as John D. Rockefeller, Bernard Baruch, Paul Warburg [late arrival from Germany] and Jacob Schiff, whose family ties with the Rothschilds were more than a century old. These men knew exactly what was needed to gain full control of money, and what to do with that control.

Their chief representative in Washington was Senator Nelson Aldrich [whose daughter married John D. Rockefeller Jr.]. Aldrich chaired the National Monetary Commission created by Congress in 1910 in answer to the 1907 crisis. The commission studied the issues for two years, particularly the workings of central banking in Europe, clearly the most sophisticated in the world. With no great surprise the Aldrich Commission, unofficially but *directly guided*[41] by the Morgan-

---

[41] One instance of such guidance came during a secret retreat at Morgan's hunting club on Jekyll Island off the coast of Georgia. It was at this time that the US Federal Reserve System was devised, according to one of the participants, Frank Vanderlip, then president of the Rockefeller National City Bank.

Rockefeller banking political action group, adopted the basics of the European model as our own.

The skullduggery and manipulations that made Federal Reserve legislation possible are an interesting aside to our current political process, but for now the fact of its creation in 1913 and its consequences to ourselves as individual sheep are of the most relevance. The major changes to American banking that came about with the creation of the Federal Reserve were THREE. These were the far-reaching powers handed over by Congress. As a preamble, however, please note particularly that the Federal Reserve label is merely a *name* given to a *privately held* group of banks. It is **NOT** a federal institution. It is *not* a branch of the federal government. The banks are run by private individuals whose *first* responsibility is to themselves and a handful of very rich individuals and foundations.

The 1913 Changes to American Banking
- First: The *Federal Reserve*, the new central banking system of the United States, was granted control over interest rates. Specifically, it is the *discount rate* which is under direct control of the Fed. This is the interest charged by the Fed when they lend money to banks in their district. Changes to the discount rate cascade down throughout the entire banking system, directly affecting the availability of money to any and all borrowers for any purpose. It has a direct, and immediate affect on the market value of stocks. Please note that *the men turning this valve which controls stock prices are themselves the biggest holders of such securities*. One might begin to be a little suspicious of motives and actions when the conflict of interest is so blatant. **The potential for manipulation to their own advantage is absolutely unlimited**, and the means of constraint against such manipulation is completely nonexistent. This is item one.

- Second: The Fed was granted control over the *size* of the national money supply. The means granted was the ability to *set reserve requirements* on member banks according to rules and formulas under Fed control. Reserves are non-interest-bearing deposits [at each member bank] which, therefore, change the gross amount of money in circulation. When a change in inflation rate becomes important to the *Fed owners*, all they need do is change the reserve requirement. A forceful warning about how this power might easily be misused came right along with the passage of the Federal Reserve Act itself.

The Congressional Record for Dec. 22 1913, Vol. 51, p 1446, contains the following quote of Congressman Charles Lindbergh Sr., father of Lucky Lindy.
'The new law will create inflation whenever the trus ts want inflation. It may not do so immediately, but the trusts want a period of inflation because all the stocks they hold have gone down..... Now, if the trusts can get another period of

inflation, they figure they can unload the stocks on the people at high prices during the excitement and then bring on a panic and buy them back at low prices..."

'The people may not know it immediately, but the day of reckoning is only a few years removed."

Lindbergh's prediction came true within a decade, when our greatest speculative bubble began in the roaring twenties, brought on by money supplies that seemingly had no end. The end did come, however, in 1929 after loose money policies had done their inflationary, ruinous deed. As prices of everything plummeted, big money was able to re-accumulate any security it wanted at costs far below where they had sold during the frenzy. Thus the first test of the new monetary control system, a system which was 'sold" as the preferred means of *preventing* panics, bank runs and wild swings in the economy, was a dismal failure. But more than failure, it showed once again for those who were capable of connecting cause and effect, the catastrophic consequences of amateur government meddling in affairs far beyond their ken. Most of the voting congressmun had been led like babes by a few savvy, and well-indoctrinated big money professionals into doing something that makes no sense at all.

The point of most interest in this discussion, however, is the effect of this particular government failure on all the rest of the one hundred and fifty million Americans who had a right to expect far better from their elected representatives. Two whole generations endured economic privations that would not have happened had the Federal Reserve Act not been passed in the form it was. How could people carry on in their pursuit of happiness when government actions not only didn't ensure stable economic conditions but actually contributed directly to subvert those prerequisites to stability?   This is item two.

- Third: There is the monopoly granted the Fed, meaning the Fed owners, to be the exclusive lenders of money to the federal government. The process is a bit indirect, but the effect is to lend money to government. Government issues securities which the Fed is empowered to buy and sell. Thus, any time a spending Congress raises the debt ceiling to accommodate yet more spendthrift programs, the Fed simply buys new government securities and lends money to member banks to do the same. The money the Fed uses for this is *newly created* money which today, has absolutely no backing of assured value *except* the collective word and honor of the United States Government.   This is item three.

The mountain of monetary machinations we now live beside, a mountain created by irresponsible legislators, and I say this deliberately, mostly for their own personal gain in power, these are the people who stand behind the pledge to repay those who ultimately financed the loans, namely private individuals, including

278

citizens of other countries. How does one view the pledge of such people? *We are witness and party to the greatest pyramid scheme ever run.* As long as there are new willing lenders who will buy *new* government securities from the Fed, which is the amount of *increase* in the national debt, there will be money available for the interest payments government has to make on the previous debt increase. There is no difference whatsoever between this legal government process and the illegal, con-artist scam which pays old 'investors" with part of the take from the next batch of 'investors."

Income Tax

The great bulk of interest payments, of course, are covered by revenues collected from *income taxes. The ability of government to levy an income tax was the second critical turning point of 1913*, and the final piece of the puzzle to gain unfettered control of US money by The Money Trust. If the twelve district Federal Reserve were to lend money to government, the bankers wanted to be sure such loans could be repaid. It took a Constitutional Amendment, but by February 3, 1913 enough of the States had ratified the *Sixteenth Amendment*, and the income tax was born. The transition to private control of American money and its economy was finally completed when legislation was passed which dumped an income tax on all working Americans. The progression of confiscation from that time to now has been relentlessly upwards in an attempt to satisfy the money gluttony of government. Sadly, there is no amount of money that can satisfy a system of spending and taxing which is *inherently* unstable. It will continue upward, exponentially, until failure is final and complete. It may seem ironic that the bankers' concern about repayment of loans to government will most likely end up not ever being satisfied since repayment is not a condition government has placed on itself. But the sop of repayment, with taxation as the means, was necessary to convince *individuals* to become the final holders of government securities.

Note carefully that once sold to us as individuals the Fed [and therefore the Fed owners] have no further liability in case of default.

For them there is no possible way to lose as a result of any of these transactions. They have no concern that their wealth can be compromised no matter what government does. National debt size is not a factor; they are merely middle-men. Bankruptcy is not a factor; they will merely buy up the best of what is left when the crisis subsides. Riots or even wars are not a problem for the same reason. And obviously they have no concern for which bunch of power-seekers is actually running the government. Their position is so secure that I can think of only one thing that could even affect it — and that is to abolish the Fed as it is structured now. Perhaps a case can be made favoring Fed control based on an undisputed NEED for control of some sort. One would think, however, that a means of control could be devised that doesn't pander to the biased interests of one powerful group over all others whose need is clearly greater but is far too diffuse to contest the issue.

*   *   *

There remains only to characterize the failure of the 1913 Congress so there will be no misunderstanding about it. The Constitution defined the structure of the central government to consist of three independent branches. The Congress, in its unfathomable lack of wisdom, chose to create a fourth independent branch which we can view as the Financial Branch of government. It did this by overt legislation which was not intended to define a fourth branch, but by legislation which was effectively nothing but a *contract* with a private banking institution, owned and controlled by private individuals. Congress, in this inexplicable mode, granted total monopoly powers over money to these people and made essentially zero provisions in this contract for the Monopoly to operate within specified guidelines or with specific goals to be monitored by Congress. In effect, the Congress, and therefore we the people, received nothing in return for granting this monopoly. We must understand that the Monopoly was granted almost total freedom of action, has never been audited, and reports to Congress, not for any kind of approval, but for limited information purposes only. A more advantageous arrangement for the bankers can not be imagined. In fact even the bankers could not have imagined better contract terms. If anything more advantageous were possible, you can be sure it would have been part of the contract, since the bankers themselves wrote it. Conversely, a more disastrous contract can not be imagined from the perspective of the individual citizen who needs *stability of living conditions*, and who naively expected government to supply that stability.

A Conclusion To Bear In Mind

It becomes clearer by the moment that one law-making body, with legislative powers that are all-encompassing, is not, and can not be sufficiently competent to produce the rules of national intercourse with the wisdom needed. What has resulted from this branch of government, to which far too many powers were granted, has instead become a catalogue of subgroups of experts, responsible to no set of citizen voters, who decide matters and then merely bargain with other legislators who know nothing of how their own vote becomes subverted and shamefully exploited. We are now a nation whose rules are not made even by a majority of representatives, let alone voters, but by the smallest of minorities, to the benefit of no one except special interests. The *prototype* special interest group was the early 1900 version of The Money Trust, later legitimized, seemingly in perpetuity, as the Federal Reserve System.

*   *   *

I have used mainly two references for the basic facts and background needed to tell this Fed story. The first is a 1996 high school term paper by Lori J. Blomer titled, 'The Federal Reserve System and Its Power." The importance of this, and the thing most heartening about this short report is that it shows that the foolishness of our government's activities is no longer taboo in teaching our young people truth. I am more and more convinced that the teaching of truth - in all things - is the only hope to correct the problems we have created, and which warp the lives of us all. The second reference, of the many that might have been used, is the book by James Perloff called, 'The Shadows of Power," a report on the Council on Foreign Relations and the American Decline, and a book that all Americans would benefit from because of the background information it contains. It isn't necessary to agree with Perloff's conclusions, [my own reservations are discussed later], but it is very important to be aware of some of the details he presents of government operations.

3 - Corporate Welfare and the Archer Daniels Midland Saga

The Federal government would have us believe that it champions free enterprise. Indeed, if it has any constitutional charter regarding business, it is to assure equal opportunity for everyone. Their actions belie that responsibility. The face they turn toward voters is a lie. We have already looked in some detail at the distortions inflicted on the United States agricultural industry. We know that the decades-long meddling in agriculture has served no useful purpose whatsoever — to citizens. Any benefits derived accrue solely to government as a means of extending itself and of wielding power, none of which is a proper constitutional goal. Bending agriculture into a crazy quilt form far from that of normal business, however, is not the limit of government meddling. Their unwanted and unconstitutional efforts extend throughout the entire business spectrum. Wherever government senses political gain, meaning control of money and expansion of itself, that is where it meddles most, regardless of the consequences to those they serve or, as we will see shortly, the basic economies of foreign neighbors.

Collectively, and somewhat erroneously, this bit of government foolishness has been labeled "corporate welfare". The companies that benefit from this ill-conceived policy are hardly destitute, but the stage is draped that way for the benefit of Joe and Josephine Public. The loudest sounds are meant to convince the Public that some home-grown industry is in need of protection of various sorts from unfair foreign competition. Actually, convince is the wrong word. All that' s necessary is to air a reason and almost any reason will do. Placate is probably more accurate. Home goods are subsidized, tariffs are set, quotas meted out and government gets to administer the whole enterprise. The lucky producers have guaranteed markets at hefty prices, competition is nil and their corporate future is as good as it gets. These "business men" are so pleased, in fact, that they devise an endless stream of ways to share their good fortune with those who make it all happen, mainly advocacy groups and the politicians themselves.

Mr. bureaucrat gets to spend money, make decisions that give him endless influence, and assures himself of longevity in government service as campaign money and other forms of gratitude pour in.

Joe Public, on the other hand, gets to pay higher prices for all the subsidized products, pays the ever-increasing tax bill for the subsidies and the bureaucracy, and then can' t quite understand why our foreign neighbors hate us. We get a hint from the following. Sugar production is directly subsidized in the US with a minimum support price to US growers of 22 cents per pound while world prices vary between 4.5 and 10.5 cents/lb. Tariffs, added to foreign sugar, keep supermarket prices high. Furthermore low quotas are set on foreign growers so that our import tonnage is far less than it had been before the meddling or would be in a free market. This stupid policy has caused great economic harm to the world's real sugar producers notably the Philippines and the countries of Central America. The only ones who benefit are a few US growers [with one company supplying 80 % of all corn sweeteners], advocacy groups and politicians addicted to power.

Look further at one more example of the foolishness of corporate welfare to see how bad it has become for those of us who pay the bill. Archer Daniels Midland is a powerhouse of corporate America, a multi-billion dollar enterprise marketing corn sweeteners, seed oil, flour, biochemicals, ethanol, and other products. Prudential Securities estimated Archer Daniels Midland profits for 1995 at $746 million, of which *at least 43%* came from products subsidized or protected by the United States federal government. The estimate report notes that the complexity of United States crop support programs make it extremely difficult to know the full extent of profits derived through subsidies, so the 43% figure is a minimum. ADM lobbying and direct political campaign contributions quite likely were decisive in extending the Federal sugar subsidy program. The result was that, for 1995, consumers paid about $3 billion more than they would have in a free market. The final effect was that for every $10 extra that Joe and Josephine Public spent to buy corn sweeteners another dollar of profit went to ADM. We are not surprised at all to learn that ADM is the company which alone supplies 80% of the domestic corn sweetener

The skullduggery of the corn sweetener debacle is far exceeded in foolishness by the ethanol subsidy programs carried out by our generous federal government. For this one, a comparable metric is three times as bad for the tax-paying consumer. For every dollar of ADM ethanol profit, Americans pay more than $30 in *extra* cost.

A few more facts will help to show how illogical the whole ethanol subsidy thing is.

Ethanol is distilled corn alcohol. Add one part ethanol to 9 parts gasoline to make gasohol, which is nothing but a sop to energy independence. Even if it gave the same energy output as gasoline, a 10% reduction in gasoline use is next to meaningless as an energy substitute. The fact that it is one third less fuel efficient means that about 4% more fuel must be burned to go the same distance. The next jolt is the cost in fuel to distill the alcohol from the corn, which is greater than the cost in refinery fuel to make the same amount of gasoline.

The real jolt to logic, however, is the cost to make ethanol. Notice first that it could be sold as another alcohol product where the cost to consumers would easily cover processing and return a profit. Instead, government power motives dominate. It costs $1.60 per gallon to produce ethanol (1986 USDA estimate)[42] while gasoline at wholesale was priced at 60 cents per gallon. (The 1995 price was 55 cents per gallon). For every gallon produced ADM got a 54 cent tax reduction against profits, so the cost to gasohol blenders was $1.06 per gallon. This is where direct government subsidies come in. Blenders receive a 60 cent federal subsidy and a state subsidy between 30 & 40 cents for each gallon. Therefore, the net cost to blenders of the ethanol additive ranges between 6 and 16 cents per gallon, which is considerably less than their own refinery cost of 60 cents per gallon of gas. That is an outright gift of about 8%, paid directly from our income taxes.

These are not companies struggling to help us realize energy independence. They are giant, highly profitable businesses which have learned to play the American political game, benefiting themselves and government bureaucrats with huge returns gouged from the earnings of tax-paying Americans.

This information about corporate welfare is taken from the CATO Policy Analysis No. 241, by James Bovard. It was published in September of 1995 and gives many more details of the whole sordid story. A quote from this report is very enlightening concerning the attitude of those businessmen and politicians willing to steal from the public treasury. The political strategy, attributed to ADM, "has long been based on the ideas that politicians should control prices and markets, and that ADM and [chairman] Andreas should control politicians."

Between 1980 and 1995, the cost to American taxpayers for all ADM-related lobbying activities has been more than $40,000,000,000 dollars, that for just one segment of American industry receiving "corporate welfare."

* * *

---

[42] Actual cost to Archer Daniels Midland may have been lower, but this figure will be used to be more conservative.

283

This whole disgusting, criminal, self-serving, arrogant and degrading lie goes on with impunity under our very noses. Without exaggeration it has the potential to destroy the Republic. No force to date has been seriously raised against it. Nor have we even mentioned here the equally criminal funding, with tax money, via this insidious government conduit, of special religious, environmental, anti-energy and anti-nuclear interests. The leak in the public money dike, opened with those first government gifts of tax money in the time of Congressman Davy Crockett, has indeed become a torrent of money that threatens to drown our country and us along with it.

APPENDIX F
Equality & Inequality

1 – Examples of Local Government Oppression

This appendix elaborates on the noble concept of Equality summarized in Chapter 14. The fact that the cases cited here are but a very small fraction of the scurrilous actions against our fellow Americans should make us all uncomfortable with the way government has evolved.

In our fondest hopes and dreams for achieving a society that advances steadily, we envision this magnificent governmental structure being led by the best among us. They are people whose wisdom is far beyond the norm, people coming from the same molds that gave us George Washington, James Madison, Thomas Jefferson, Harry Truman, and a few others. We see such leaders as pointing the way when the fuss and clamor of our complex societies won't let us see straight. The problem is that such leaders are very very rare and the great gaps in time without true leadership have been more than enough to assure our own mediocrity as a nation trying to live its ideals.. Not only have we not advanced from the tremendous platform build by the Founding Fathers, but we have assuredly regressed in ways that should no longer betolerated.

Think again about the American Civil War. Its *fundamental cause* came from our attempt to hold some people as mere property, unequal in every respect. The two, irreconcilable ideas created two factions which, coupled with grossly inadequate leadership *on both sides*, spelled death for 624,000 young men. The **practice** of equality among people was certainly non-existent from 1791 to 1865.

"Reconstruction" merely added more hate to the defeated, and triggered petty resolve — at every level of government and society — to prevent there being equality of anything for Black compared to White. Even the United States Supreme Court didn't understand the *concept* of EQUALITY and lacked the wisdom needed during that long period. Bad law, ramroded onto the statute books at *all levels* of government was condoned and upheld by the court. And when the foolish notion of separate-but-equal came into vogue they were incapable of seeing that separate-but-equal is inherently unequal, as is surely self-evident to anyone without hate or fear of someone who only looks different than ourself. Adolph Plessy was jailed in 1896 in Louisiana for attempting to board a railroad car reserved for White travelers. One of Plessy's four grandparents was half Black, giving him a blood inheritance of one-eighth Black and seven-eighths White, thereby rendering him unfit to ride in cars with those having eight eighths White blood. The notion and the law propagating it are preposterous, but when the Supreme Court upheld *Louisiana's right to deny equality*, our purity as a nation disappeared completely via failed legal decisions.

There is nowhere to turn when the highest tribunal of the land refuses to honor the very foundation ideals of government.

Nowhere except back to the people themselves, which at the time was not only impractical, but a loser as well. Any answer derived via referendum would surely have been the same. We should ask ourselves now whether such a test among the people would be different.

On 18 May 1896, the US Supreme Court did its deed to keep the racial wound open. Justice Henry Billings Brown (1891-1906), siding with six other Justices, rejected the argument that Louisiana violated the 13th Amendment, which he claimed pertained *only* to the institution of slavery itself (another error). And he rejected the argument claiming violation of the 14th Amendment, the guarantee of equal protection, since separate-but-equal accommodations were required. [Please note that such a law added a cost to the Louisiana and Nashville Railroad for extra cars, a demand by government which itself stepped beyond the proper bounds of government]. Justice Brown muddied the waters even more when he tried to justify his decision by equating such segregation to 'long-established customs of society..... To require mixing of the races would be futile in the face of strong public sentiment as shown by laws requiring separation of races in educational facilities, for example."

The lone dissenter to this latest *judicial* crime was John Marshall Harlan (1877-1911) whose wisdom in this was ignored by the rest of the court. His was the only right answer, but since the majority has its (wrong) way, we lived for another 58 years **practicing inequality** instead of the equality that distinguished America at the founding. Justice Harlan's words should be memorized by all young students, and by their parents as well.

The 'Constitution is colorblind, and neither knows nor tolerates classes among citizens."[43]

The *practice* of inequality began by ignoring the Constitution as approved by the 13 states and Commonwealths in 1791. It continued even after the Civil War by ignoring both Amendments 13 and 14, which sadly enough should never even have been needed. The *philosophy* of equality was established before the 19th century ever began, but petty little people and leaders refused to be guided by the ideal. The

---

[43] The Oxford Companion to the Supreme Court of the United States, edited by Kermit L. Hall.

Plessy decision, a serious miscarriage of justice, allowed inequality to continue being practiced full force into the 1950s. The kind of inequality practiced during that whole long era was not restricted to symbols, however, but extended into every facet of life as southern state legislators enacted laws designed specifically to deny such basic rights as freedom of contract, property ownership, and economic liberties. None of this changed until Chief Justice Earl Warren's Court began to unravel the laws that condoned the practice of inequality. The path, however, was anything but direct.

It took most of the decade of the 1950s to divert the *Federal* conscience from unequal and segregated, Black and White, to equality and oneness of society. The sequence of judicial steps to make that philosophical shift are perhaps secondary to understanding why our history is one of inequality, but a look briefly at some of those steps gives us a way of understanding how mediocrity and pettiness, not profound truths, have ruled our social progress throughout most of our nation's existence. Consider this short list:

- 1938, Gaines vs. Missouri[44] - The Supreme Court denied Missouri's offer to pay Gaines' tuition to law school out of state instead of permitting entrance to Missouri's all-White law school.
- 1948, Shelley vs. Kraemer - The Supreme Court held that radically restrictive covenants were unconstitutional, a decision helped in part when the United States Attorney General added its weight to the petitioner, the NAACP.
- 1950, McLaurin vs. Oklahoma State Board of Regents - The Supreme Court invalidated segregation in graduate schools.
- 1950, Sweatt vs. Painter - The Supreme Court invalidated segregation in Law Schools.
- 1952 to 1954, Brown vs. Board of Education I, - The Supreme Court finally decided on the *merits* of Public School segregation, ruling it unconstitutional, but saying nothing about the manner or timing to correct the problem of existing segregation in public education.
- 1955, Brown II - A Supreme Court decision to guide desegregation itself, only succeeded in being ambiguous with its "all deliberate speed" proviso. The phrase, which says nothing, gave State and local officials all the latitude they needed to block real rework. While the Supreme Court decision was unanimous, the do-nothing phrase was included at the insistence of Justice Felix Frankurter, and delayed real change further. Perhaps it also minimized violence.

---

[44] The case is recorded by the Supreme Court as 'Missouri ex rel. Gaines vs. Canada, 305 U S 337 (1938)."

- 1956, Gayle vs. Browder - Finally, the Supreme Court got around to overruling the 1896 Plessy decision which allowed separate but equal. It did this by invalidating segregation in state parks, beaches, bath houses, golf courses as well as public transportation.
- 1958, Cooper vs. Aaron - This was the first real test of the desegregation decision of Brown I (note the 4-year hiatus). The Supreme Court ruled that a further delay of 2 1/2 years, requested by Little Rock school officials, would violate Black student rights, thus putting time into desegregation. It also ruled on the question of whether state governors and legislators were bound by Supreme Court decisions. This is amazing; 167 years after adoption of the Constitution, this fundamental question needed serious court time to straighten out government officials. Obviously this was merely part of the never-ending delaying tactics used to prolong inequality in America.

The **habit** of Americans to maintain inequalities had lost its Federal voice and its "legal" justification. The practic e, however, didn't go away, it merely shifted to a thousand scattered sites as state legislatures and city governments resisted decent and just living with every conceivable trick, legal or otherwise. We will list just a few presently, but the important thing to realize is that *even with US Supreme Court decrees, very little actually changed.* For example, by 1964, ten years after all Americans were clearly told that segregated schools violated the law of the land and the Unalienable Rights of citizens, less than two percent of segregated school districts had complied with this most fundamental of laws. I haven't seen information about how many school districts there are in total, and what fraction were actually segregated to begin with, but I see no reason at all to assume that the problem of inequality was anything but huge, spread throughout the country, and shameful.[45]

* * *

The practice of legalized inequality, to our everlasting shame, is not confined to the issue of segregation. There is at least one other episode of American history that we would do well to recall often. We *must* remind ourselves how easy it was for our honorable, constitutional guardians in government to toss out the very basis of our national heritage. Very soon after the United States was thrust into the Second World War, the Federal government, without hesitation, decided that a whole collection of citizens could be stripped of every single Unalienable Right GUARANTEED by the Constitution, except life itself. Property, freedom of

---

[45] I know of at least one public school system that didn't practice segregation as far back as the 1920s, namely Connecticut, where I was taught. Perhaps that is why I found the whole segregation issue to be so strange, when the answers are truly self-evident.

movement, free expression, freedom to work, and the pursuit of happiness were summarily stolen from them for the remainder of the war. About 120,000 Japanese-Americans were suddenly viewed as infiltrators and spies. Without the merest hint of "due process" or "equal protection under the law" this whole segment of American citizens became non-citizens, trucked off to internment "camps" hundreds of miles from their homes and businesses. "Relocation camps" at Gila River, Arizona, and Heart Mountain, Wyoming, became home and all there was to life was only to wait.

How was it possible for such dictatorial dereliction of duty to go on in our beautiful America, our haven from oppression? An answer to that is probably as complex as human intercourse can be. Unreasoned fear? A knee-jerk reaction to the Pearl Harbor attack, which had no connection with this blameless bunch of men, women and children? Another failure of leadership? There is no acceptable excuse, but the fools who caused it to happen got away with it without censure of any kind.

Two More Reluctant Conclusions
I am inclined to see at least two faults deep within our governmental structure, faults serious enough to allow the deed. The first we have discussed before. It is the provision within the Constitution that *provides* government with the power to suspend all individual rights in a time of declared national emergency. This is *a major fault in the document*, because it takes away the very thing that is only *threatened* by the emergency. The implications are obvious. I contend that there is no conceivable emergency that could justify such an abrogation of Rights.

The second fault is the lack of true safeguards among the branches of government to undo a mistake or prevent another branch from exceeding its authority.

Sweeping up Japanese-Americans was a huge mistake — at the very least — or a crime that other Americans should have challenged immediately. No such action was even contemplated against Italian-Americans or German-Americans, because none was needed. Enemies in our midst cannot be identified by the shape of their eyes, but the *habit* of inequality, **so long practiced in America**, rationalized the crime into necessity. The Japanese-American internment was perhaps one of our four most depraved actions as a nation, and in the same class of shame as slavery and segregation, the treatment of America's Indian people and the American war in Vietnam. The ONLY consolation possible in the Japanese-American crime is that murder was not used as a tool of government.

The dignity with which these 1942 Americans conducted themselves far outshines the morally destitute men who forgot completely why we became one nation. In all the 63 years since the crime, restitution never became a matter

289

seriously considered. That should have been the very first order of governmental business the day after Japan formally surrendered on 2 September, 1945. As it was, these people were ignored, as if the whole debacle had never happened. But of course they were granted the Right once again to pursue happiness.

Lest Americans forget what was done in our name, consider visiting the Museum of Tolerance at the Simon Wiesenthal Center, 9786 West Pico Boulevard in Los Angeles, the site which commemorates the Holocaust, and with that somber mood, go then to 369 East First Street near Union Station in downtown Los Angeles where the Japanese-American National Museum sits ready to remind us of part of our past.

*　　*　　*

But surely, all that intolerance is a thing of the past. What is the condition of equality today in America? The quick answer is that **inequality** is still dominant. No matter what the Federal courts have ruled, no matter what even the US Supreme Court has ruled, progress is still sporadic and diffuse. The monster is a multi-headed hydra with no single point of vulnerability. City and State officials continue to find ways to thwart the spirit of equality. And the sad thing is that even when a city is finally forced to change, it does so only in the very specific situation ruled upon by the courts. The very next opportunity that denying an Unalienable Right becomes the new battleground, different people suffer and more precious time goes by. Consider the miserable record of the city of Yonkers, New York.

For fifty years beginning in the 1930s, Yonkers deliberately forced segregation as official policy by manipulating school zone boundaries which satisfied the letter of segregation laws but consigned Black students to the worst schools. For housing, approvals for low-rent construction just happened to concentrate these projects within Black, residential areas. These decisions were found by the trial judge to be the direct result of pressure by Whites for the avowed purpose of maintaining segregation. The hateful attitude spread itself into almost every point of contact with the Black community. School facilities were the most run down; the teaching staff was the least qualified; guidance counseling aimed students into dead-end jobs; schools were chronically overcrowded; the work force was limited to jobs with little future; and the decades of inequality turned southwest Yonkers into an American ghetto. The picture of the Warsaw ghetto of the 1940s is closer to the truth of that region than the city's description as just a poor neighborhood.

Finally, the Federal government sued the city in 1980, and after a trial of more than three months, Federal District Court Judge Leonard Sand ruled that *the city was guilty of discrimination* in education and in housing. Any victorious feelings this judgment might have evoked, however, were dissipated like fog under a rising sun, when the court ordered that 200 low-cost housing units be built in non-minority neighborhoods. The hatefulness of Yonkers' record was matched by the foolishness of higher government's heavy hand, and no one really benefited.

If there was progress within the Yonkers school system but no change within the city government, then Yonkers continues to be a source of inequality. It seems strange in the extreme that city officials can willfully violate the Constitution, be found guilty, and yet not be held *criminally* liable for the harm they have done to thousands of people. The lop-sidedness of justice shows its distorted shape once again. Removal from office, and imprisonment seem appropriate. Acts that do harm should become a criterion for dealing with the crimes of public officials. *The schooling of Public Servants* needs much more emphasis on that part of the curriculum that deals with duty and responsibility.

There are many other sources that still do not champion equality, constitutional pillar or not. Here are a few more examples:[46] Take particular note of the dates. Little has changed.

• May 1987, Fontana, California: Demond Crawford could not be given an IQ test 'because Demond is Black". However, if he were registered as Hispanic, the test could be given. It was official California state policy to prohibit Black students from taking standard intelligence tests. (Such tests are beneficial in helping students progress, but the state set up the ban, for Black students only, to avoid discrimination suits. Logic was turned upside down.

• December 1986, California: State Superintendent of Public Instruction issued a directive stating in part —
    "An IQ test may not be given to a Black pupil even with parental consent."
Such tests may not be used with Black students:
    - to plan a program of advancement;
    - to gain diagnostic information;
    -to develop goals and objectives;
    -to determine special education needs;
    -to find strengths and weaknesses.
    All these sensible objectives were denied only to Black students, but were available for constructive use with all others. The discrimination quagmire had won out over equality and common sense.

• 1988, Starrett City, New York: Housing authorities kept units vacant, in spite of a long waiting list of Black applicants, hoping that Whites would apply and thereby 'preserve the racial balance". (Another contrary result from that intended.)

---

[46] All these instances of practicing inequality were taken from Clint Bolick's 'Grassroots Tyranny".

- 1992, Washington Post article: Adoptions of Black orphans into loving, non-Black families are often prevented on strictly racial grounds.

- 1990, Prince George's County, Maryland: Arbitrary transfers of White and Black teachers were made by the Board of Education, regardless of qualifications, in order to maintain a racial balance of faculty members.

- 1980, Flint, Michigan: A strict racial quota caused Stuart Marsh to be demoted solely because he is White, in spite of his very high ratings as an educator or even his seniority. (When fundamental principles are abandoned, a society cannot function peacefully or, indeed, with honor.)

Both kinds of injustices are still with us today. As ordinary citizens, we must ask why there is still so much OFFICIAL discrimination in government decisions and actions. Regardless of the incessant rationalizations for all the shoddy treatment we have seen, I don't believe that *most* Americans feel that it is necessary. Even more strongly, I think Americans do not *want* such government oppression against their neighbors, knowing full well that it can easily be turned against any one of us. In a *clear* warning, US Supreme Court Justice Robert H. Jackson (1941-1954) had this to say about the unconscionable Supreme Court decision to inter Japanese-American citizens.

Once a judicial order rationalizes the Constitution to show that it sanctions such an order, the Court for all time has validated the principle of racial discrimination.

The changing nature of government, both federal and local, is most noticeable in matters of discrimination. The Federal mind-set has by now been forcibly altered to see inequality for the scourge it is. Local and State politicians, however, still are a long way from understanding the disservice they continue to dispense. Unfortunately, a skirmish won here for justice must be repeated elsewhere many times over before real change can become a reality.

Conclusion: The Battles Won For True Equality Have Not Changed The Practice of Inequality

2 - The State and Local Government Millstone

If we look for relief from the overbearing weight of federal authorities in our lives, hoping that state and local officials might be our refuge, then we will be disappointed and our trials with government will continue. In a very real sense, local government is even more intrusive because its power is most often aimed directly at individuals. Their actions are very personal, while the oppression of Federal officials is usually aimed at the amorphous multitude. The Federal government *steals money* and overspends mostly for their own benefit. Local politicians aim at *your freedoms*, and their aim has been very good.

Local and State governments, like the Feds, have been granted and have unilaterally assumed far more authority than is necessary, either for national or personal well-being. All levels of government have taken on too much decision-making and directing, to the point that they no longer represent the great bulk of individuals. Instead, they represent themselves and the uncountable special interest groups that distort the landscape.

A Conclusion Forces Its Way Into Our Consciousness
In my thoughts about government misdeeds and possible ways to govern ourselves better, it seems quite clear that an overhaul must begin with the very foundation document itself, the Constitution.

I would point out that to solve our problems with the local and State bodies of government, a very different condition exists. As such, any solution will be much more involved. Merely rewriting 50 state constitutions and innumerable Charters for every city fiefdom might be an option, but is probably a never-ending task. We are confronted, once again, with the issue of the division of governmental responsibilities between States on the one had, and central government on the other. From the very beginning, States saw the need to centralize certain functions of government for mutual benefit and security, but were clearly of a mind to retain all other powers to themselves. In agreeing to the Ninth Amendment, which lumps the State and the People together, to the States, it was merely an afterthought to include the masses. The US Supreme Court has been sparring with the States ever since 1791 at every issue involving the prerogatives of State versus Federal government.

The court has, in fact, deferred to the States on a great many important issues of regulation and control, so much so that State powers are clearly dominant with regard to individuals.

This process has created such variability among laws and regulations that one has the impression of dealing with independent, sovereign nations instead of cloned miniatures of the whole. The subject of Federalism, the balance between State and Federal powers, is integral with the structure of government. For the moment, however, I would simply point out the obvious.

293

No debate aimed at creating an improved self-governing society can succeed unless the sovereignty of individuals has highest priority.

What Conclusion Do You See Concerning Equality In America???

Economic Liberty – Again   (Ref. Chapter 14)

As of 1985, there were in the United States, more than 82,000 different units of local government.[47]   Most of these are not elected and, therefore, can only be controlled indirectly by voters, who should have learned by now that even "direct control" of *elected* officials is an impossibility.   Included in this overwhelming number of governing entities that do, in fact, control us are 40,000 municipal governments, 15,000 school districts, and 26,000 *special* districts. These governing bodies are comprised of 500,000 *elected* officials and more than 13 million tax-paid employees, a monstrous number that dwarfs the mere two-plus million Federal civilian employees. We are inundated with people who control everything we want to do or must do in our own pursuit of happiness. The confrontation between individuals just trying to get along and the controlling regulators became one-sided when the divide-and-conquer strategy was first instituted at about the time Roosevelt's New Deal was inaugurated. Since that time the specifics of living have steadily become worse.

Here is a particularly disturbing example, again taken from Bolick's *Grassroots Tyranny*, which shows the interplay among our overseers, and shows the *extremes of control* that can be exercised by government. Please note that none of the restrictive elements of control contributed anything positive or worthwhile to anyone collectively or individually in the struggle to progress, but do in truth hinder personal advancement at every crossroad. The sole beneficiary: Government.

New Jersey regulators created an economic nightmare for auto insurance companies with a 1983 law written to provide insurance to high-risk drivers for the same cost charged to sensible drivers (mistake #1).   The gift to bad drivers amounted to a subsidy to them, a welfare-like benefit that was to be funded by traffic fines and a surcharge on insurance policies (mistake #2, a theft from every driver). A new *government* agency was set up to administer this farce, and within five years, the subsidized low-priced insurance had attracted more than half of New Jersey motorists to the government agency, called the Joint Underwriting Association.   By 1990 this economically stupid endeavor had generated a new public debt for New Jersey of over $3.3 billion, (mistake #3, another debt to taxpayers who had no need of it and derived no benefit from it).

---

[47] Again, the facts come courtesy of Clint Bolick's 'Grassroots Tyranny'.

The government's response to this new fiscal disaster was to legislate additional taxes in the form of annual assessments ($150 million) on insurance companies and a greater surcharge on insurance policies (mistake #4). *By the new law*, these costs were not allowed to be passed along to policy holders, so the insurance companies had to absorb them all as business losses (mistake #5). This mistake is the inevitable result of earlier meddling into business whenever fiat is invoked selectively to replace economics. The imbalance of normally stable supply-demand actions always requires further meddling, which then only adds to the imbalances. And so it was that the insurance companies themselves realized they could not continue to subsidize New Jersey political larceny, and tried to withdraw from a business that was no longer a business.

Here is where the excesses of New Jersey political errors became extreme, making any pretense of protecting Rights a complete sham. As embattled insurers tried to minimize losses by getting out of the New Jersey auto insurance business, New Jersey passed a LAW that was specifically designed to prevent that (mistake #6). This move was much more than a mistake, however. *It was a crime against insurance companies; a crime against free enterprise, and a crime against the very fundamental Right to earn a living.*

Which makes the next step in this sad saga of American government all the more devastating to individual and collective liberty. New Jersey then made it unlawful (more of mistake #6), retroactively (mistake #7), for a company to surrender its insurance license in their sensible attempt to quit a losing business. To quit, a company had to obtain *permission* from the Commissioner of Insurance and meet any *conditions* he might impose (mistake #8). Twin City Fire Insurance Company gave up its license to sell before the legislation was passed. When it was passed, New Jersey got a court-ordered injunction forcing Twin City to remain in business. To be "allowed" to quit, the Commissioner imposed 14 conditions on Twin City's parent corporation, ITT Hartford, including:

- continue selling for 5 more years
- accept new clients during that time, and therefore increase losses;
- then surrender licenses for all other types of insurance;
- and then surrender all licenses of five other ITT Hartford companies doing business in New Jersey.

This tyrannical, heavy-handed thumping of an American business by local government was upheld by the New Jersey Supreme Court (mistake #9), with both the *law* and the *conditions* judged to be appropriate actions of local government.

The ultimate authority, the US Supreme Court, added its approval indirectly by *refusing* to hear the case (mistake #10).[48]

We've been tallying up a list called mistakes in an oversimplified attempt to quantify a bad situation caused by local government. At virtually every opportunity where official actions had a choice, the one selected caused direct harm to businesses operating in New Jersey. So far the list has ten entries, but one can easily accept that if the complete set of details were known about this one case alone, that the list of "mistakes" would be much greater. Nevertheless, our ten will do nicely, because they represent every *major* turning point. I have a very simple test as to whether an event is an unfortunate accident OR a criminal act. The test is whether it is willful, and does it harm someone. We can test New Jersey's culpability in this case rather easily, and as we will see, very disturbingly.

- **Mistake #1** - Same cost of insurance to all drivers - Good intent; very likely no willful desire to harm.
- **Mistake #2** - Surcharge on all policyholders - A typical tax event, with the usual (moderate) intent to harm the taxpayer but without malice. I've labeled it a theft of money from good drivers by forcing them to pay the insurance bills of bad drivers. Theft qualifies as a crime, but Americans have become so inured to such *arbitrary* tax increases, (i.e. if we even know about them), that we easily forget that most of them are thefts and, therefore, crimes.
- **Mistake #3** - Incurring a needless public debt - This hurts every taxpayer and the value received is non-existent. We need not quibble about its being criminal. (Any payments of claims against drunk drivers, for example, hardly make up for the removal of such drivers from the road.)
- **Mistake #4** - Forcing insurance companies to pay the debt - A deliberate intent to force business to pay for a government mistake. A crime with intent.
- **Mistake #5** - Disallowing increased rates to consumers - Not only is this a ridiculous move from a basic business economics viewpoint, but there is willful intent to harm insurers by forcing increased service without compensation, a penalty taken directly from profits, the only reason that a company exists in the first place. The insurance industry, like all others, is not an altruistic enterprise and is not a source of infinite funds. Willfully eliminating profit will surely kill any company. A crime with intent.
- **Mistake #6** - A law to prevent quitting a business - A clear, willful intent to harm the companies economically and to *deny rights*; a crime by any logical definition. New Jersey also showed contempt for the *concept* of creating just laws, those rules we must have to live peaceably.

---

[48] The US Supreme Court makes a strange fundamental distinction between Freedoms or Rights, pertaining to economic matters and those Rights pertaining to individuals. By refusing to hear cases involving economic rights, the US Supreme Court has abdicated half of its responsibilities and has been a major factor in allowing the growth of economic subjugation by local and State government agencies.

• **Mistake #7** - Retroactively? - The strategy of using bogus law to cover government mistakes compounds those mistakes and shows how low little people will sink to force acceptance of government power. This crime adds to the earlier crimes, subverting the whole system of government instituted by *the people* for their mutual benefit.

• **Mistake #8** - Conditions of Withdrawal? - New Jersey first denies that companies can quit, i.e., they have no RIGHT to quit, but in the next breath, they say the State will confer that right upon the companies provided they pay certain bribes and penalties. The extortion locked up in this chilling example is so blatant that one is flabbergasted, almost speechless when confronted with such distortions of the public trust. Extortion is a crime!

• **Mistake #9** and **Mistake #10** - Approval from the Courts, the last refuge of citizens - To make a thing legal or illegal, all that is required is agreement from the courts. With that approval, any crime can be legalized. This New Jersey crime is an example of the *extremes of oppression* that now occur in the US because the philosophy of this 'people's" government has changed from one of *service* to one of **exercising power**.

*   *   *

Given this very informal listing of mistakes made by New Jersey in dealing with insurance companies, I have argued that many of these 'errors in judgment" have the requisites to brand them as crimes. In my opinion the composite character of these government actions is a criminal one, and is a crime that has gone uncontested as such, a crime that has absolutely no *dedicated* instrument of justice pursuing it to put it right. When acts of government at any level are such that they meet the simple criteria of criminal acts, then it seems quite obvious that they are crimes that need to be undone. Yet the American system of government *provides no mechanism to undo such crimes that is not part of the offending branch(es) of government.*

We individually are not all insurance companies by any means, but we are all definitely victims of these crimes, citizen of New Jersey or not.

This crime committed in New Jersey is the same one being committed in varying degrees throughout the United States by all the other 81,999 local agencies of government. They are stealing the *Rights* of individuals, effecting a systematic and relentless degradation of every facet of American life. Yes, there is almost always money involved as well, and that is most likely the main reason that local government does what it does. The chief loss to We the People, however, is not money but Rights, and while we can quantify the money stolen by all these government escapades, Rights are measured in a far different and personal way.

297

Please bear with me on this, because we have finally arrived at an *understanding* of local/state government operations that tell us just how much the grand idea of self-government has been subverted. We need to go back to the very beginning of this destructive farce. The idea of uniform auto insurance rates came either from government or from lobbyists for high-risk drivers, most probably from government. There is absolutely no doubt that the general New Jersey citizenry did not demand such a change. There was no overriding goal, agreed to by all voters, or drivers, or adults, that compelled government to begin this intrusion. Citizen clamor for uniform cost was non-existent. Even more telling is the realization that no argument of logic can be made — from the standpoint of New Jersey citizens — which shows the change to be good or necessary to preserve some citizen benefit in danger of being lost.

The logic from government's viewpoint, however, is also clear, provided only that law should benefit government first. More money would flow through government. More government administrators and regulators were needed; and a lot of new money was involved. Once the farce began, compounding that first mistake became inevitable as the stupidity of the economic intrusions grew. Instead of canceling or undoing the damage, government's answer was simply to apply more and more repressive power.

The worst blows against our Rights, however, were the actions of the courts. It is all too obvious that *the guiding criteria being used have little to do with upholding citizen Rights* when government "rights" are involved. As we review this case, it is relatively easy to understand how government has allowed itself to evolve to increase **its** own benefits at the expense of We the People. It is not at all so easy to see why or how the same destructive transition has occurred within the American Justice System.

Conclusion: Our Rights Exist At The Whim Of Government

There is a key addendum that goes along with this New Jersey example of government failure. It has to do with an attitude of government which, in the extreme, becomes the New Jersey insurance-control crime just dissected. The attitude is that almost all human activities, whether personal or business, are things to be allowed or disallowed by decisions from government.

It hardly matters whether a person wants to drive a taxi, start a radio station, cut hair, or fly an airplane, government conducts itself as if it alone has the right of decision. The giving of licenses for a fee — for just about every activity, has become a fixture in American life, so much so that all of us sheep have become wary of any salesperson without a license. The issuing of licenses by a control agency — for a fee — is a control mechanism that assures nothing to a customer except that government has gotten its cut from every business.

Such licensing is too often also a means of *limiting competition* and has come about through an "arrangement" between government and special -interest enterprises. I call that collusion and conspiracy to defraud, and that's a crime.

Practicing law without a license has bad connotations. The same holds for medicine, at any level of service. We might recall the turf battles chiropractors and physical therapists have been subjected to, to know what the real purposes of licensing are; controlling competition, increasing government size and increasing the amount of money under control.

The government, at any level, was never handed the charter to dispense anything, because no *source* exists that originally held that responsibility. Individuals could only agree to yield their individual Rights to such things as *choice* of trade or profession, and that certainly was never done. The Constitution doesn't grant such power because it has no such authority to grant.

Yet States, cities and counties unilaterally ignore this implied limitation on their powers, as does the Federal government, and through this single opening have gained unprecedented control of all Americans.

The result has been one of the biggest thefts of Unalienable Rights of all individuals. For all practical purposes we no longer live under a system of government of the *people*, but instead are controlled in our daily activities by a system of power-holders who have replaced the Unalienable Rights of individuals with rights bestowed by government. **And that is our true condition today.**

This next example follows from the discussions in Chapter 14, adding more to the way local governments have flaunted their power at the expense of those rights of people they were sworn to protect.

Warped Philosophy, Bad Law and Majority Rule, vs. Privacy and Free Choice
(Ref. Chapter 14, example 4)

Consider how government-think has become so dominant when it comes to decision-making. Whether the rights of people are involved or not, they are secondary to the goals government has set for itself, and their decisions bear this out almost universally.

Philosophy — In spite of our supposed American beliefs in the equality of individuals, the Rights to property and freedom from search and seizure without due process, the Right to free expression and sovereignty of the individual, there is a contradictory philosophy which denies these foundation stones as the ones by which we should build our lives together.

The opposing philosophy contends that a simple" majority" has a right that supersedes that of the individual on questions of individual choice if that majority opinion differs.

The "logic" says that a majority of some undefined subset of Americans can outlaw behavior that they find objectionable, even though the same behavior is acceptable elsewhere. The reference truth, the criterion for deciding, the fundamental Right seems to permit someone other than yourself to decide whether your choices are to be allowed under *conditions* which change depending on the OPINION of that someone else. The foundation of that philosophy is, therefore, not a fixed one, but depends on someone else's opinion concerning what you may or may not do.[49]

This in turn says that individuals are not equal and that there is no such concept as individual sovereignty.

In its stead there is the nebulous belief that there is a someone else more equal and more qualified to rule on things that pertain only to yourself.

The issue here is a classic case of a self-evident truth, a solid, unequivocal dictum, being completely abandoned by flawed logic and irrelevant details which obscure the untenable nature of the argument. A solid basis for the creation of law is thrown away and is replaced with mercurial opinion that is an ever-changing reference, subject only to the collected group currently doing the deciding. You cannot espouse equality and sovereignty and then simply deny them when your mood is shifted by something you find distasteful. Be glad that *you* are not being forced into acts you find objectionable, as your right *not to act* is still being respected.

---

[49] One recognized spokesman for this majority-based philosophy is Robert Bork, one-time candidate to the Supreme Court. He states that 'the major freedom ... of our kind of society is the freedom to choose to have a public morality." Thus homosexual acts are not victimless because the 'knowledge that an activity is taking place is a harm to those who find it profoundly immoral."

There are gaping flaws in this position on social justice, including such questions as: (1) How is this harmful knowledge obtained if Right to privacy is preserved? (2) What portion of American society sets the moral standards, all citizens, those of one State, or one city, or one enclave or just the neighborhood? (3) How do you reconcile State coercion to enforce a 'public morality" with the Rights of free choice , privacy and equality? (4) And lastly, what reference does this nebulous 'society" use as its foundation for 'morality", and is that reference universal, meaning accepted by all living persons?

The philosophy of living together in America is based on equality and sovereignty, not just sometimes or under conditions chosen by government or, worse yet, by a majority of something. It is based on equality *always* and *under all conditions*. It cannot be otherwise and still be a viable concept.

The application of this new oppressive philosophy, however, in unending variation, is exactly why there are so many bad laws in America pertaining to 'morality," laws that are ambiguous in the extreme and oppressive beyond all common justice.

Bad Law — There are as many versions of the counter-equality philosophy as there are bad laws against privacy on the books. It's fair to say that each was contrived to deal with a particular situation perceived *locally*, when someone took offense. As each such law attempted to accommodate the outraged opinion, all it could possibly do was to deprive everyone of an inherent right in some measure, and in complete disagreement with another law somewhere else. Bad law comes in so many forms, and deals with so many issues that seem to be different but are not, that there is never any closure on the questions and rights involved. *Each becomes an independent crisis test case and progress in the general sense nationwide is never accomplished.* The bad law in East Cleveland [case 1 below], in one warped *application* of that law, actually denied the Right of a woman to have her grandson live with her. That travesty was never matched either in preparation, application, or evaluation, with living conditions in Georgia, for example, which has no such constraint. Georgia is certainly no model for ideal living, but it never condoned the restrictions of East Cleveland.

Summarized below are the bare-bones highlights of a few cases researched by Bolick. In his descriptions of these crimes by government, Bolick has shown the contradictions inherent in them all and the confusion that continues in American courts, all the way to the top. His work also gives me further justification for an opinion of mine that has been growing stronger as these revelations unfold. It is becoming more and more clear that we Americans are living in a country which is ruled not by one code of law, well-conceived and improving with every decision, but by 52[50] separate and distinct codes which differ in specific and very significant ways. Nor is there anything inherent in our system of justice which causes these myriad codes to converge; *in fact, the differences are becoming greater with time.* We should stop ignoring those differences, and decide among ourselves whether we want a unified set of rules for the entire country or if we want to continue the untenable condition of one country with 52 different references for conduct.

Now to Bolick's samples of injustice, with emphasis on local governments' failures in legislating bad law.

---

[50] Fifty states, one federal and Washington DC make up the fifty-two codes.

301

CASE 1 Location - East Cleveland, Ohio, 1973

The Bad Law - Criminal by Definition Only - Residences are restricted to 'Family" only, with Family defined as traditional: owner, their parents and their children

Foolish & Unjust Effects of a Bad Law - A grandmother was convicted and sentenced to 5 days in jail and a $25 fine for having two orphaned grandchildren living with her who were cousins, not siblings.

CASE 2 Location - Tazewell County, Illinois - Eight local high schools

The Bad Law - The 'War on Drugs" - again -

Unjust Effects - Without any prior *indication* of a drug problem in any of these schools, authorities (namely Sheriff James Donahue) decided to raid all 8 schools simultaneously "...to find out if the re was a problem. You never know until you go in to take a look," Donahue explained.

Courts are routinely upholding such raids (e.g., a 1990 Washington Post survey of 200 'drug" raids, all upheld.)

Random detention and searches at public transportation stations without probable cause. One can conclude, correctly, that the *crimes* committed against the Rights of individuals and the harm done by AUTHORITIES in so-doing, far outweigh any benefit derived by society from these police actions. The so-called 'Drug Problem" has been transmuted into a real *police problem* and our ability to combat the harmful *effects* of drugs hasn't been improved one single iota as a result.

CASE 3 LOCATION - United States Supreme Court hearing

THE BAD LAW - A local zoning law forbidding unrelated persons from living together! Upheld by the court.

UNJUST EFFECTS - Just imagine the effects of applying this spurious philosophy nationwide.

CASE 4 LOCATION - Georgia

THE BAD LAW - Georgia's anti-sodomy law, which states that a 'person commits the *offense* of sodomy" (not the crime), 'when he performs or submits to *any sexual* act involving the sex organs of one person and the mouth or anus of another." (My emphasis added).

Georgia is one of 24 backward States with some version of law proscribing 'sodomy" which is *defined* differently by those states. Georgia's bad law provides a maximum punishment (for this offense against someone's sensibilities) of 20 years. We should note that the law is NOT an elaboration of the CRIME of Rape, because it is applied against consenting partners.

COMPOUNDING BAD LAW - The United States Supreme Court upheld the Georgia law by rationalizing it as an issue different from the real one involving the Right to privacy, to be left alone (more on this presently).

UNJUST EFFECTS - Michael Hardwick was subjected to arrest, prosecution, conviction, and four years of legal mayhem culminating in a 5-4 loss at the Supreme Court and finally jail for actions that harmed no one, for actions that only opinion justified as 'objectionable."

So much for the background on a few of the hundreds of samples of government assaults on privacy.

Confusion in the Courts

The terrible injustice dumped on Michael Hardwick [Case 4 above] was made worse by the rationalizations and confusion of the United States Supreme Court Majority Opinion rendered in the case. Four justices sided with Justice Byron White to uphold the bad law and Hardwick's conviction, but that majority opinion resulted from their inability to understand the fundamental Rights being contested. White, and the four others, posed the question as 'whether the Federal Constitution confers a fundamental right" upon 'homosexuals to engage in acts of sodomy". This majority further stated the Constitution protects only those rights 'implicit in the concept of ordered liberty or that are deeply rooted in this Nation's history and tradition."

There is *no such equivocation in the equality of people* or the *Right to privacy* which were thus denied by giving preference to opinion. The rhetoric describing what the Constitution does guarantee is meaningless, a misleading fusillade of words offered to obscure their confusion. 'Deeply rooted in ... tradition"? Is not the tradition of equality and that of Right to privacy as basic as can possibly be? Five Justices of the Supreme Court, people appointed for life, were *incapable* of understanding the fundamentals of this sad case. One of those five later admitted his error (Justice Lewis Powell), but the terrible damage to Michael Hardwick had been done.

There is absolutely no excuse for such a terrible crime by government against a blameless man, especially when the flaw in the logic of the majority of justices was vehemently pointed out to them by the four who disagreed. Justice Harry Blackmun correctly showed that the issue concerned the Right to be left alone — and nothing else.

At this point we must seriously ask ourselves about the way things are structured within American government in our attempt to preserve the ideals and concepts that raised America in 1791 far above the concepts of rule throughout history. Our REFERENCE for justice, for preservation of ideals and for advancement of society is plagued by all the frailties and inadequacies of humans, yet we:

- make no provision for review or evaluation of the performance of Justices;
- appoint fallible people for life;
- permit decisions of monumental import to be based on simple majority.

The process of invoking an ultimate arbiter is deficient for all those reasons and cries out for change. It brings us to my last concern regarding the condition of our Right to privacy.

Majority Rule Can be the Ultimate Tyranny

This single case against Michael Hardwick would never have gotten beyond the stage of being just personally distasteful to some of his neighbors if it had not been for the warped manner in which majority rule is applied in the United States. That effect dominated the issue twice, once at the time Georgia created its 'Sodomy" law, and once when the United States Supreme Court ruled on the constitutionality of the law. Thinking only of the Georgia State legislature, it became law merely because a simple majority of legislators approved. There had been no voter initiative or referendum with whole-hearted agreement of an overwhelming majority. It is safe to say that most of the Georgia electorate were not even aware of the debate concerning the issue. Even more obvious is the deduced fact that the opinions of all those legislators who *disagreed* with the law ended up being totally ignored.

Like it or not, the 'democratic process" also bound all dissenters to something that was distasteful to them. We use a Go, No-Go criterion on issues that are so terribly complex that Yes or No answers can't possibly serve the concept of justice for all. One vote more than half the number of legislators is all it takes to cram bad law onto the books, and Georgia did just that. They were able to cloud the issue enough to hide the fact that an Unalienable Right was being shattered — for everyone — by using a morality campaign where morality is not really involved. While this is an opinion, it is one I hold very strongly. The loss of Rights to people not troubled by their own gender identity is not as visible as to those targeted by that law, but the *privacy* of everyone has become a non-right by the actions of government.

The day (or the night) that police decide to invade your own bedroom on suspicion of 'distasteful" conduct, then you will have no more doubt of the very real loss of Rights.

A majority vote of the nine Justices of the Supreme Court is a mere five individuals. When a judicial "answer" has the backing of only five Justices, but also has the strong *disagreement* of the remaining four Justices, then one would think that some recognition of that shaky answer would be appropriate. I contend that the importance of judicial decisions that pertain to our fundamental Unalienable Rights are every bit as important, if not more so, as a decision concerning the life of an accused murderer is in the balance.

For the murderer, the verdict of guilty must be *unanimous*; anything less, and guilt has not been established.

When considering Rights, no such requirement exists, and with as few as five fallible Justices, we have all lost Rights that must be viewed to be as important as one life. Far too many men and women have given up their own lives defending those Rights for us ever to think otherwise.

Another Conclusion We Must Finally Accept
We must stop holding ourselves hostage to the unworkable concept of rule by simple majority. Privacy is a precious Right we all once had, a Right recognized 200 years ago, but which has been taken from us, *mostly* by local government bodies in hundreds and hundreds of actions over the decades. The remnants would be unrecognizable to any of those men who first spelled it out for us.

APPENDIX G
Unalienable Rights & Government's Performance

Table 6 follows the hierarchy of Appendix C, condenses the statement of each Right and offers the grade I would give to government for its performance so far. The grade you yourself would give will have much more meaning for you because it will be your own evaluation.

Table 6 THE HIERARCHY OF UNALIENABLE RIGHTS -
Rights That Come With Life

1. LIFE (Declaration of Independence)

  1.1 <u>Right to life, to their own person, the property of no one else.</u>   **[grade: -3]**

  1.2 <u>Right to join with others for security.</u>

    1.2.1 Right to pay for protection and to change agreements   **[grade: -4]**

      1.2.1.1 Right to decide compensation.   **[-10]**

    1.2.2 Right to define government.   **[-6]**

      1.2.2.1 Right to remove individuals and change a contract.   **[-6]**

      1.2.2.2 Right to change the Constitution.   **[-3]**

      1.2.2.3 Right to Representation.   **[-8]**

      1.2.2.4 Right not to be ruined by government.   **[-5]**

      1.2.2.5 Right to revolt.   **[-8]**

    1.2.3 Right not to be deprived of Rights.   **[-7]**

    1.2.4 Right to defend life.   **[-4]**

      1.2.4.1 Right to learn.   **[-2]**

      1.2.4.2 Right to own and bear arms.   **[-4]**

    1.2.5 Right to truth and honesty from government officials.   **[-4]**

      1.2.5.1 Is there an Unalienable Right to truth ? [A conundrum not yet answered by humanity.]

    1.2.6 Rights of individuals to be placed *ahead* of the goals of government. **[-5]**

  1.3 <u>Right not to be the object of hate by government.</u>   **[-5]**

  1.4 <u>Right to be secure, and Right to Privacy for their persons, homes, papers, information and possessions, including reputation.</u>   **[-5]**

    1.4.1 Right against unreasonable searches and seizures (Amendment IV). Security **From** government excesses   **[-4]**

    1.4.2 Right to Privacy.   **[-5]**

1.5 Right to control elements of government through restraints, rules of operation and change.   **[-6]**

1.6 The Right to change government   **[-8]**

1.7 Right to resist oppression   **[-8]**

1.8 Right of equality of human class with all other people.   **[-5]**

1.9 Right of individuals not to be dictated to in matters of the individual. [See also Items 3.]   **[-8]**

1.10 Right of individuals not to be dictated to through law based on religious grounds.   **[-6]**

1.11 Right to Citizenship.   **[grade neither + nor -]**

1.12 Right to decide life or Death for self.   **[-4]**

1.13 Right to be free of physical and mental abuse from any other person.
        [-3]
        (for example, husbands do not own their wives, nor may children be abused by parents.)

2. BASIC FREEDOMS

2.1 Right to life and freedom from subjugation   **[-2]**

2.2 All people are born with equal Individual Sovereignty, possessing exactly the same Unalienable Rights.   **[-4]**

2.3 All power is derived from the people   **[-7]**

2.4 Freedom of Speech.   **[-3]**

2.5 Freedom to create, print and preserve. **[-3]**

2.6 Freedom to assemble peacefully.   **[-2]**

2.7 Freedom to confront and petition government for a redress of grievances
        [-5]

2.8 Freedom to keep and bear arms for security and with the approval of no one else.   **[-4]**

2.9 Freedom to make all decisions regarding use of home and property so long as the rights of others are not threatened or violated.   **[-5]**

2.10 Freedom honestly to buy and sell.   **[-5]**

2.11 Freedom to pursue happiness as defined by self.   **[-6]**

3. DECISIONS FOR SELF

3.1 Liberty   (Declaration of Independence)
    3.1.1. Right to make own decisions.   **[-6]**
    3.1.2 Right to let others decide or not.   **[-10]**
            one of government's worst failings
    3.1.3 Right to defend liberty against security organizations such as government and courts.   **[-5]**

A new mechanism is needed.

3.1.4 Right to meaningful choices - particularly with regard to existing conditions at time of reaching the age of responsibility. **[-9]**

There are no choices that come with adulthood.

3.1.5 Right of following own conscience in all matters of religion and belief. **[-3]**

Waco proves the failing.

3.2 <u>Right not to be bound by decisions of others from before own life</u> - or not actually agreed to by self. Thomas Paine noted that no one has the power to barter away the rights of the unborn, or for that matter, those already alive [Thomas Paine #1]. **[-7]**

3.3 <u>Right not to accept responsibility</u> **[-1]**

Government has not yet evolved to the stage of subverting this Right.

3.4 <u>Right to decline military service on decision of conscience.</u> **[-4]**

Vietnam is still our best indicator of a Right lost.

4. FRUITS OF LABOR

4.1 <u>Pursuit of Happiness</u> (Declaration of Independence)

4.1.1 Right to acquire property. **[+1]** A rare expanded right to undo earlier wrongs.

4.1.2 Right to keep possessions. **[-7]** Taxes, confiscation and inheritance confiscation still prevail.

4.1.2.1 Derived directly from the rights to acquire and keep possessions, *is the right not to be taxed*. (See also 4.1.2.2.) **[-10]**

Clearly one of the worst failures of government.

4.1.2.2 Right to be free of confiscation **[-10]**

The limitations to confiscation remain a thing set by government, which shows there is no remaining Right to property

4.1.3 Right to defend possessions. **[-8]**

4.1.4 the right of disposing of wealth after death. **[-10]**

4.2 <u>A person' s úalienable Right of ownership is not subordinate to any other claim.</u> **[-10]**

4.3 <u>The right to acquire, keep, sell or use property of any kind is coupled with the right to engage in the free trade of property</u>, within a framework established by society. **[-6]**

4.4 <u>The pursuit of happiness does not only depend on acquiring property</u>. Also part of that basic right are the following:

4.4.1 The ability to exercise all Unalienable Rights with a minimum of intrusion. **[-5]**

4.4.2 The right to choose and pursue any occupation or profession in any locale. **[-4]**

4.4.3 Right to find a mate.   **[-2]**

4.4.4 Right to create.   **[-2]**

4.4.5 Right to conceive and to rear offspring. [see also 4.4.8]
[neutral]

4.4.6 Right of choice of recreation and the manner in which to spend wealth.
[-1]

4.4.7 Right not to do any of these things.   **[neutral]**

4.4.8 Right of parenthood.   **[neutral]**

4.5 Right not to have to compete with any monopoly created by government.
[-4]   Subsidies to industry are clear violations.

---

5. RIGHTS IN LAW AND JUSTICE

[Refer to companion volume on Law & Justice]

5.1 Right to fairness by the law and law enforcement.   **[-7]**
The failings of our judicial system stem from the inadequacies of the defined system. The grade, therefore, is more for the failings of the Constitution than of government per-se.

5.2 Amendment IV states:
"The right of the people to be secure in their persons, houses, papers, and effects, against unreasonable searches and seizures, shall not be violated, and no Warrants shall issue, but upon probable cause, supported by Oath or affirmation, and particularly describing the place to be searched, and the persons or things to be seized."   Refer also to item 1.4.2   **[-5]**

5.3 Fairness under the law is expanded through the enumeration of Rights covered by Amendment V of the Bill of Rights. Refer also to items 4.2, 4.1.4 and 5.4   **[-8]**

5.3.1 Right to indictment only by a Grand Jury. [*"No person shall be held to answer for a capital, or otherwise infamous crime, unless on a presentment or indictment of a Grand Jury, except in cases arising in the land or naval forces, or in the Militia, when in actual service in time of War or public danger;......"*]   **[-8 ?]**

5.3.2 Not to endure Double jeopardy; [*"....nor shall any person be subject for the same offense to be twice put in jeopardy of life or limb,   "*]
[-5]
The error derives from excessive, literal adherence to a noble concept, even in the face of truth and justice. A *balance* has not yet been reached.

5.3.3 Not to incriminate self; [*"....nor shall be compelled in any criminal case to be a witness against himself,...."*]   **[neutral]**

309

5.3.4 Due process to be deprived of life, liberty, property; [*"....nor be deprived of life, liberty, or property, without due process of law;...."*] (Refer to comments in Item 4.2.) **[-10]**

    Fault here lies more with process than with intent, although malicious intent can be present.

5.4 <u>Just compensation for confiscated private property</u>. [*".... nor shall private property be taken for public use without just compensation."*] [Refer to Item 4.2.] **[-10]**

5.5 <u>Amendment VI is further elaboration of the Rights of individuals under the law</u>. Rights enumerated under Items 1., 2., 3. and 4. are all *Unalienable Rights*, while Rights pertaining to the Law are derived from them. As such they are much more subject to opinion as we shall see. With the benefit of two hundred more years of experience under the Bill of Rights, we are now in a better position to evaluate those early opinions and to offer changes.

5.5.1 Speedy public trial; [*"In all criminal prosecutions, the accused shall enjoy the right to a speedy and public trial,...."*] **[-7]**

5.5.2 Trial by jury - a must ??? [*"....by an impartial jury of the state and district wherein the crime shall have been committed; which district shall have been previously ascertained by law,..*] **[-6]**

    Juries are increasingly incapable of relating complex information to the guilt or innocence of defendants. The dictum of JURY can no longer assure justice or control of law by the people.

5.5.3 Informed of charges and witnesses; [*".... and to be informed of the nature and cause of the accusation; to be confronted with the witnesses against him;...."*]**[-8]**

5.5.4 Compulsory process (subpoena) for defense; [*"....to have compulsory process for obtaining witnesses in his favor,...."*] **[neutral ?]**

5.5.5 Counsel; [*"....and to have the assistance of counsel for his defense."*] **[-6]**

    The justice system allows and even encourages misleading testimony and representation instead of *demanding* truth from both sides.

5.6 <u>Amendment 7</u>: *"In Suits at common law, where the value in controversy shall exceed twenty dollars, the right of trial by jury shall be preserved, and no fact tried by a jury shall be otherwise re-examined in any Court of the Unites States, than according to the rules of the common law."*

5.6.1 Civil Suits **[-4]**

5.6.2 Re-examination of facts. **[-3]**

5.7 <u>Amendment 8</u>: *"Excessive bail shall not be required, nor excessive fines imposed, nor cruel and unusual punishments inflicted."* **[-6]**

5.7.1 Right to fairness in bails and judicial rulings **[-6]**

    The ways in which government (i.e. the system of law and justice) warrants a failing grade are legion.

5.8 Right not to be accused, imprisoned or held under arrest except as prescribed
by law. [French Declaration of Rights of Man]   **[-2]**
One may argue that the intent of government is usually proper.
The main fault is a failure to prosecute officials when they do not preserve
this Right. Waco is a clear example case where government criminals
continue in power.

5.9 Right to humane treatment by police. [French Declaration of Rights] Any
person accused of any crime is to be presumed innocent until proven
guilty. **[-7]**

5.10 Right to just punishment, free of cruelty.   **[-4]**
I take it as an obvious fact that murders inside of prisons
constitute cruel punishment. Our record is unacceptable.

5.11 Victims of crimes have a Right to expect from the Criminal Justice System
restitution of losses suffered, to the fullest extent possible.   **[-8]**

6. SPECIAL RIGHTS.

6.1 Habeas Corpus - The Great Writ of Liberty.   **[-8]**

6.2 All Unalienable Rights that are accepted as self-evident by a society have
another attribute namely that they apply permanently and without
interruption.   **[-10]**
This failing has been discussed thoroughly in this book
concerning the War and Emergency Powers Act of 1933.

*   *   *

A disclaimer seems appropriate. The particular grades attached to the
performance of government for its stewardship of our Rights are obviously not
rigorous. Their importance rests not on those values but only on the clear fact of the
loss of precious Rights. The losses have been due *to the overt acts of government*
itself at all levels through slow but direct, relentless legislative erosion. No foreign
detractors have yet added to our loss of Unalienable Rights — with the question of
the UN still undecided.

A CONCLUSION NOT TO BE AVOIDED
Once again we must remind ourselves that government is not created by the
people to legislate Rights. Its purpose is to preserve those rights in the face of ALL
potential detractors.

***The 200-year record of American government, however, shows unequivocally
that our losses have come only from the actions of our own government and no
other source.***

311

The conclusion regarding what must change is absurdly obvious.

*   *   *

APPENDIX H

A Better Way to Finance Government

The United States Government is the largest spending organization in the entire world. In all its years of operation, however, government officials have not learned even the most basic means of managing the huge piles of money that flow through their agencies. Instead, the process they always use is simply to *collect* and to *spend*. Everything that is collected is spent outright, along with more besides, as the political winds dictate. Even when their profligate legislation commits them to future expenditures, provisions are never made to handle sensibly the added expenses to come, meaning that segregated funds are never part of the plan. Every expense becomes a direct draw on money to be collected through taxes.

A simple change in philosophy about the control and use of money could remove the perpetual agony of confiscation from citizens to satisfy the legitimate and not-so-legitimate expenditures of government. Suppose instead, there were an endowment fund, nation-sized, that could be tapped [by proper authorization procedures] to meet on-going expenses. Suppose that fund were invested, in the limiting case invested throughout the world, so that a return is realized which is large enough to meet current expenses. The effect would be monumentally different than mere spending. The principal would never be lost, certainly never become negative, and would be made more beneficial through its use as investment capital. Any amount added to it from gifts, or one-time taxes, would directly increase the amount of the principal sum.

Such a drastic departure from history need not be a pipe dream, as a few simple numbers will show.

- Assume a nominal return of 6 % per annum from the **National Fund**.
- Assume also that yearly expenditures become more sensible, and are 'merely' $1 trillion; [actually they should be les s, but the example is almost reasonable].
- 6% of a $17 trillion National Fund equals about $1 T, and the fund remains to yield next years needs.

The question to answer is: where can the National Fund principal come from?

313

• Suppose as part of **each citizen's decision** to accept a more responsible government, that he or she also agrees to donate a gift to government of   say $10,000 over ten years. This is a **one time only** gift, and ultimately all other taxes would be phased out to zero, after which no further tax of any kind would ever be levied for the rest of that person's life. It can be viewed as an obligation of citizenship, and one well worth the really essential services provided by government.

• 200,000,000 citizens, at $10,000 each will ultimately create a fund of $2,000,000,000,000. Within 40 or 50 years, each person will have made the gift, and the fund has become a viable, healthy national resource.

That amount is about one eighth of what a completed fund should be for the US under current conditions. But suppose the expenses were more sensible, somewhere around half a trillion dollars? Or what if the return were closer to 10 % , or the number of gift-givers was closer to 300,000,000 ? suddenly the insurmountable doesn't se em quite so impossible. Each new generation will add to the total as well. During whatever transition period is required to accumulate a totally sustainable, nation-sized endowment fund, other means of income might still be needed to turn the tide. Hefty, one time corporate 'gifts', sales taxes , etc., all of which would have specific termination dates, are possible. Then too, the period over which that **National Fund** need be built up is completely under our own control, and anything which can ultimately rid us of the foolishness of our present 'system" will be far more acceptable. As the saying goes, in the fullness of time, the fund can be anything that the collective wisdom of the entire citizenry wants to make it, and the potential for the constructive use of such an asset for true 'national goals' is almost unlimited. A time will also come when the initial input from each person could be lowered, even though it never was oppressive.

The exact same approach can also be used for local government expenditures. For this, an entirely separate fund could be devised, which would again receive contributions from each US citizen — one time during the person's life. Each city's share of that fund's return would be b ased on its population for that year according to some agreed formula. If people still insist that *States* are also a necessary element of government, then the same rules would suffice for them as well. I still contend, however, that from an administrative standpoint, States are obsolete, even though some restructuring might be needed in law enforcement. Most of the confiscation by cities and States are even more regressive than federal taxes. Real estate taxes, assessments and others merely add inflationary pressures and are arbitrary in the extreme.

Taxes are an antiquated, repressive and destructive way of financing the collective needs and desires of people who have joined together to improve all aspects of their lives. To add to that process the power of the gun to **force** the surrender of personal wealth, is clearly unenlightened if not actually barbaric, and exactly opposite to the purpose for which government is formed in the first place. Just because **taxation** has been the method used throughout history, does not mean it is the only way or the optimum way to organize ourselves. Clearly there are other, better alternatives, and funding government as it is presently structured is feasible by this different method.

A few other points are appropriate to make regarding the process of financing government. Suppose finally that we carry the notion described in this book of a restructured government one added step. Funding the expenses of such a restructured government via a National Fund brings out the following additional points.

- The National Fund is under the **exclusive** control of the people via referendum, administered by the Citizens Advocacy Agency.
- The CAA is authorized to negotiate contracts with each of the several, independent Agencies of government, per Constitution II, setting funding levels for each.
- Payments are made to theses agencies, per the contracts, by the Funding Agency in accordance with CAA directions.
- Payments drawn from the National Fund can be no greater than the limits approved by **REFERENDUM**.
- Independent Firms are used to manage the National Fund, and are paid a small but reasonable fee related to the size and the increase of assets under their direction. The incentives are set for **safety** and for **long-term return**.
- Once the National Account is self-sustaining, AND begins to generate surpluses, the National Debt is paid down to the level set by referendum.
- By referendum, the one-time payment from citizens to the National fund can be changed, even to lower the initial amounts. One reason for such a change might be, for example, that the national debt has finally been reduced to zero.
- Every other source of taxes, e.g. an interim sales tax, will be phased-out to zero over the transition period.
- The ultimate taxing authority rests with the people, via referendum, not with government, whatever its structure.

INDEX

319

risk20, 24, 29, 37, 38,
75, 78, 90, 93, 158,
159, 194, 235, 294,
298
RNC   18
Robert H. Jackson292
Roosevelt34, 72, 110,
217, 260, 294
Rothschilds   77, 276
Ruby Ridge 9, 41, 42,
87, 139, 194
Rudman   6, 30

S

second-class
American   214
self-evident   12, 134,
138, 143, 216, 234,
254, 260, 285, 288,
300, 311
skullduggery   199,
277, 282
Social Security10, 20,
31, 32, 58, 60, 97,
108, 109, 110, 111,
112, 113, 114, 124,
144, 211
sockdolager   264
solution   10, 13, 31,
44, 56, 58, 77, 88,
98, 101, 108, 110,
113, 121, 124, 156,
161, 170, 171, 190,
193, 206, 212, 214,
216, 221, 222, 254,
276, 293
special interests   11,
99, 102, 144, 166,
232, 280
spending binge24, 91,
104
squander   65

squandered 1, 32, 53,
137, 169
stability 8, 10, 15, 20,
21, 26, 39, 54, 69,
70, 72, 74, 87, 141,
148, 167, 168, 172,
174, 193, 207, 225,
278, 280
Stanley Wolf117, 122
Starrett City 135, 291
stranglehold   235
Strawman   163, 164,
167, 171, 173, 177,
182, 186, 220, 235
striation   249
structure   4, 6, 7, 21,
24, 30, 46, 87, 101,
102, 124, 125, 126,
141, 146, 148, 154,
159, 163, 167, 170,
171, 180, 183, 185,
186, 189, 190, 193,
194, 195, 196, 197,
201, 202, 203, 205,
207, 208, 209, 213,
235, 280, 285, 289,
293, 315
Susan Lee   81

T

Tammy O. Tengs   90
taxation 9, 24, 55, 56,
57, 82, 87, 108,
138, 147, 170, 190,
235, 253, 254, 279,
315
taxes9, 10, 11, 18, 19,
22, 29, 31, 46, 54,
55, 58, 60, 61, 84,
86, 87, 95, 108,
110, 111, 113, 118,
128, 144, 145, 220,
235, 254, 269, 279,

283, 295, 313, 314,
315
testing 121, 123, 148,
222, 226, 230, 232
thefts   10, 11, 19, 98,
113, 296, 299
Thomas Kean   128
Thorstein Veblen   72
Threats   34
threshold   40, 55, 60,
64, 74, 108, 144,
161, 182, 198, 200,
208, 235, 252
Thurgood Marshall
149
Tiananmen Square 44
Tobacco   43, 47
tolerance   225
Tolerance   290
Tom Bethell   76
Transition 165, 214,
215
Transition Plan 165
treasure   1, 8, 14, 52,
138, 205, 225, 231,
269
Trial by jury 258, 310
trust 1, 11, 31, 32, 70,
83, 103, 108, 112,
113, 139, 155, 181,
205, 233, 267, 297
truth 1, 21, 32, 34, 42,
48, 98, 100, 115,
117, 130, 142, 170,
193, 218, 222, 224,
225, 226, 234, 249,
252, 258, 264, 271,
281, 290, 294, 300,
306, 309, 310
TRUTH   224, 226
tyranny   11, 16, 89,
127, 132, 133, 160,
213